Troubleshooting and Repairing Camcorders

Homer L. Davidson

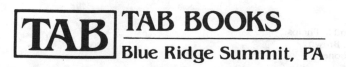

TAB TAB BOOKS
Blue Ridge Summit, PA

FIRST EDITION
SECOND PRINTING

© 1990 by **TAB Books**.
TAB Books is a division of McGraw-Hill, Inc.

Library of Congress Cataloging-in-Publication Data

Davidson, Homer L.
    Troubleshooting and repairing camcorders / by Homer L. Davidson.
       p.   cm.
    ISBN 0-8306-8337-2   ISBN 0-8306-3337-5 (pbk.)
    1. Camcorders—Maintenance and repair.   I. Title.
  TR882.D39   1990
  621.388′337—dc20   89-29141
                                  CIP

TAB Books offers software for sale. For information and a catalog, please contact TAB Software Department, Blue Ridge Summit, PA 17294-0850.

Questions regarding the content of this book should be addressed to:

Reader Inquiry Branch
TAB Books
Blue Ridge Summit, PA 17294-0850

Acquisitions Editor: Roland S. Phelps
Production: Katherine G. Brown
Book Design: Jaclyn J. Boone

Contents

I would like to dedicate this book to my brothers and sisters:
Carl, Cecil, Thelma, Edgar, Walter, Lena, Hubert, Charles, and Janet.

Acknowledgments

Without the help of many electronic technicians and 10 camcorder manufacturers, this book would never have been written. A great deal of thanks goes to the national service managers of the following manufacturers who provided service data for this book:

Canon
General Electric (Thomson Consumer Electronics)
Mitsubishi
Minolta
Olympus
Pentax
Radio Shack
RCA
Sony
Zenith

See the Introduction for a list of makes and models discussed in this book.

Introduction

*S*ervicing a camcorder is just as exciting as using it to take those memorable pictures. Troubleshooting the camcorder is a whole new ball game, so to speak, if you have never touched one. With out the service literature, you have one strike against you when attempting tough repairs. The camcorder is nothing more than a camera and a video cassette recorder in one package.

Like any electronic and mechanical device, the camcorder can break down. The purpose of this book is to provide practical and technical data to help make camcorder repairs much easier. Troubleshooting and repairing camcorders has opened up another new field in consumer electronic maintenance. Primarily, this book was written for the electronic technician, except the intermediate and experienced electronic student can also learn from each chapter.

This book contains 14 chapters, beginning with the various camcorder and video cassette formats. Chapter 2 provides service data and the required tests equipment. The camera section is described thoroughly in Chapter 3. The video circuits are described in Chapter 4. Chapters 5 and 6 describe how the system control, detection, and servo systems perform. How the motor circuits operate and how to repair them is in Chapter 7. The audio circuits are described in Chapter 8. Chapters 9, 10, and 11 describe how the mechanical VCR section operates, how to remove and replace mechanical components, and the required mechanical adjustments. The electrical adjustments are given in Chapter 12. The most important chapter in the book, Chapter 13, tells how to troubleshoot and repair the various sections of the camcorder. Finally, Chapter 14 covers servicing the power supply and battery charger.

Servicing the camcorder takes a steady hand. Like other compact electronic devices, parts are crammed together. Sometimes you must remove many components and boards before getting to the defective part. Troubleshooting the camcorder requires a lot of patience and dedicated workmanship. But then this is what successful electronic technicians are made of.

Besides required test equipment, the schematic diagram and service literature is a "must" item. Over 10 different camcorder manufacturers have provided valuable service literature and schematics for this book. You can save a lot of valuable service time by having the correct schematic diagram. These camcorder manufacturers have provided the required service information, and this book could never have been written without their help.

Like the compact disc player, the camcorder is loaded with special components such as integrated (IC) processors surface-mounted parts, CCD and MOS image devices, and special optical components. These parts must be obtained from the manufacturer. Always replace these special parts with that of the original part number. These components are listed in the manufacturer's service literature.

Servicing the camcorder might force a change in the attitude of the electronic technician, but it also can be a lot of fun. All electronic products that arrive on the scene might seem different at first, but each day it becomes a lot easier.

The following table lists the makes, models, and formats of the units discussed in this book.

Make	*Model*	*Format*
Canon	VM-E2NA	8 mm
General Electric (Thomson Consumer Electronics)	9-9605	VHS
Mitsubishi	HS-C2OU	VHS-C
Minolta	C-3300	VHS-C
Olympus	VX-801	8 mm
Pentax	PV-C850A	8 mm
Radio Shack	Realistic 150	VHS-C
RCA	CPR100	VHS-C
	CPR300	VHS
Sony	CCD-M8E/M8U	8 mm
Zenith	VM6150	VHS-C

Chapter **1**

Camcorder and Video Cassette Formats

Camcorders are nothing more than a combination electronic camera and video recorder in one package (FIG. 1-1). Most of the tools found upon the electronic technician's bench are all that is required to service the VCR section. Use the same tools you would use to repair the VCR recorder. Besides those found upon the service bench, you'll need a good vectorscope, color monitor, lighting equipment, refection charts, and a light meter. You can do a lot of camcorder maintenance with just the reflection charts and dual-trace oscilloscope for electronic adjustments.

When video cameras were first used with color TV sets, the instant picture was seen directly on the TV screen or monitor (FIG. 1-2). With camcorders, the scene can be recorded, played back at once, or seen at a later date. Some camcorders have playback features while the smaller units record only. Like the VCR, there are several different tape formats to service.

BETA

The Beta camcorder matches up with the Beta VCR machines and cannot plug into a VHS recorder. Basically, the Sony Beta format was one of the first VCRs on the market with the best quality recordings. Beta camcorders can take pictures on a Beta cassette but have no playback features. The Beta camcorder has about 280 lines of resolution compared to the 250 lines of VHS machines. The Beta cassette can play from 15 minutes up to 5 hours of recording. The L-750 cassette is slightly smaller than the standard VHS cassette (FIG. 1-3).

VHS

The video home system (VHS) camcorder employs the same cassettes as the VHS video tape recorder (VCR), making this unit the most stable and popu-

1-1 The RCA CC275 VHS camcorder with electronic viewfinder.

1-2 Early video cameras required a TV receiver for a monitor and had no recording or playback feature as in this Newvicon 3150 model does.

1-3 *The Beta video cassette is slightly smaller than the VHS cassette.*

lar unit (at present). The VHS cassettes are low in price and can be played back in camcorders or VCRs. The VHS tape is not interchangeable with the Beta cassette. Many of the VHS camcorders can be played directly through the TV set or monitor. In standard play (SP) you can get two hours of recording on the standard T-120 cassette (FIG. 1-4). You can get up to six hours of recording in extended play (EP) mode.

Since the early VHS format, the cassette and VCR have been improved. The HQ recording system improved the picture with sharper definition, truer colors, and less snow. Today, the super (S-VHS) camcorders provide

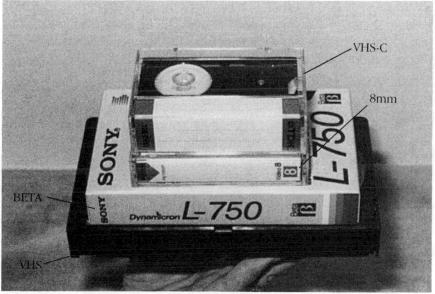

1-4 *The standard T120 (VHS) cassette is the largest.*

1-5   *The VHS-C cassette is about the same size as the 8 mm, except the tape is the same width as in the VHS cassette.*

more lines of resolution which means more detailed pictures. The standard VHS camcorder might have 240 to 250 lines while the super VHS might contain over 400 lines of resolution. The S-VHS camcorder can be played through the TV set or monitor but not the regular VCR unit. The VHS cassette can be viewed on an electronic viewfinder. Regular VHS cassettes can be played back through the super VCR machines.

VHS-C

The compact VHS-C camcorder is small in size, light to carry, and uses the small VHS-C cassette (FIG. 1-5). The VHS-C camcorder is much easier to take on vacations because of the physical size, compared to the VHS model. The VHS-C camcorder must be supported for steady pictures. The VHS-C cassette can be played directly into the TV set or color monitor but must be placed in the regular VHS-size plastic holder before inserting into the VHS VCR (FIG. 1-6).

Although the tape itself and the recorded magnetic patterns are the same as a VHS cassette, the VHS-C cassette is only one-third the size. The tape movement is actuated by a plastic, geared reel inside the regular VHS cassette. The take-up function is driven by a gear. The VHS-C cassette contains a supply-reel disk, but there is no take-up reel disk (FIG. 1-7).

1-6   *Inside view of the gear and supply reel disk of the VHS-C video cassette.*

1-7   *Inside view of the VHS cassette with supply and take-up reels.*

When the VHS-C cassette is inserted into the VHS cassette, the adaptor extracts the tape and positions it in the same manner as the full-size VHS cassette. Now the tape can be inserted into the VHS-format deck (FIG. 1-8). When inserted, the supply reel disk of the VHS deck drives the supply reel of the VHS-C cassette. Remember, the take-up reel disk of the VHS recorder drives the take-up operation via the pulley and gear of the adaptor (FIG. 1-9). A small amount of noise might be created with the VHS-C and VHS adaptor.

Naturally, with a smaller camcorder, all parts are also reduced in size. Here the regular size and weight of the 41 mm-diameter rotating head drum is about one-third the size of the full VHS format. To retain compatibility with the VHS format, the rotation speed is increased to 45 revolutions per second, while the tape-wrapping angle is increased to 270 degrees (FIG. 1-10). The conventional cylinder drum diameter is 62 mm at 180 degrees tape wrap-around angle.

8 MILLIMETER

The 8 mm cassette is the newest type of camcorder and is made by both electronics and camera manufacturers. The 8 mm camcorder operates with a small lightweight format and thinner tape. The 8 mm video cassette operates from 15 minutes to 4 hours of playing time. The 8 mm cassette can be played back through the camcorder electronic view finder, TV set or color monitor, or 8 mm VCR. The 8 mm cassette cannot be played through the VHS-C or VHS camcorder.

The 8 mm camcorder has a smaller drum head diameter with digital audio frequency modulation. The audio portion is recorded right with the video signal rather than on the edge of the tape like in VHS models. The

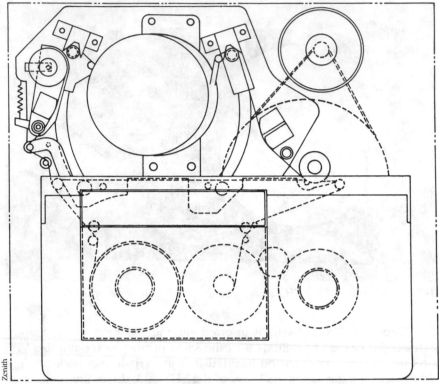

Zenith

1-8   *Detailed drawing of VHS-C cassette inside the VHS adaptor.*

horizonal resolution is between 300 and 330 lines. Most 8 mm camcorders contain a charge-coupled device (CCD) for image pickup. The flying erase (FE) head prevents the color "rainbow" effect when recording and is mounted in the same drum or cylinder as the video heads.

VIDEO CASSETTE PROBLEMS

The video cassette itself, like the audio cassette, can cause a lot of audio and video problems. Tape spilling out may be caused by improper alignment or a tape that is wound too loose or tight. Inspect the cassette before inserting it into the camcorder for a broken or bulging case to prevent jamming of

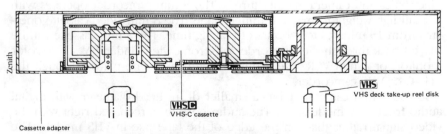

Zenith

VHS
VHS deck take-up reel disk

VHS-C
VHS-C cassette

Cassette adapter

1-9   *The VHS-C reel drive principle inside a regular VHS cassette adaptor.*

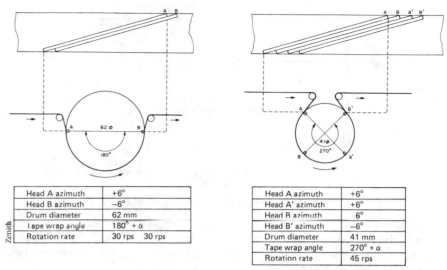

Head A azimuth	+6°
Head B azimuth	−6°
Drum diameter	62 mm
Tape wrap angle	180° + α
Rotation rate	30 rps 30 rps

Head A azimuth	+6°
Head A' azimuth	+6°
Head B azimuth	6°
Head B' azimuth	−6°
Drum diameter	41 mm
Tape wrap angle	270° + α
Rotation rate	45 rps

1-10   *The normal and reduced-size head drums of the VHS-C recorder.*

the tape or cassette. You might think poor tape recordings in both video and audio sections are a defective tape head. Try the cassette in both the VCR and the camcorder to determine whether the cassette or camcorder is defective. If in doubt, try a new recorded known cassette in the camcorder.

CAMCORDER FEATURES

Knowing how the camcorder operates is important when servicing the unit. In fact, many reported "problems" are operational; since the camcorder has become popular, there have been several new features added.

Auto Focus

The focus is always automatically and precisely adjusted when set in auto focus. Manual focus adjustment is also possible in most cameras. You may find optical focusing in small and low-priced camcorders. Most camcorders use the infrared beam for auto focus, except the NEC V50U (VHS) camcorder has a prezo auto focus circuit.

Auto focus works via infrared rays that are emitted from the camcorder to the object and reflected back to a receiving lens (FIG. 1-11). Here the reflected rays strike two photodiodes. The focus lens moves until the two photodiodes receive an equal amount of light, correcting the camera focus.

Auto White Balance

The white balance is fully automatically adjusted and continuously changes with fluctuations in illumination during shooting. The automatic white balance circuit controls the gain of the red and blue chrominance signals to maintain white balance (color temperature) under various lighting conditions in the RCA CPR300 VHS camcorder. White balance refers to the adjust-

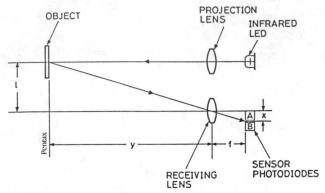

1-11   *The measurement principle of the infrared auto focus system.*

ment of the recording system to the color temperature of the light illuminating the subject. The auto white balance has white balance sensors at the front of the lens assembly.

CCD and MOS Sensor

The early TV cameras and camcorders have pickup tubes called the *vidicon, saticon,* and *newvicon* tubes. Today, most camera sections use either the CCD or the MOS sensor. A Charge-coupled device (CCD) is a semiconductor that consists of orderly arranged MOS-cell capacitors. It consists of photoelectric conversion, charge accumulation, and charge transfer and operating time.

Camcorder makes that use MOS image devices include Minolta, Pentax, Radio Shack, RCA, and Hitachi. (The others use CCDs.) The MOS image sensor operates in the same manner with picture elements (photodiodes with npn three-layer construction). The advantage of the CCD and MOS devices over the tube pickups are the former have longer life, no image lag or burn, no figure distortion, strong chip, instant on, lower power consumption, and are small and lightweight.

Automatic Iris

The automatic iris mechanism is called a *meter system*, which mechanically connects drive and brake coils. The optical signal is optoelectrically converted by the CCD images and converted to electrical components. In other cameras, the light may be controlled by electronic shutter-speed control circuits.

High-Speed Shutter Operation

During normal camera operations, photo electrons are stored in the MOS or CCD image sensor. For a one-field time period before being scanned, the photodiodes are reset. Selecting the shutter function has the effect of delaying the reset pulse. The reset pulse is set closer to the next readout. Selecting the shutter speed determines the length of time that the reset pulse is applied before the photo tube is scanned. Shutter speed is controlled by a large microprocessor (FIG. 1-12). High-speed shutter function makes it possible to catch super-fast action pictures.

Zoom Lens

The power zoom switches move the lens assembly for close-ups or distant pictures or for wide angle shots. The zoom buttons are easily controllable while operating the camera. A zoom lever manually zooms the picture in or out. A microbutton may provide for close-up scenes.

Electronic Viewfinder (EVF)

Not all camcorders have an electronic viewfinder. With the EVF, you can actually see the picture you are taking on a small screen. What you see is what you get. The electronic viewfinder is in black and white while the recording is in color (FIG. 1-13). The electronic viewfinder may be used as a monitor in playback operations. Actually, the electronic viewfinder is a tiny TV receiver with video, high voltage, deflection circuits, and a small picture tube.

1-12 *The various controls are usually located on the side and top of the camcorder.*

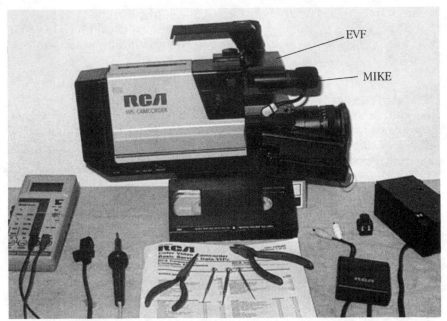

1-13   *The electronic viewfinder (EVF) is at the front of the camera. The audio mike is attached to the EVF in this RCA CPR300 camcorder.*

Audio Dubbing

The audio dubbing feature allows replacing the original recorded sound to be replaced with background music, narration, or special sound effects. Insert editing is handy for editing tapes by inserting new scenes into the already-recorded video cassette.

HQ Technology

You may find in some late camcorders the HQ symbol mark feature of the new VHS high quality picture system. HQ technology improves the picture quality while retaining VHS interchangeability. This means, in some models, raising the white clip level and detail enchancer. Remember, the HQ camcorder system will operate in the conventional VHS recording system.

HOOKUPS

Most camcorders can be connected directly to the TV set or color monitor with a VHF connecting cable and an audio/video cable (FIG. 1-14 and 1-15). The RF adaptor may be required between camcorder and the TV antenna input terminals (FIG. 1-16 and 1-17). If the TV set or color monitor has video and sound input jacks, the audio/video cord is connected between camcorder and TV set or monitor (FIG. 1-18).

When using a TV without audio/video input terminals
Connect the Video AC Adapter VF-BA81 (provided) as shown below.

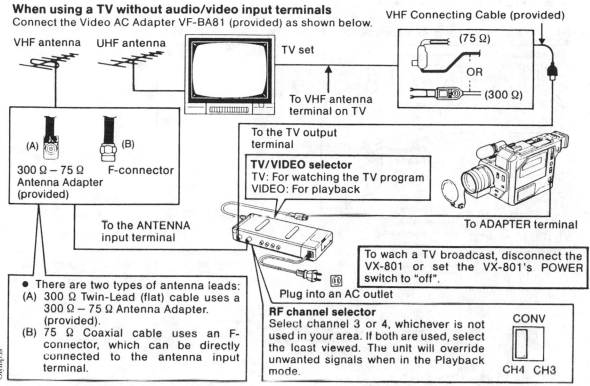

VHF antenna

UHF antenna

TV set

To VHF antenna terminal on TV

VHF Connecting Cable (provided)

(75 Ω)

OR

(300 Ω)

(A) (B)

300 Ω − 75 Ω Antenna Adapter (provided)

F-connector

To the ANTENNA input terminal

To the TV output terminal

TV/VIDEO selector
TV: For watching the TV program
VIDEO: For playback

To ADAPTER terminal

To wach a TV broadcast, disconnect the VX-801 or set the VX-801's POWER switch to "off".

Plug into an AC outlet

- There are two types of antenna leads:
(A) 300 Ω Twin-Lead (flat) cable uses a 300 Ω − 75 Ω Antenna Adapter. (provided).
(B) 75 Ω Coaxial cable uses an F-connector, which can be directly connected to the antenna input terminal.

RF channel selector
Select channel 3 or 4, whichever is not used in your area. If both are used, select the least viewed. The unit will override unwanted signals when in the Playback mode.

CONV

CH4 CH3

1-14 *How to connect an 8 mm camcorder to the television set.*

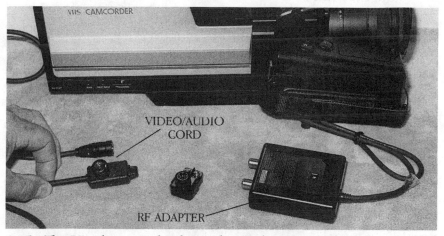

VIDEO/AUDIO CORD

RF ADAPTER

1-15 *The RF adapter and video/audio cord are used to connect the RCA camcorder (VHS) to the TV set.*

Connection to a TV set's antenna terminal

If your television is not equipped with video/audio input jacks, connect the Model 3300 and TV set using RF Output Adapter RF-M3000S.

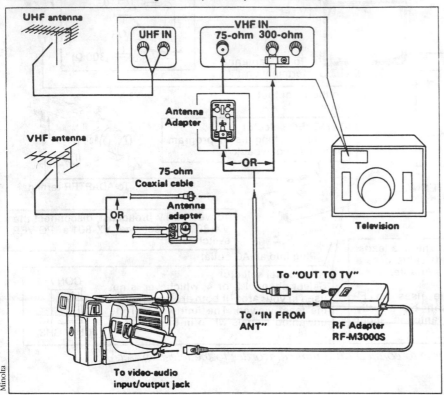

1. Disconnect the VHF antenna cable from the antenna terminal(s) of the television.

Note:

● Leave the UHF antenna leads connected to the TV.

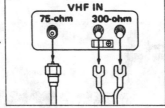

1-16   Use an RF adapter to connect the camcorder to the back of the VHF terminals of the TV set.

When recording from other equipment, the video cassette recorder is connected between the TV set and the camcorder. In some models, the ac video adaptor is used when operating the camcorder from the power line (FIG. 1-19). Editing the recording hookup may be obtained with the VCR connected between camcorder and TV set or monitor (FIG. 1-20). Dubbing intro-

1-17 *RF adapters connect the camcorder to the VHF terminals of the TV receiver for monitoring.*

duces some degree of picture quality deterioration. It is recommended that the video camcorder recorder be placed in SP mode.

BLOCK DIAGRAM

Looking at the camcorder block diagram may help to determine where the trouble is. The manufacturer's service literature is a must item in trou-

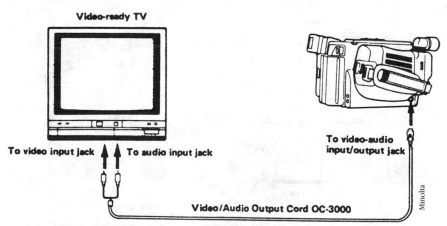

1-18 *Connect the camcorder directly to the TV set, if a video and audio jack is provided, with a video/audio cord.*

When using the Video AC Adapter

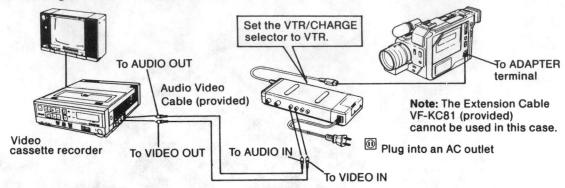

Set the VTR/CHARGE selector to VTR.

To AUDIO OUT

Audio Video Cable (provided)

To ADAPTER terminal

Video cassette recorder

To VIDEO OUT

To AUDIO IN

Note: The Extension Cable VF-KC81 (provided) cannot be used in this case.

Plug into an AC outlet

To VIDEO IN

When using the Battery Pack

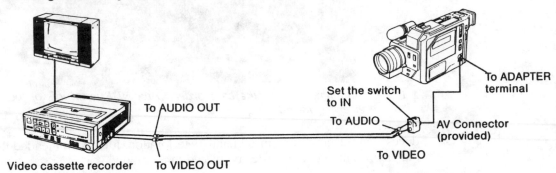

To AUDIO OUT

Set the switch to IN

To ADAPTER terminal

To AUDIO

AV Connector (provided)

Video cassette recorder

To VIDEO OUT

To VIDEO

1-19 *An ac adapter connects the video cassette recorder between the TV monitor and the camcorder.* Olympus

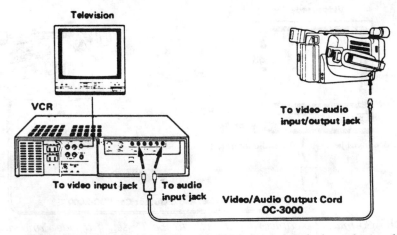

Television

VCR

To video-audio input/output jack

To video input jack

To audio input jack

Video/Audio Output Cord OC-3000

1-20 *For editing, connect the VCR to the camcorder with the video/audio cord.* Minolta

bleshooting the camcorder. Not only does it contain the block diagrams, but it breaks down each stage and shows how the components are tied together in each separate schematic. The schematic contains not only the circuits, but also voltages and critical waveforms.

VHS

The early VHS camcorder camera block diagram has a pickup tube or CCD stage, processor, AWB, auto focus, and EVF stages (FIG. 1-21). The CCD stages consist of CCD image sensor, CCD sync generator, CCD driver, and sampling hold circuits. The iris motor, AIC operation, chroma, and sync pulse generator may be found in the process circuits. The AWB circuit contains AVT sensor, AWB gain, switching and decoder. The focus lens, zener and iris motors, motor control circuits, demodulator, AGC, and clamping and digital converters are found in the auto focus circuits.

The electronic viewfinder consists of horizontal and vertical sync, horizontal and vertical oscillator, deflection coils, flyback transformer, and CRT. The input of the EVF stages connects to the video output of camera circuits. The EVF circuits are often contained in one unit.

VHS-C

The VHS-C camera section consists of the AIC circuits, autofocus, automatic white balance, chroma processing, encoder/NTSC signal processing, luminance, MOS or CCD image sensor and circuits, matrix and filter, pulse generator, preamplifier, signal processing, sync generator, power supply distribution, and electronic viewfinder circuits (FIG. 1-22). The Zenith VM6150 main board block diagram is shown in FIG. 1-23.

8 Millimeter

The 8 mm camera section contains auto focus, CBA, CBA sensor, mother CBA, detection module, delay module, AWB module, encoder matrix mod-

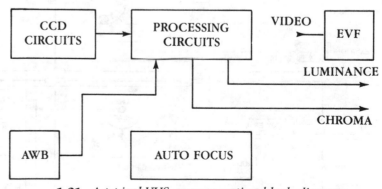

1-21 *A typical VHS camera section block diagram.*

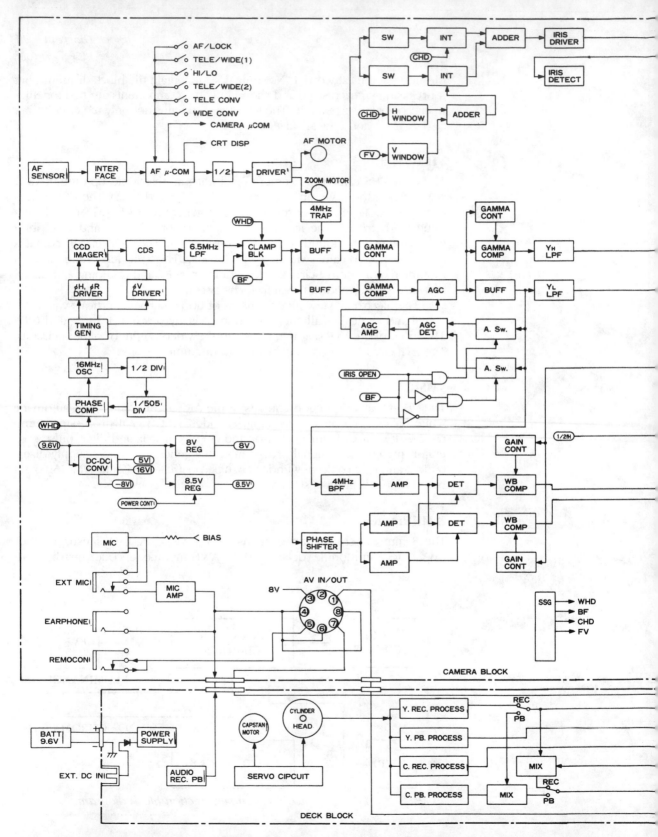

1-22 *The complete block diagram of the VHS-C Minolta C3300 camcorder.* Minolta Camera

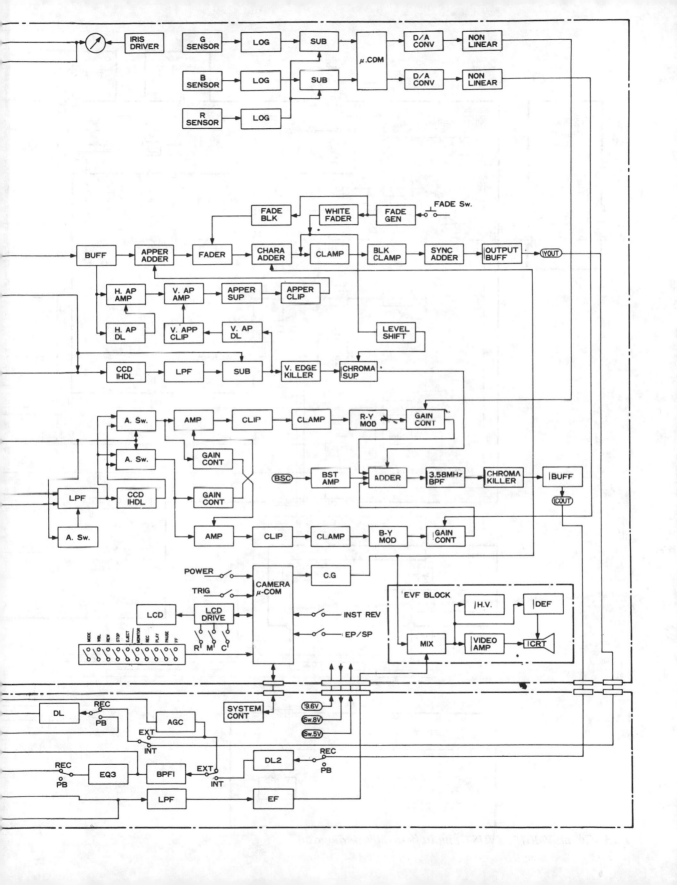

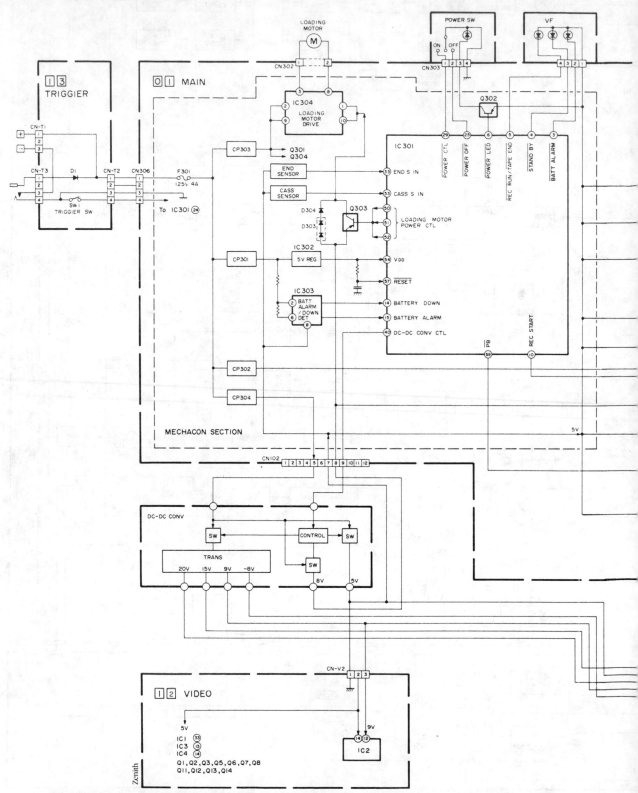

1-23 *Zenith VM6150 (VHS-C) main board block diagram.*

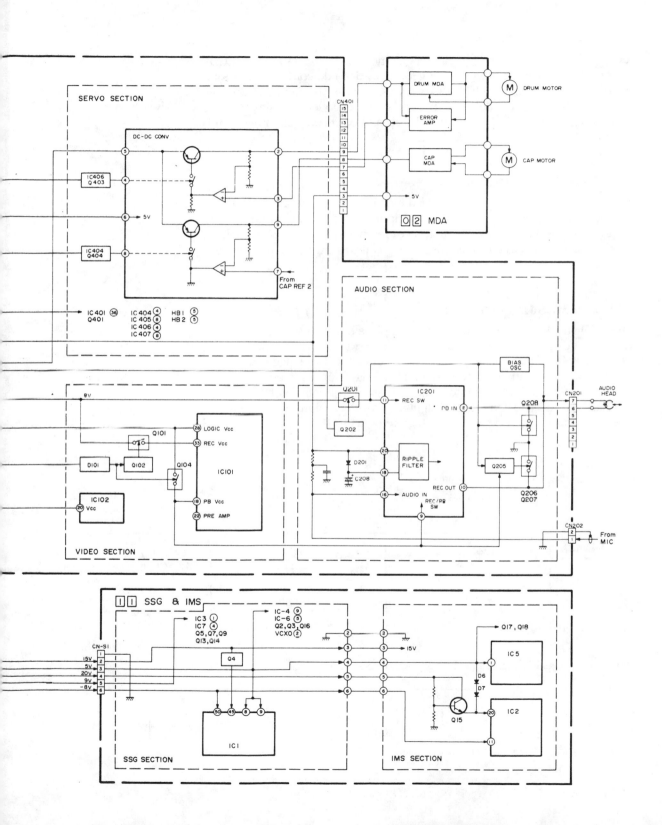

ule, and EVF (FIG. 1-24). The auto focus CBA consists of the sensor, processing, AXVS circuits, motor drive AF, and zoom motors. The CCD imager, CCDV driver, clock generator, sync signal generator, dc-to-dc converter and sample-hold circuits located on the CBA sensor board. The mother CBA contains the AGC detector, delay, AWB, matrix, and encoder modules in some units. The Pentax PV-C850A 8 mm main circuit board connection diagram is in (FIG. 1-25).

THE CAMERA SECTION

The camcorder features are broken down into the camera and the VCR sections for easy operation. A brief description of each stage in the camera section follows. Although some of these different circuits might be called by another name, the circuit functions are the same, as explained in Chapter 3 (FIG. 1-26).

CCD and MOS Image Sensor

The CCD and MOS image sensors take the place of the older pickup tube. A CCD charge-coupled device is a semiconductor that consists of orderly arranged arrays of MOS cells (capacitors). The MOS color image sensor uses picture elements with a structure of npn three-layer photodiodes. The color resolution filter arranges white, yellow, cyan and green color filters in a mosaic pattern. The four-color output improves resolution with reduced image retention. Both devices are integrated circuits.

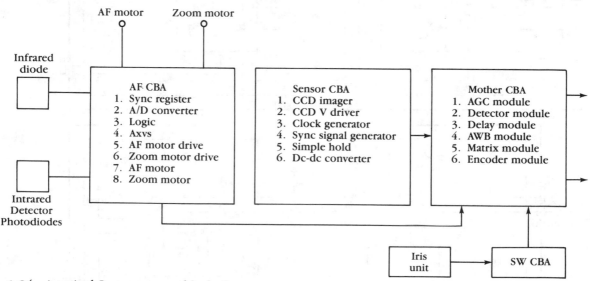

1-24 *A typical 8 mm camera block diagram.*

CCD or MOS Drive Pulse

The drive pulse generator circuit generates the pulses that drive the image sensor and signal-processing circuits. The drive pulse generator IC is often broken down into four sections: the 5.37 MHz high speed circuit, the shutter function, and the horizontal and vertical frequency circuits. The 5.37 MHz high speed section generates the horizontal shift register clock pulse. The shutter speed control determines the shutter speed. The horizontal frequency section generates the horizontal shift register start, vertical shift register clock, vertical buffer, reset, and sweep pulses. The vertical frequency section generates the vertical shift register start, vertical optical block, field discrimination, vertical start, and FA and FB field discrimination pulses.

Sync Generator

The sync generator provides signals that synchronize the operations in the color camera. It is usually one large IC component. It supplies signals to the iris driver, auto white balance, date generator, process, luminance enhancer, chroma amp filter, and MOS image sensor drive pulse.

Signal Processing

In the signal-processing circuits, the cyan, white, green, and yellow are driven simultaneously by the 5.43 MHz sampling frequency. The matrix circuit produces luminous (y) and chrominance (R, B, and G) signals.

Preamplifier

The yellow, cyan, green, and white signals from the MOS or CCD image sensor are amplified by the preamplifier circuits. The input impedance is very low and controlled by a single IC.

Matrix Color Circuits

The amplified cyan, green, yellow, and white signals are fed into the matrix IC to produce the luminance, red, blue, and green signals.

Resampling Process

The white, cyan, green, and yellow signals are fed from the preamp circuits to the sampling IC. Improved high-frequency response and signal-to-noise ratio are obtained by averaging the value of every picture element (pixel). The luminance (YL and YH) signals are fed to the process board.

Luminous Signal Processing

The luminous signal is clamped, gamma corrected, and blanked to eliminate noise during the blanking period. Also, the signal is white- and dark-clipped and fed to the automatic iris control circuits and to the AGC amplifier.

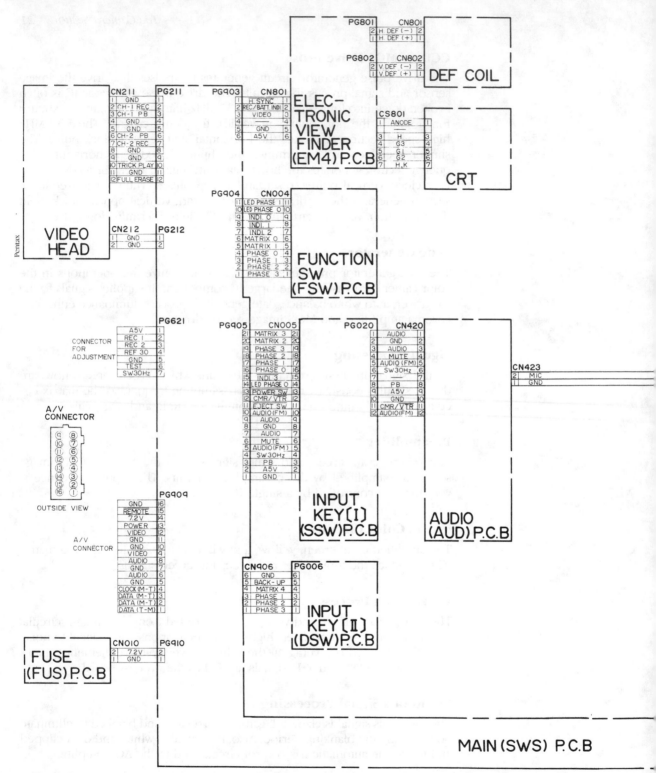

1-25 *Pentax PV-C850A (8 mm) circuit board connection diagram.*

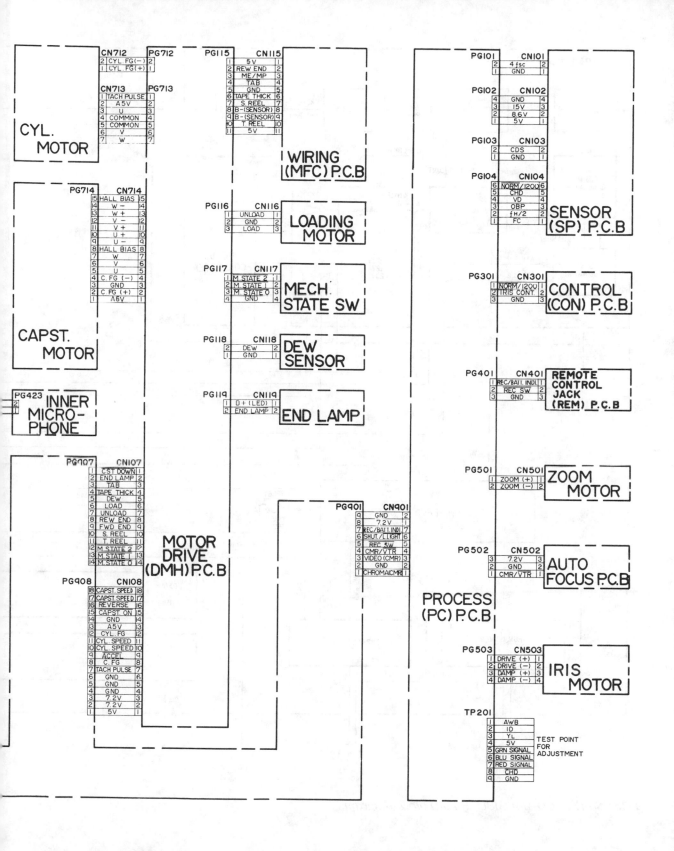

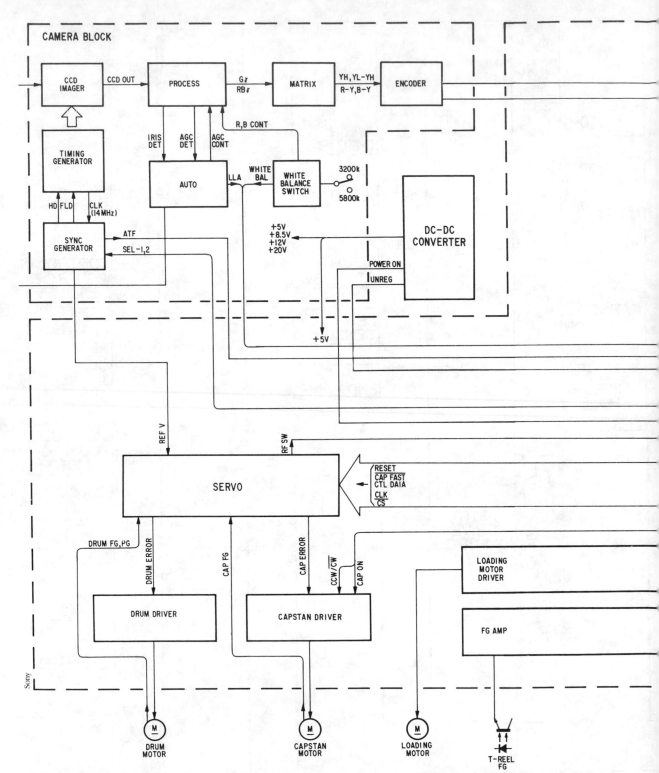

1-26 Sony's CCD-M8E/M8U (8 mm) block diagram.

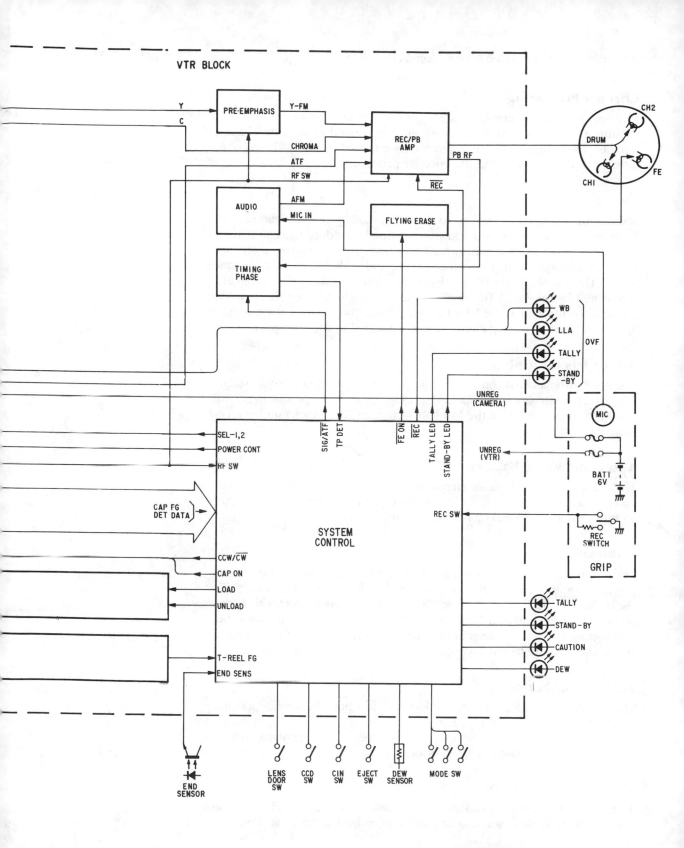

Chroma Processing

The red, green, and blue signals are applied to the input of the color processing IC. Here the red and blue signals are applied to the white balance circuits. These signals are mixed to produce the –R –YL and –B –YL color difference signals applied to the encoder processing circuits.

Encoder

The luminance signal is applied to the NTSC signal-processing circuits. The luminance signal is clamped and white clipped to reduce the color output in the bright areas of the picture. The white-clipped luminance signal is blanked, applied to the YC mixing circuit, and added to the chrominance signal. The –R –YL and –B –YL signals are applied, clamped, and balance-modulated by the 3.58 MHz signal. These two modulated signals are added and applied through a 3.58 MHz bandpass filter. The reduced noise signal is applied to the Y/C mixing circuits and then added to the luminance signal.

AIC or Iris Control

The AIC (automatic iris control) circuit controls the level of the video signal. This circuit controls the iris opening as detected from the processing circuit. The AIC circuit consists of the low light detection, AGC killer, and iris motor drive circuits.

Automatic White Balance

The automatic white balance circuit maintains correct white balance under various lighting conditions. These circuits correct the white area of a picture so it does not have a red or blue cast or tint.

Automatic Focus

The automatic focus circuits transmits an infrared signal that strikes the subject and bounces back to the infrared receiver located on the camera. This signal is detected by two photodiodes that produce electrical current according to the infrared light received. The auto focus circuit uses these two signals to move the lens in the proper direction. When the two signals become equal, the lens is focused and the auto focus motor stops.

Power Distribution

The power distribution circuits regulate and distribute the operating voltage to the various camera circuits. For instance, a 12-volt source might need to be regulated into separate 9- and 5-volt sources. These regulated voltages are routed to the various camcorder operations.

VTR OR VCR SECTION

The VTR or VCR section consists of the video head, head switching, system control, trouble detection circuits, on-screen display, servo system, luminance record, chroma record process, luminance playback, chroma play-back and audio circuits. Although there are many other smaller circuits within the VTR, the most important ones are given here. Plus, besides these circuits, there are many mechanical movements that are given in detail in Chapter 9.

Video Heads

The upper cylinder or drum in the VHS and VHS-C video recorders have a 41 mm diameter with four heads (FIG. 1-27). The tape wrap for this system is 270 degrees and rotates at a speed of 2700 rpm. This system produces a more compact camcorder, providing compatibility with previous VHS re-corders (FIG. 1-28). The 8 mm drum is smaller in diameter and contains two channels and a flying erase (FE) circuit. The FM audio signal is recorded along with the video rather than at the edge of the VHS tape (FIG. 1-29).

System Control

The system control microprocessor controls the reset, clock, power, battery detection, function switch, capstan, on-screen display, servo, luma/chroma, trouble detection, tape run, loading motor, mechanical control, and charac-

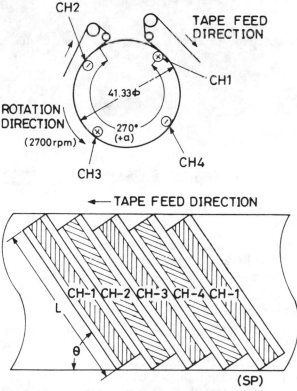

1-27 *The VHS/VHS-C video head configuration.* RCA

1-28 *The head assembly is smaller in the VHS RCA CPR300 camcorder than in the regular VCR.*

ter generator in most camcorders. Usually, one large IC operates all of these functions.

Head Switching

The head-switching circuits consists of a preamp and the switches of the four head channels in the VHS and VHS-C models. Head switching is done in the record and playback modes.

Trouble Detection Circuits

The VHS and VHS-C trouble detection circuits consist of the end circuit, dew sensor, mechanism switch, take-up reel sensor, supply reel sensor and supply end circuit. The battery detection circuit is usually controlled by the system control IC. The clog head detection circuit warns that there is accumulation of magnetized tape dust in the head gap of the 8 mm head assembly.

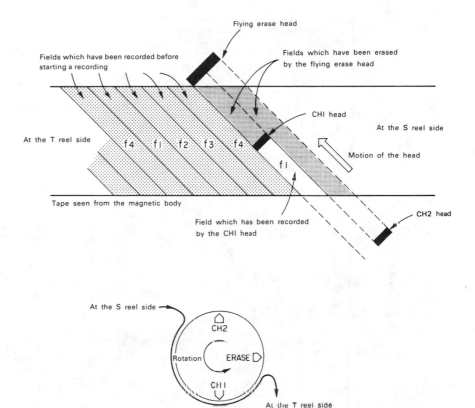

1-29 *The magnetic tape field with flying erase head in the 8 mm camcorder.* Zenith

On-Screen Display

When the display switch is on, the system control IC produces a low signal that is applied to the character generator in the VHS-C camcorder. This signal from the character generator displays the battery level, tape counter, shutter speed and operation mode. This character signal is amplified and mixed with the video in a video amp IC. From here, the video signal is fed to the EVF and AV output.

Servo System

In the VHS-C, the upper cylinder must rotate at 2700 rpm in playback and record in the VHS-C circuits. This means the phase and speed of the capstan and cylinder motors must be controlled. The $^1/_2$ V sync, REF 30 Hz, 30 Hz PG pulse, cylinder FG (CYL FG) pulse, capstan FG (CFF) pulse, and CTL pulse signals are in the servo system.

    The servo system in Sony's CCD-M8E/M8U model consists of the drum, capstan FG sensor amp, capstan servo, drum motor drive, and capstan motor drive (FIG. 1-30). The drum motor and capstan motor are controlled by the drum/capstan main servo IC.

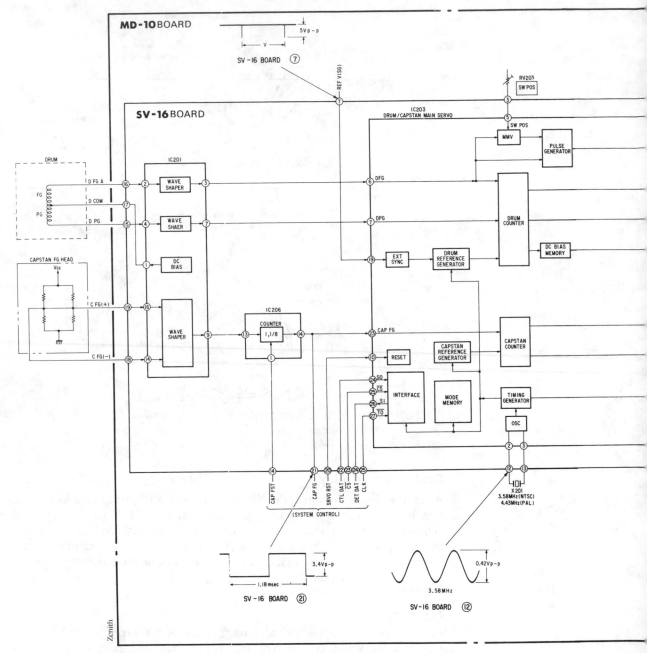

1-30   *The servo block diagram in the Sony M8E/M8U camcorder.*

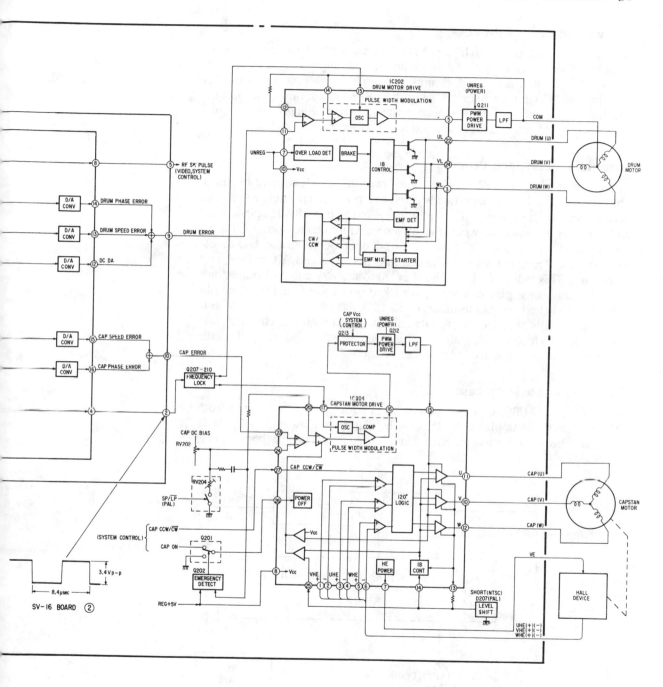

SV-16 BOARD ②

Luminance Record Process

The luminance IC, in the VHS and VHS-C units, contains the record AGC, luminance signal extractor, detail enhancer, preemphasis, clipping, frequency modulation, and the E-E amplifier circuits (FIG. 1-31). The signal is sent through a high-pass filter (HPF) to the record mixer and amp circuits. The luminance and chroma signals are mixed before going to the record amp. The record amp signal is applied to the video heads.

Luminance Playback Process

In the 8 mm luminance playback circuits, two different ICs might be used. The pick-up signal of the tape heads is fed to a preamp, channel switch, and AGC circuits in the preamp IC. This signal is fed to the 5.8 MHz peak, trap, and phase comparator between the preamp and luminance processing IC. The luminance processing IC contains the HP limit, demodulator, DO detector, dynamic deemphasis, noise cancel, line noise expand, Y/C mixer, and video amp. This video playback signal is fed to the EVF and AV connector.

The luminance playback signal is picked up by the four heads, amplified, and switched to the luminance playback IC in the VHS and VHS-C camcorders. This signal is demodulated and mixed with the chroma playback IC to produce a video signal. The video signal is fed to a character mixer IC and out to the EVF and AV out connector.

Chroma Playback Process

In the Pentax PV-C850A (8 mm) chroma playback circuits, the signal from CH1 and CH2 are amplified by IC201. The signal goes through a 1.3 MHz LPF, AGC, burst deemphasis, PB balance modulator, chroma comb filter,

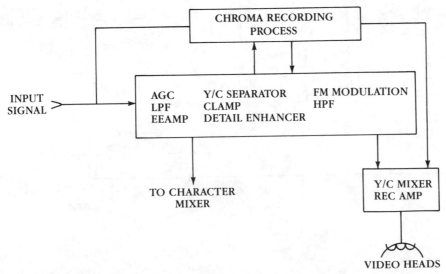

1-31 Block diagram of the VHS/VHS-C luminance record process.

chroma deemphasis, and a PB color killer and is mixed with the luminance signal in the Y/C mixer. The video signal is amplified to the EVF and AV connector circuits.

The chroma playback signal in the VHS and VHS-C chroma playback circuits are quite similar to the 8 mm. The signal from the four channels are switched and amplified in the preamp stage. The signal passes through a 1.3 MHz LPF, PB balance modulator 3.58 MHz BPF, AGC, burst deemphasis, and a comb filter and is mixed with the luminance playback signal in the Y/C mixer. This signal is fed to the character mixer to the EVF and AV out connector.

SERVICE NOTES

Like the video tape recorder, there are only a few original manufacturers who make camcorders. You might be working on one model that looks somewhat like another brand on the sales floor, but inside the camcorder body, the components are the same, except a different part number. Most camcorders are made in Korea and Japan (TABLE 1-1).

There are a few precautions the electronic technician should take before attempting to repair the camcorder. The camcorder is small, with parts jammed together. To get at one defective component you might have to remove 10 others. You need steady fingers and small thumbs. Sometimes it's the little things that save valuable service time and money.

Tab Lock   Make sure the tab at the back of the cassette is in or "turned on" for recording. If the tab is out, the cassette cannot be used for recording. Often when customers bring in the camcorder for repair because it will not record, it's because the tab is broken out of the cassette. Place a piece of tape across the opening where the tab was to record. Then remove it to prevent recording over a recording that you want to keep intact.

Write it Down   Place the components in a regular order or write down where the parts go as you remove them. If you have to leave the bench or order a part, you might not remember where it belongs after you return or when you receive the part, which could be months.

Service Cloth   It's best to place a servicing cloth down on the bench, even if the bench is carpeted, to prevent damage to the camcorder's plastic body. Even small scratches might not polish out. Also, you don't want to lose a small screw or nut underneath the camcorder.

Service Literature   This is a "must" item. You cannot troubleshoot the various stages, provide adequate electronic adjustments, replace components, take critical voltage measurements, or find the correct part numbers without the service literature. Camcorder service literature is not cheap, but it will pay for itself in the first repair.

Wrist Strap   Always wear a wrist strap when servicing and replacing delicate components such as image sensors, microprocessors, and ICs.

Know When Not to Touch   Do not attempt electrical adjustments when you do not have the correct test equipment to make these tests. Don't hap-

Table 1-1.   Camcorder Manufacturers

Manufacturer	Makes	
Canon	Canon	
Goldstar	Goldstar	
Hitachi	Hitachi	
	Kyocera	
	Minolta	
	Mitsubishi	
	Pentax	
	RCA	
	Realistic	
	Sears	
JVC	JVC	
	Samsung	
	Toshiba	
	Zenith	
Matsushita	Chinon	Olympus
	Curtis-Mathes	Nikon
	Elmo	Panasonic
	General Electric	Philco
	Instant Replay	Quasar
	J.C. Penney	Sylvania
	Kodak	Technika
	Magnovox	
	NEC	
NEC	NEC	
Sanyo	Fisher	
	Sanyo	
	Vivitar	
Sharp	Sharp	
Sony	Aiwa	Ricoh
	Fuji	Sony
	Kyocera	
	Pioneer	

hazardly tear into the camcorder when you do not have the correct service literature. If you cannot locate the defective component, check with the field service representative, wholesaler, service depot, or your fellow electronic technician. Ask for help—it's out there.

Chapter *2*

Tips and Techniques

*T*here are several service precautions to take while servicing the camcorder. Always unplug the power source when removing or installing a component, circuit board, or module. Remove the battery or ac power source when disconnecting or reconnecting plugs and electrical connections. Shut off the power and discharge electrolytic capacitors before shunting them with another. Always remove one end of any fixed diode for accurate leakage testing.

SERVICE PRECAUTIONS

Keep chemical or lubrication sprays away from the camcorder. Do not spray chemicals on or inside the unit. Clean off switch contacts with cleaning sticks and alcohol (FIG. 2-1).

Do not defeat the purpose of plugs, sockets, or interlocks. Always replace the component to its original position and order. Do not forget to replace heatsinks and shields after replacing components. Keep loose screws and nuts out of the unit.

Keep the camcorder and test equipment grounded. Connect the ground lead first and always remove it last.

When replacing a chassis in the plastic case, all the protective devices must be put back in place, such as barriers, nonmetallic knobs, adjustment and compartment shields, isolation resistors, etc.

When service is required, observe the original lead dress. Take extra precaution to assure correct lead dress in the high-voltage circuits.

Always use the manufacture replacement components, especially crucial components. These parts were designed for that particular camcorder and should be replaced by the same part number.

Before returning the camcorder to the customer, the service technician must thoroughly test the camcorder for safe operation. Clean the case and outside components, too.

Take a hot and cold leakage test on the camcorder for safety.

2-1 *Clean off switches, guide poles and roller assemblies with cleaning sticks and isopropyl alcohol.*

Cold Current Leakage Test

With the power cord pulled from the socket, place a wire jumper across the two plug prongs. Turn the ac switch on. Using an ohmmeter, connect one lead to the jumpered ac plug and touch the other lead to metal screws, metal envelopes, and control shafts that are exposed to the operator. You should measure no less than 300 kΩ measurement. Any resistance value below this figure may indicate a shorted component or wire.

Hot Current Leakage Test

Plug the ac line cord of the power pack into the 120 Vac outlet. Turn on the ac power switch. Select a metal, exposed component or shaft and take a current measurement between the camcorder and a good water ground. Recheck the camcorder if the current measured is above 0.5 mA (FIG. 2-2). Any measurement not within these limits indicates potential shock hazard and must be corrected before returning the camcorder to the owner.

ELECTROSTATIC-SENSITIVE DEVICES

Electrostatic-sensitive devices may damaged by static electricity. Some of these sensitive devices may be ICs, field-effect transistors and semiconductor components (FIG. 2-3). Carefully handle all sensitive devices in their original electrostatic packet. Do not unwrap until they are ready to be mounted.

Keep your body drained of electrostatic charges by keeping all clothing at ground potential. Wear a conductive ground wrist strap. Make sure the camcorder and test equipment are grounded. Use a grounded-tip soldering iron and solder removal tool to prevent antistatic build-up. Keep freon-pro-

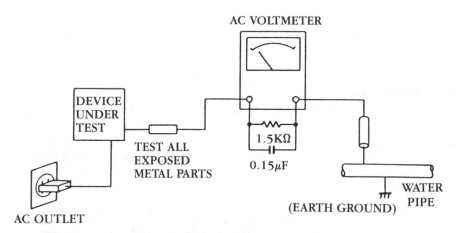

2-2   *Check the camcorder for hot leakage test after repairs.*

2-3   *Sensitive ICs and ES microprocessor devices should be handled carefully. Leave in the original electrostatic packets until installed.*

pelled chemical spray cans away from the camcorder. Prevent extra body motion that might create static electricity from a carpeted floor. Store the MOS IC in the black foam pocket it came in.

SOLDERING TECHNIQUES

Always use a grounded-tip, low-wattage (35 watts) or less iron so not to overheat ICs or transistors. A battery-operated solder iron is ideal for IC and transistor terminals. Thoroughly clean all surfaces, especially pc wiring, to be soldered. A small wire brush is ideal. Do not use freon spray cleaners for cleanup. Heat the small terminals until the solder melts and then suck up the melted solder with an antistatic suction-type solder remover. Mesh solder braid may do the job.

After the component has been removed and surface-cleaned of excess solder, mount the component. Recheck all terminal leads. Hold the iron tip against the terminal lead and apply solder. Keep a heatsink on transistor and IC component leads to protect the mounted component. Do not overheat the pc wiring, because it will lift up. Now inspect the soldered joint for a good bond and brush out rosin and excess solder with a small wire brush.

Flat-Pack and Leadless Chip Removal/Replacement

To remove the flat-pack IC, heat up each terminal and gently pry up the lead as the solder melts (FIG. 2-4). Remove all excess solder with the anti-static suction solder device or solder braid before trying to remove the IC. Run solder braid down over the terminals with the soldering iron. Clean off all excess solder and rosin from the wiring with a wire brush and remove the IC.

Carefully place the new IC in place. Note if terminal one is in the right corner (double check the correct IC mounting position). Press each IC lead against the foil and solder. Do not leave the iron on too long. Clean off the solder areas with a small wire brush. Do not use freon spray to clean these connections.

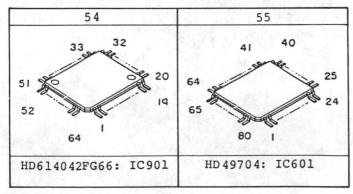

2-4 *The flat-mounted IC or microprocessor may have many leads. Heat each terminal and carefully pry up for removal.*

Remove leadless chips with a round-nose tweezer and pencil-type soldering iron. Do not heat any soldered connections for more than three seconds. Heat the soldered electrode connections, grasp the component with the tweezers and carefully twist the component to break the epoxy bond (most chip-type components are banded or glued to the board's surface with epoxy; see (FIG. 2-5). Make sure the epoxy bond is broken before trying to pick up the part with the tweezers.

Tin each wiring area or pad on the board before installing a new component. Check for correct orientation. Place the component into position on the circuit board with the tweezers and solder the terminals. Do not reinstall a component that has been removed from board.

Circuit Foil Repair

It is very easy to damage the pc foil when removing chip or IC components. Sometimes the foil or pieces of it pull up with the terminals being removed. Excessive heat applied to the pc wiring may "pop" off the foil wiring. Simply remove the defective foil pattern with a sharp knife. Locate the components tied together, and connect a piece of hookup wire from one lead of the nearest component to the other one. Make a hook in the bare hookup wire and place it over the IC pin that has pulled up the foil. Route the hookup wire to the nearest common junction of components.

SERVICE DATA

Before digging into the camcorder with any difficult symptoms, obtain the correct service diagram. Many of the present-day camcorders are made by only a few manufacturers and sometimes the same circuits are in other camcorders. However, it is very difficult to service servo, video, system control, and camera circuits without a schematic. This service literature can be obtained through the camcorder manufacturer or servicing depots. It's extremely difficult to make electrical and mechanical alignment procedures without the manufacturer's service literature. Mechanical adjustments are explained in Chapter 11 and electrical adjustments are in Chapter 12.

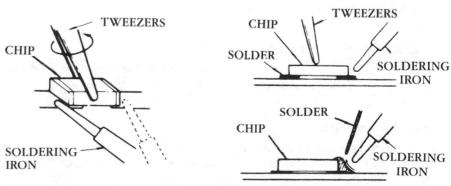

2-5 *Removing submounted flat chips from circuits.* RCA

VOLTAGE MEASUREMENTS

Most voltage measurements in camcorders are taken from the negative side of the power supply. If in doubt, locate the main filter capacitor's negative source. In the Pentax PV-C850A camcorder, the voltage measurements shown on the schematic in the camera section are measured when the VTR is in the record mode. Voltages in the VTR section are measured in both the record and play modes. The voltages in parentheses are those measured in the record mode. Voltages may be listed in black or bright red on the schematic diagram. usually, voltages should be taken with the lens cap on.

SIGNAL PATHS

When servicing the camera, VTR, and servo sections, use the signal path arrows or colors. In the NEC-VM50U VHS camcorder, the servo block diagram uses gray and red colors to identify the different servo signals. The cylinder servo speed loop is marked with a solid gray line and capstan servo speed loop with dotted gray lines. The cylinder servo phase loop is marked in a solid red line with the capstan servo phase loop in dotted red lines.

In the Radio Shack 150, different signal paths are marked blue and green. In the process schematic, the "yellow" signal is marked in solid blue lines with the white signal in dotted blue lines (FIG. 2-6). The cyan signal is alternating solid and dotted blue lines, and the green signal is a solid green line.

The chroma circuits in the Minolta C3300 chroma circuits show the chroma signal with a clear arrow and the luminance is marked with a solid arrow (FIG. 2-7). Where both color the and luminance signals are found, one-half of the arrow is clear and the other part is solid.

CONNECTIONS

Wiring connections with plugs may be marked in various sizes of boxes (FIG. 2-8). The dual box is where a connector ties on. The board connections show boxes at each end while direct wiring connections have circles with numbered connections. Double-check all connectors for poor contact if there is intermittent operation.

SURFACE-MOUNTED COMPONENTS

Surface-mounted components often consist of more than one component in the signal chip, such as transistors and base and bias resistors.

Leadless Transistors

The leadless or surface-mounted transistor number is located by a code on its surface. The code is either two alphabet letters, one number and two alphabet letters, or one alphabet letter and one number in the Pentax PV-C850A camcorder (TABLE 2-1).

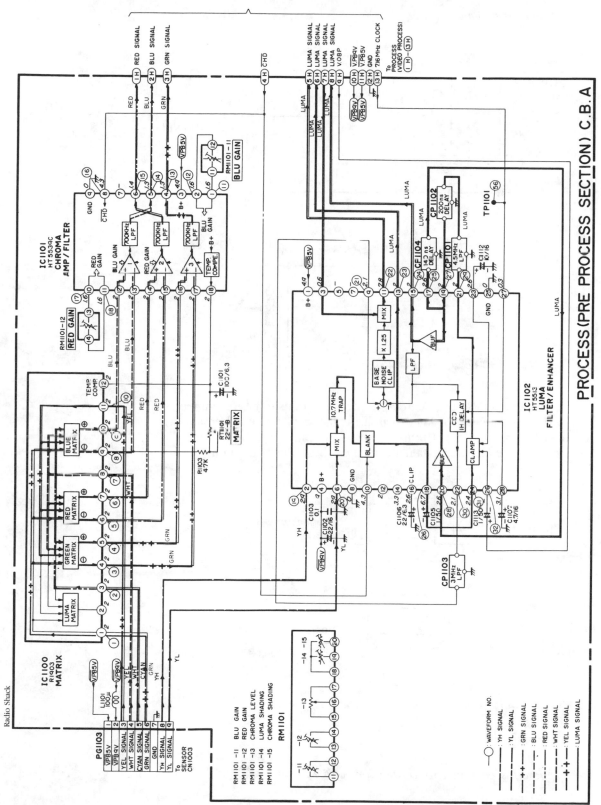

2-6 *The yellow and white signal paths are marked in blue and green in the Radio Shack 150 process circuits.*

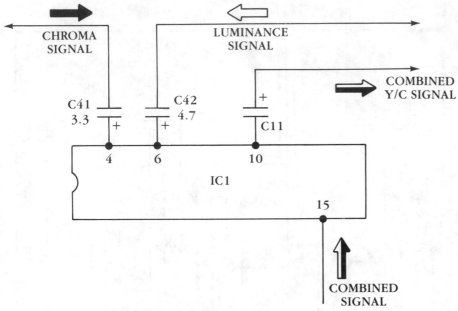

2-7 *Minolta C3300 chroma circuit signal path arrows.*

In the RCA CPR100 camcorder, the leadless transistors are numbered with a code on the body using two alphabet letters or one number and two alphabet letters (TABLE 2-2). The first letter is the transistor number and the second letter the dc current gain. Remember, these letters and numbers are

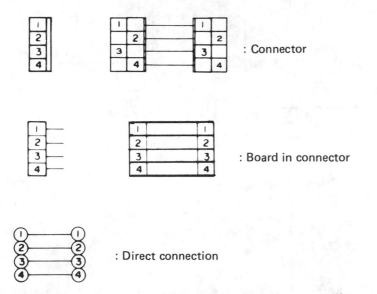

2-8 *Different schematic wire connections of the Zenith VM6150.*

Table 2-1. Leadless Transistor Identification (Pentax PV-C850A)

Letter	Transistor No.	Letter	Transistor No.
A	2SB709	P	2SD814
B	2SC1621	Q	2SC2620
BR	2SC2412KR(BR)	R	2SC2618
BS	2SC2412KS(BS)	S	2SA1121
C	2SC1122	U	2SC2404
CR	2SB710R(CR)	WQ	2SK322Q(WQ)
CQ	2SC2412KQ(CQ)	W	2SD602
D	2SC2463	X	2SK157
E	2SA1022	Y	2SD601
F	2SC2619	1F	2SK321
FR	2SA1037KR(FR)	1M	2SA1052
H	2SC1036K	1K	2SK316
I	2SB792	2B	2SK374
K	2SK160	13	DTA143K
L	2SC2462	15	DTA124K
L(6)	2SC1623(6)(L6)	25	DTC124K
M	2SA1052	26	DTC144K
N	2SC1653		

Pentax

Example:

Code	Number
CD	2SA1122D
LD	2SC2462D

Rank of DC Current Gain (h_{FE})

Transistor Number

different in different camcorders. Use the letters and numbers for that model and compare them to the chart for the correct part or component. Transistors can be npn or pnp (FIG. 2-9).

Digital Transistors

You may find digital transistors in some camcorder surface-mounted components. The digital transistors are either npn or pnp with base and bias

Table 2-2. Leadless Transistor Identification (RCA CPR100)

Letter	Transistor	Letter	Transistor
A	25B709	Q	2SC2620
C	2SA1122	R	2SC2618
D	2SC2463	S	2SA1121
E	2SA1022	U	2SC2404
F	2SC2619	W	2SD602
I	2SB792	X	2SK157
K	2SK160	Y	2SD601
L	2SC2462	1F	2SK321
M	2SA1052	1M	2SA1052
P	2SD814	L-#	2SC1623(#)

Example:

Code	Number
CD	2SA1122D
LD	2SC2462D

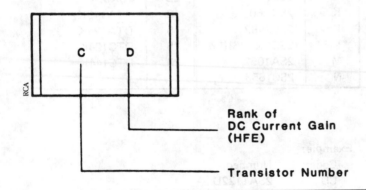

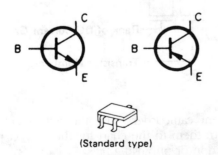

2-9 *The chip or leadless transistor can be an npn or pnp.*

Table 2-3. Digital Transistor Chart (Mitsubishi HS-C2OU)

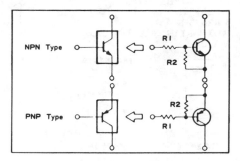

RESISTOR VALUES

JUNCTION	Part No.	R1 (kΩ)	R2 (kΩ)
PNP	DTA124EK	22	22
NPN	DTC144EK	47	47
	DTC124EK	22	22

Mitsubishi

resistors. In the Mitsubishi HS-C200 camcorder inverter, interface, and driver circuits contain the digital transistors. The advantages are their small size and high reliability. Notice the different resistance values of R1 and R2 (TABLE 2-3). Replace the entire component with either a defective resistor or transistor.

Chip Diodes

The leadless diode is identified by a code on the surface, using two alphabet letters or numbers in the Pentax 8 mm camcorder (TABLE 2-4). You might find one or two fixed diodes in one chip. Also, the zener diode is in some models. Chip diodes often have three terminal leads, except only two are used when one diode is contained within (FIG. 2-10). Correct polarity must be observed.

Table 2-4. Leadless Diode Chart (Pentax 8 mm)

Code	Diode No.	Code	Diode No.
MH	MA151K	6.8	MA3068
MT	MA151WK	6.8M	MA3068M
MU	MA152WK	9.1	MA3091
MN	MA151WA	27	RD2.7M-B
MO	MA152WA	30	RD3.0M-B
MC	MA153	56	RD5.6M-B
NT	DAN202K	91	RD9.1M-B

Pentax

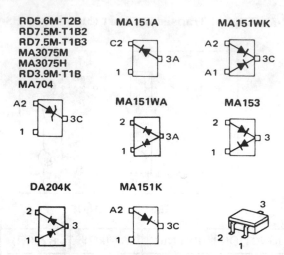

2-10 *Chip diodes in the Mitsubishi HS-C2OU camcorder.* Mitsubishi Electric

Table 2-5.   Leadless Resistor Values (RCA VHS-CPR100)

Letter	Value	Letter	Value
A	1	N	3.3
C	1.2	Q	3.9
E	1.5	S	4.7
G	1.8	U	5.6
J	2.2	W	6.8
L	2.7	Y	8.2

Example:

Code	Value		
L 0	2.7×10^0	=	2.7 ohms
S 3	4.7×10^3	=	4.7K ohms

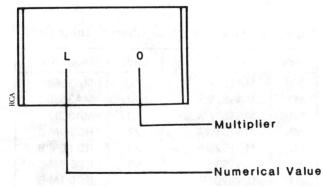

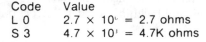

Leadless Resistors

The value of some leadless resistors is indicated on the surface of the component by a two-position alphanumeric code in the RCA CPR100 camcorder (TABLE 2-5). Here the letter is first, which indicates the numerical value, and the multiplier the second number. Double-chip resistors are found on the Zenith VM6150 unit (FIG. 2-11). These devices contain two different resistors

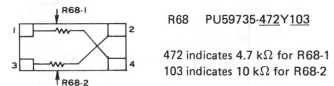

R68   PU59735-472Y103

472 indicates 4.7 kΩ for R68-1
103 indicates 10 kΩ for R68-2

2-11   *Double-chip resistors in the Zenith VM6150 VHS C camcorder.* Zenith

in one chip. Here resistor R68-1 (4.7 kΩ) has lead terminals of 1 and 4, while resistor R68-2 (10 kΩ) is connected with terminals 2 and 3. The double-chip resistor can be installed with either end interchanged, but if the chip is turned over or mounted upside down, it will result in the wrong resistor values. Remember, each manufacturer has its own code.

Leadless Capacitors

The capacitive value is indicated on the surface of the surface of the component, using body color and one letter, or one letter and one number in the Pentax 8 mm camcorder (TABLE 2-6). For example, a leadless capacitor with a red body and coded with letter A is a 1 pF capacitor. If the body was black with code letter A, it equals 10 pF. A chip resistor listed as L3, equals $2.7 \times 10^3 = 2700$ ohms. The alphanumeric-coded leadless capacitor in the RCA CPR100 model are found on the surface (TABLE 2-7).

TEST POINTS

Various test points are shown throughout most circuits in the camcorder from which to take voltage or waveform samples. For example, measure the regulated 5 V out from the power circuits at TP1 (FIG. 2-12). TP401 provides the waveform signal applied to the end sensor IC407 at pin 10.

Voltage and signal waveforms may be taken at the input and output terminals of IC or microprocessor components to determine if the correct signal is passed on to the next component. The oscilloscope is a very valuable tool when troubleshooting the mechanism, servo, video, luminance, and color circuits and in making electrical adjustments.

CLEANING

The camcorder is a complicated piece of equipment. It contains belts, rollers, heads, etc., which become worn and deteriorated under extensive usage. Dust and dirt also cause the camcorder to malfunction. Regular and

Table 2-6. Leadless Capacitor Values (Pentax 8 mm)

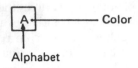

Body Color	Alphabet	Value
Red	A	1 (PF)
	C	2
	E	3
	G	4
	J	5
	L	6
	N	7
	Q	8
	S	9
Black	A	10 (PF)
	C	12
	E	15
	G	18
	J	22
	L	27
	N	33
	Q	39
	S	47
	U	56
	W	68
	Y	82

Example:

Color	Code	Value
Red	A	1 PF
Black	A	10PF

Pentax

periodic maintainance should be performed upon the camcorder to keep it in tip-top shape.

Keep the lens assembly clean with a regular camera cleaning brush kit. Clean the video, full erase, and audio/control heads with a cleaning kit and solvent. Periodic cleaning of the tape mechanism's moving parts may prevent greater damage.

Table 2-7. Leadless Capacitor Values (RCA CPR100)

Alphanumeric Coded Capacitors

The value of some leadless capacitors is indicated by an alphanumeric code on the component surface. Use this code and the following chart for component identification.

Code	Value	Code	Value
A0	1pf	L1	27pf
H0	2pf	N1	33pf
M0	3pf	Q1	39pf
d0	4pf	S1	47pf
f0	5pf	U1	56pf
m0	6pf	W1	68pf
n0	7pf	Y1	82pf
t0	8pf		
y0	9pf	A2	100pf
		C2	120pf
A1	10pf	E2	150pf
C1	12pf	G2	180pf
E1	15pf	J2	220pf
G1	18pf	L2	270pf
J1	22pf	N2	330pf
Q2	390pf	A4	0.01µf
S2	470pf	E4	0.015µf
U2	560pf	J4	0.022µf
W2	680pf	N4	0.033µf
Y2	820pf	S4	0.047µf
		U4	0.056µf
A3	0.001µf	W4	0.068µf
E3	0.0015µf		
J3	0.0022µf	A5	0.1µf
N3	0.0033µf		
S3	0.0047µf		
W3	0.0068µf		

Q2 — 390pf   d0 — 4pf

RCA

Cleaning the Video Head

First use a cleaning tape to keep the heads and tape guides free of tape oxide. If the dirt on the video head is too stubborn to be removed by the tape cleaning cartridge, use a cleaning stick and solvent to clean the audio head. Some manufacturers recommend a chamois leather cleaning stick with solvent.

Do not try to clean the head down through the cassette cover vent (FIG. 2-13). Remove the front cassette cover to get at the video head to clean it. Some manufacturers recommend that you hold the cleaning stick at right angles and holding the top part of the head only, gently turn the rotating cylinder to the right and left (FIG. 2-14). Do not move the stick vertically or you may damage the head. Thoroughly dry the head after cleaning. If cleaning fluid remains on the video head, the tape may be damaged when it comes in contact with the head surface. The cleaning cassette may clean up some of the rollers and guide pins, but they should also be cleaned with alcohol and cleaning stick (FIG. 2-15).

Tape Transport

The tape transport system consists of parts that come in contact with the running tape. The drive system consists of those parts that run the tape (FIG. 2-16). Periodic cleaning of the components is necessary to ensure good performance of the tape mechanism (TABLE 2-8). Clean with gauze or lint-free

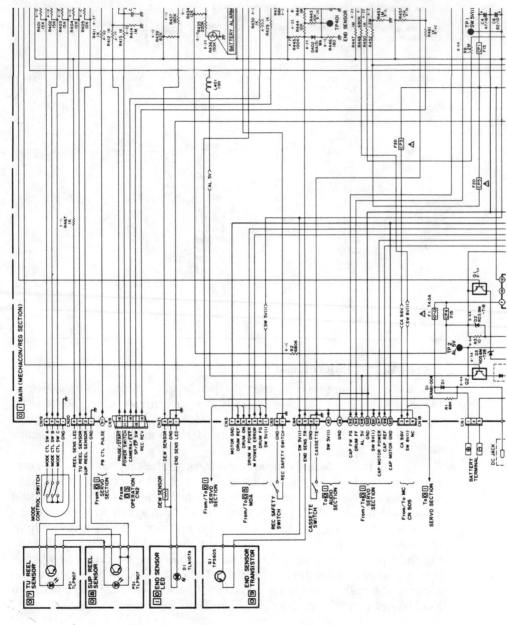

2-12 *Test points and voltage measurements are found throughout the Mechacon and Regulator circuits in the Minolta C3300 camcorder.* Minolta Camera

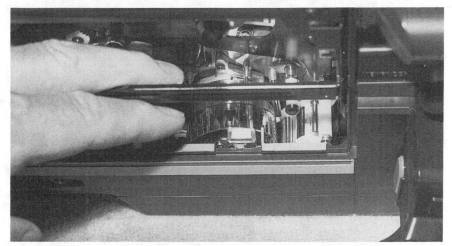

2-13 *Remove the front loading cover to get at the video heads to clean.*

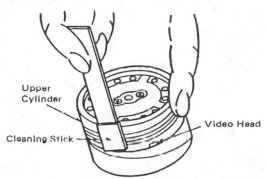

Upper
Cylinder

Cleaning Stick

Video Head

2-14 *Rub the video head horizontally with cleaning stick and solvent.*

2-15 *Clean all rollers and tape guides with cleaning stick and alcohol.*

1. Capstan Motor
2. Pinch Roller
3. TG1 Arm
4. TG1 Band
5. TG1 Release Arm
6. Soft Brake
7. Lever A
8. Lever A Release Pin
9. LM Motor
10. Drum Motor
11. Pendulum Gear Arm

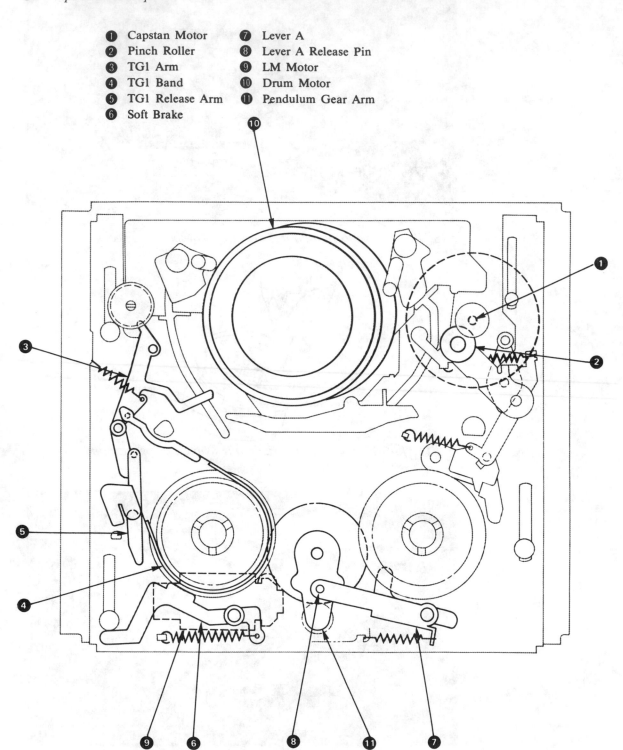

2-16 *Clean drive system, which are the parts that run the tape.*

Table 2-8. Mechanical Parts Maintenance

Use following table as a guide to maintain the mechanical parts in good operating condition.

Parts \ Maintained every	1000Hrs	2000Hrs	3000Hrs	4000Hrs	5000Hrs
Video head	R C	R C	R C	R C	R C
Audio/Control (A/C) Head	C	C	C	C	R C
Full Erase (FE) Head	C	C	C	C	R C
Capstan flywheel	C	C	C	C	C
Center pulley	C	C	C	C	C
Supply guide pole	C	C	C	C	C
Take-up guide pole	C	C	C	C	C
Tension band	C	R C	C	R C	C
Supply reel disk	C	C	C	C	C
Supply gear	C	C	C	C	C
Take-up gear	C	C	C	C	C
Impedance roller	C	C	C	C	C
Pressure roller	C	R C	C	R C	C
Pulley belt	C	R C	C	R C	C
Capstan belt	C	R C	C	R C	C
Capstan motor		R		R	
Loading motor		R		R	
Cylinder motor		R		R	
Between both guide roller bases and gutters on chassis		H		H	
Pressure roller arm		H		H	
Loading gear		H		H	
Catcher block		H		H	
Shaft of cassette holder switch		H		H	
Gear of supply loading ring		H		H	
Gear of take-up loading ring		H		H	

Table 2-8. Continued.

Parts \ Maintained every	1000Hrs	2000Hrs	3000Hrs	4000Hrs	5000Hrs
Shaft of FE head	S	S	S	S	S
Shaft of supply reel disk	S	S	S	S	S
Shaft of supply sub gear	S	S	S	S	S
Shaft of supply gear	S	S	S	S	S
Shaft of take-up gear	S	S	S	S	S
Shaft of take-up reel gear	S	S	S	S	S
Shaft of pressure roller	S	S	S	S	S
Shaft of pressure roller arm	S	S	S	S	S
Shaft of cam gear	S	S	S	S	S
Shaft of A/C head base	S	S	S	S	S
Shaft of loading gear (1)	S	S	S	S	S
Shaft of loading gear (2)	S	S	S	S	S
Shaft of center pulley	S	S	S	S	S
Shaft of ring idler gear (1)	S	S	S	S	S
Shaft of ring idler gear (2)	S	S	S	S	S
Shaft of loading ring spacers	S	S	S	S	S

Note 1: R: Part replacement
C: Cleaning (For cleaning, lint-free cloth dampened with pure isopropyl alcohol).
H: Grease refilling (The indicated point should be lubricated with Hitazol or Froil grease every 5000 hrs).
S: Oil refilling (The indicated point should be lubricated with pan motor or Sonic Slidas oil every 1000 hrs).

cloth dipped in isopropyl alcohol or freon. Also, Kim wipes and solvent does the job on the following parts:

- Capstan shaft
- All idler wheels
- Impedance roller
- Pressure roller
- All tape guide posts
- Supply reel
- Capstan belt

- Pulley belt
- Capstan motor pulley
- Center pulley
- All gear assemblies

Cleaning the EVF

After using the camcorder outdoors, where dust and dirt blows freely, the electronic viewfinder CRT surface must be cleaned. Remove the EVF from the camcorder. Clean the outside lens and remove covers if necessary to get at the CRT surface. In some models, the front eyepiece comes off and the CRT surface will then be in sight. Wipe off the dust of the tube lightly with a cotton swab or stick. Reassemble the EVF assembly and replace it on the camcorder.

LUBRICATION

The tape transport mechanism is properly lubricated at the factory, and additional lubrication should not be needed during the first year of operation. Periodic inspection for lubrication may be followed as shown in (TABLE 2-8). Remove the old lubricant first. Do not over-oil; only a drop will do. A squeaky bearing should be lubricated. It's best to not lubricate at all than to over-oil, where it could drip down on other moving parts. Wipe off excess oil with cleaning stick and alcohol. Place a drop or two of light oil on the moving parts. Many camcorder manufacturers have their own grease and lubricants. Before replacing a moving part, apply oil or grease.

Apply a light grease, for example Hitazal or Froil, with a small stick or brush on sliding areas (FIG. 2-17). Do not use excess grease. Keep it away from the tape transport or drive system components. Wipe up any excess with cloth and alcohol. Periodic greasing may be applied every 1000 or 5000 hours in these places:

- Between pressure roller bar and shaft
- Between pressure roller and gear assembly
- Between the base of guide rollers and gutters
- Gutter of cam gears
- Gutter of chassis
- Loading gear shaft
- Loading gears
- Ring idler gear
- Shaft of loading rings
- Shaft of idler gears

TEST EQUIPMENT

Most electronic service establishments already have many of the needed test equipment for camcorder repair (FIG. 2-18). If you are already servicing VCRs,

2-17 *First clean off old grease, then apply light grease with a small stick or brush on all sliding areas.*

2-18 *Most electronic service establishments already have the needed test equipment for camcorder repair. Only a few special tools, such as lighting equipment and other test jigs, are needed.*

you have most of the test equipment and hand tools needed. You might only need a few additional test instruments and cable adapters. Here is a list of basic test equipment needed for camcorder repair:

- Oscilloscope
- Digital voltmeter and/or multimeter
- Frequency counter
- Vectorscope
- Color video monitor
- Tripods
- Light box (3200 degrees)
- Waveform monitor
- Light meter
- 0-to-12-volt power supply

Besides the schematic diagram and required service literature, there are many small tools, adaptors, jigs, and color scale charts. Some manufacturers provide a back focus chart, a gray and white chart, and a hunting chart in the service literature (FIG. 2-19). Each manufacturer has a complete list of servicing jigs and tools listed in the service literature for each camcorder.

The Oscilloscope
The dual-trace scope should have a minimum bandwidth of 25 MHz. Delayed sweep is necessary for camera alignment procedures. Most service establishments have a dual-trace scope of higher bandwidth for TV and VCR servicing.

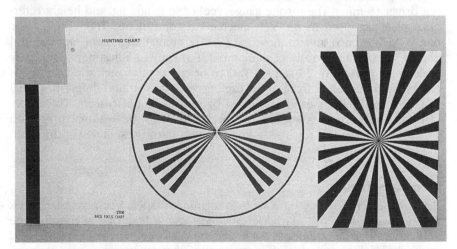

2-19 *Several different adjustment charts are often included in the service literature.*

Meters

Accurate voltage and resistance measurements are needed in checking microprocessor, IC, and transistor voltages. Choose a meter with at least 1200 to 1500 volts dc to read the high voltage on the anode of the pickup electronic viewfinder tube. If you are using a VOM, make sure it is at least a 20 kilohm/volt type.

Frequency Counter

If you are going to purchase a frequency counter, make sure it will read above 20 MHz.

Vectorscope

Some manufacturers use the vectorscope in making black and white balance adjustments, auto white balance, chroma level adjustments, shading adjustments, red/blue/green setup, and red and blue signal gain (some of these adjustments can be made with the oscilloscope). The vectorscope was used many years ago in servicing the TV chassis.

Light Box

Although the light box is more expensive than wall charts for camera servicing, it is the best. The light box with 3200-degree light source provides even lumination of test patterns over a white opaque screen. The light box may contain a fixed or variable light output. These light test boxes may be obtained through the various camera manufacturers or wholesale part dealers.

Special Test Jig and Tools

The special tools for the RCA CPR100 camcorder consist of a head adjust driver, special driver bit (3 mm), hex key, hex nut driver (3 mm) and hex nut driver (5 mm). The torque gauge, reel table height jig, and height reference plate are used in the VTR mechanical adjustments. The VHS-C color bar (1 kHz mono) and monoscope (7 kHz mono) alignment tapes round out the electrical adjustment equipment. For camera adjustments, the gray scale chart with 10 or 11 steps, NTSC color chart, autofocus, and back focus charts are mounted in front of the camcorder. You will find different special jigs, tools and harnesses are required by various manufacturers. These special jigs and harnesses should be purchased from the manufacturer. You might be able to put together some of these harnesses after working with the various camcorders.

Test Cassettes

Each manufacturer may have its own alignment tapes. Use a regular blank tape for recording and playback tests. Most use at least one alignment tape and others use an additional color cassette (TABLE 2-9). These tapes are used in mechanical, electrical, and camera setup adjustments.

Table 2-9. Test Cassettes

Mfg.	Test Cassette	Part Numbers
Minolta	Alignment tape M+C1	7982-8012-01
Mitsubishi	Alignment MH-C1	859C35909
NEC	VHS alignment tape	79040302
Pentax	NTSC alignment tape	20HSC-2
RCA	Color bar 1 kHz mono	180434
	Monoscope 7 kHz mono	180435
Zenith	Alignment tape MY-C1	868-206
	EP mode check tape CY-CIL	868-247

Chapter **3**

The
Camera Section

The basic camcorder circuit can be broken down into the camera and VCR sections. The camera section may consist of the lens assembly, image sensor, luminance and chroma processing, and the electronic viewfinder. The different circuits within the camera section have many different operations (FIG. 3-1).

VHS/VHS-C CAMERA CIRCUITS

The VHS and VHS-C camera section may contain the lens assembly, automatic focus, iris or AIC control, and zoom motor assembly. The image sensor might have a pickup tube, as in the early VHS camcorders, or the later VHS and VHS-C models use a CCD or MOS pickup device. The drive pulse generator and preamplifier circuits are contained in the MOS or CCD circuits. Other VHS and VHS-C camera circuits are the sync generator, sample and hold, signal processing, matrix and filtering, luminance processing, chroma processing, automatic white balance, encoder, and power distribution systems (FIG. 3-2).

8 mm CAMERA CIRCUITS

The 8 mm camera lens assembly may consist of the focus, lens, automatic focus (AF), iris control, and zoom lens assembly. The image sensor may consist of a color filter, a CCD pickup sensor, and a CCD driver. The light signal from the CCD image device feeds to the process circuits which consist of signal separation (S/H), AGC, AGC detector, color separation S/H, and white balance. The timing generator combines the original oscillator signal and generates various timing pulses. The matrix signals are fed to the encoder circuits, which supply chroma and luminance signals to the video circuits (FIG. 3-3).

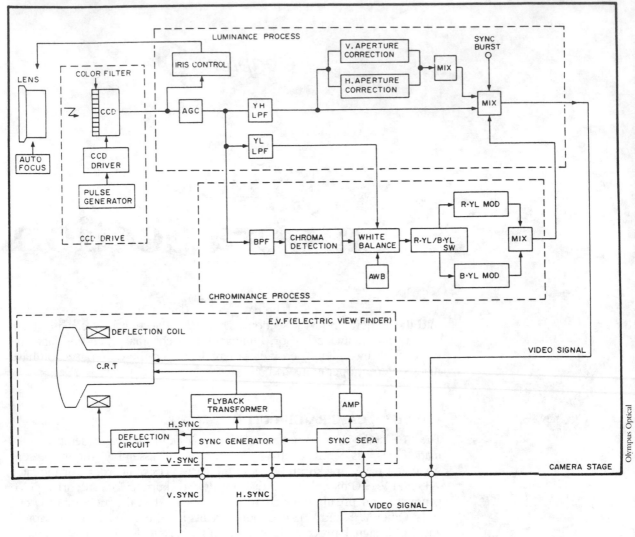

3-1   *The overall block diagram of the camera stage in the Olympus VX-801U 8 mm camcorder.*

PICKUPS

In the early VHS, VHS-C, and Beta camcorder, a pickup tube was used to detect the image and convert it to a electrical signal. However, the tube's disadvantages have been overcome by CCD or MOS pickup devices.

Pickup Tubes

The early commercial video cameras contained a small pickup tube called the Videcon, Saticon, and Newvicon. The Newvicon pickup tube was in the

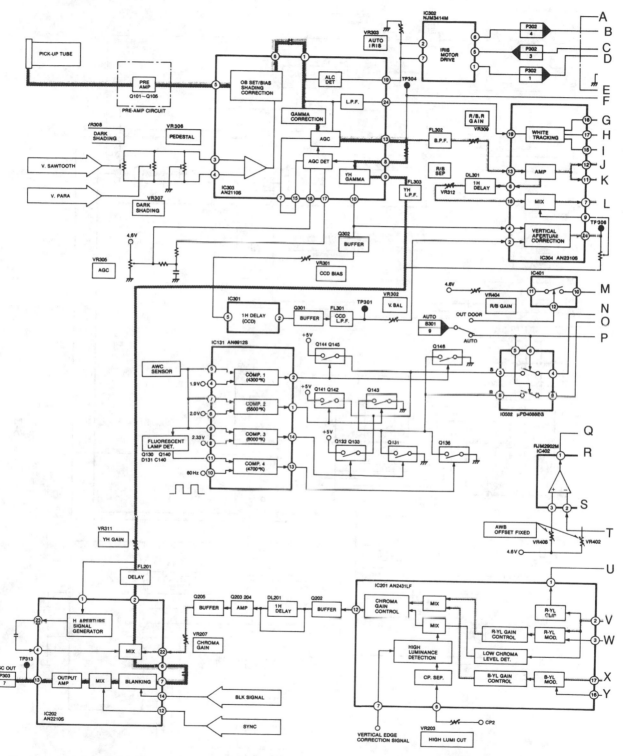

3-2 *Camera process block diagram in the General Electric 9-9605 camcorder.* Thomson Consumer Electronics

A
B
C
D
E
F

IRIS MOTOR.

M

L 306, L 307
C 322, C 323

YL L.P.F.

4.6V
VR310
YL PEDESTAL

CLAMP
Q306~Q308

V. SAWTOOTH/PARABOLA
H. SAWTOOTH/PARABOLA
γ1~γ3

VR313~VR319
GAMMA SHADING
CORRECTION

G → γ1
H → γ2
I → γ3

21   22

C 339
R/B SEP

J
K
L

2

RED/BLUE
SEPARATOR

24

IC305
AN2320S

RED
GAMMA
SHADING

BLUE
GAMMA
SHADING

GAIN
CONTROL

GAIN
CONTROL

DET.

DET.

R-YL MATRIX

B-YL MATRIX

14

13

11

YL

3   4   5   20   6   19

V. SAWTOOTH/PARABOLA
H. SAWTOOTH/PARABOLA
γ1~γ3

GAMMA SHADING
CORRECTION

VR320~VR326

VR327
VERTICAL
EDGE

M
N
O
P

IC401
μPD4066EG

6   7
4   3
8   9

γ3

9   11

IC403
MN4053BS

Q

R   14   5   8   10   9

5   4   3   14   13   12

S   12   13   7   8

T

2.5V

U

Q402 Q403
COLOR
MATRIX

BUFFER
Q401

SC FOR CCD

VR205
COLOR PHASE

VR204
COLOR
PHASE

6   SC1
7   SC2

VR401
R-YL
PED.

V

W

VR403
B-YL
PED.

COLOR
MATRIX
Q407~Q412

SYNC

BF

BSC

CP1

CP2

WHD

BLK

CP1+WHD+BLK

CP2+WHD+BLK

18   SYNC
12   BF
13   BSC
10   CP1
11   CP2
8   WHD
15   BLK
17   W. BLK

IC203 MN6064RS

4

X201

5

C230
SC

X
Y

LUMINANCE INFORMATION SIGNAL PATH
COLOR INFORMATION SIGNAL PATH

3-2 Continued

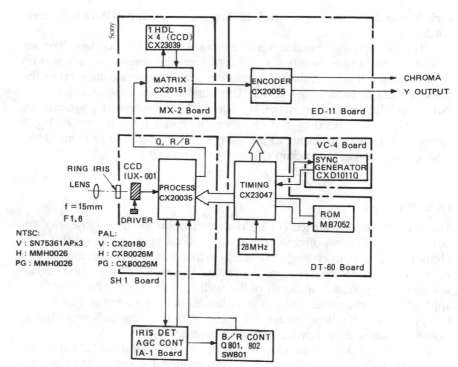

3-3 *Block diagram of Sony's CCD-M8E/M8U 8 mm camera section.*

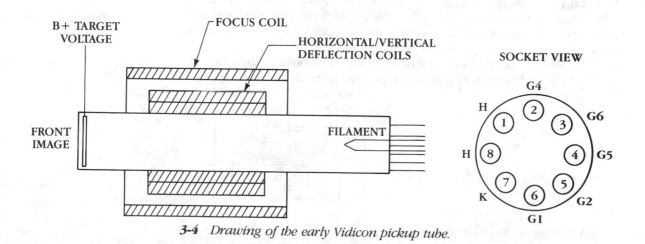

3-4 *Drawing of the early Vidicon pickup tube.*

early General Electric 9-9605 and the Saticon was in the RCA CLR200 camcorder.

The pickup tube contains heater elements and higher voltages, like any tube, for normal operation (FIG. 3-4). The pickup tube needs time to warm up before using. Of course, the tube has many disadvantages compared to the present CCD or MOS image device. The camcorder with the pickup tube is bulky, weighs more, has image lag, has higher power consumption, has short life, is influenced by the electronic magnetic field, is easy to break (glass body), and it is easier to burn the screen. Today, the CCD and MOS devices are used as the pickup device in all camcorders.

CCD Pickups

The charge-coupled device (CCD) is a semiconductor that consists of orderly arranged arrays of cells (capacitors). When light shines on the CCD element, an electric charge is developed that varies with the intensity of light. The CCD device can store the charge in a well or hole when certain voltages are applied. The depth of the well or hole varies with the voltage applied to the electrode. The charge collected in the adjacent cell or hole is moved to the cell where voltage is applied. With the many different cells or holes, the self-scanning process keeps repeating.

The surface area of the chip is divided into thousands of light-sensitive spots called *pixels* (picture elements). For example, the Zenith VM6150 camcorder charged-coupled device utilizes 223,368 pixels with a resolution in excess of 270 lines. The Pentax PV-C850A unit consists of 250,920 picture elements with 330 lines or more. The most recent camcorder CCD picture elements average between 200,000 and 300,000 pixels.

Pentax PV-C850A (8 mm) CCD   The CCD image sensor consists of 250,920 picture elements (510 horizontal and 492 vertical), giving the camera a horizontal revolution of 330 lines or more. The device also has the function of a $^{1}/_{1200}$-sec and shutter. The CCD is a semiconductor device in which MOS capacitors are in arrays. The photoelectric function converts light into a charge. When light comes in, an electric charge occurs that depends upon the intensity of the light. (FIG. 3-5).

The storage function occurs when a voltage is applied to the CCD under certain conditions. A region where positive holes do not exist appears

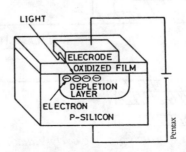

3-5 *Pentax 8 mm CCD construction.*

and charges gather there. This region is called a *depletion region* or *potential well*. The greater the potential difference, the deeper the potential well (FIG. 3-6).

The charge transfer function occurs with an appropriate voltage. The charge moves from one device element (register) with a lower potential to the adjacent element (register) with a higher potential as the charge tends to fall into a potential well. Now the charge moves from element to element if an appropriate voltage is applied to it. The CCD operation is in all camcorders using the charged-coupled device pickup element.

MOS Pickups

The MOS image sensor is a semiconductor chip device. When light falls on the picture element, the electron/hole pair is generated inside the NT layer and PT layer, which forms the photodiode. As the elections flow out, the NT layer in the PT layer the hole remains. With positive and negative voltages applied to the metal electrodes, the electrons are moved through the silicon base, providing vertical and horizonal picture scanning. Low infrared and well-balanced sensitivity is obtained by using photodiodes as the picture element (FIG. 3-7). The MOS (metal-oxide silicon) image pickup device is in the Hitachi, RCA, and Realistic camcorders. You may find the MOS device in some Kyocera, Pentax, and Sears models.

Realistic 150 (VHS-C) MOS Image Sensor   The HE98245 MOS color image sensor has an image size of 8.8 (II) × 6.5 (V) mm matching a $^2/_3$-inch optical system. The chip size is 9.9 (H) × 8.0 (V) mm. The number of picture elements are 570 (H) × 485 (V) with a total of 276,450 pixels. With this type of MOS color image sensor, sensitivity in the infrared region is low and well balanced spectal sensitivity characteristics are obtained by use of picture elements (photodiodes) with an npn three-layer structure. Blooming is also suppressed with this structure.

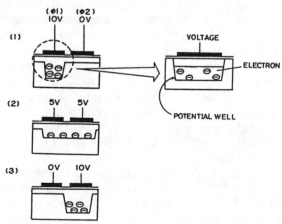

3-6 *Principle charge transfer in the CCD pickup device.* Pentax

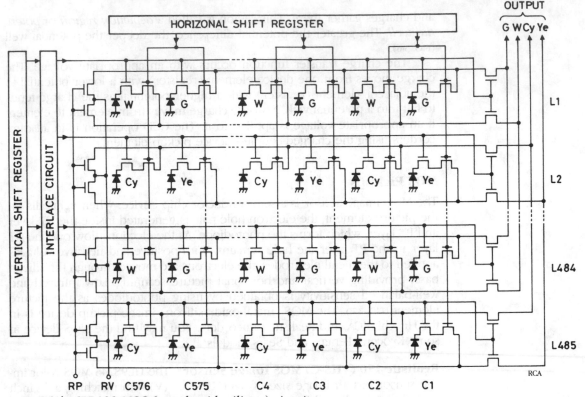

3-7 *RCA's CPR100 MOS (metal-oxide silicon) circuit.*

The color resolution filter is made by arranging complementary white (W), yellow (YE), cyan (CY) and green (G) color filters in a mosaic. The four color signals, W, YE, CY and G, are read out via four output lines, so interlaced scanning with high resolution and without residual image can be performed.

When light falls on a picture element, an electronic hole pair is generated inside the n^+ and p^+ layer. In the n^+ layer, the electron remains and the hole flows to the p^+ layer. The photoelectrons are stored in the n^+ layer as the photoelectroic conversion signal (FIG. 3-8).

A positive pulse is applied to the gate of the vertical switching transistor (TV). When reading the signal, the barrier of the gate lowers, the photoelectron stored in the n^+ layer is drawn into the n^+ layer as drain. When a positive pulse is applied to the gate of the horizontal switching transistor (TH), the barrier of the gate lowers, the photoelectron in the n^+ layer as source is drained into the n^+ layer as a drain connected to the signal line and is derived as the output.

When the positive scanning pulse generated from the vertical scanning circuit opens the gates of the vertical switching transistors (TVs) and the horizontal scanning circuit opens the gates of the horizonal switching transistors (THs) beneath them from left to right in sequence, the photoelectrons of the photodiodes of two horizontal lines are output in sequence

3-8 *MOS picture element of Realistic image sensor.*

to perform horizonal scanning. When the gate opened by the vertical scanning circuit is changed in sequence and the same is repeated, the photoelectrons of all the photodiodes are output in sequence and all the picture elements are scanned.

Pentax PV-C850A (8mm) Sync Signal Generator   The sync generator produces 15 sync signals and clock pulses that the camera and VTR need for timing. The encoder/sync signal generator (IC1206) generates these signals with correct timing (FIG. 3-9). IC206 receives four FSC clock pulses at pin 22 from pin 26 of the drive signal generator IC1102, which produces sync sig-

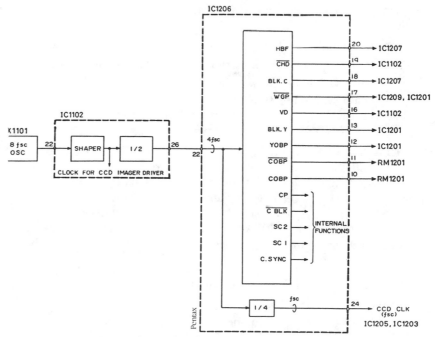

3-9   *Pentax PV-C850A (8 mm) sync signal generator circuits.*

nals with the aid of dividing and logic circuits. The following signals are generated by the sync generator:

- Horizonal burst flag (HBF) pulse determines when to insert the subcarrier (fsc).
- Camera horizonal drive (CHD) pulse times the horizonal drive of the image sensor.
- Chrominance blanking pulse (BLKC) times the blanking of the chroma signal.
- Window gate pulse (WGP) determines the sampling time for AGC and iris detector.
- Vertical drive pulse (VD) times the vertical drive of the image sensor.
- Luminance blanking pulse (BLKY) times the clamping of the luminance signal.
- Luminance optical block pulse (YOBP) times the sampling of optical block level from the image sensor outputs.
- Chrominance optical block pulse (COBP/COBP) times the sampling of RGB signals.
- Clock pulse.

The following sync signals are used inside IC206 and are not supplied outside:

- Clamp pulse (CP) times the sampling of R-Y and B-Y signals.
- Composite blanking pulse (CBLK) times blanking for the encoder in IC1206.
- Sub carrier pulse (SCI) is amplitude-modulated by the B-Y signal.
- The 90-degree delayed sub carrier (SC2) pulse is amplitude-modulated by the R-Y signal.
- Composite sync pulse (C.SYNC) determines when to apply horizontal and vertical sync signals during the blanking period.

RCA CPR100 (VHS-C) Sync Generator Circuit   There are many operations within the color camera section that are synchronized to provide correct operation. IC1107 provides the generated signals to synchronize the different operations in the color camera circuits (FIG. 3-10).

The reference frequency signal inside IC1107 is controlled with a crystal oscillator (14.31818 MHz). All start and synchronization output signals are counted down from the reference frequency. IC1107 generates the following signals:

- Composite sync (C.SYNC), pin number 16
- Blanking pulse (B.BLK), pin number 9
- Clamp pulse (CP1), pin number 11
- Composite Sync (C.SYNC), pin number 12

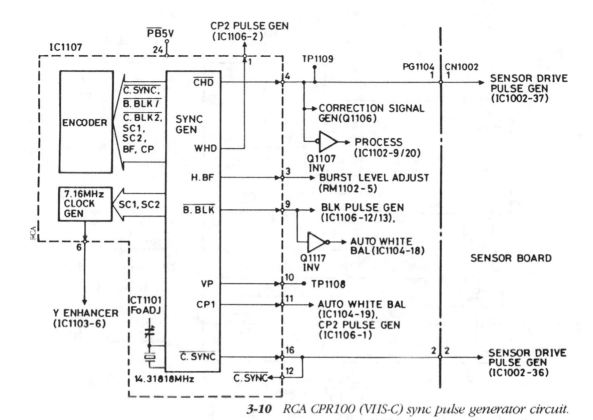

3-10 *RCA CPR100 (VIIS-C) sync pulse generator circuit.*

- Wide horizonal drive pulse (CP2), pin number 1
- Horizontal burst flag pulse (H.BF), pin number 3
- Vertical pulse (VP), pin number 10
- Camera horizonal drive pulse (CHD), pin number 4
- 7.16 MHz clock pulse (CLK GEN), pin number 6

Pentax PV-C850A (8mm) CCD Image Drive Circuit The charged-coupled device (CCD) image sensor is driven by the horizontal drive signals (H1 and H2) with two phases, vertical drive signals (V1 through V4), with four phases, output reset signal (PG), and three fixed dc bias voltages (VOFD 9-15 V, VPD 14 V, VSG − 12 V).

H1 and H2, applied to the H register, time the transfer of charge from the H register to the output circuit during the horizonal scan period. The high (Hi) output level is 1.6 V and the low (Lo) level is − 6.5 V (FIG. 3-11).

The precharge gate (PG), applied to the output circuit, times the resetting charge, which remains in the output circuit after the previous scanning before charge is transferred from the H register to the output circuit during the horizontal scanning period. The high (Hi) output level is 9 V, and the low (Lo) level 1 V.

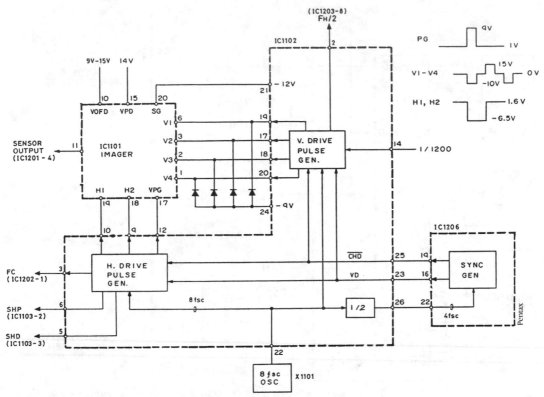

3-11 *Pentax (8mm) CCD image sensor drive circuit.*

V1 through V4 time the transfer of charge from the V register to the H register during the horizonal blanking period. Also, they time the transfer of charges from the sensor to the V register and their mixing during the vertical blanking period. The output levels of V1 and V3 take three values, Hi, Mid and Lo. V2 and V4 take two values, Mid and Lo. The high (Hi) level is 15 V, Mid level 0 V, and low (Lo) level −10 V.

The voltage of overflow drain (VODF) determines the overflow drain voltage. There is a well of electrons (overflow drain) between adjacent sensor elements. If excess charge occurs at an image highlighted, it will be injected into the (well) to prevent V register, reducing blooming. The varying voltage of the image sensor is set between 9 and 15 volts.

The voltage of precharge drain (VFD) determines the reset level of the precharge drain in the output circuit. Charge remaining from the previous scanning period will be reset by applying this voltage (14 V) to the output circuit before charge is transferred from the H register to the output circuit.

The voltage of sensor gate (VSG) determines the depth of the potential well in the storage section of the sensor. This voltage is −12 V.

IC1102 produces the drive signals and VSG. The sensor drive signal generator (IC1102) receives the fsc clock pulse generated by the clock generator X1101. The horizontal and vertical drive signals (CHD) and (VD) generated by the sync generator/encoder (IC1206) through pins 22, 23 and 25 produce the synchronized drive signals. These signals drive the CCD image sensor.

Radio Shack 150 (VSH-C) MOS Color Image Sensor Drive Pulse Generator The MOS color image sensor drive pulse generator (IC1005) consists of the 5.37 MHz high-speed section, horizontal frequency section, vertical frequency section and shutter control section (FIG. 3-12). You may find the shutter speed section only on some camera circuits.

The CHD pulse is input to operate the horizontal counter (COUNTER) to synchronize operations with the sync generator (IC1104). Also, the CHD pulse with the C.SYNC pulse is used to detect fields and operate the vertical counter (COUNTER).

The 5.37 MHz high-speed section consists of the 10.7 MHz voltage-controlled crystal oscillator (10.7 MHz VCXO) and generates a reference frequency of 10.7 MHz, adjusted with trimmer capacitors (CT1001). This 10.7 MHz reference frequency is applied to the phase detector (PHASE DET), and its phase is compared with the trailing edge of the CHD pulse (FIG. 3-13). The error voltage generated by the phase detector (PHASE DET) is applied through the low-pass filter (LPF) and pin 3 to the Varicap diode (D1001) of

3-12 *The MOS color image sensor circuits are in a shielded compartment in the RCA CPR300 camcorder.*

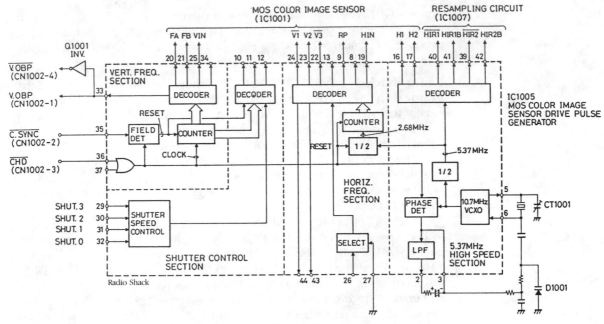

3-13 *Realistic 150 MOS color image sensor drive pulse generator.*

the 10.7 MHz voltage-controlled crystal oscillator and to control its frequency. The 10.7 MHz reference frequency is divided by 2 and is applied to the decoder (DECODER) and divider ($\frac{1}{2}$) of the horizontal frequency section.

The decoder (DECODER) generates 5.37 MHz horizontal shift register clock pulses (H1 and H2), which are applied to the MOS color image sensor (IC1001), and the horizontal integration pulses (H1R1, H1RB, H1R2 and H1R2B), which are applied to the resampling circuit (IC1007).

The horizontal frequency section generates the 15.734 kHz horizontal frequency from the reference frequency of 2.68 MHz, which is divided by 2. The counter (COUNTER) is reset after the delivery of the last H1N pulse every 1H and stop operation. It resumes operation at the leading edge of the CHD pulse. The selection circuit (SELECT) inputs 2 bits of data from pins 26 and 27, determining the horizontal frequency.

The vertical frequency section determines the field by receiving CED and C.SYNC pulses from the sync generator (IC1104) and generates the 60 Hz vertical frequency.

The shutter control circuits (SHUTTER SPEED CONTROL) input 4 bits of data from pins 29 to 32 (SHUT. 3 to SHUT. 0) and determine the sampling periods (shutter speed). In this unit, these four inputs are high (Hi), and the sampling period (shutter speed) is fixed to 1.60 second.

The shutter speed (storage time) of the CCD image sensor is normally $\frac{1}{60}$. At this speed, pictures of a fast-moving object would be distorted in slow or still playback. A higher shutter speed is needed to reduce this picture movement. However, such a higher shutter speed results in a lack of exposure and lighting (a video light of 160 lux or more at $^1/_{1200}$ is necessary indoors). With lower shutter speeds ($^1/_{750}$), lower than the blanking pulse period, switching noise appears at the bottom of the picture because reading and releasing changes occur in the middle of the picture. Rotate the shutter speed at $^1/_{1200}$ so that switching noise is not noticeable. At $^1/_{1200}$, the storage time is about $^1/_{20}$ of the ordinary value ($^1/_{60}$) and is within the vertical blanking period.

SIGNAL-PROCESSING CIRCUITS

The VHS and VHS-C signal-processing circuits may consist of the CCD or MOS image sensor, preamplifier, resampling, chroma, and luminance circuits. The 8 mm signal-processing circuits may consist of CCD image sensor, signal separation S/H, AGC, AGC detector, color separation S/H and white balance (FIG. 3-14). In the 8 mm signal-processing circuits, a CCD image sensor picks up the images and feeds them to the signal separation S/H and AGC circuits. The output of the camera processing circuit consists of a luminance (Y) and chroma (C) signals. The camera has two video output signals that ae applied to the EE video signal processing circuits in the VCR or VTR. The other is the chroma signal, which is supplied to the chroma signal-processing circuit in the VTR.

Pentax PV-C850A (8 mm) CDS and AGC Circuits   The signal-processing circuits consist of the output from the image sensor (IC-1101) through buffer (Q1102) to pin 1 of IC1103 and the Y/C separation of IC1201 (FIG. 3-15). These circuits do two things: one is to make the signal output from the image sensor continuous and the other is to keep the level input to the processing circuits appropriate while the intensity of incoming light varies. IC1103 (CDS) performs the first function. IC1201 (AGC) performs the second. In addition to these circuits, there is a clamping circuit that regenerates the DC component for the sensor output signal and a blanking circuit that regulates the blanking period and removes noise.

The CDS circuit (IC1103) samples reset noise. The signal including reset noise separates from the sensor output and subtracts the reset noise

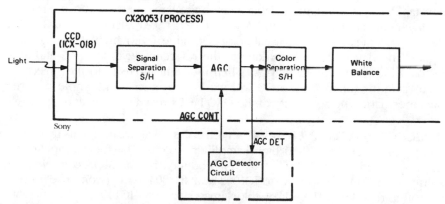

3-14 *Sony's CCD-M8E/M8U (8 mm) signal-processing circuits.*

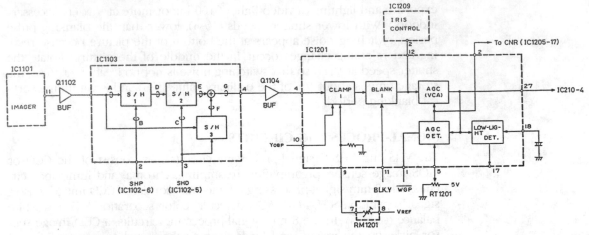

3-15 *Pentax (8 mm) CDS and AGC circuits.* Pentax

from the signal to remove it and makes the signal continuous by replacing the reset noise signal. This removes low-frequency noise and leakage of the sample-hold pulse.

The clamp 1 circuit (IC1201) samples the black level (optical black level) of the sensor output and clamps each line equally to regenerate DC components lost in C coupling before the sensor output is applied to the AGC circuit. Clamp 1 is a keyed clamp with feedback. It samples the optical black level of the sensor output applied to pin 4. The black level of the sensor output is always clamped to the reference level and is applied to the blanking circuit (BLANK-1).

The blanking circuit regulates the blanking period and removes noise occurring during this period before the sensor output is applied to the AGC circuit in the next stage. This clamps the sensor output to a fixed level (approximately 1.8 V). The blank sensor output is applied to the AIC control (IC1209) and the AGC circuit (IC1201).

The AGC circuit keeps the input level to the signal-processing circuits constant by controlling gain, depending on the light intensity. It consists of a voltage-controlled amplifier and AGC detector (AGC DET). The AGC DET detects the mean value (normal) or peak value (with high input) of the signal. The detected level is added to the reference level at pin 5 and applies to the gain combat of VCA. When the light intensity to the object is high (bright sunlight), the AGC will work "too much" and whole picture becomes dark. The sensitivity of the GAC DET prevents this action.

Realistic 150 (VHS-C) Preamplifier Circuits   The weak signals from the image sensor are amplified by preamplifier circuits. The four complementary-color signals (W, YE, G, and CY) produced by the MOS color image sensor (IC1001) are applied to IC1002 and IC1003, which compose a preamplifier (FIG. 3-16). The MOS color image sensor (IC1001) is a current source with a low output at about 200 mA. Therefore, the camera's overall signal-to-noise ratio (S/N) depends on the preamplifier.

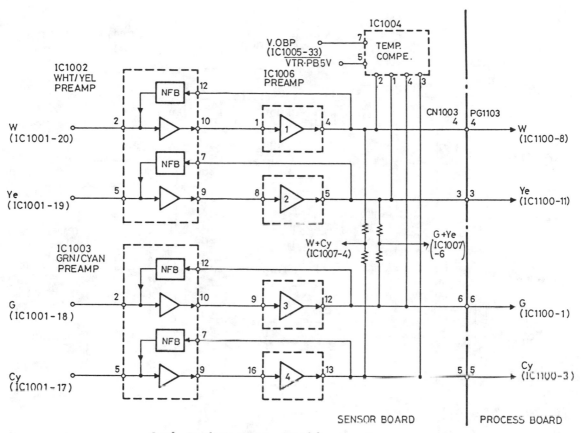

3-16 *Realistic 150 preamplifier circuits.* Radio Shack

The preamplifier has the low input impedance of about 500 ohms, as it must read signals with the short clock interlude of 186 ns (5.37 MHz). To reduce the input impedance, the dc output of the second-stage preamplifier (IC1006) is negatively fed back to the FET amplifier in the first stage (IC1002). The amplified color signals come out of pins 4, 5, 12, and 13 and enter the resampling circuit (IC1007) and matrix circuit (IC1100).

RCA CPR100 (VHS-C) Matrixing and Filter Circuits The matrix and filter circuits in the RCA camcorder may be called the resampling circuits in other VHS and VHS-C models. Here the amplified cyan, green, yellow, and white signals are applied to the matrixing circuits, producing the luminance, red, blue, and green signals (FIG. 3-17). Q1101 controls the dc bias of the matrix circuit according to the ambient temperature to compensate for drift in the preamplifier output. A low-power filter network (LPF) is found in each color amp output. The complete RCA CPR100 sensor schematic is found in FIG. 3-18.

LUMINANCE SIGNAL PROCESSING

The purpose of the luminance circuits is to separate the luminance signals and form the composite video signal. The VHS and VHS-C luma circuits

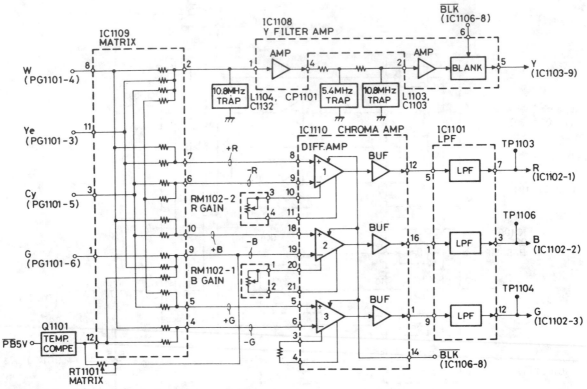

3-17 *RCA CPR100 (VHS-C) matrix and filter circuits.* RCA

consists of a shading correction, setup, feedback clamp, gamma correction, blanking and linear clip, AGC, AGC detector, and gamma control circuits. While the 8 mm luminance (Luma) circuits may consist of a low-pass filter, blank correct, Y clamp, gamma correct blanking, horizontal aperture, base noise clip, Y enhancer, Y/C mix, VCA, and sync mix (FIG. 3-19).

Realistic 150 (VHS-C) Luma Process Circuit   The luma signal enters the process circuit (IC1103) at pin 18. The luma shading correction circuit corrects the horizonal shading signal from IC1105. The correction signal passes pin 11 (IC1105) and enters the luma shading control, which adjusts the signal level. This output is added to the luma signal to correct shading.

To fix the black level of the luma signal, the control RM 1101-5 determines the set-up voltage, which is added to the luma signal.

The black level of signal, which serves as the reference level, must be fixed to perform gamma correction and white clipping. The feedback clamp feeds back a sampled voltage to the input signal to fix the black level. The black level of the output of the gamma correction circuit is sampled and held at the timing of the vertical optical block pulse from pin 15 (FIG. 3-20). The sampled voltage is compared to the set-up voltage generator. This difference voltage is fed back to the input signal when the V.OBP pulse is applied. Now the black level of the luma signal is fixed.

The gamma correction circuit amplifies the luma signal nonlinearly according to the gamma (1) and gamma (2) (dc voltages) supplied by the gamma control circuit in order to set the overall gamma characteristic value.

The blanking (BLANK) and linear clip (white/dark clip) circuits remove the high-level noise produced by the MOS color image sensor and perform linear clipping to limit the white level within the rated range. The output is applied to a dark clip circuit (DARK CLIP) that performs linear clipping during the blanking period, in which synchromous noises remain so that noise is removed and black level limited. The luma signal is applied to the mixer (MIX). The iris detect signal (IRIS DET) is found at pin 4 and enters the iris control circuits (IC1404).

When the object brightness varies, the automatic iris control circuit controls the lens iris to vary the amount of light striking the MOS image sensor. If the object brightness fails, the automatic iris control circuit opens the lens iris and the video signal output level remains unchanged. The AGC circuit (AGC) raises the gain to keep the video signal level constant at all times.

CHROMA PROCESSING CIRCUITS

The red, blue, and green signals are fed to the luminance (luma) and chrominance (chroma) signal-processing circuits from the LPF or chroma amp circuits. The red and blue circuits are applied to the white balance circuits in the RCA CPR100 chroma circuits (FIG. 3-21). These three color signals are corrected like the luminance signal through the various blanking and clipping circuits. After the matrix stage, R-YL appears at pin 24, and B-YL comes from pin 23 of the chroma process (IC1102). These signals are fed to the chroma encoder processing circuits.

Pentax PV-C850A (8 mm) Chroma Signal-Processing Circuits   The chroma signal-processing circuits separate the YL, 2RG, and 2B-G signals and generate a composite video output signal. The 0.7 MHz LPF (IC1210) separates the narrow-band luminance signals to create the R, G, and B signals from the image sensor output. This signal applies to pin 5 of IC1204 (FIG. 3-22). The 4.77 MHz BPF (IC1210) separates the high-frequency variations and modulates this signal from the sensor output. The output (pin 8) is applied to pin 4 of the sync det (IC1202).

The RGB matrix (IC1204) demodulates the R, G, and B signals and adjusts the gain and balance on the modulation axis. The gain of each signal is adjusted so that the R-Y and B-Y become zero when a white object is viewed. The modulation axis is similarly adjusted when shooting a black object. When the gain of the G channel is fixed, those of the R and B channels are equalized to the G channel. The output pins 6, 8, and 10 are applied to 8, 9, and 10 of the clamping circuits (IC1207).

Before the R, G and B signals are sent to the auto white balance control circuit (AWB) and gamma correction circuit (GAMMA CORRECT), this circuit regenerates the dc components last due to C coupling by keyed clamping and equalizes them for every line. The clamp pulse is applied to pin 13. The

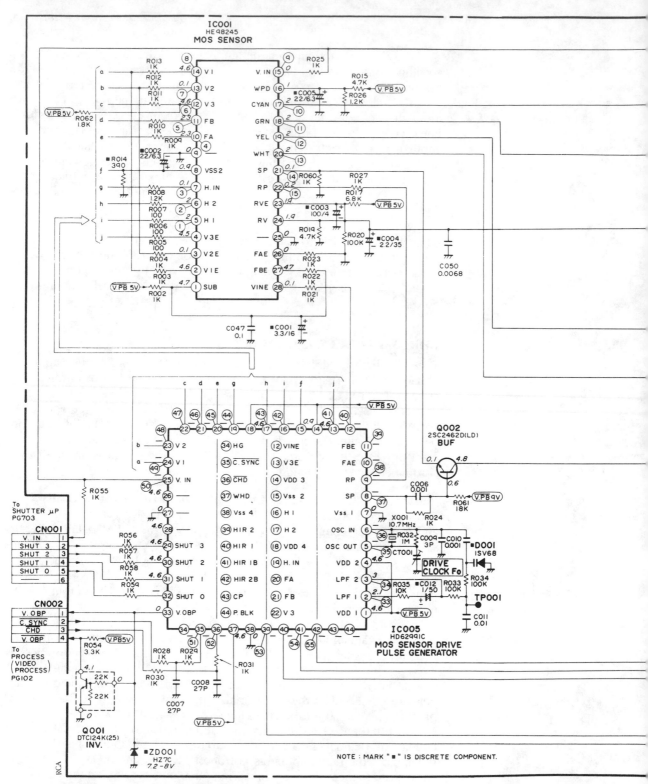

3-18 RCA CPR100 sensor schematic.

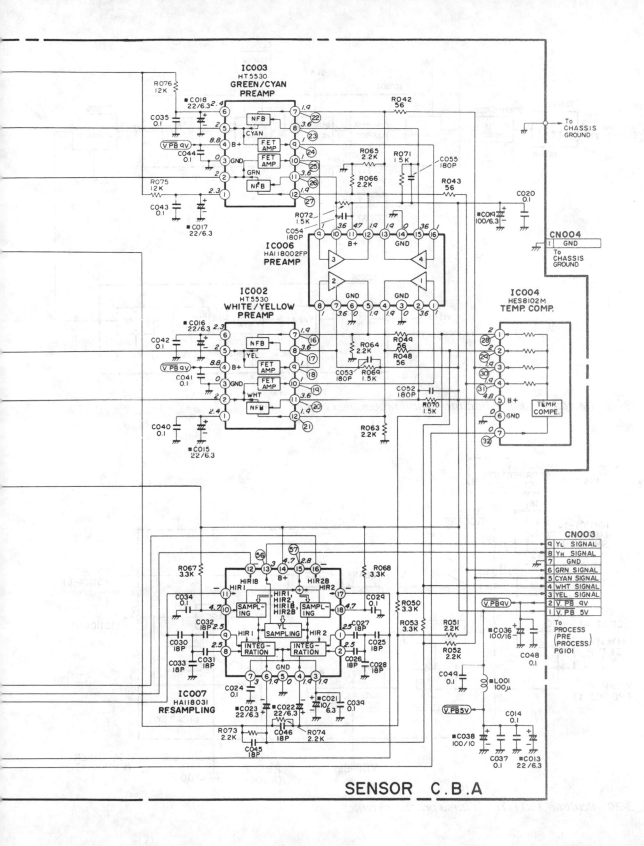

SENSOR C.B.A

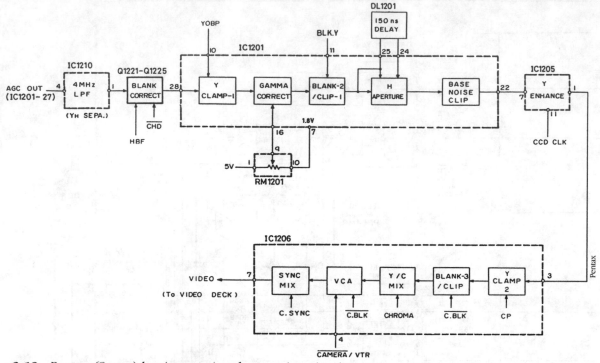

3-19 *Pentax (8 mm) luminance signal-processing circuits.*

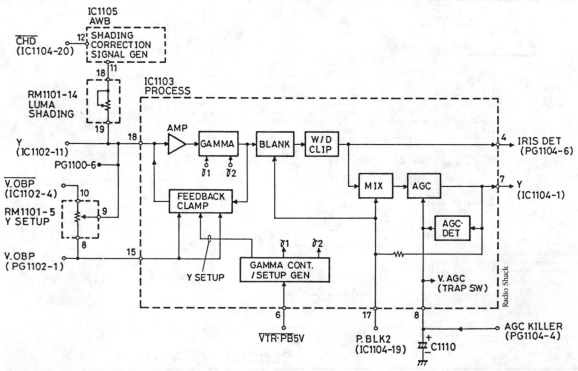

3-20 *Realistic 150 (VHS-C) luma process circuits.*

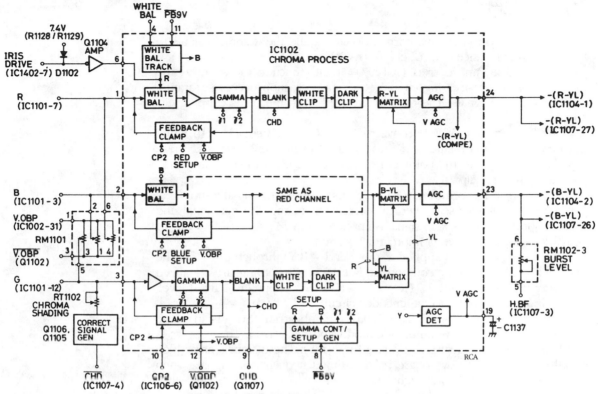

3-21 RCA CPR100 (VHS-C) chroma processing circuit.

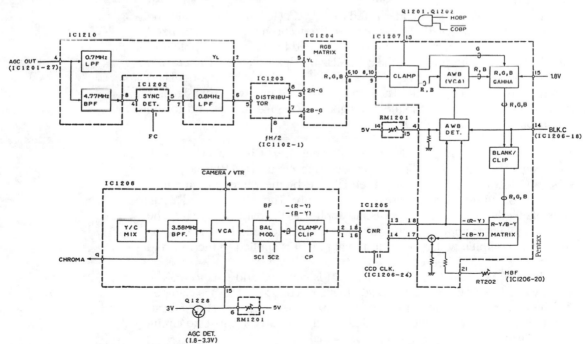

3-22 Pentax PV-C850A (8 mm) chroma signal-processing circuits.

G signal is fed to the gamma correction circuit and the R and B signals to the auto white balance control circuit (AWB).

The RGB gamma correct (IC1207) circuits function the same as the luminance signal-processing circuits. Gamma correction occurs separating the R, G, and B signals. The outputs are applied to the blank/clipping circuits.

R-Y/B-Y matrix (IC1207) converts the R, G, and B signals with white balance adjustments resulting in (R-Y) and (B-Y) difference signals. These signals are applied to the color noise remover (CNR) with (B-Y) at pin 17 and (R-Y) through pin 18.

The color noise remover (CNR) circuits improve the signal-to-noise ratio (S/N) by making use of vertical correlation of the chroma signal and color resolution. The −(R-Y) signal is applied at pin 13 and −(B-Y) at pin 14 of IC1205. The S/N signal is improved 1.4 times.

The −(R-Y) signal is applied at pin 7 and −(B-Y) through pin 16 of the clamp/clip IC1206. The dc component, last due to C coupling, are equalized for every line, and then the − (R-Y) and − (B-Y) are clipped to a fixed level. The outputs are applied to the encoder circuit.

In the encoder (BAL MOD IC1206), the subcarrier (SC1) is in phase with the burst signal and amplitude-modulated by − (B-Y). The subcarrier (SC2) is 90 degrees delayed in phase by − (R-Y). These signals are added together, providing a two-phase balance-modulated chroma signal. When the burst flag pulse (BF) is high (Hi), during burst period, blanking stops and SC1 is amplitude-modulated by − (B-Y), which is present during the burst period to obtain the burst signal.

The output from the encoder is fed to the VCA (IC1206). VCA limits the maximum amplitude of the balance-modulated chroma signal to a fixed value controlling the gain. The gain is determined by the dc bias applied to pin 15. The output is applied to the 3.58 MHz bandpass filter (BPF) network.

The 3.58 MHz BPF limits the bandwidth of the balance-modulated chroma signal to a fixed value. The output is divided into two. This signal is applied to the Y/C mixer for the YH signal-processing circuits and to the VTR through the buffer (pin 9).

RCA CPR100 Encoder/NTSC Signal-Processing Circuit The luminance signal is applied to the signal-processing circuit (IC1107) at pin 28 (FIG. 3-23). This luminance signal is then clipped by the white clip circuit to reduce color output in bright areas of the picture. The white-clipped Y signal is blanked by the blanking pulse and applied to the dark clip circuit. The clipped Y signal is applied to the MIX/fade circuit and added to the chroma signal. The complete video signal found at pin 19 is applied to the EVF and character generator when connected.

The − (R-YL) signal (pin 27 of IC1107) is clamped and balance-modulated by the 3.58 MHz signal. The − (B-YL) signal (pin 26 IC1107) is clamped and then balance-modulated by the 3.58 MHz 90-degree phase shift subcarrier signal. These two signals are added and applied to the mix/fake circuit where it is then added to the luminance signal.

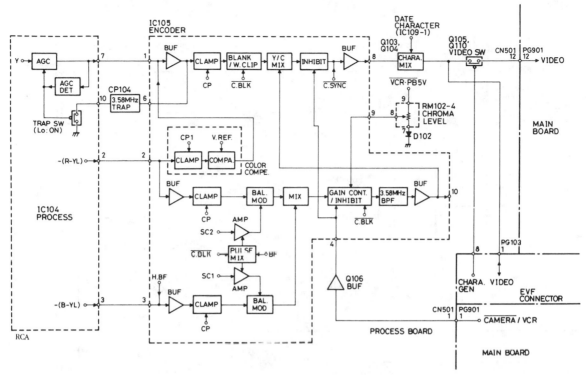

3-23 *RCA CPR100 encoder/NTSC signal-processing circuits.*

AUTOMATIC IRIS CONTROL (AIC)

The AIC circuit controls the opening of the lens iris according to the object brightness. The AIC circuit may consist of controlling IC, iris motor, and manual iris control. The iris detect signal is applied at pin 2 of the AIC control (IC1404). The gate cuts off the signal during low (Lo) periods and permits the signal to pass during high (Hi) periods (FIG. 3-24). The level detector provides an average iris detected signal. If the luma signal level falls, the iris motor operates to close the iris. The AIC (IC1404) controls the iris motor at pin 9.

Pentax PV-C850A (8 mm) AIC Circuit The auto iris control circuit (AIC) keeps the input level to the signal processing circuits constant by controlling gain, depending on light intensity (8 lux minimum, 200 lux saturation). When the light intensity is higher than 201 lux, this circuit operates to fix the input level of the signal-processing circuits by controlling the iris so that the light intensity to the image sensor is lower than saturation at 200 lux. The circuit consists of AIC detector/driver (IC1209, RM 1201, and RT1301 to adjust the iris motor and exposure (FIG. 3-25). IC1209 contains the gate, iris detector and iris driver circuits. Outputs of pins 8 and 9 (IC1209) are fed directly to the drive and clamping coils of the iris motor.

RCA CPR100 (VHS-C) AIC Circuits The AIC circuit controls the iris opening, depending on the level of the iris detect signal from the process-

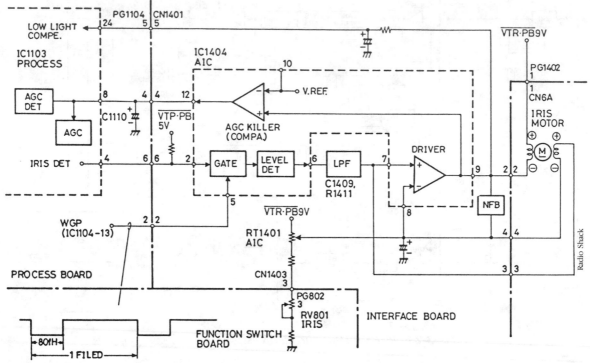

3-24   *Realistic 150 automatic iris control (AIC) circuit.*

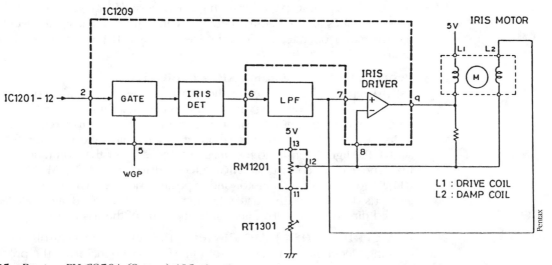

3-25   *Pentax PV-C850A (8 mm) AIC circuit.*

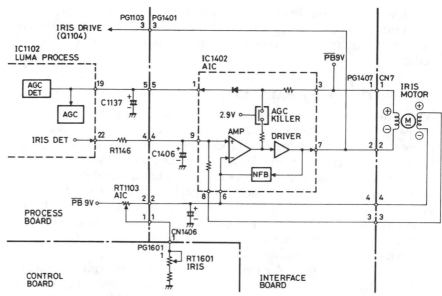

3-26 *RCA CPR100 (VHS-C) AIC circuits.* RCA

ing circuit at pin 4 (IC1402). The output level of the video signal is also controlled by this circuit (FIG. 3-26). The AIC circuit consists of IC1402, iris motor, AIC control (RT1103), and iris control (RT1601).

The reference voltage is adjusted by the AIC control (RT1103) and iris control RT1601. When the average lighting in the camera decreases, the comparison voltage decreases, resulting in the decrease of the output circuit. When the average lighting increases, the output of AIC also increases (FIG. 3-27).

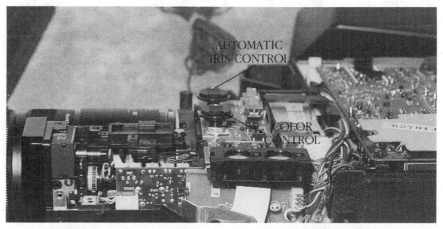

3-27 *Location of automatic iris and color controls in the VHS RCA CPR300 camcorder.*

The video output level is controlled by the AIC and AGC circuits. The AIC control (RT1401) sets the crossover point of the automatic iris and automatic gain controls. This control is adjusted during camera set-up procedures.

AUTOMATIC WHITE BALANCE

White balance refers to the adjustment of the recording system to the color temperature of the light illuminating the subject to be recorded. When properly adjusted, white balance produces accurate recording of the colors in the scene. Keep the camcorder set at automatic white balance at all times.

Automatic white balance generates gain control signal of the R and B signals from the two color difference signals and feeds them back to the gain-control circuit. Now a white object is white, regardless of the light source (color temperature). – (R-YL) and – (B-YL) signals from the process circuits are fed to the automatic white balance control circuit (IC1103) through pins 2 and 3 (FIG. 3-28).

The dc level of the color temperature signal is fixed with a clamp pulse at pin 9. The gate permits the input signal to go to the following stage only when the preblanking pulse is at pin 5. The clip circuit clips the color difference signals at the high and low levels. The color temperature detector consists of a differential amplifier which that subtracts the – (R-YL) from

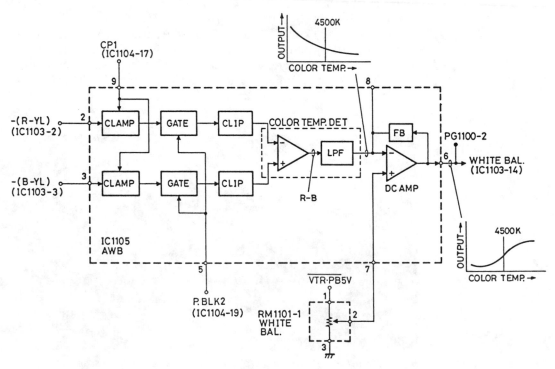

3-28   *Realistic 150 (VHS-C) automatic white balance control circuits.* Radio Shack

– (B-YL) to generate the color temperature R-B. The dc amp controls the white balance control voltage to control gain of the R and B signals.

Pentax PV-C850A (8 mm) White Balance Circuit (AWB)   The AWB (IC1207) corrects the level of the R and B signals to reproduce a white object properly according to the color temperature (2800-7000K) of the light source. The VCA gain is controlled by the AWB detection voltage (FIG. 3-29). The AWB DET detects the difference where $R - B = -(B-Y) - [-(R-Y)]$, compares it to the AWB correction voltage, and produces an error voltage. The error voltage is applied to the VCAs of the R and B channels. The outputs of the R and B channel VCAs are applied to the R and B channel gamma correction circuits.

AUTOMATIC FOCUS CONTROL

The auto focus system measures the distance from an object by emitting infrared rays towards the object and detecting the reflection, using the principle of triangulation. Infrared rays from an infrared LED pass through a protecting lens to the object (FIG. 3-30). The infrared rays hit the object and reflect back through a receiving lens and enter the sensor. The sensors consists of two photodiodes. Now the autofocus system moves the receiving

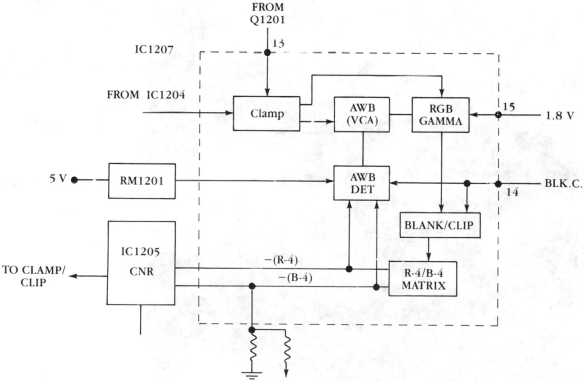

3-29   *Pentax PV-C850A (8 mm) white balance circuits.*

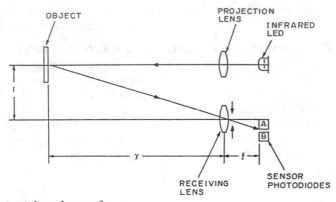

3-30   *Principles of auto focus.*

lens to equalize the light intensity of the photodiodes. The object lens is moved by the same amount as the receiving lens (FIG. 3-31).

Pentax PV-C850A (8 mm) Auto Focus Control Circuits   The sensor (D2, a photodiode) converts the 9 kHz infrared rays from the object into a current whose intensity depends on the strength of the infrared rays. This

3-31   *The macro lever on the RCA CPR300 camcorder is for close up shots.*

current is applied to a preamplifier (IC4), which converts current into voltage. The voltage signal is applied to pins 23 and 24 of IC1 (FIG. 3-32).

The 9 kHz bandpass amplifier separates the reflected infrared components of channels A and B, which are amplitude-modulated by 9 kHz from the input signal. These outputs are applied to the adder and subtractor. The adder and subtracter generate two reflected infrared signals (A and B). By adding B to A, a far-end detection signal (A + B) is generated, and by subtracting B from A, a focus error detection signal (A – B) is generated. The A + B signal shows whether the object is in the in-focus range or not. The (A – B) signal shows whether the object is in the infocus range. The output is applied to the sync detector circuit.

The infrared LED drive circuit drives the infrared LED. The motor drive circuit drives the autofocus motor. The switching transistors (SW1 through SW4) are controlled by the signals near-on and far on, which is supplied by IC1. The AF motor terminals are connected to pins 5 and 8 of IC1.

RCA CPR100 Autofocus Block Diagram With the focus switch in the auto position and with the power switch in, + 5 volts is applied to auto focus circuits. The infrared circuit generates an 8 kHz infrared signal and is applied to LED drive (Q3). Now the infrared signal travels to the object and reflects back to the photodiodes and sensor preamp circuit (IC1). The reflected signal is detected by the two photodiodes producing electrical current. Both signals are amplified by the preamp circuits and applied to IC2 (FIG. 3-33). The signals are synchronized by the 8 kHz clock signal and applied to the comparator circuits. The resultant connection signal is applied to

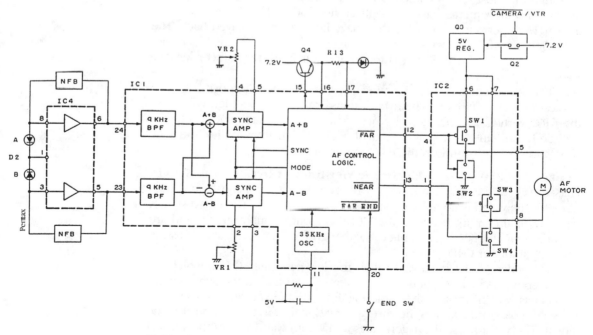

3-32 *Pentax PV-C850U (8 mm) auto focus circuit.*

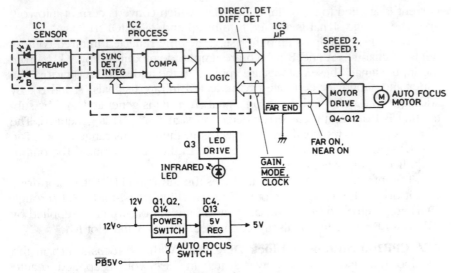

3-33 *RCA CPR100 auto focus block diagram.* RCA

microprocessor IC3. The output signal from IC3 is applied to the motor drive circuits (Q4 through Q12), operating the auto focus motor (FIG. 3-34).

THE ELECTRONIC VIEWFINDER

Although the most recent camcorders have the electronic viewfinder, some of the smaller cameras have the optical viewfinder. The electronic view-finder (EVF) permits monitoring the image being shot or played back. The electronic viewfinder looks and acts somewhat like the small black-and-white TV chassis. The EVF unit is found at the front of the camcorder (FIG. 3-35).

The EVF circuits consist of a miniature picture tube with horizontal and vertical deflection circuits. The flyback transformer provides high voltage to the CRT. Vertical and horizontal sync circuits are generated and fed to the EVF deflection and VCR system control circuits. A small amplifier and sync separation circuit round up the EVF circuits (FIG. 3-36).

Pentax PV-C850 (8 mm) Electronic Viewfinder Circuits   The EVF circuits consist of the video, vertical and horizontal deflection, and high-voltage circuits. The video is applied at pin 10 of IC1801 (FIG. 3-37). The video signals from the main circuit board in the VTR come out through pin 11, and are amplified by IC1801 and applied to the grid of the CRT after passing through amplifier Q1802.

The video signal passing through the low-pass filter (LPF), which removes spurious high-frequency components, is applied to the sync separator circuits, which separate the vertical and horizontal sync signals. The vertical sync separator separates the vertical sync signal from the composite sync signal. The vertical oscillator generates a sawtooth waveform to the vertical drive, which produces vertical drive signal (pins 16 and 17) to the vertical deflection coils.

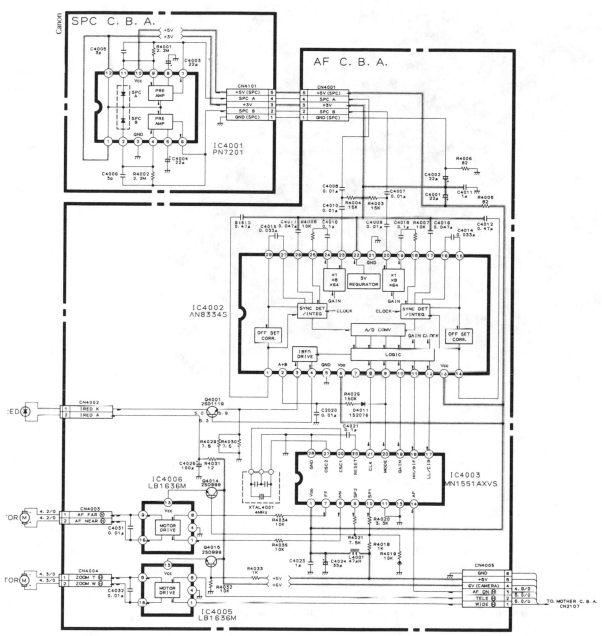

3-34 *Canon VM-E2A auto focus sensor schematic.*

The phase detector compares the phases of the separated horizontal sync signal with the horizontal drive pulse generated in the horizontal oscillator circuits. The synchronized horizontal drive pulse is applied to the driver (Q1803), which drives the horizontal defection coils. L1802, R1813, and C1825 improves the linearity of current flowing through the horizontal deflection coils.

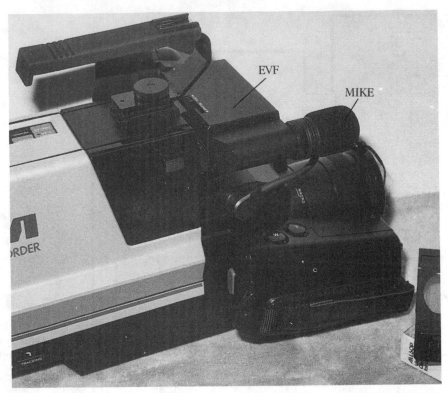

3-35 *Location of the electronic viewfinder (EVF) in the RCA CPR300 camcorder.*

In the high-voltage circuit, the horizontal drive circuit generates the high voltage for the CRT (FIG. 3-38). Pin A of T1801 supplies 2.5 kV to the anode of the CRT. Pin B supplies approximately 500 V to the focus circuits. R1823 and R1824 provide a dividing circuit that supplies 250 V to grid 2. Pin 4 supplies approximately 70 V to the brightness circuits. Pins 1 and 6 supply a flyback pulse to light the filament of the CRT.

Realistic 150 (VHS-C) Electronic viewfinder (EVF)   In some camcorders, the EVF assembly is locked in place with a sliding plastic lock assembly (FIG. 3-39). The EVF assembly may be adjusted to either side for easy viewing. Push the lock to one side and the EVF assembly can be removed after removing the EVF plug-in cable to the camera section.

IC1801 amplifies the video signal and provides sync separation, vertical oscillator, vertical drive, and horizontal oscillator circuits in one IC. The video output at pin 5 of IC1801 is applied to the video grid 1 through a driver (Q1802) (FIG. 3-40).

After the video signal enters the low-pass filter (C1818, R1817, LPF), which removes high-frequency components, it enters IC1801 at pin 11. The sync separator separates the composite sync signal from the sync signal and is applied to the vertical sync separator and H sync phase detector circuit

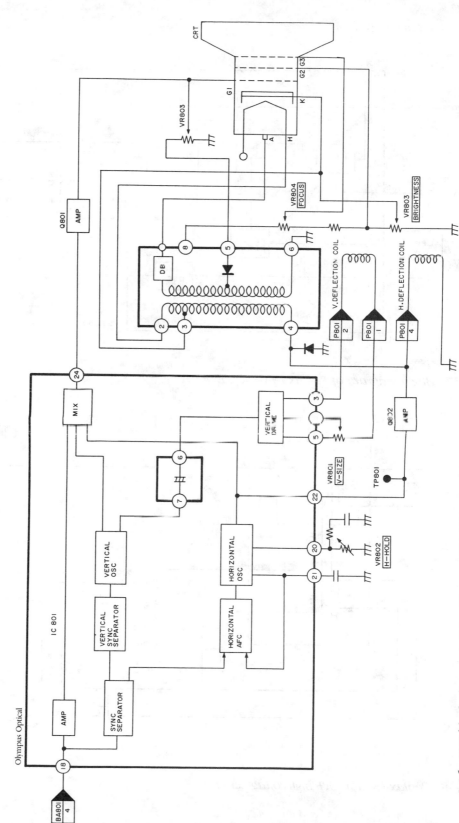

3-36 EVF block diagram of the Olympus VX-801 camcorder.

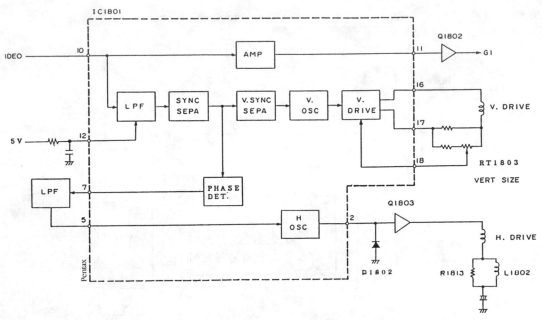

3-37 *Block diagram of Pentax PV-C850A EVF circuit.*

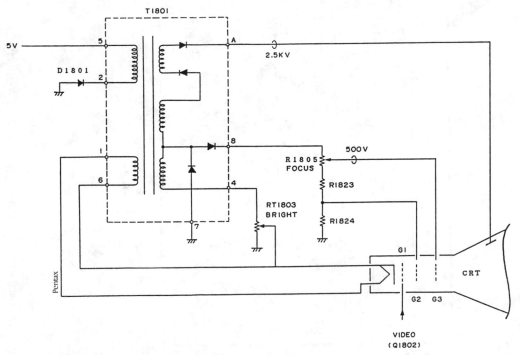

3-38 *Pentax (8 mm) EVF high-voltage circuits.*

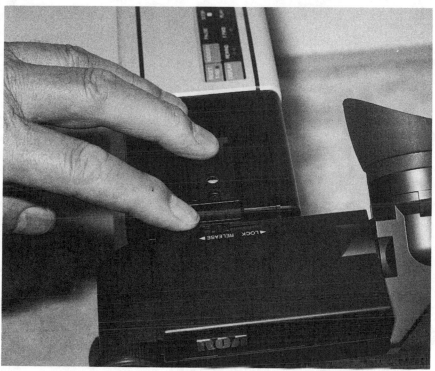

3-39 *The lock/release button of the EVF on the RCA CPR300 camcorder.*

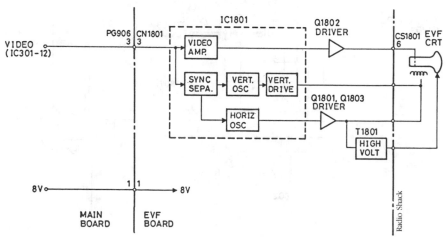

3-40 *Realistic (VHS-C) EVF circuit configuration.*

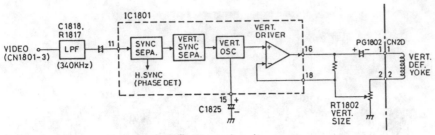

3-41   *Realistic EVF vertical deflection circuits.* Radio Shack

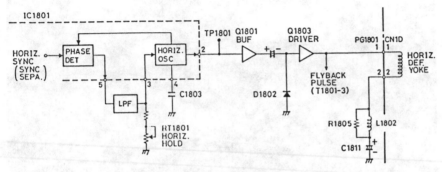

3-42   *Realistic (VHS-C) EVF horizontal deflection circuits.* Radio Shack

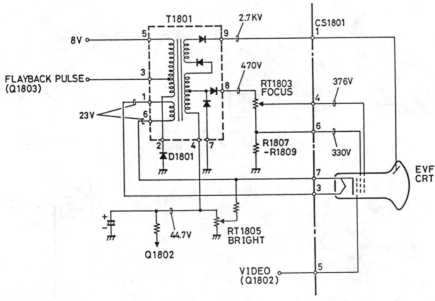

3-43   *Realistic (VHS-C) high-voltage circuit of the EVF.* Radio Shack

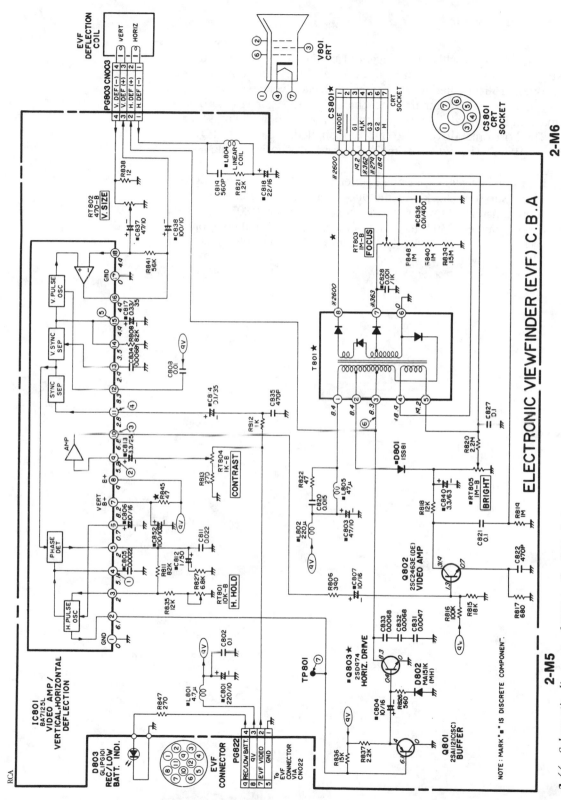

ELECTRONIC VIEWFINDER (EVF) C.B.A

2-M6

2-M5

NOTE: MARK "■" IS DISCRETE COMPONENT.

3-44 Schematic diagram of EVF in the RCA CPR100 camcorder.

(FIG. 3-41). The vertical oscillator is triggered by the vertical sync and produces vertical sawtooth waveform to the vertical driver. The vertical waveform out of pin 16 is applied to the vertical deflection yoke winding.

The phase detector compares the phases of the separated horizontal sync signal and horizontal drive pulse generated by the horizontal oscillator (FIG. 3-42). The horizontal drive pulse (pin 2) is applied to the buffer (Q1801) and driver (Q1803). The output from Q1803 drives the horizontal deflection yoke.

The horizontal driver output pulse generates the high voltage in flyback (T1801). Pin 9 supplies 2.7 kV to the anode of the CRT (FIG. 3-43). Pin 8 supplies approximately 470 V to the focus circuits. Divider R1807 and R1803 generates approximately 330 V to grid 2 of the CRT. Pins 1 and 6 supply the filament voltage. (The RCA CPR100 VHS camcorder electronic viewfinder schematic is in FIG. 3-44.)

Chapter **4**

Video
Circuits

*T*he video circuits consist of the video in and out circuits, head switching, operations in the record and play modes, luminance signal recording and playback circuits, and color signal recording and playback circuits. All of these circuits appear in most camcorders, while the flying erase head drive circuit is found only in the 8 mm units, and the bias oscillator circuits are located only in the VHS and VHS-C camcorders (FIG. 4-1).

VIDEO SIGNAL INPUT/OUTPUT CIRCUITS

The video signal input circuits are switched into the input either from the camera or external devices connected to the AV connector. Usually, the RF device (RF converter) is converted to the AV input circuits. Video signal directly from the TV or VCR recorder may be connected to the video circuits. The video output signal is supplied to the electronic viewfinder and external devices connected to the AV connector. Figure 4-2 shows the AV input cable connection for the RCA CPR300, and FIG. 4-3 shows the output connector.

Pentax PV-C850A (8 mm) Video Signal Input/Output Circuits   Either the camera video signal (pin 1) or the external device video signal (pin 5) will be selected according to the camera/VTR signal and external device (FIG. 4-4).

The camera/VTR signal supplied from IC908 is high (Hi) during camera mode. The high voltage from the camera sets the switch to Hi through the OR circuit (D201), so the camera video signal applied to pin 1 is selected.

When the video signal detector (VIDEO DET) detects the video signal coming from the external device, its output is low (Lo) and sets a switch (SW) at Lo (external device to select the external device video signal applied to pin 5).

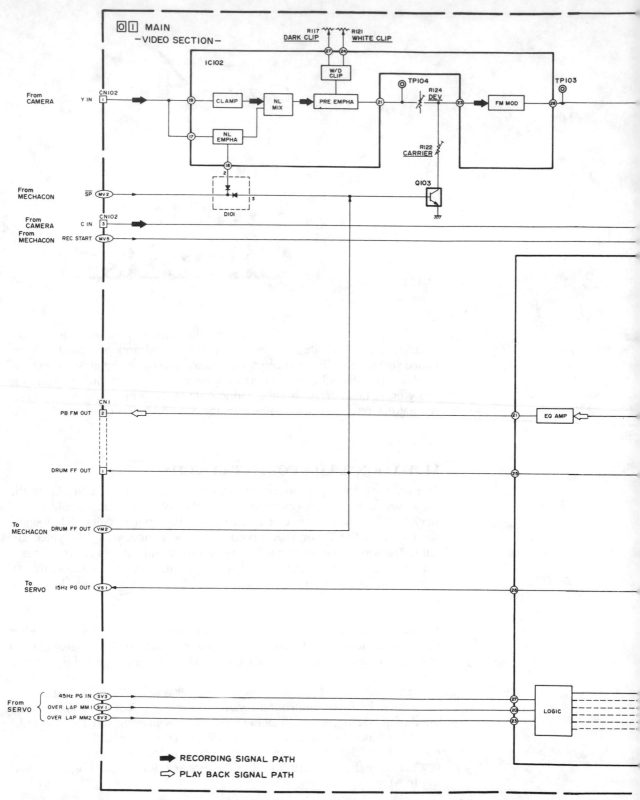

4-1 *The video block diagram of a Zenith VM6150 camcorder. The video recording signal path is*

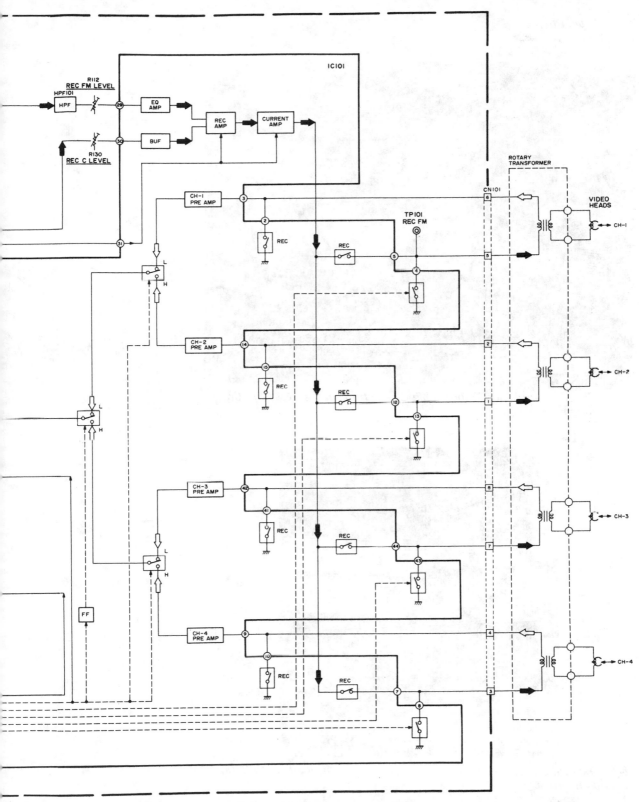

shown with a black arrow, and the playback signal path with a white arrow. Zenith

4-2   The AV (audio/video) input cable connection on the RCA CPR300 camcorder.

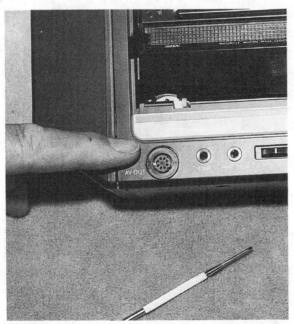

4-3   The audio/video (AV) output cable connection in the RCA CPR300 camcorder.

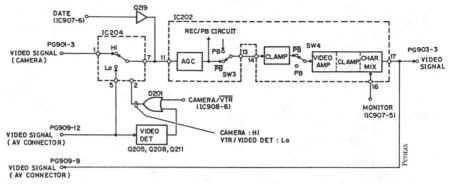

4-4   *Pentax PV-C850A (8 mm) video signal input/output circuits.*

The video signal selected by the signal-selecting circuit (IC204) comes out through pin 7 and, after the date signal (DATE) has been added, enters the luminance signal-processing circuit (IC202). Character signals (OSD) are added to the video signal processed in the video circuits. The output is supplied to the electronic viewfinder (EVF) and the external device (RF converter) connected to the AV connector.

RCA CPR100 Input/Output Video Circuits   Pin 14 of the encoder IC (IC1107) is low (Lo) when the electronic viewfinder (EVF) is connected to the EVF connector during camera recording (FIG. 4-5). SW1 is on and SW2 is off, allowing video to pass through to the luminance (luma) process section (pin 1 of IC201). When SW2 is off, the chroma signal passes through the buffer to the chroma processing circuits.

Pin 10 of the electronic viewfinder (EVF) is grounded and the PB 9V and PB 5V are turned off when the AV input adaptor is connected to the EVF connector. Likewise, the video signal from the adaptor goes through pin 6 of the EVF connector to the luminance/color (luma/chroma) circuits.

Pin 14 of IC1107 becomes high (Hi), SW1 turns off, and SW2 turns on during character generation operations. The camera video signal goes through the interface and wiring board with pin 4 of the EVF connector to the character generator where the two video signals are added.

Realistic 150 Input/Output Video Signal Circuits   The luminance and color (luma and chroma) signals from the camera, passing through the main board, enter the luma/chroma board (FIG. 4-6). The luma and chroma signals are output when a VTR/camera signal is applied to pin 4 of the encoder (IC1104), located on the process board. It is high (Hi) in camera input mode. The luminance enters the luma signal-processing circuit (IC201) and the color enters the chroma signal-processing circuit (IC202) through buffer (BUF). The chroma signal is also supplied to a video amplifier (IC301), which generates the EE video signal.

In the output circuits, after processing in the luminance (luma) signal-processing circuit (IC201), the luma signal is supplied to the main board and enters the video amp (IC301), which mixes the character signal (CHAR-

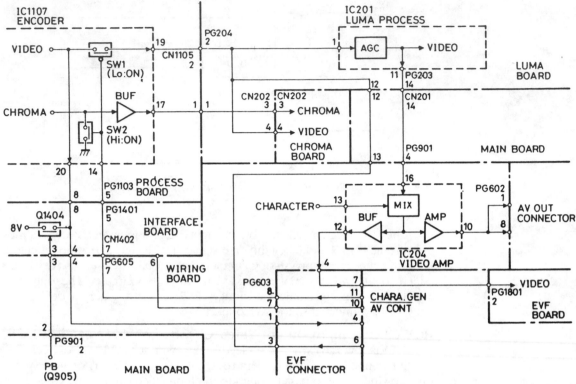

4-5 *RCA CPR100 (VHS-C) video signal input/output circuits. Remove the EVF connector to plug in the cable.* RCA

ACTER) coming in through pin 13. This luma signal passes through a buffer (BUF), out of pin 12 before being suplied to the electronic viewfinder (EVF), and applies a luma/chroma mixer (Y/C MIX). The chroma signal applied from pin 2 is mixed with the luma signal to generate the EE video signal because the switching circuit (SW) in the IC is activated by applying low (Lo) PB 5V. The output passes through an 6 dB amp and out of pin 10 before being output from the AV OUT connector.

The video playback signal reproduced by the luma signal processing circuit (IC201) exits pin 19. The output video signal is also applied to the video amp (IC301) and is processed in the same way as the EE signal except luma/chroma mixing.

HEAD-SWITCHING CIRCUITS

The head-swtiching circuits in the camcorder are often controlled by an IC component. The head-switching circuits set the video heads in the record or play mode with several control signals.

Pentax PV-C850A (8 mm) Head-Switching Circuits   The head-switching control signals in this model are: REC INHIBIT, SW30Hz, ASBL/PB, REC SIGNAL, SQUELCH and HEAD SW signals (FIG. 4-7).

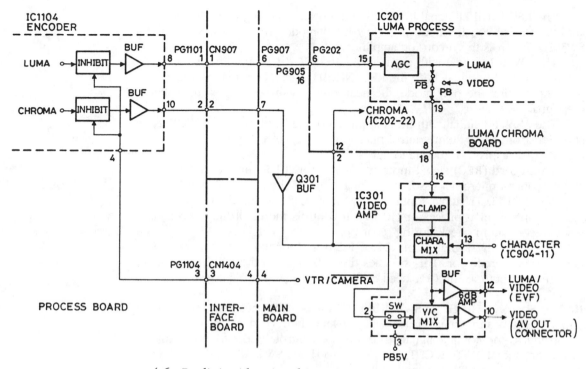

4-6 *Realistic video signal input/output circuits.* Radio Shack

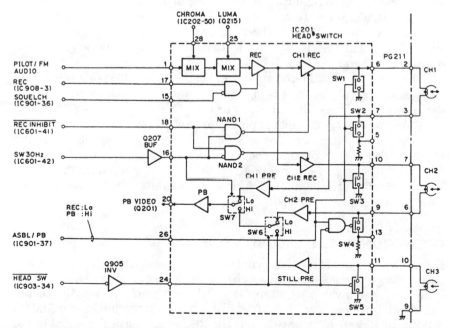

4-7 *Pentax PV-C850A (8 mm) head-switching circuits.* Pentax

The REC INHIBIT signal in pin 18 of the head-switching IC201 is generated by the servo circuit during the record mode. This signal, with the SW30Hz, controls the recording amplifier.

The SW30Hz signal with input at pin 16 of IC201 is supplied from the servo circuit. This signal, with the REC INHIBIT signal, controls the recording amp. during the play mode, the head output will be selected to make the signal continuous.

The ASBL/PB signal with input at pin 26 of the head-switching IC201 is supplied from the system control microprocessor, selecting the mode (either record or play) of the video heads.

The record (REC) signal input at pin 17 of IC201 is supplied from the system control microprocessor. This signal controls the recording amplifier.

The SQUELCH signal input at pin 15 of IC201 is supplied from the system-control microprocessor (IC901). It controls the recording amp and holds recording in check during record pause.

The head SW signal at pin 24 of IC201 is supplied from the system control microprocessor. This switches the CH2 head to the still head with the same azimuth as the CH1 head during the slow and still modes.

Radio Shack 150 Head-Switching Circuits The head-switching IC (IC203) switches the video heads over between the record and play modes, according to the control signals (FIG. 4-8). The control signals found in this model are the MONITOR CUT, HEAD SW1 to HEAD SW4, REC 5 V, SW30Hz and SW 15 Hz, and PB 5V signals.

The MONITOR CUT signal at input pin 3 of the head switch (IC203) is supplied from the system control circuits. This controls the recording amplifier to inhibit recording during record pause and loading.

The HEAD SW1 to HEAD SW4 signals input at pins 17, 13, 11, and 9 of the head switch IC (IC203). The head switch signal is supplied from the servo circuit and selects the CH1 to CH4 video heads, one after another during record and playback.

The REC 5 V signal input at pin 2 of head switch IC203 is supplied from the system control circuit. It is high (Hi) during the record mode to set up the recording circuits with the video heads.

The SW30Hz signal input at pin 22 and SW 15 Hz signal input at pin 23 of IC203 is supplied from the servo circuit. These two signals select the video head output to obtain a continuous signal during play mode.

The PB 5V signal input at pin 25 of IC203 is supplied from the system control circuits. It is high (Hi) during play mode to set up the playback circuits with the video heads.

OPERATION IN THE RECORD MODE

During record mode in the General Electric 9-9605 VHS luminance and chrominance circuits, the video signal is fed in at the line-in video jack or from the camera video signal to the switching IC3002 (FIG. 4-9). The output signal is fed to the character MIX signal to pin 5 of the luminance REC/PB process or IC3001 to the AGC amp. The REC switch turns the signal to the Sub Amp inside the luma IC. The video signal may be switched by the EE

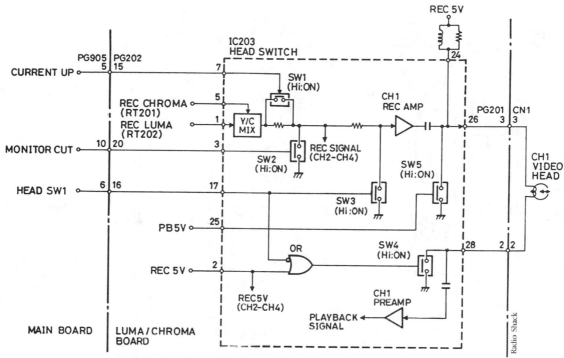

4-8 *Realistic 150 (VHS-C) head-switching circuits.*

amp to the character mix (Q3006) and Q3003, Q3004, and Q3005 amps to the video out jack and to the electronic viewfinder (EVF).

From pin 28, the signal goes externally to the low-power filter network FL3001 and back into IC3001 at pin 61. Here is a 12 dB amp, and the signal proceeds through the nonlinear emphasis deemphasis stage to the clamp amp. The luma video signal goes through the main emphasis section to the white-dark clip stage through the FM modulator.

The recording current level control VR3001 adjusts the FM recording signal and is fed through a high-power filter (HPF) network to a MIX transistor (Q3007) to the recording amps Q3009 and Q3010. The REC FM signal is fed to the head-switching transistors Q3506, Q3511, Q3516, and Q3521 and applied directly to the four heads (R1, L1, R2, and L2).

The video signal is also fed to the chroma section after splitting at pin 5 of the switching IC8001. The video signal enters pin 32 of the chrominance REC/PB processing IC and is amplified and fed out pin 31 to the 3.58 MHz BPF circuits and fed back into IC8001 at pin 23. Internally, the video signal is switched to record, passes through AGC, PB buffer, rec burst, 6 dB boost, LP/SLP and switched by REC switch through the color killer and out pin 17. The video/chroma signal passes through a low power filter (630 kHz LPF) and is mixed with the luminance/video signal at mixer Q3007.

Pentax PV-C850A (8 mm) Operation During Record Mode The pilot/FM audio signal (pin 1) coming from the main circuit board mixes first with the chroma signal (pin 28) and then with the luminance signal (pin 25)

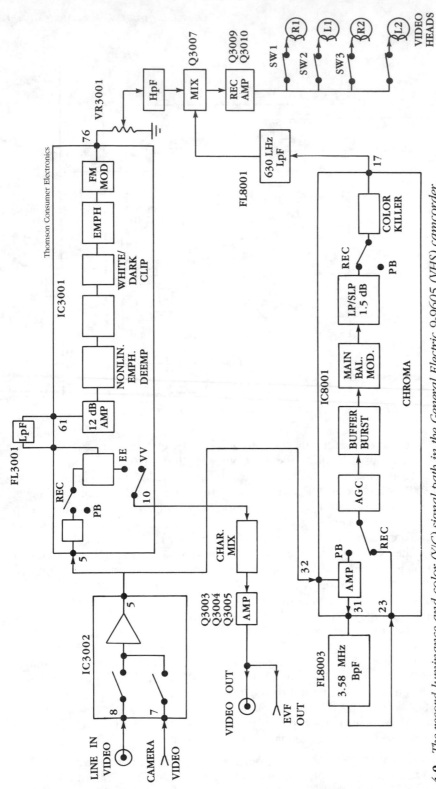

4-9 The record luminance and color (Y/C) signal path in the General Electric 9-9605 (VHS) camcorder.

of head switch IC201 before entering the recording amp (REC). It operates with the REC signal high (Hi), at pin 17, to supply the video signal to the CH1 and CH2 recording amplifier (CH1 REC/CH2 REC). (See FIG. 4-6.)

During recording, the ASBL/PB signal (pin 26) is low (Lo). Now the switching circuits (SW2 and SW4) turn on to ground the playback circuits of the CH1 and CH2 heads and form the recording circuit. The recording amplifier (CH1 and CH2 REC) is selected according to the output of the recording amp control circuit (NAND), and recording current is supplied from the recording amplifier to the head through a rotary transformer.

The recording amplifiers (CH1/CH2 REC) control circuit generate recording amp control signals from REC INHIBIT (pin 18) and SW30Hz (pin 16) signals and consist of two NAND gates. The CH1 control circuit (NAND 1) generates the control signal of the CH1 recording amp when SW30Hz is low (Lo) at CH1. The CH2 control circuit (NAND 2) generates the control signal of the CH2 recording amplifier when 30 Hz is high (Hi) at CH2. The recording amp operates when the control output is Hi.

Sony CCD-M8E/M8U (8 mm) Video Signal Recording System   The Y signal (luminance) and C signal (chroma) are fed from the camera block to the various circuits (FIG. 4-10). The Y signal from the camera is delayed 650 ns by DL501, 502 and time matching of Y and C is performed. This delayed signal is fed to the YM-2 board. Here the preemphasis circuit is composed of a subemphasis and main emphasis circuit. In the subemphasis circuit, the nonlinear emphasis and deviation settings are performed. In the main emphasis circuit, the linear emphasis circuit and AC clip are in operation.

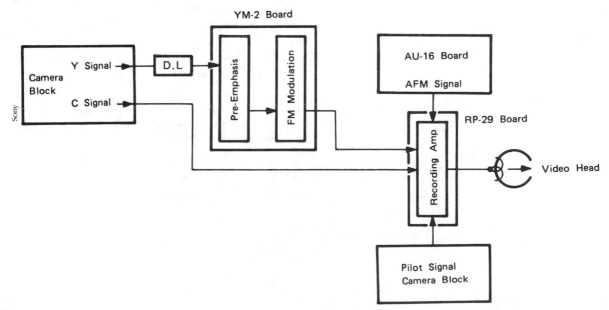

4-10 *Sony CCD-M8E/M8U (8 mm) video signal recording system.*

The Y signal is fed from the YM-2 board to the recording amp circuits. Likewise, the C signal is fed directly to the recording amp circuits. The AV-16 board contains the FM modulator circuit, which feeds to the recording amp. Also, the pilot signal camera block feeds to the same recording amp.

The Y and C (luminance and chroma) signals enter Q101 mixed and feed to pin 3 (FIG. 4-11). The Y FM signal is fed into pin 1 of recording amp CX 20034. The Y signal is controlled by the dc voltage at pin 21 and the mixed signals are controlled by the dc voltage at pin 44. ME tape/MP tape switching is also operated at pin 44.

The four mixed signals are converted from voltage to current, pass the recording amp and rotary transformer, and are then supplied to the video heads.

Realistic 150 (VHS-C) Y and C Record Mode   The luma/chroma mixer (Y/C) stages comprise a record current control circuit SW1, luma/chroma mixer (Y/C MIX), and monitor cut circuit (SW2) (see FIG. 4-6). It is common to CH1 to CH4. Receiving the chroma signal at pin 5, the luma/chroma mixer (Y/C MIX) mixes the chroma signal with the luma signal applied to pin 1. The output comes to the recording current control circuit (SW1), which increases the recording current when the CURRENT UP signal applied to pin 7 is high (Hi) when recording is to restart. The output is applied to a recording amp (REC AMP) of CH1 to CH4.

The monitor cut signal (SW2) following to the recording current control circuit (SW1) cuts off the recording signal when the MONITOR CUT signal (pin 3) is high (Hi), during record pause and loading.

The REC 5 V signal (pin 2) of the head-switching circuit is Hi during the record mode so that the switching circuit (SW4) turns on, grounding the playback terminals of the head through resistors to establish the recording circuit.

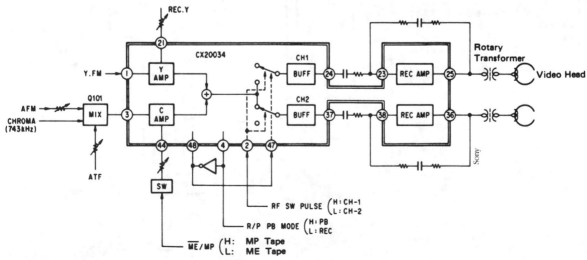

4-11 *Sony CCD-M8E/M8U (8 mm) recording amp circuit.*

When the HEAD SW1 signal applied to the switching circuit (SW3) via pin 17 is low (Lo), the switching circuit (SW3) is off, the recording signal enters the recording amplifier (REC AMP), and recording current flows to the heads through a rotary transformer.

When the HEAD SW1 signal is high (Hi) during recording CH2 through CH4, the switching circuit (SW3) is on and the video heads are short circuited to prevent crosstalk occurring in other channels. The CH2 through CH4 video heads are switched with HEAD SW signals, HEAD SW2 to HEAD SW4, one after another, like the CH1 video head.

OPERATION IN THE PLAY MODE

In the General Electric 9-9605 VHS luminance and chrominance circuits in play mode, the signal is picked up by heads R1, L1, R2, and L2. The play heads feed the signal to the head amp IC3501. The luminance signal is fed from pin 20 and 21 to the phase compensator circuits of Q3501, L3501, and C3526, while the chroma signal path comes out of pin 15 of IC3501 and feeds to Q3502 amp through a 630 kHz low-power filter (LPF) going to pin 34 of IC8001, the chrominance processing IC.

The chroma signal at pin 34 feeds to the internal buffer stage out of pin 30 through the 3.58 MHz BPF circuit and back to pin 23 of IC8001, to the burst 6 dB ATT and onto the playback switch. With the switch in playback mode, the chroma signal is switched to the color killer stage, out pin 17 to pin 20 of the luminance IC3001, where the chroma signal is mixed with the luminance video signal.

The playback luminance FM signal from the phase compensator circuits is fed to pin 56 of IC3001 through the DOC SW, DOC AMP, drop-out detector to the 1H delay and limiter circuits inside IC3001. It passes through the FM demodulor, out pin 42 through the low-pass filter (FL3002) into pin 36 and is amplified, deemphasised, and goes through picture control to output pin 29 of IC3001.

The luminance signal path in playback mode with output at pin 29, enters pin 7 of IC3001 to the PB switch. The luminance video signal is switched to a SUB CLAMP, out pin 28 through a low-power filter network (FL 3001) into pin 61. Here it is amplified by a 12 dB amp and fed to the nonlinear emphasis/deemphasis to the mixer stage, mixing with the chroma video signal.

The VV signal is switched inside IC3001 and the output appears at pin 10. The chroma/luma video signal goes through a character MIX and is amplified by Q3003, Q3004, and Q3005. The luma/chroma video signal playback mode path feeds to the video out jack and the electronic viewfinder (EVF) (FIG. 4-12).

Pentax PV-C850A (8 mm) Operation During Play Mode   During play, the ASBL/PB signal (pin 26) is Hi. So, switching circuit (SW1 and SW3) turns on to ground the recording terminals of the heads to form the playback circuit (FIG. 4-7). Signals that have passed through preamplifiers (CH1/CH2 PRE) come to a switching circuit (SW7), which forms a continuous signal by selecting the CH1 signal when SW30Hz is low (Lo) and the CH2 signal when

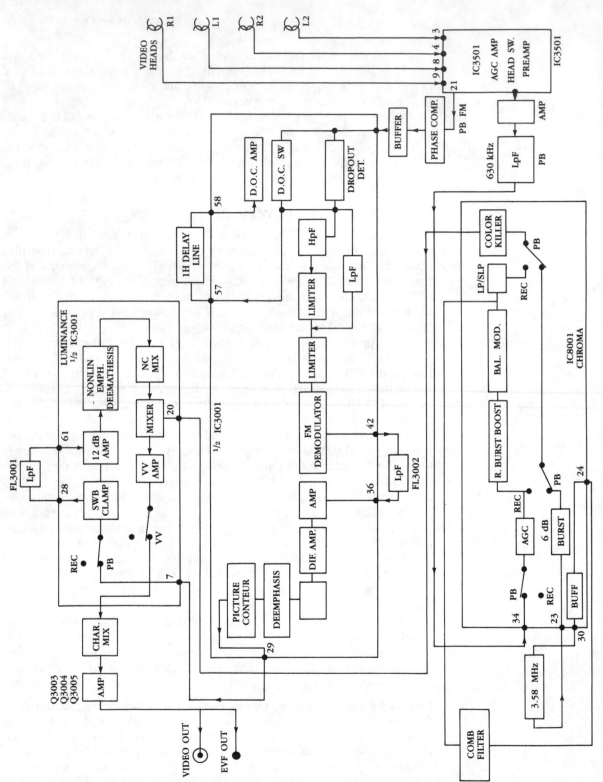

4-12 *The playback luminance and chroma (Y/C) signal path in the General Electric 9-9605 (VHS) camcorder.* Thomson Consumer Electronics

SW30Hz is high (Hi). The continuous signal passes through a playback amplifier (BP) before coming out through pin 20.

During the play, the output of the still head is grounded by SW5 while a switching circuit (SW6) selects the output of the CH2 preamplifier. During the slow or still modes, the HEAD SW signal (pin 24) is high (Hi). Now SW5 does not ground the still head, and the switching circuit (SW6) selects the output of the still preamplifier. In place of the CH2 head, the still head picks up the signal. The output of the CH2 head is grounded by SW4.

Radio Shack 150 (VHS-C) Operations in Play Mode   The PB 5 V (pin 25) is Hi during the play mode so that the switching circuit (SW5) turns on, grounding the recording terminals of the heads to establish the playback circuit (see FIG. 4-8).

When the head SW1 signal applied to the switching circuit (SW4) through an OR gate is low (Lo), the switching signal is produced and enters the preamplifier (CH1 PREAMP). To play back through other channels (CH2 to CH4), the HEAD SW1 signal is high (Hi), SW4 is on, and the video head is short-circuited to prevent crosstalk. The CH2 through CH4 video heads are switched with HEAD SW signals (HEAD SW2 to HEAD SW4), one after another, like the CH1 video head.

IC205 is a switching circuit to prevent crosstalk. Each switching circuit in the IC turns on and grounds the playback terminals of each channel by applying low (Lo) HEAD SW signals (HEAD SW1 to HEAD SW4) when the other channel is played back.

PENTAX PV-C850A

The following section applies to the circuits of the Pentax PV-C850A camcorder.

Luminance Signal Recording Circuits

The luminance signal recording circuits consist of IC204, IC202, and IC201 (FIG. 4-13). IC202 operates in the record mode when the playback (PB) signal is Lo and in play mode when the playback signal is Hi. IC204 is the Camera/external device video signal selector. IC202 does the function of luminance signal record/processing (recording AGC, luminance signal separator, pre-emphasis, clip, FM modulator, and EE amp). IC201 is the recording Y/C mixer and recording amplifier.

AGC Circuit

The AGC circuit detects the input level of the video signal and controls the gain to keep the output level fixed (FIG. 4-14). The input video signal is applied to the AGC circuit luminance signal separator (Luma COMB FILTER), pin 6, the 3.1 MHz low-pass filter (CP204), pin 25, the equalizer (EQ), through SW6 to the sync separator (SYNC SEPA), and through a clamping circuit (CLAMP) to the AGC detector (AGC DET) (FIG. 4-15).

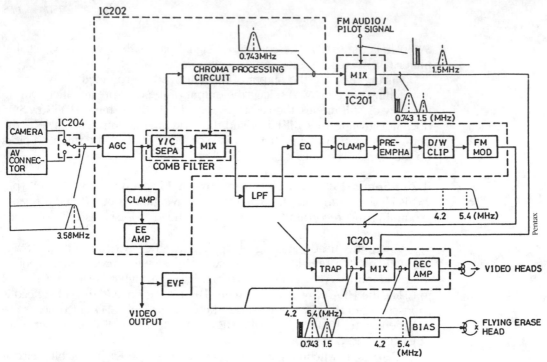

4-13 *Pentax PV-C850A (8 mm) luminance signal recording circuits.*

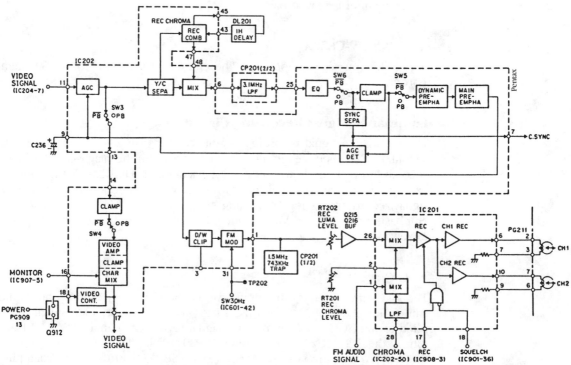

4-14 *Pentax PV-C850A (8 mm) luminance signal recording circuits.*

Sync Separator

The sync separator (SYNC SEP) separates the sync signal from the luminance signal and applies it to pin 7 and the AGC detector (AGC DET).

Clamping Circuit

In the clamping circuit (CLAMP), the sync signal level at its top (SYNC TIP) must be fixed at (4.2 MHz) independently of the video signal to frequency modulate the luminance signal. The luminance signal is applied to the AGC detector (AGC DET) and goes through SW5 to the preemphasis circuit (PRE EMPHA).

Referring again to FIG 4-15, the AGC detector (AGC DET) generates the key pulse (3), which has a fixed level by delaying the horizontal sync signal (H SYNC) applied from the sync separator (SYNC SEPA) until the back pulse, and adds it to the clamped luminance signal (4). The AGC detector (AGC DET) detects the sum level of the key pulse (fixed level) and the horizonal sync (H SYNC-VARYING level) and generates an AGC voltage that is inversely proportional to the sum level. C236, connected to pin 9, holds the output and supplies it to the AGC circuit (AGC), and it controls the gain to fix the level of the horizontal sync signal.

Luminance Signal Separator

The luminance signal separator (REC LUMA COMB FILTER) consists of a comb filter, removes the chroma signal from the input video signal, and extracts the luminance signal (FIG. 4-16).

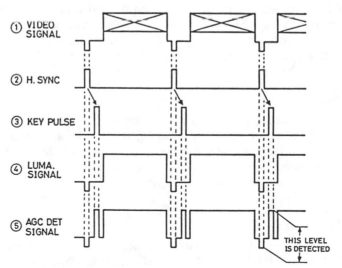

4-15 *Pentax PV-C850A (8 mm) operation of the AGC circuit in the luminance signal recording circuits.* Pentax

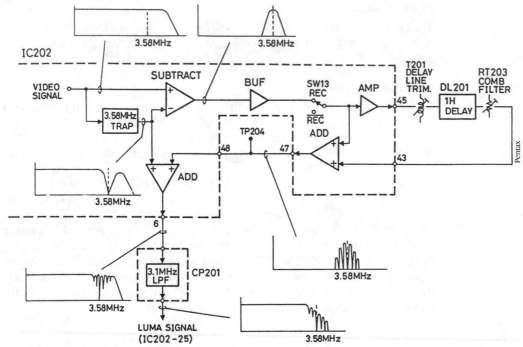

4-16   *The luminance signal separator circuits in Pentax PV-C850A (8 mm) camcorder.*

Luminance Signal Separator (Y/C SEPA)

This consists of a subtractor (SUBTRACT) and a 3.58 MHz trap that extracts the 3.58 MHz chroma signal by subtracting the video signal (inverting input—from which the 3.58 MHz chroma signal is removed) from the video signal (noninverting input). The 3.58 MHz chroma signal is applied to the chroma signal-processing circuit through a buffer stage.

Comb Filter

The comb filter circuit consists of a 1H delay line (DL 201-1H DELAY) and an adder (ADD). The output of the adder, which adds the original signal with the 1H = delayed signal is the 3.58 MHz luminance signal from which the 3.58 MHz signal is removed. The output comes out of pin 47 and enters the adder (ADD) in IC202 through pin 48.

Delay Line Trim

The delay line trim (T201) is connected to the 1H delay line. It matches the impedance and the level of the 1H-delayed sync. It is adjusted to balance the signals added together so that characteristics of the separator are optimized.

Mixer (ADD)

The mixer adds the video signal from which the 3.58 MHz chroma signal is removed to the 3.58 MHz luminance signal. The output is a luminance signal with a frequency response extending to high frequencies and comes out of pin 6.

Video Equalizer

The video equalizer raises the luminance signal level at about 2 MHz (edge) by about 1.5 dB to let the luminance signal preshoot so that the amount of clipping by the subsequent clipping circuit (CLIP) is actually reduced (FIG. 4-17). During play, preshooting of the signal waveform is corrected by an overshoot circuit to improve signal-to-noise (S/N).

Preemphasis Circuits

The dynamic and main preemphasis circuit emphasizes high-frequency components during recording so that noise is removed when the original frequency response is restored during play. The dynamic preemphasis (DYNAMIC PRE-EMPHA) varies the amount of emphasis, depending on the level of the input signal. The amount of emphasis is increased when the level is low and reduced when it is high to prevent excessive clipping in the subsequent clipping circuit (CLIP) and overmodulation in the FM modulator (FM MOD).

The main preemphasis circuit results in a fixed amount of emphasis that is independent of the input level. The preemphasis luminance signal comes to a clipping circuit (D/W CLIP).

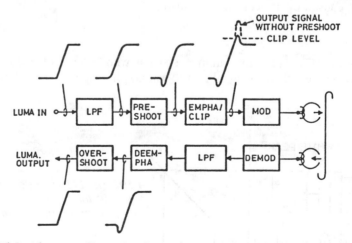

4-17 *The video equalizer circuits in the Pentax PV-C850A (8 mm) camcorder.* Pentax

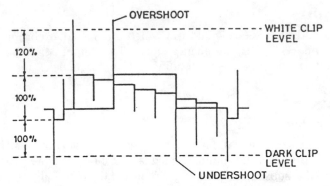

4-18 *The dark/white clip chart in the Pentax PV-C850A camcorder.* Pentax

Dark/White Clipping Circuit

The preemphasis luminance signal overshoots or undershoots at the rising or falling edge because the level of high-frequency components is enhanced. If this were to be frequency modulated, overmodulation would occur, resulting in inversion of black and white. To prevent this, the clipping circuit clips the signal at 100 percent for the dark level and at 120 percent for the white level (FIG. 4-18).

FM Modulator

The FM modulator (FM MOD) modulates the input signal so that the sync tip corresponds to 4.2 MHz and the white peak, to 5.4 MHz (FIG. 4-19).

The FM carrier frequency is offset by $\frac{1}{2}$ FH alternatively from field to field according to the SW30Hz applied to pin 31. This prevents beat interference caused by adjacent tracks during play.

Mixer

The mixer (MIX) mixes the luminance signal, with its level adjusted with the down-converted chroma signal and FM audio/pilot signals.

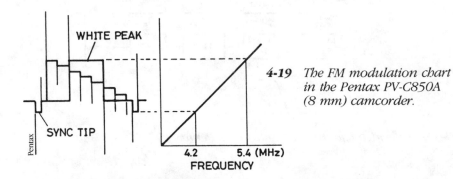

4-19 *The FM modulation chart in the Pentax PV-C850A (8 mm) camcorder.*

The mixer (MIX) mixes the 743 kHz down-converted chroma signal with the 1.5 MHz FM audio/pilot signals. The output, after having its level adjusted by RT201 (RED CHROMA LEVEL), is connected to pin 2 and again mixed with the luminance signal. The output passes through a recording amp (AMP) and comes to the CH1 and CH2 recording amplifier.

The recording amplifier (REC) is controlled by the (SQUELCH) signal applied to pin 15. It is high (Hi) during record pause and the leading time for restarting record. A switching circuit turns on and the recording amp stops.

EE Video Signal Output Circuit

The EE video signal is supplied from the AGC circuit (AGC) and is applied to a clamp (CLAMP) through pins 13 and 14. After being clamped, it is applied to the video signal (FIG. 4-20).

The video signal amplifier (VIDEO AMP) is a feedback amp consisting of an operational amp (VIDEO AMP) and a transistor. The output is 2 V_{p-p} video signal.

The clamping circuit clamps the dc level of the 2 V_{p-p} video signal and applies it to the character signal adder. The character signal adder (CHAR MIX) adds the character signals (data of tape counter, counter memory, available remaining time, and battery level) to the video signal. The output is applied to the electronic viewfinder (EVF) through pin 17 and to the RF converter unit connected to the AV connector.

The video output control circuit (VIDEO CONT) consists of a constant-current circuit and a switching circuit that controls output video signal. If the RF converter unit is not connected to the AV connector, the switching circuit (Q912) on the main circuit board is held off, together with constant-current circuit, so that current consumption is reduced.

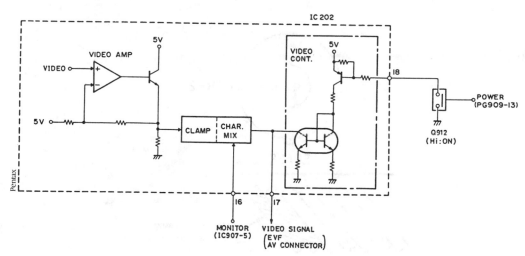

4-20 *The EE video signal output circuit of Pentax PV-C850A (8 mm) camcorder.*

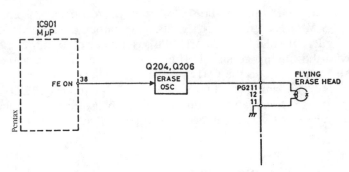

4-21 *Pentax PV-C850A flying erase head circuit.*

Flying Erase Head

The erase head is mounted on the upper cylinder, like a video head. It erases the CH1 and CH2 video tracks simultaneously 90 degrees before the CH1 video head during recording. The drive circuit Q204 and Q206 are an oscillator (OSC) supplying the erase head with erase current (FIG. 4-21). It is controlled by the FE CONT signal supplied from the system-control microprocessor. When the record mode is entered, the FE CONT signal becomes high (Hi), and the oscillator (OSC) generates the erase current of about 7 MHz.

SONY CCD/M8E/M8U ROTARY TRANSFORMER AND VIDEO HEAD

The rotary transformer has a three-channel structure. The inner side contains the erase head, the middle side is CH2, and the outer side CH1 (FIG. 4-22).

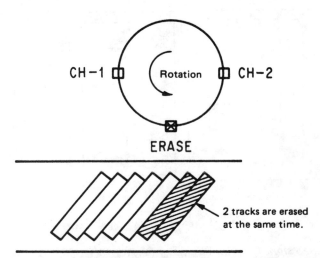

4-22 *Erase head channels of Sony's CCD-M8E/M8U (8 mm) camcorder.*
Sony

The video head contains two pieces, while the erase head one piece. Here two tracks are erased at the same time. Erasing is performed along the track by a rotary, rather than a stationary, erase head. Only the 8 mm camcorders have the flying erase head system.

RCA CPR100 LUMINANCE RECORD PROCESS CIRCUIT

The luminance record process is the same as the conventional VHS system except for the head-switching circuits of the four-head recording system. To select the record or playback mode, 5 volts (PB 5V) is applied to pin 12 of the luminance signal record processor (IC201). When the PB 5V signal is present, the play mode is selected (FIG. 4-23). The record mode is selected when the PB 5V signal is low (Lo). IC201 contains the Y/C separator, AGC, preemphasis, clipping, frequency modulation, and EE amp circuits. IC203 contains the luminance/chroma (Y/C) mixer and the recording amp. IC206 is the detail enchancer circuit.

CHROMA SIGNAL RECORDING CIRCUITS

During the camera mode, the 743 kHz down-converted chroma signal is generated from the 3.58 MHz chroma signal coming from the camera. In the

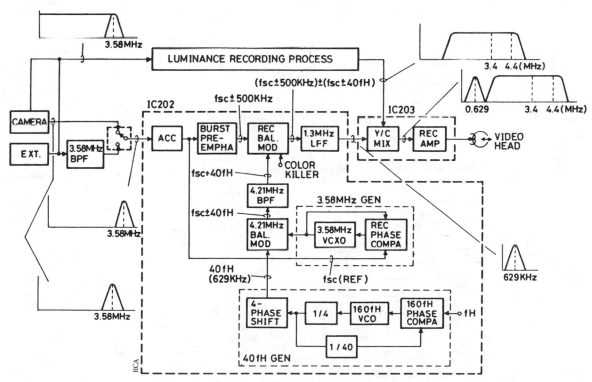

4-23 *RCA CPR100 (VHS-C) luminance record process circuit.*

VTR mode, the 3.58 MHz chroma signal is extracted from the input video signal, and the 743 kHz down-converted chroma signal is generated. IC202 operates in the record mode when the REC signal is high (Hi), and in play mode, when it is low (Lo) (FIG. 4-24).

IC204 and IC205 contain the camera/external device video signal selector. IC202 contains the luminance signal record/processing (AGC and chroma signal separator), chroma signal record/processing (AGC, burst preemphasis, chroma preemphasis, frequency converter, 3.58 MHz generator and 47 1/4 FH generator). IC201 contains the recording Y/C mixer and recording amplifier.

Pentax PV-C850A Chroma Recording Circuits If you select the recording signal in the camera mode, the 3.58 MHz chroma signal from the camera is received. In the VTR mode, the 3.58 MHz chroma signal is extracted from the composite video signal coming through the AV connector. This selection is performed in IC205 (FIG. 4-25). In the camera mode, the CAMERA/VTR signal is high (Hi) and IC205 selects the 3.58 MHz chroma signal coming from the camera through pin 4. The chroma signal for the camera passes through a 400 ns delay circuit, which adjusts the timing of the luminance signal before entering IC205. In the VTR mode, the CAMERA/VTR signal is low (Lo), and IC205 selects the 3.58 MHz chroma signal applied to pin

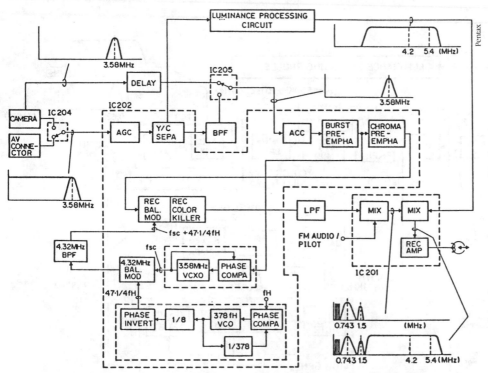

4-24 *Configuration of chroma signal recording circuits in the Pentax PV-C850A camcorder.*

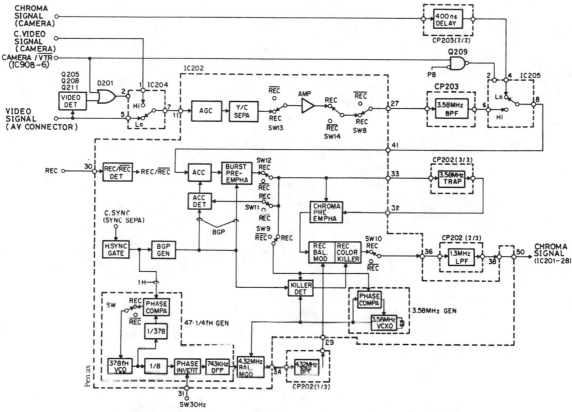

4-25 *The chroma signal recording circuits of Pentax PV-C850A (8 mm) camcorder.*

6 after being extracted from the composite video signal. The output of IC205 is sent to the AGC circuit in IC202.

The AGC circuit consists of the AGC Amp and AGC detector and fixes the output burst signal level regardless of variations in the input level (FIG. 4-26).

The burst gate pulse (BGP) is generated by the burst gate generator (BGP GEN) with the burst signal extracted from the input chroma signal, and the gain of the AGC amp is controlled so that the level of the burst signal remains constant.

The burst preemphasis circuit is used to reduce color irregularities and noise appearing as horizontal lines this raises the burst level by 6 dB when the burst gate (BGP) is input (FIG. 4-27).

The chroma preemphasis circuit consists of a 3.58 MHz trap connected across pins 32 and 33, an amplifier (AMP), and a subtractor (SUBTRACT). It emphasizes low-level sideband components during recording so that the signal-to-noise (S/N) can be improved when emphasized components are deemphasized during play (FIG. 4-28). The subtractor (SUBTRACT) subtracts the original signal (inverting input) from the inverted-and-amplified signal

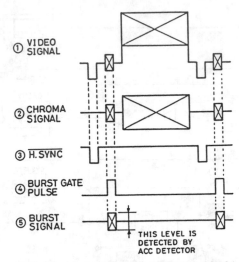

4-26   *Operations of the ACC circuit in Pentax PV-C850A (8 mm) camcorder.* Pentax

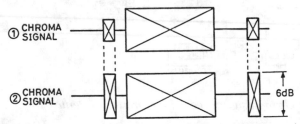

4-27   *The burst preemphasis chart in Pentax PV-C850A (8 mm) camcorder.* Pentax

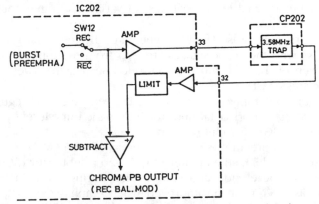

4-28   *Pentax PV-C850A (8 mm) chroma preemphasis circuit.* Pentax

(noninverting input), and the output is the sum of the input signals added together in phase.

In the main converter, the frequency of the 3.58 MHz chroma signal is converted by the 4.32 MHz signal from a 4.32 MHz bandpass filter (CP202). From the output, the 1.3 MHz low-pass filter (CP202) in the later stage removes the sum signal (4.32 MHz + 3.58 MHz) and outputs the difference signal, that is, the 743 kHz down-converted chroma signal (4.32 MHz − 3.58 MHz).

The color killer (KILLER DET) detects the burst signal in the input signal, and the output is the 743 kHz down-converted chroma signal. When a burst signal is not detected, the chroma signal will not be output.

RCA CPR100 Chroma Record Process Circuit The chroma recording circuit (IC202) extracts the 3.58 MHz chroma signal from the video signal, which generates a 629 kHz down-converted signal for recording. The PB 5V signal is switched between record and playback operation (FIG. 4-29). The playback operations take place when the PB 5V is high (Hi). Record operations begin when the PB 5V is low (Lo). The following circuits are found inside IC202, AGC, burst preemphasis, 3.58 MHz VCXO and REC PHASE comparator, 40 FH signal generator, and frequency converter. The luminance chroma (Y/C) mixer and record amplifier circuits are in IC203.

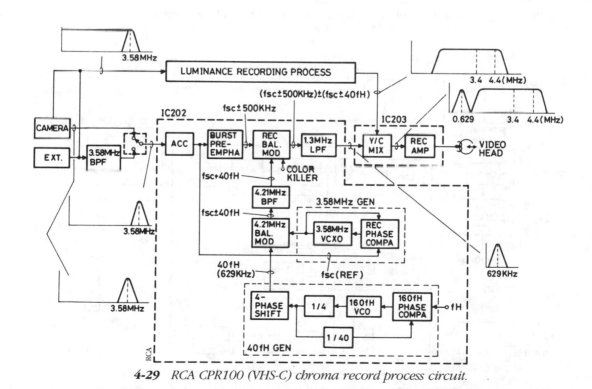

4-29 *RCA CPR100 (VHS-C) chroma record process circuit.*

LUMINANCE PLAYBACK PROCESS CIRCUITS

The luminance playback circuit consists of the video heads, preamplifiers, demodulated and playback, signal synthesizer, AGC, deemphasis, dropout compensation, luminance mixer, and 1H delay for drop-out compensation. In the RCA CPR100 VHS-C luminance playback process circuits, the RF signal picked up by the heads is amplified by IC203 (FIG. 4-30). Also, the PB 5V signal is switched between playback and record in IC203. When the PB 5V signal is high (Hi), playback is in operation, and when the PB 5V signal is low (Lo), recording operation is switched in. IC203 contains the luminance chroma (Y/C) mixer and preamplifier. The FM demodulator, deemphasis and Y/C circuits are contained in IC201. IC204 amplified the luminance playback signal and is fed to the electronic viewfinder (EVF) and AV out connector.

Pentax PV-C850A Luminance Signal Playback Circuit   The luminance signal playback circuits consists of IC201, IC202 and IC203 (FIG. 4-31). IC202 enters the play mode when the signal PB turns high (Hi). IC201 contains the preamplifier, signal synthesizer and AGC. IC202 contains the luminance signal playback processing (FM demodulator, deemphasis, dropout compensation, noise canceler, and Y/C mixer. The 1H delay dropout compensation is found in IC203.

Realistic 150

The following circuit descriptions pertain to the Realistic 150 camcorder.

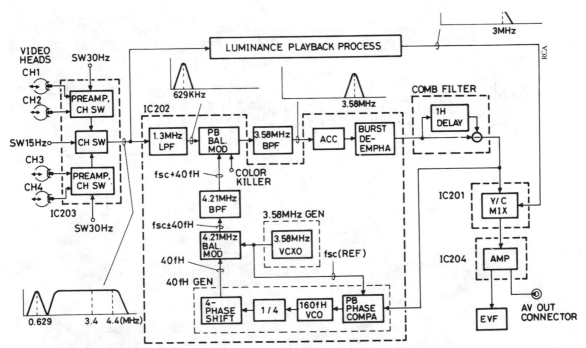

4-30   *Luminance playback process circuit of the RCA CPR100 (VHS-C) camcorder.*

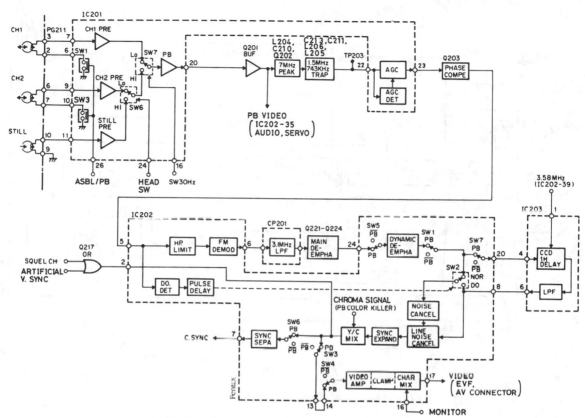

4-31 *Luminance signal playback circuits of Pentax PV-C850A (8 mm) camcorder.*

Luma Signal Playback Circuits The signal picked up by the tape heads is preamplified and switched by IC203 (FIG. 4-32). It is then fed to a 4.6 MHz PEAK playback equalizer (CP201). As the preamplifier has a flat frequency response, this performs correction of the head frequency response playback output. It raises the response around the upper limit (4.6 MHz) of the FM carrier to flatten the overall frequency response.

AGC Circuit The AGC circuit corrects the deviation, including interchannel deviation, of the outputs of the video heads (FIG. 4-33). The AGC detector (AGC DET) detects the input level and feeds the output back to the AGC circuit to control gain. The signal passes through the dropout (SW8), SW4, and pin 4 before coming to the phase equalizer Q201, DL201, and dropout detector (DO DET) included in the IC.

Phase Equalizer Q201 is the phase equalizer stage. This circuit corrects phase distortion occurring when the playback equalizer (CP201) equalizes the amplitude so that distortion of the playback waveform is reduced. The output passes through a buffer (Q214) and input at pin 2 before entering IC201 once again.

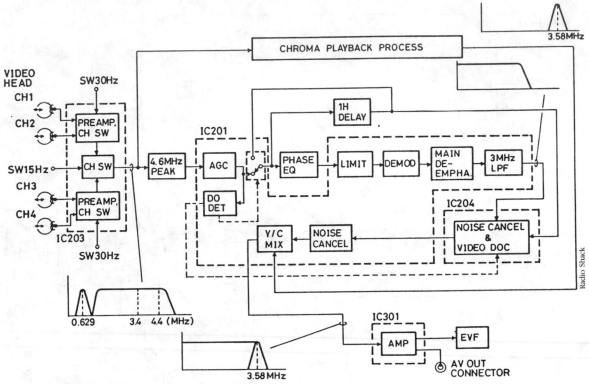

4-32   *Realistic 150 (VHS-C) luma signal playback circuits.*

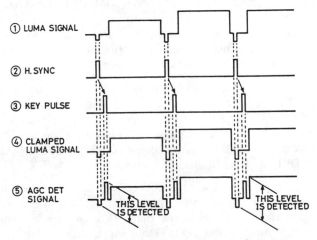

4-33   *Realistic 150 (VHS-C) luminance AGC operation.*   Radio Shack

High-Pass Limiter The high-pass limiter suppresses lower side-band components to prevent black/white inversion. If the recording is done with preemphasis applied to that part of luma signal where the black level changes to white level, the carrier would be subject to dropout at the edge during playback, and inversion between black and white would occur together with deterioration of S/N.

Main Deemphasis Circuit The effect of this circuit is reversed compared to that of the main preemphasis circuit during recording. It restores the original signal level by alternating the high-frequency components that were boosted during recording. The output goes through SW1, pin 14 and the 4.1 MHz bandpass filter (L213 and C252). The output is at pin 13 of IC201 and goes through a low-pass filter (3 MHz).

Playback Equalizer The playback equalizer contains Q207, Q208, and Q213. This circuit operates when the PB 5V is applied to the base of Q207. The output enters the H-correlation noise canceller/dropout compenator IC204. The luma signal goes out of pin 6 to pin 23 of IC201.

Noise Canceler The noise canceler circuit removes high-frequency noise (random noise) in the played-back luma signal to improve the S/N. The greatest effect occurs with the low-level luma signals. The output luma signal passes through SW5, pins 24 and 28, before coming to the sync expander (SYNC EXPAND) and passes through SW2 before coming to the sync separator (SYNC SEPA).

Sync Separator In the sync separator (SYNC SEPA), the output video signal passes through SW2 and comes to the sync separator (SYNC SEPA), which separates the sync signal as in recording. The output appears at pin 20 and feeds to chroma sync (IC202).

Sony CCD-M8U Luminance Signal Playback System

The signal is picked up by the video heads passing through the rotary transformer and fed to the head amp at pins 26 and 35 (FIG. 4-34). The head and RF amp are found in each channel. At playback, the frequency characteristics are tuned around 6.5 MHz to 7.5 MHz, with feedback damping and the signal is flattened. The RF SW pulse fed in at pin 2 of CX20034 switches the playback signal. When it is high (Hi), channel CH1 is selected, and when it is low (Lo), CH2 is selected with a continuous signal obtained at pin 12.

CHROMA SIGNAL PLAYBACK CIRCUITS

After being processed in IC202, the chroma signal mixes with the luma signal and becomes the video signal in the Radio Shack 150 chroma playback circuits (FIG. 4-35). IC203 contains the preamp and continuous signal generator. The chroma playback processing, which contains chroma signal separator, AGC, burst deemphasis, playback balanced modulator, and crosstalk cancel, is contained in IC202. The luminance and color (luma/chroma) mixer is found in IC201 with the output video amplifier (IC301).

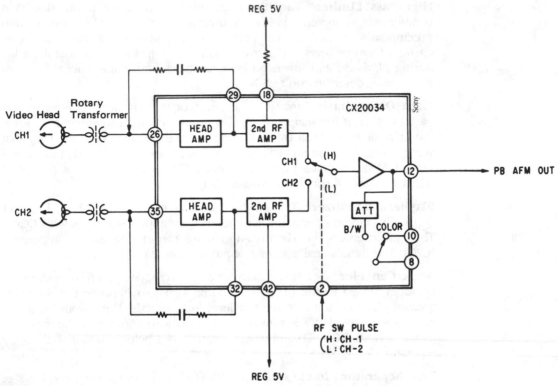

4-34 *Sony CCD-M8E/M8U (8 mm) luminance signal playback amp circuit.*

Pentax PV-C850A Chroma Playback Circuits　The playback signal enters pin 35 of IC202. A 100 kHz trap removes pilot signal (FL-F4). After pilot signal removal, the playback signal enters a 1.3 MHz low-pass filter (CP202) through SW10 (pin 36). The 1.3 MHz low-pass filter removes the FM audio and FM luminance signals from the playback signal to extract a down-inverted chroma signal (743 kHz + 500 kHz). The AGC and AGC DET controls the gain of the chroma signal to keep the burst level fixed (FIG. 4-36).

The burst deemphasis circuit alternates the burst signal. The main converter mixes the down-converted chroma signal (743 kHz + 500 kHz) with 4.32 MHz to convert the frequency. A 3.58 MHz and bandpass filter extracts the chroma signal by removing spurious components. The playback chroma comb filter adds the 1H-delayed signal to remove crosstalk. The chroma deemphasis circuit alternates the sideband components. A color killer detects the burst signals synchronized with the burst gate pulse (BGP) and 3.5 MHz continuous signal to detect whether it is present or not.

During playback, the burst frequency fluctuates due to jitter, etc. and is removed by the 47 ¼ FH generator. After the playback color killer, the luminance and color (Y/C) is mixed and the result is the video signal. The video amp amplifies the video signal and feeds it to the electronic viewfinder and AV connector. The complete luminance and color (LUMA/CHROMA) schematic of the Pentax PV-C850A camcorder is shown in FIG. 4-37.

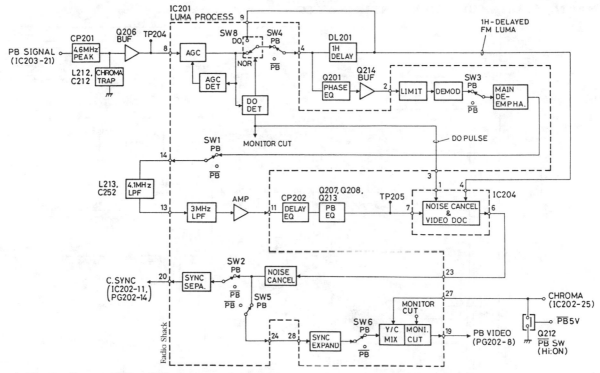

4-35 *Realistic 150 (VHS-C) chroma playback circuits.*

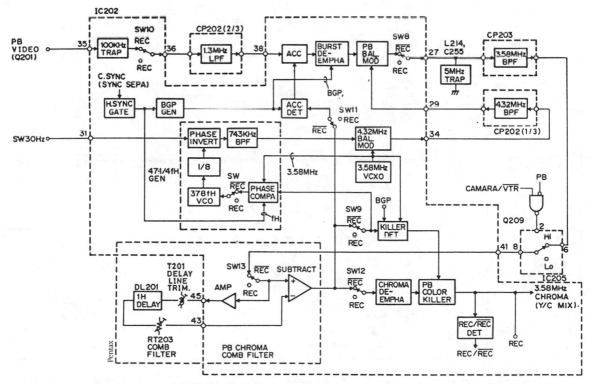

4-36 *Pentax PV-C850A (8 mm) chroma playback circuits.*

MAIN (LUMA/CHROMA) SCHEMATIC

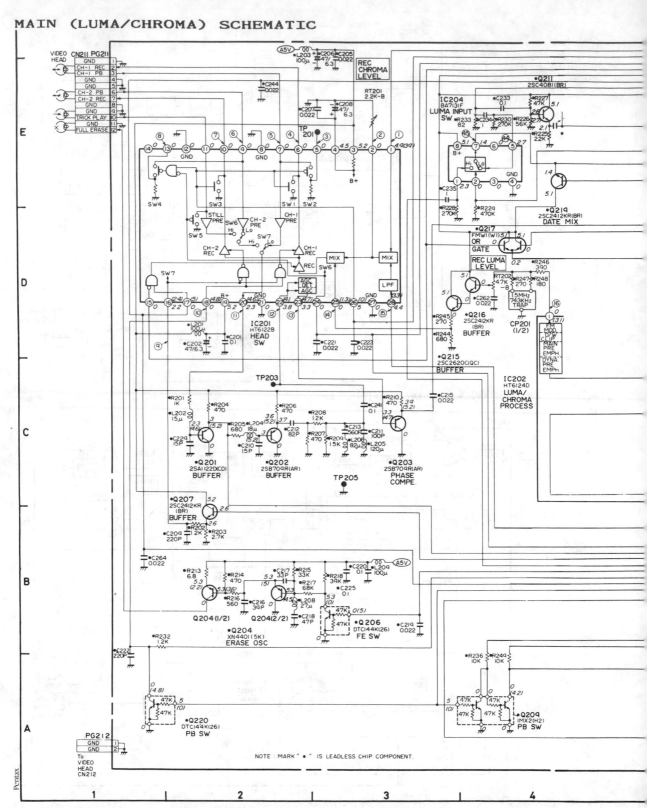

4-37 *The main luma/chroma schematic of Pentax PV-C850A (8 mm) camcorder.*

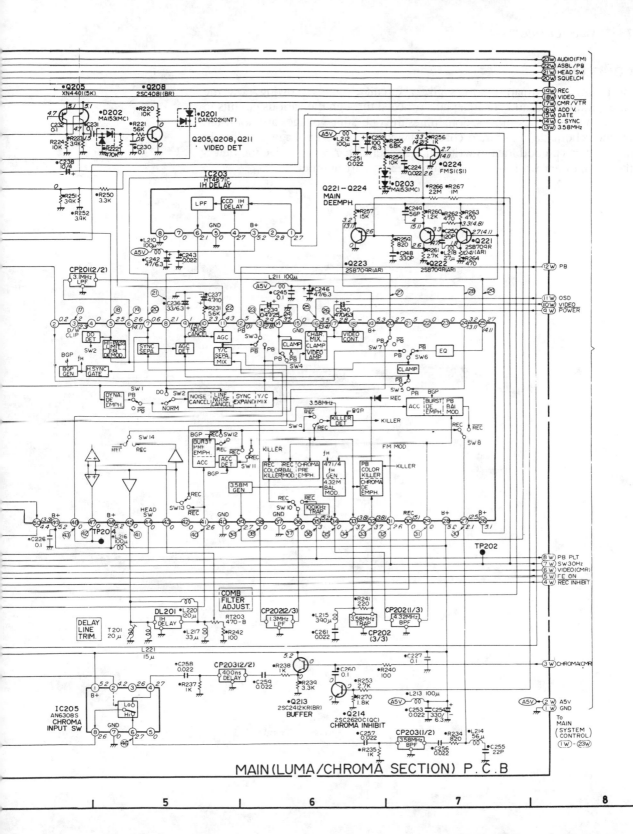

MAIN (LUMA/CHROMA SECTION) P.C.B

CONCLUSION

Most camcorder manufacturers give a circuit diagram showing how the video, luminance, and chroma paths proceed through the various circuits in record and playback modes. Sometimes the operating voltages are not listed on the schematic; a separate chart showing the correct voltage is given. In this case, it's a good idea to write on the schematic. Always replae the defective component with the manufacturer's exact part number.

Chapter **5**

System Control

*T*he most important component in the system control circuits is a microprocessor, also called a microcomputer or integrated IC. This system control IC may have from 48 to 82 connecting terminal leads (FIG. 5-1). Usually, the microprocessor controls all functions of the camcorder, including the camera and VCR functions. In the VHS models, the system control microprocessor may control the loading motor, trouble detector, camera control, power control, battery overdischarge detector, servo control, function control, luma/chroma control, character generator and audio circuits (FIG. 5-2).

All of the above functions are controlled in the VHS-C camcorders with added tape run control, mechanism control, tape speed detect, and on-screen display.

SYSTEM CONTROL CIRCUITS

The system control microcomputer in the 8 mm camcorders control may control the warning detection, loading motor, sync generator, D-D converter, continuous recording, video, digital servo, capstan signals, LED indication, and key and mode switch circuits. The CPU or microprocessor IC is a very delicate component and must be handled with care. Make sure all possible tests are made before replacing this system control component. Besides, it is very expensive to replace.

Pentax PV-C85OU (8 MM)

Although IC901 (main system control NP) controls the system control circuits, there are three different microprocessors in these circuits (IC901, IC902, and IC903). IC901 controls the following functions (FIG. 5-3).

- Controls the power latch relay to turn the power on and off according to power switch input.

5-1 *System control microprocessors can have from 48 to 82 terminals.*

- Calculates the length of tape wound and controls the character generator to display the data in the electronic viewfinder.
- Transfers counter data to calendar generator (IC906) and maintains data just after the power is off.

The sub-system control IC (IC902) controls the following:

- Receives key commands through a matrix switch circuit and supplies it to IC901.
- Detects battery terminal voltages and sends the signal to IC901. IC901 controls power source and character generator IC907 to display battery status in the electronic viewfinder.
- Detects $1/1200$ shutter speed mode and sends signal to IC901. IC901 controls the character generator IC901 to display the shutter speed in the electronic viewfinder.
- Receives mode data from IC901 and controls the matrix driver to the drive mode indicator.

The functions of the slow/still SS UP (IC903) are the following:

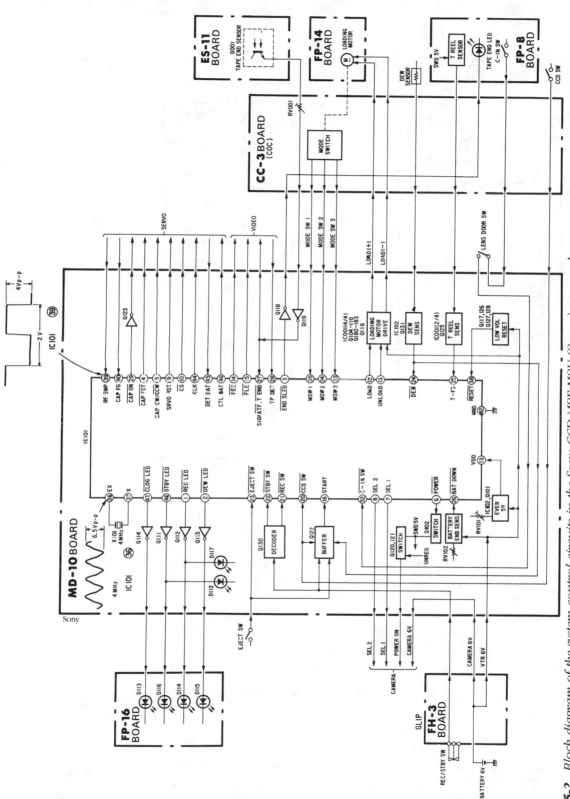

5-2 Block diagram of the system control circuits in the Sony CCD-M8E/M8U (8 mm) camcorder.

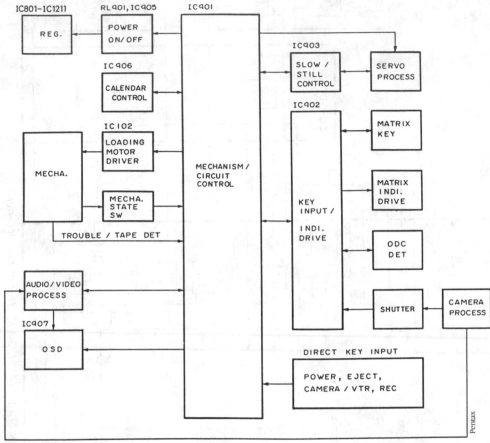

5-3   *Pentax PV-C850U (8 mm) configuration of system control circuits.*

- Receives still, slow, frame advance and play data and controls the servo circuit in place of IC901.
- Communicates with the calender generator (IC906) to correct and read the date, adds the date to the video signal in the character generator (IC8907), and record it as required.
- Controls the loading motor and mechanism mode.
- Detects trouble in the mechanism to protect the tape and mechanism.
- Controls the signal-processing system.
- Transfers display data to the character generator (IC907).
- Controls the mode of the servo circuit.
- Communicates with the slow/still microprocessor (IC903) to match commands and operation.
- Communicates with the sub microprocessor (IC902) to match commands and operation.

- Directly inputs operation of the POWER, EJECT, CAMERA VTR, and REC switches.
- Calculates the remaining tape time and controls the character generator to display data in the EVF.

RCA CPR100 (VHS-C)

Microprocessor IC901 controls the system control operation. IC901 controls the power operation, function switch control, overdischarge detect power control, tape speed detect, servo luma/chroma control, trouble detection, tape run, loading motor, clock generator, mechanism control, and on-screen display control circuits (FIG. 5-4). The system control microprocessor is usually found on the main chassis board (FIG. 5-5). In most RCA camcorders, the system control circuits control the camera assembly, VCR assembly, power control, and distribution.

The loading motor control drives the loading motor circuitry, which in turn mechanically operates levers and gears to control the mechanisms. The

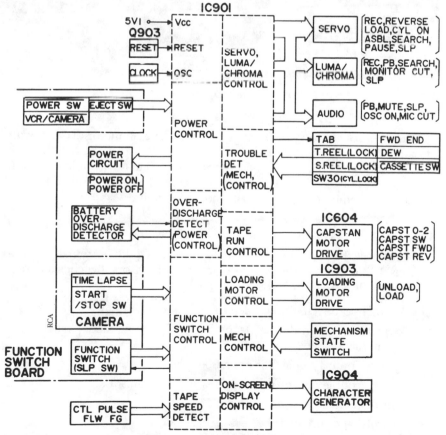

5-4 *RCA CPR100 (VHS-C) system control circuits.*

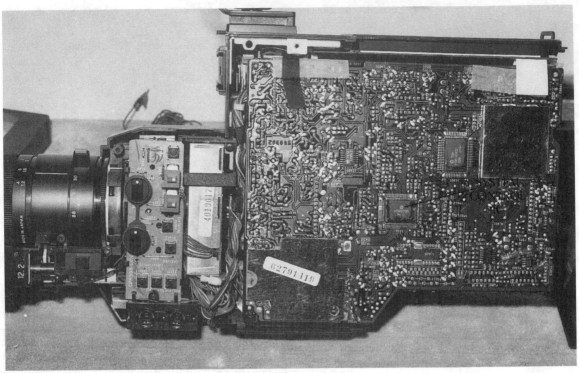

5-5 *The system control microprocessor in the RCA CPR300 VHS camcorder on the main circuit board.*

tape run control section provides signals to the capstan motor drive IC with capstan switch, capstan forward and capstan reverse procedures. In the VCR system, various trouble and monitor devices are fed to the trouble detection mechanism control of IC901. The system control circuitry found here is similar to all camcorders in the VHS and VHS-C units.

Realistic 150 (VHS-C) System Control Circuits

IC901 controls the system control circuits and has 64 thin terminal pin connections. IC901 controls the circuits composed of sensors, switches and motors (FIG. 5-6). IC901 controls the following:

- Controls power circuit and detects battery discharge.
- Controls on-screen display (tape counter, operating mode, battery voltage, and tape speed).
- Outputs control signals for operating mode.
- Detects trouble and protects circuits and mechanisms.
- Controls loading and unloading.
- Controls tape running.
- Detects tape speed during playback and sets the tape speed.

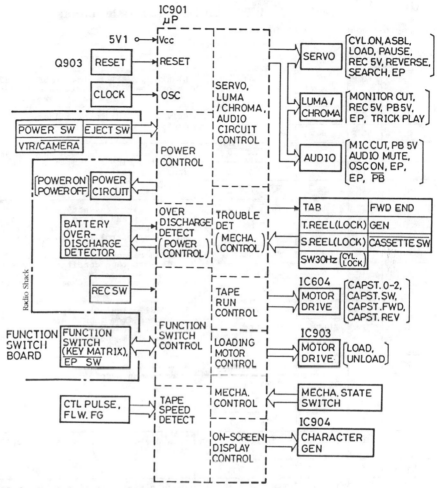

5-6 *Realistic 150 VHS-C system control configuration.*

IC901 is a flat component with 64 leads. See TABLE 5-1 for the different pin number assignments.

Sony CCD-M8E/M8U (8 MM)

CPU IC101 handles the system control circuits (FIG. 5-7). IC101 controls the loading and unloading of the loading motor. The sync generator and D-D converter are controlled by the system control microcomputer IC. IC101 controls the continuous recording and video circuits. The system control (MB88501) controls the digital servo, capstan, and drum motor assemblies. All the sensing, detection, switch modes and key board are tied to the system control microcomputer. IC101 controls the output LED indication control units.

Table 5-1. IC901 Pin Terminal Assignments

Main system control μP (IC901)

Pin No.	I/O	Active level	Abbreviation	Function
1	O	L	REC/BAT. INDI.	Lights REC/BAT indicator of EVF during record, and flashes it when battery terminal voltage is at lower limit.
2	O	H	LOAD	Drives loading motor and sets mode of mechanism.
3	O	H	UNLOAD	
4	I	L	M. STATE 0	IC901 detects mode of mechanism and indicates time during which loading motor should operate.
5	I	L	M. STATE 1	
6	I	L	M. STATE 2	
7	I	L	CST DOWN	IC901 detects cassette holder status (open or closed) and sets mechanism to stop or record pause mode when closed, and inhibits control input when open.
8	I	H	FWD END	1. When cassette holder is closed, IC901 detects tape condition from sensor inputs. 2. IC901 detects tape end and sets device to stop mode.
9	I	H	RWD END	
10	I	PULSE	S REEL	1. IC901 calculates tape length left unused from inputs and state of pin 61. 2. IC901 sets device to stop mode when reel disk speed has fallen below certain value.
11	I	PULSE	T REEL	
12	I	PULSE	DATA (S-M)	Communicates with sub μP and matches command and mode.
13	I	PULSE	DATA (S-M)	
33	O	PULSE	CLOCK (M-S)	
34	O	PULSE	DATA (M-S)	
14	I	L	CYL LOCK	Sets device to stop mode when cylinder status signal is Lo.
15	I	L	LP	
16	I	PULSE	SW30Hz	Adjusts timing to synchronize record and erase when restarting recording.
17	I	PULSE	CFG	Counts a pulse when restarting recording to determine the back-space amount.
18	O	L	REVERSE	Sets servo circuit to reverse mode.
19	O	L	CAPST ON	Activates capstan servo circuit.
20	O	H	CYL ON	Activates cylinder servo circuit.
21	O	H	SEARCH	Sets servo circuit to search mode.
22	O	L	HALT	When Lo, record pilot signal output mode is selected. When Hi, G4 signal output mode is selected.
23	O	H	FF/REW	Sets ervo circuit to FF/REW mode.
24	O	H	REC START	Times when to start recording pilot signal.
25	O	L	PAUSE	Sets servo circuit to pause mode.
26			VDD	Connect to 5V.

Pin No.	I/O	Active level	Abbreviation	Function
27	O	PULSE	CLOCK (M--)	Selects chip according to pins 50 and 51. IC901 communicates with slow/still µP, receives/transfers data from/to calendar generator, or transfers data to character generator through these common bus lines.
28	I	PULSE	DATA (--M)	
29	O	PULSE	DATA (M--)	
30	O	L	RESET (M--)	Resets slow/still µP, sub µP and character generator.
31	O	PULSE	REMOTE	When connected to VTR with remote pause input, timing of recording is adjusted during dubbing.
32		PULSE	DATA (T-M)	Communicates with timer adaptor through A/V connector. Pins 33 and 34 are used for IC901 to communicate with sub µP.
33		PULSE	DATA (M-T)	
34		PULSE	CLOCK (M-T)	
63		PULSE	DATA (T-M)	
35	O	H	REC	Sets servo circuit to record mode.
36	O	H	SQUELCH	Stops recording video signal or outputting play signal.
37	O	H	ASBL/PB	1. Sets servo circuit to play mode after release of record pause until restart of recording. 2. Sets video signal system to play mode.
38	O	H	FE ON	Times erasing.
39	O	H/L	USA/JAPAN	Changes date mode according to the units destinated to the U.S.A and Japan.
40	I	L	REC SW	When supplied, alternates between record and pause.
41	I	L	EJECT SW	Comes in at power-on to set mechanism to eject mode via the loading motor.
42	I	L	POWER SW	When supplied, alternates between power on and off.
43	I	H	RESET	Reset signal.
44	I	L	TEST	
45			OSC	Sets system clock frequency to 4.1 MHz.
46			OSC	
47			Vss	GND
48	O	H	MUTE	Stops output of playback audio signal.
49	O	H	PLAY	Sets circuits to play mode.
50	O	L	CS (SS)	Selects slow/still µP as destiantion of data sent along data bus (pins 27-29).
51	O	L	CS (CG)	Selects character generator as destination of data sent along data bus (pins 27-29).
52	O	H	CS (CAL)	Selects calendar generator as destination of data sent along data bus (pins 27-29).
53	O	L	STROBE	Latches data transferred to calendar generator.
54	O	L	OE	Sets the output pins of calendar generator to the high-impedance state.
55	O	H	POWER OFF	Turns OFF power latch relay.

Table 5-1.   Continued.

Pin No.	I/O	Active level	Abbreviation	Function
56	O	H	POWER ON	Turns ON power latch relay.
57	O	H	A5V ON	Keeps power (5V) of system control circuits ON.
58	I	H		NC
59	I	H/L	CAMERA/VTR	Record pause mode is selected when Hi and stop mode when Lo, immediately after power-on.
60	I	H	NO TAB	Inhibits record mode.
61	I	H	TAPE THICK	Indicates tape thickness needed for tape length calculation. Hi indicates 10 μm and Lo, 13 μm.
62	I	H	DEW	Condensation in mechanism is detected. Key input is inhibited when Hi.
64	O	PULSE	END LAMP	Drives end lamp with pulse.

Microcomputer IC101 is a flat surface-mount component with 48 pin terminals. The terminal connections and functions are shown in FIG. 5-8. Check TABLE 5-2 for terminal connections of IC101.

FUNCTION SWITCH KEY INPUT CIRCUITS

Some of the function switch input circuits are tied into the system control microprocessor. Usually, the function input switch circuits consist of the key matrix, the input to the camera section, and the system control microprocessor. The VCR section of the switch key input is connected to the PAUSE, STOP, REWIND, PLAY, F.FWD, RESET, DISPLAY, and receiver buttons (FIG. 5-9). The clock output pulses may place diodes in series with the key input switches in some camcorders, supplied by two phase signals from system control IC.

IC901 supplies two phase signals to the key matrixing circuits (FIG. 5-10). When the function switch is pressed, IC901 detects the switch by monitoring the data input. IC901 now sends out the required signals to carry out the function of the key pushed. Often, the key input buttons are mounted on a separate pc board that slides into position with one of the side panels removes (FIG. 5-11).

In the more expensive camcorders, a shutter and shutter speed circuits are tied into the function switch input circuits. Shutter switches S607 and S608 are only accepted in the record or record pause modes in the RCA CPR300 VHS camcorder (FIG. 5-12). With S607 set in normal position, the shutter speed is $1/60$ second. When S607 is in the high-speed position, switch S608 can be used. Each time S608 is pressed, the shutter speed advances to the next sequence $1/120$ to $1/250$ to $1/1000$, etc. Now this shutter high speed is registered in the electronic viewfinder. The shutter speed switches (S608 and S607) key inputs are applied to the shutter IC701, and these signals are applied to IC901 at pins 19, 20, and 21.

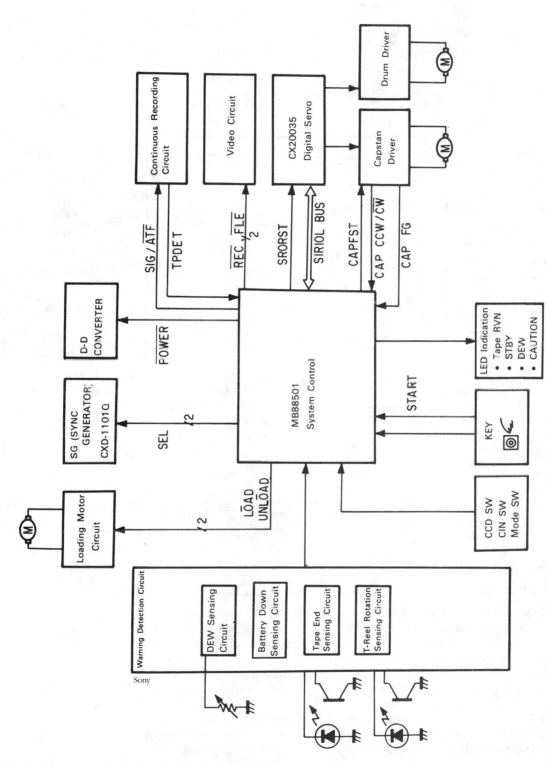

5-7 *Sony CCD-M8E/M8U (8 mm) system control block diagram.*

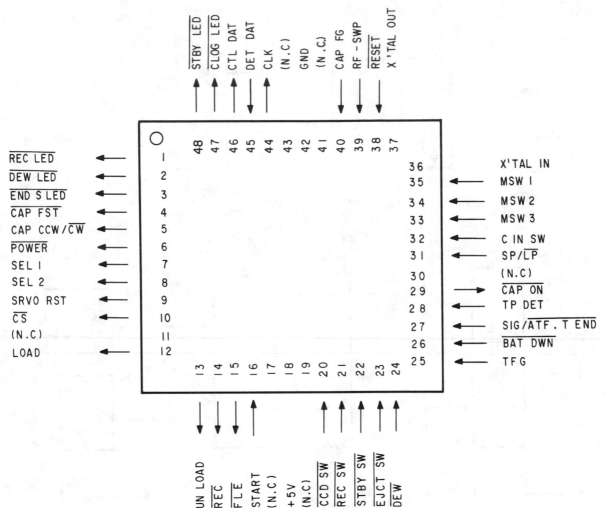

5-8 *Sony CCD-M8E/M8U system control (IC101) pin connections.* Sony

Pentax PV-C85OU (8 mm)Control Key Input Circuits

Four out of 20 control keys on the case are directly connected to IC901: CAMERA/VTR, EJECT, POWER, and REC (FIG. 5-13). The remaining key buttons are connected to IC902 through the matrix key through the key input circuits. The matrix key input circuit generates a five-phase key scan signal, timed by the four-phase signal (phases 0 through 3), developed at pins 9 through 12 of IC902 and feeds it back to pins 15 and 16 and 19 through 21 of IC902.

Out of the eight mode indicators on the case, the REC/BAT is directly driven by pin 1 of IC901. The rest are driven through the matrix drive circuit. In the matrix drive circuit, phase 0 and 1 of the four-phase signal (phase 0 through 3) pass through D901 while phases 2 and 3 pass through

Table 5-2. Sony CCD-M8E/M8U CPU Terminal Connections

Terminal numbers	Port names	IN/OUT	I/O circuit types	Signal names	Functions
1	O2	OUT	OPEN DRAIN	REC LED	Turns on during a REC (recording) time and when the battery is down.
2	O3	OUT	OPEN DRAIN	DEW LED	Turns on when dew is present.
3	O4	OUT	OPEN DRAIN	END SENS LED	Turns on the tape end detection LED.
4	O5	OUT	OPEN DRAIN	CAP FST	This drives the capstan motor with eight times of speed during the unloading period.
5	O6	OUT	OPEN DRAIN	CAP CCW/CW	Direction of the capstan motor rotation ("H"= counterclockwise, "L"=clockwise. Seen from above)
6	O7	OUT	OPEN DRAIN	POWER	Switch signal for the D/D converter (ON/OFF of the power supply)
7	P0	OUT	OPEN DRAIN	SEL1	ATF Pilot Signal switchover signal for the sink generator (CXD-1101Q)
8	P1	OUT	OPEN DRAIN	SEL2	
9	P2	OUT	OPEN DRAIN	SRVO RST	Reset signal for the servo IC (CX20035)
10	P3	OUT	OPEN DRAIN	CS	Chip select signal for the communication with the servo IC (CX20035)
11	(N.C)	—	—	—	—
12	R0	OUT	OPEN DRAIN	LOAD	Loading motor drive signal ("H" while driving)
13	R1	OUT	OPEN DRAIN	UNLOAD	Loading motor drive signal ("H" while unloading)
14	R2	OUT	OPEN DRAIN	REC	Switchover signal between REC and PB amplifier (CX20034). "L"=during REC time
15	R3	OUT	OPEN DRAIN	FLE	Flying and erase oscillation control signal ("L"= during oscillation)
16	START	IN	300 kΩ Pull down	START	Microcomputer standby mode reset signal
17	(N.C)	—	—	—	—
18	Vcc			+5V	
19	(N.C)	—	—	—	—
20	R4	IN	OPEN DRAIN	CCD SW	Cassette compartment down detection switch
21	R5	IN	OPEN DRAIN	REC SW	REC switch
22	R6	IN	OPEN DRAIN	STBY SW	Standby switch
23	R7	IN	OPEN DRAIN	EJECT SW	Eject switch
24	R8	IN	OPEN DRAIN	DEW	"L" while dew is preset
25	R9	IN	OPEN DRAIN	TFG	Take-up Reel FG

Sony

Table 5-2. Continued.

Terminal numbers	Port names	IN/OUT	I/O circuit types	Signal names	Functions
26	R10	IN	OPEN DRAIN	$\overline{\text{BAT DWN}}$	Battery down signal ("L"=during a low voltage)
27	R11	IN/OUT	OPEN DRAIN	SIG/$\overline{\text{ATF}}$ · $\overline{\text{TEND}}$	Continuous recording signal/ATF mode changeover output and Tape end signal input
28	R12	IN	OPEN DRAIN	TPDET	Continuous recording signal
29	R13	IN/OUT	OPEN DRAIN	$\overline{\text{CAP ON}}$	Capstan motor ON/OFF
30	(N.C)	—	—	—	—
31	R14	IN	OPEN DRAIN	SP/$\overline{\text{LP}}$	SP/LP speed selection switch (only for PAL model)
32	K0	IN	300 kΩ Pull up	$\overline{\text{CIN SW}}$	This becomes "L" when both the cassette-in switch (detects a mis-erasing protection claw) and the lens shutter switch are at ON position.
33	K1	IN	300 kΩ Pull up	MSW3	
34	K2	IN	300 kΩ Pull up	MSW2	Mode switch (3-bit construction, for mechanic position detection)
35	K3	IN	300 kΩ Pull up	MSW1	
36	EX		300 kΩ Pull up	X'tal IN	4 MHz ceramics generator (for clocks)
37	X		300 kΩ Pull up	X'tal OUT	
38	$\overline{\text{Reset}}$		300 kΩ Pull up		External reset signal
39	$\overline{\text{IRQ}}$	IN	300 kΩ Pull up	RF SWP	RF switching pulse
40	$\overline{\text{TC}}$	IN	300 kΩ Pull up	CAP FG	CAPSTAN FG (for determining a rewinding quantity in continuous recording period)
41	(N.C)	—	—	—	—
42	Vss	—	—	GND	
43	(N.C)	—	—	—	—
44	$\overline{\text{SC}}$/$\overline{\text{TO}}$	OUT	10 kΩ Pull up	CLK	Timing clock for the communication with the servo IC (CX20035)
45	SI	IN	300 kΩ Pull up	DET DAT	Serial data from the servo IC (CX20035) (status signal input)
46	SO	OUT	10 Ω Pull up	CTL DAT	Serial data to the servo IC (CX20035) (control data output)
47	O0	OUT	OPEN DRAIN	$\overline{\text{CLOG LED}}$	This turns on the LED for the clogging (head clogging) (Caution LED)
48	O1	OUT	OPEN DRAIN	$\overline{\text{STBY LED}}$	This indicates the standby atatus and turns on the LED.

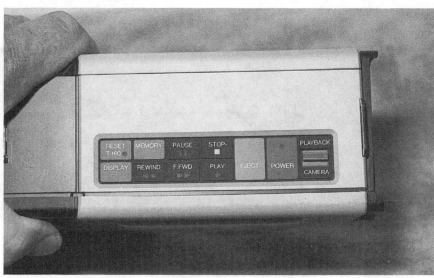

5-9 *Top function switch assembly of the RCA CPR300 VHS camcorder.*

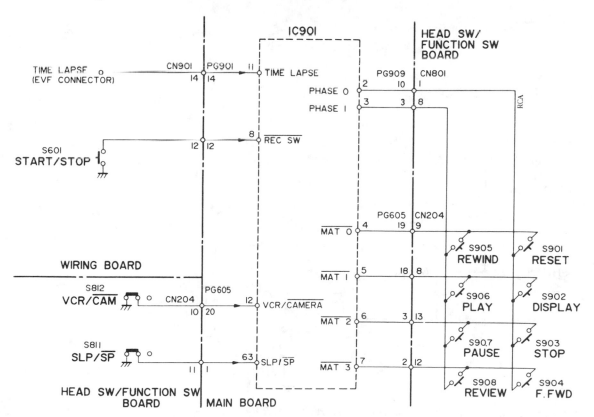

5-10 *RCA CPR100 (VHS-C) function switch input circuit.*

5-11   *Top key input button board from RCA CPR 300 camcorder.*

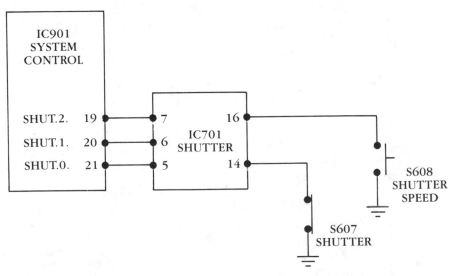

5-12   *Function shutter input speed circuits in RCA CPR300 VHS camcorder.*

D902 so that a two-phase indicator drive signal is generated. This signal is applied to each indicator. The cathodes of the indicators are connnected to pins 22 through 25 of IC902. IC901 controls the output levels at pins 22 through 25 to drive the LEDS, synchronized with the four-phase signal (phases 0 through 3).

RCA CPR100 (VHS-C) Function Switch Input Circuits

The function switch input circuits consist of the input camera section, key input, and system control microprocessor. The start/stop and camera input receiver signals are at pins 8 and 7, respectively. Pin 11 of IC901 receives the time input lapse signal (see FIG. 5-10). The start/stop, receiver, and the time lapse operations are accessible when the camcorder is switched to camera position. Matrix signals from pins 2 and 3 (IC901) are applied to the function switches. When one of the function switches is pressed, the signal is routed through the switch back to IC901. Then the microprocessor sends the necessary signal to perform the function.

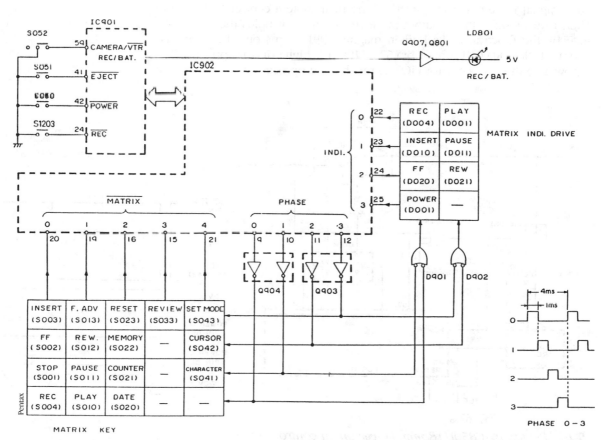

5-13 *Control key input circuit of Pentax PV-C850U (8 mm) control circuits.*

POWER CONTROL CIRCUITS

The power supplies for the camcorder are also controlled by the system control microprocessor. The correct voltage source is furnished by batteries or the ac power line via the ac adaptor/charger. Often, these voltages are regulated with IC or transistor components. A relay may be found in some models to apply the regulated voltage to the function control microprocessor. In turn, these output voltages are fed to the various camcorder circuitry. The power control operation consists of turning the power off and on, VTR power, camera power, and eject operations.

Pentax PV-C85OU (8 MM) Power Circuits

The main power supply is cut off automatically when the battery terminal voltage falls below a certain level or when the motor and mechanism causes trouble. The main system control (IC901) controls the on/off switching of the main power (FIG. 5-14). The main power (7.2 V) is supplied to the power latch relay (RL901) and microprocessor power switch (Q911). RL901 supplies 7.2 V to the regulators when the power is on. RL901 turns on when a pulse signal is output from pin 56 of the main system control IC (IC901). Then it turns off with an output pulse from pin 55. It holds the on or off state by the function of its built-in magnet. Q911 turns on when S050 is operated. Now RL901 is on, or pin 57 or IC901 is high (Hi) to supply the 7.2 V power to the 5 V regulator (IC905) for the microprocessor.

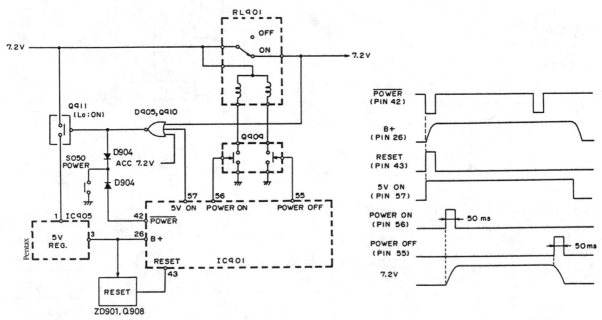

5-14   Pentax PV-C850U (8 mm) power on/off control circuits.

When the power is on, the power switch (S050) also turns the power off. Q911 turns on as its base is grounded through D904 and S050. The power voltage (7.2 V) is applied through Q911. IC905 generates a 5 V output and supplies it to IC901 and the reset circuit. Now IC901 is active. After being reset it detects power operation using the input pin 42, sets pin 57 at high (Hi), and generates a pulse of 50 ms wide at pin 56. The output at pin 57 holds Q911 on. Q911 is held on by relay (RL901) or the output at pin 57.

The power switch (S050) activates to turn the unit off when the battery terminal voltage has fallen below a certain limit or the motor or mechanism is in trouble. IC901 provides counter data to the calendar generator (IC906) and then supplies a pulse 50 ms wide to pin 55.

Relay (RL901) is now turned off by the pulse from IC901 (pin 55) and stops the 7.2 V to the regulators. Pin 57 of IC901 turns low (Lo), so Q911 turns off and IC905 stops the supply of 5 V. The output at pin 57 holds Q911 on in place of S050 until all processing is complete before switching the power off.

Realistic 150 (VHS-C)

The main board generates power supplies for all circuits. The battery or external battery pack (12 V) applies power through fuse F970 to the latch relay (RL901). The system control (IC901) controls RL901 to supply power to the various circuits.

For VTR power, the sliding power switch (S809) grounds the base of the 12-volt switch (Q904) through ZD901 and D803, turns Q904 on, and applies 12 V of power to the 5.6 V regulator (IC905). When the 5V2 source is applied from D914 to pin 26 (V$_{CC}$) of the system control IC (IC901), 5V3 source from D914 is also applied to the reset circuit (Q903, ZD902, and RESET) at the same time to reset the system control (IC901) (FIG. 5-15).

Because input pin 14 (power switch) through D903 is low (Lo), the system control (IC901) determines that the power is on and outputs a high (Hi) power-on signal from pin 54 (POWER ON) for 100 ms. The power-on signal output turns relay driver (Q901—POWER ON SW) on and switches relay (RL901) on to supply 12 V to the voltage regulators and generate power as shown in TABLE 5-3.

The 5.6 V regulator (IC905) inputs power via D902 and maintains the system control V$_{CC}$ power (5V2). When the power is on and the power switch (S809) is in position, the system control (IC901) determines that power has been switched off and outputs a high (Hi) power-off signal with a duration of 100 ms from pin 55. The power-off signal turns relay driver Q902 on and switches relay RL901 off to cut the 12-volt power supply (enters stop mode).

During the eject operation of the VTR, when eject switch S810 is pressed in the power-off state, the system control IC901 operates because 12 V switch (Q904) is on as it was with the power on. At the same time, the system control (IC901) outputs a high (Hi) power-on signal with a duration of 100 ms through pin 54, because pin 15 (EJECT SW) input is low (Lo) and

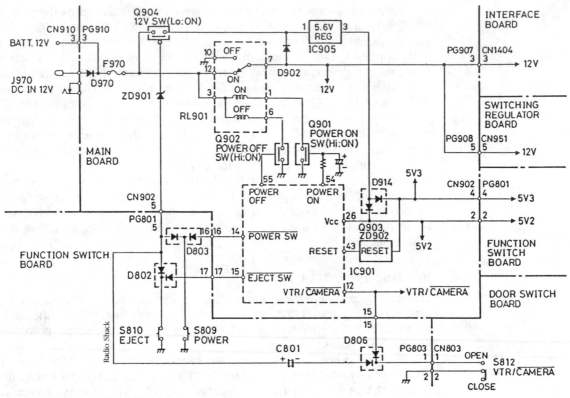

5-15 *Realistic 150 VHS-C power circuit.*

eject is detected. The high (Hi) POWER ON signal raises each power source during power on and operates the eject function (FIG. 5-16).

When the eject operation is completed, the POWER OFF signal sets the power off (STOP) mode. With the power on, eject operates in all modes except record. The power-on state is held after eject is completed.

In camera power operation, the lens door is opened during camera recording, the VTR/CAMERA switch (S812) interlocked with the door is set to open. This grounds the base of the 12 V switch (Q904) through ZD901, D806, and S812 until C801 is charged in the same way when the VTR power is turned on. Since pin 12 (VTR/CAMERA) receives a low (Lo) input via S812, the system control (IC901) detects power on in the camera mode. The power-off mode is detected when the lens door is closed, S812 is switched to close, and pin 12 is set to high (Hi) (FIG. 5-17).

Radio Shack 150 (VHS-C) Switching Regulator Circuits

The sawtooth generator (IC951) generates a sawtooth-wave signal around 100 kHz and applies it to the pulse width modulator (PWM COMPA). The PWM outputs from each driver are applied to switching transistors Q951 to

Table 5-3. Realistic 150 Power Supply Sources

Supply Power	Generator	Supply Destination	Application
12V	RL901-7	Camera	*
		AV OUT connector	For RF converter
		System control circuit	IC903
		Servo circuit	IC604, IC551
8V	SWR	Camera	*
		Luma/chroma circuit	IC301
		EVF (Camera)	
5V1	SWR	Audio circuit	IC401, IC402, Trouble sensors
		Servo circuit	Main power (IC601 - IC603, IC605)
		Luma/chroma circuit	Main power (IC201 - IC204)
		System control circuit	IC904
PB5V	Q908-C	Camera	*
		Luma/chroma circuit	IC201 - IC203
REC5V	Q909-C	Luma/chroma circuit	IC202
		Servo circuit	IC601
5V2	IC905-3	System control circuit	μP (IC901)
		Function switch circuit	Backup detector
5V3	IC905-3	System control circuit	IC902
		Function switch circuit	POWER LED B+/Backup detector
B+ CYL.	SWR	Servo circuit	IC551
B+ CAPST.	SWR	Servo circuit	IC604

Radio Shack

Q954. Q951 to Q954 supply the power sources, 8V, 5V1, B+ CAPSTAN and B+ CYL via the independent filter network (FIG. 5-18). The PWM comparators (PWM COMPA) supply 8V and 5V1 power source comparing the sawtooth signal as applied to the positive input with the feedback signal as applied to the positive input with the feedback signal as applied to the negative input and change the output pulse width to vary the power supplies. The PWM comparator for the B+ capstan applies the capstan servo signal from the servo circuit to the inverting input and outputs the variable power supply for the capstan motor according to this CAPST. SERVO signal.

The PWM comparator for the B+CYL. inputs the CYL.FB signal, the

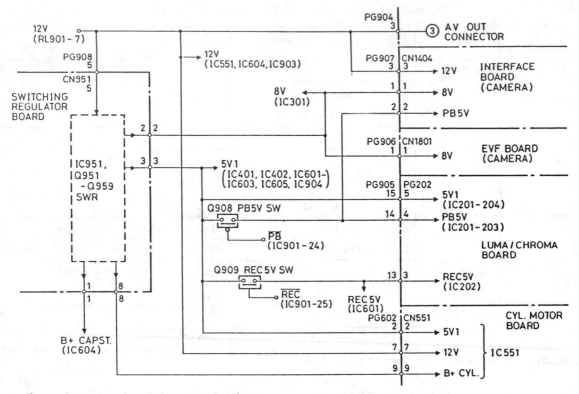

5-16   *Realistic 150 (VHS-C) power distribution circuits.* Radio Shack

feedback from the cylinder motor driver, via the noninverting input and outputs variable power supply for the cylinder motor according to this CYL.FB signal. B+CYL. goes high (Hi) when the CYL.FB signal is low (Lo). When a high load is applied to the cylinder motor (during starting, etc.), Q956 (LOAD SW) and Q957 (CAPSTAN SW) turn on and ground the CYL.FB signal to maximize the B+CYL. power. Zener diode (ZD953) limits the maximum value of B+CYL. D955 protects the B+CYL. power line from short circuits. When the B+CYL. goes low (Lo) because the load circuit is short-circuited, Q955 turns off and causes the CYL.FB signal to go high (Hi) with D955 to shut off the B+CYL. output.

Sony CCD-M8E/M8U (8 MM) Standby Sleep Mode

The purpose of the CPU standby sleep mode is to conserve battery consumption. The system control microcomputer IC consumes most of the power. The battery power should be conserved at all times, especially when the camcorder is not in use. With the standby sleep mode circuits, the system control CPU cuts off the power when not required.

The system control CPU controls the signal (POWER) for the dc-dc converter and turns the 5V switch off when in the high (Hi) state. The system

5-17 *Power circuits are mounted on the main circuit board of RCA CPR300 VHS camcorder.*

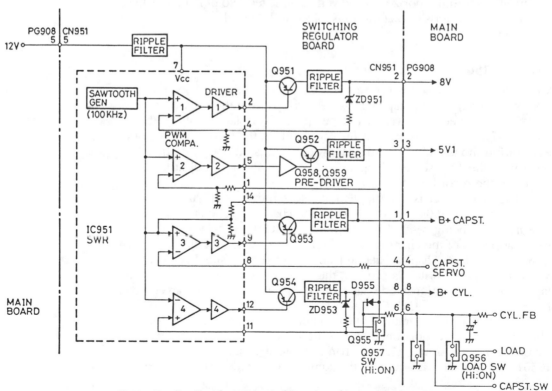

5-18 *Radio Shack 150 switching regulator circuit.* Radio Shack

control is now in STANDBY mode. When the input pulse is applied at the START PORT (pin 16) of IC101, the STANDBY mode is released (FIG. 5-19). The system control enters the STANDBY mode with the cassette door up or the LS (linear skating) becomes a READY state. The system control goes into the STANDBY mode when the LS chassis stops during error detection.

ON-SCREEN DISPLAY CIRCUITS

When the display button is pressed, the system control IC generates a signal to a character generator that the system control microprocessor applies the data to display battery level and tape counter in the electronic viewfinder (EVF) of many camcorders. In the RCA CPR300 camcorder, the system control microprocessor provides the display of battery level, tape counter, shutter speed, and operation mode. The signal from the character generator IC is fed to the video amp IC for on-screen display in the electronic viewfinder.

RCA CPR100

The system control microprocessor generates a low (Lo) signal at pin 25 with the display switch pressed (FIG. 5-20). This signal is fed to the character generator (IC904). The system control (IC901) applies data to the character generator (IC904) in displaying battery level and tape counter indications. The character signal at pin 10 is fed to pin 13 of the video amp (IC204) and synchronizes with the horizontal and vertical sync fed into pins 14 and 15 of IC904. The character signal at pin 13 is mixed with the video signal at pin 16 and applied to the EVF.

Realistic 150

When the DISPLAY switch is pressed, the battery voltage, tape speed, operation mode and four-digit tape counter are displayed in the electronic viewfinder (EVF) screen (FIG. 5-21). The tape speed is displayed only in the SP mode and the operation mode is displayed only in the record, fast forward, and rewind modes. When the display switch is pressed one more time, the display in the EVF screen disappears. However, the REC indicator is displayed in the record mode.

When the power is first supplied, the system control (IC901) and character generator (IC904) are reset. When the character generator (IC904) is activated after being reset, the system control (IC901) provides a high (Hi) signal at pin 28 of the character generator (IC904). When the display switch is not pressed, no display data and no output data is supplied (FIG. 5-22). When the display switch is pressed, the character signal data showing the tape counter, operation mode, tape speed, and battery voltage are output, synchronized with the C.G. CLOCK pulse.

The character generator (IC904) outputs a character data signal, synchronized with the horizontal and vertical sync signals (H. and V.SYNC) input from pins 14 and 15. The character signal is supplied to pin 13 of IC301 and is mixed inside with the luminance or video signal at pin 16.

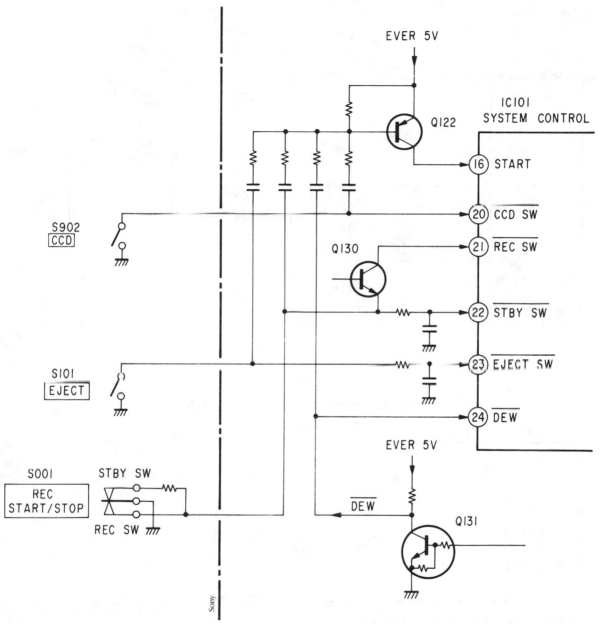

5-19 *Sony CCD-M8E/M8U (8 mm) standby sleep mode.*

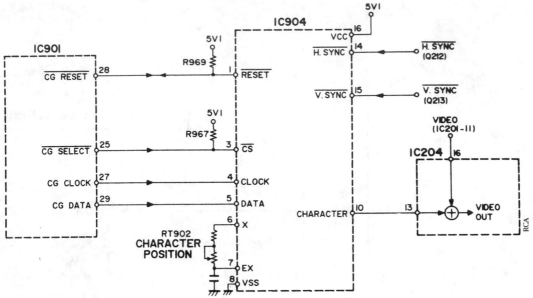

5-20   *RCA CPR100 on-screen display circuits.*

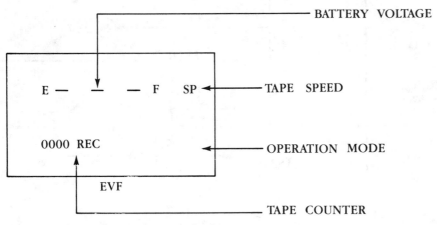

5-21   *Realistic 150 EVF screen display.*

When the display mode is changed, the system control (IC901) outputs low (Lo) at pin 28 to reset the character signal generated by the character signal generator (IC904). The character generator (IC904) makes pin 1 (RESET) low (Lo) when there is no V.SYNC signal input at pin 15 to inhibit the display data output of the system control (IC901).

A complete main system control section in the RCA CPR100 VHS-C camcorder is shown in FIG. 5-23. The system control microprocessor also controls the trouble detection (Chapter 6) and capstan and loading motor circuits (Chapter 7).

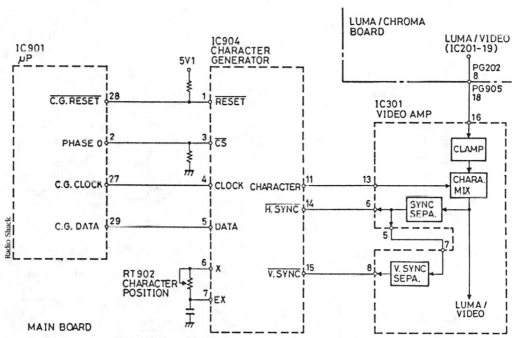

5-22 *Realistic 150 (VHS-C) on-screen display circuits.*

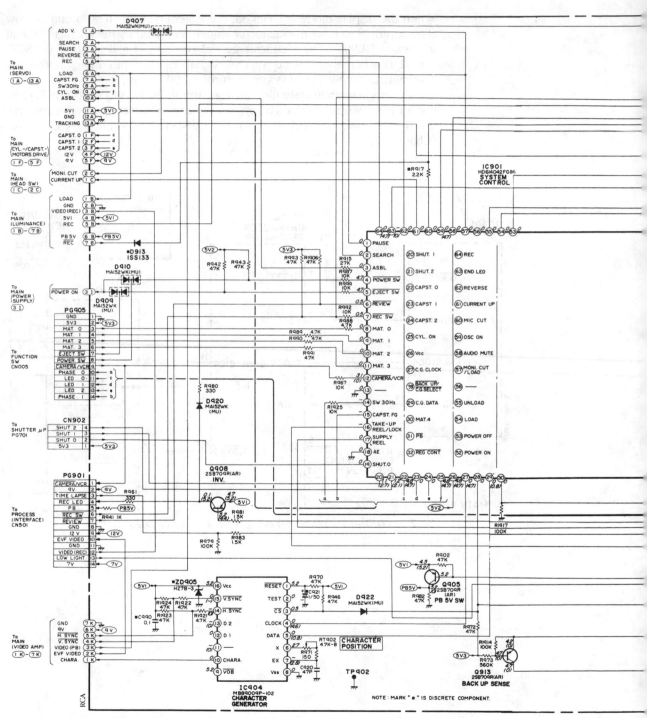

5-23 *Complete RCA CPR100 system control schematic.*

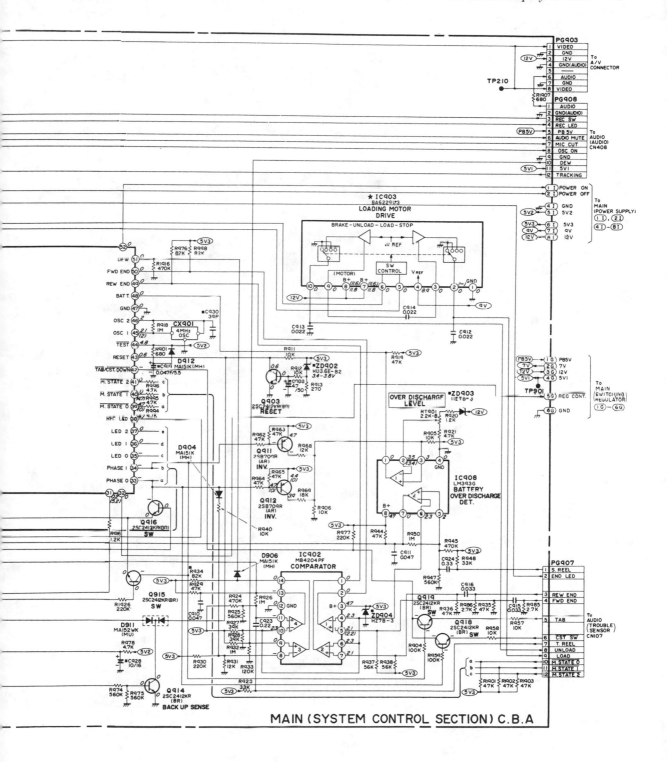

MAIN (SYSTEM CONTROL SECTION) C.B.A

Chapter *6*

Trouble Detection and Servo Circuits

*T*he trouble detection circuits troubleshoot the tape transport system, mechanism, tape type, and recording condition for tape protection, mechanisms, and recording. Usually, the various sensor indicators are controlled by one large microprocessor. The system control microprocessor monitors the supply-end sensor, take-up reel sensor, dew sensor, supply reel sensor, safety tab switch, cassette switch, and mechanism state mode switch (FIG. 6-1). The VTR will stop functioning if the correct signals are not applied to the system control microprocessor.

TAPE-END SENSOR

Basically, when the tape reaches its end, the clear leader of the tape lets the end sensor light shine through the tape to fall on the end photo sensor. The end photo sensor then applies a voltage to the system control IC and the control microprocessor stops the tape movement. Now the operator knows when to change the cassette.

Pentax PV-C850A (8 mm) Tape-End Sensor

Sensors that detect failures in the tape transport system are the tape-end sensors (Q104 and Q105) on the take-up and supply sides, reel sensors (Q102 and Q103), and cylinder lock sensor. The condensation sensor and cassette holder sensor (S103) detect the mechanism condition. Added to these are the tape thickness sensor (S101) and the tab sensor (S102) (the latter detects whether there is a tab on the cassette).

For tape-end sensors (Q104 and Q105) on the take-up side, phototransistor Q104 detects light from an LED (D101) through a transparent part at the end of the tape (FIG. 6-2). Likewise, phototransistor Q105 checks for the end of the tape at the supply side. D101 is driven by the pulse signal developed at pin 64 of IC901 to save power.

6-1 *Top view of the VTR RCA CPR300 (VHS) showing the different detection sensors.*

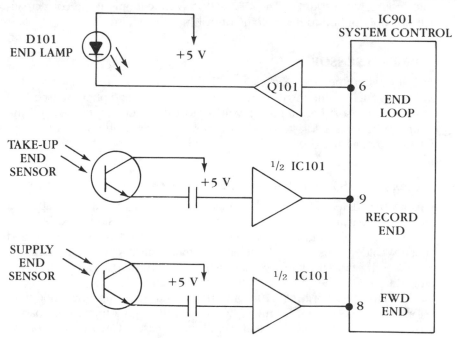

6-2 *Pentax PV-C850A (8 mm) end sensor circuits.*

After being shaped by comparator IC101 to protect against optical noise, the outputs of Q104 and Q105 are applied to pins 9 and 8 of IC901. The IC901 checks the inputs at pins 9 and 8 synchronously with the LED drive pulse and sets the input to the stop mode as soon as pin 9 or 8 turns high (Hi). Also, it detects how the tape is installed from both inputs.

RCA CPR100 (VHS-C) End-Sensor Circuits

When the tape reaches the end while moving in the forward direction, the light shows through the clear leader of the tape and allows light to shine on the surface of the supply-end photo sensor. The end-sensor lamp is turned on by control microprocessor IC901 (FIG. 6-3). Now the supply-end photo sensor applies 5 volts to pin 5 of the comparator IC902. A high signal from IC902 is applied to pin 18 of IC901. Then IC901 detects this high signal and shuts off the tape movement.

Realistic 150 (VHS-C) End Sensor

System control IC901 outputs a low end-sensor lamp drive pulse (pin 30) with a duration of approximately 1 ms. This low end lamp pulse turns the driver (Q907) on and lights the end-sensor lamp (D125). Since the transparent section at the tape end activates the supply-end sensor (Q123) to apply high to the noninverting input (pin 5) of comparator 1 of IC902, the output at pin 2 goes high. This causes pin 18 (FWD END) of the system IC901 to input high and the end of tape is detected (FIG. 6-4).

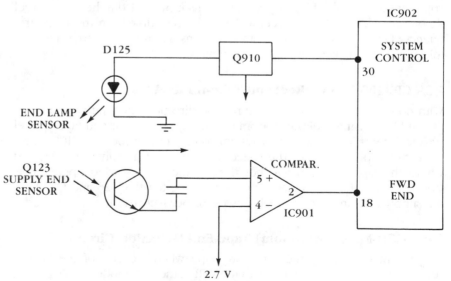

6-3 *RCA CPR100 (VHS-C) end sensor circuits.*

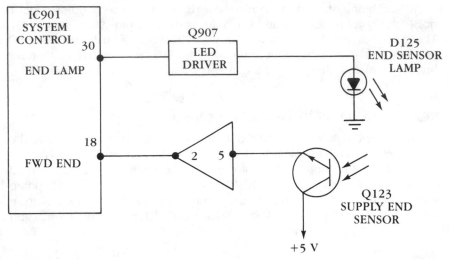

6-4 *Realistic 150 (VHS-C) end sensor circuits.*

Pentax PV-C850A (8 mm) Reel Sensors

On the take-up side, phototransistor Q102 detects a beam of light reflected by eight reflector plates fitted at equal intervals on the underside of the reel disk. Phototransistor Q103 works similarly on the supply side. The speed of the reel disk rotation is obtained from the rate of the reflected pulses. The light source (LED) is integrated in the same reel sensor chip. After being shaped by comparator IC101 to protect against optical noise, the outputs of Q102 and Q103 are applied to pins 10 and 11 of IC901 (FIG. 6-5). Here IC901 computes the length of tape by counting sensor pulses from the take-up reel sensor and detects failure (reel lock) of the reel disk from the pulse frequency. Detecting the inputs from both sensors and at pin 61 (tape reel thickness), it calculates the tape remaining time.

RCA CPR100 Supply Reel and Take-up Reel Sensors

With no take-up end sensor in the reverse direction, the tape is stopped at the end by sensing reel pulses from the supply reel sensor and take-up reel sensor. Input pins 20 and 21 of system control microprocessor (IC901) receive the applied pulses. The speed is reduced at a point near the end where the tape can stop and not damage the tape. Rewind operation is stopped when the tape reaches the end of tape travel. Q126 and Q119 are the supply reel and take-up reel sensors, respectively (FIG. 6-6).

Sony CCD-M8E/M8U (8 mm) Tape-End Detection Circuit

To prevent damage to the drum and tape when the end of the tape is reached, the tape-end sensor places the VTR in the stop mode. This tape-end detection in the 8 mm VTR is the same system as in the VHS models. There's an LED at the center of the cassette half, and a small window lets the light

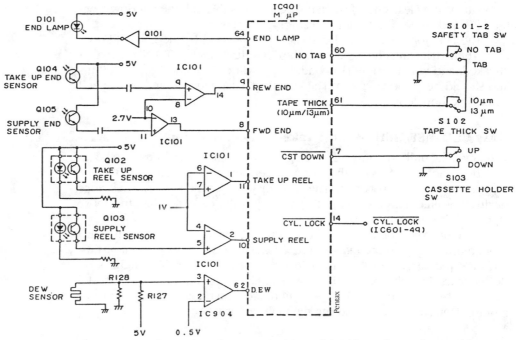

6-5 *Pentax (8 mm) reel sensor Q102 and Q103 in the main trouble detection circuits.*

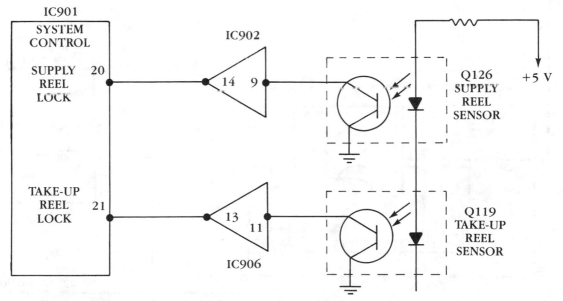

6-6 *RCA CPR100 (VHS-C) supply and take-up reel sensors.*

through. At the clear end of the tape, light comes through the window from the LED and shines on a phototransistor (FIG. 6-7).

The LED for the tape-end detection is controlled by the END LED signal. When detecting the tape end, the logic level of the T END signal is checked, and when in low (L) condition, it will continue for about 300 ms and should be at the tape end. The tape length, tape leader, and tape speed determine how long it takes.

Sony CCD-M8E/M8U (8 mm) Take-Up Reel Rotation Check

The tape may pull out, unwind, or clog up the mechanism when the take-up reel does not rotate. With the take-up reel detection circuit running, the tape is stopped to protect it. The tape may be jammed if the reel stops during the unloading period and cannot eject the cassette. Now the loose tape must be removed from the VTR.

Take-up reel detection is done with a phototransistor and LED mounted underneath the take-up reel (FIG. 6-8). The LED shows light against the reflected surface of the underside of the take-up reel. This light is reflected back into the phototransistor. The LED and phototransistor are located in one component. When the reel rotates, the phototransistor contains a pulse. Detection is done during the REC, PB, or GG mode (FIG. 6-9).

DEW SENSOR

The dew sensor detects moisture in the VCR or VTR section of the camcorder. With moisture increasing, the dew sensor resistance increases, send-

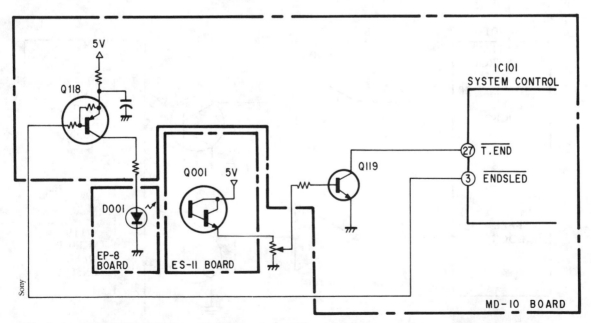

6-7 *Sony CCD-M8E/M8U (8 mm) tape end detection circuits.*

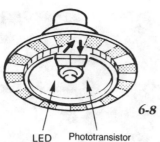

6-8 *The take-up reel rotation check with LED and photo-transistor in the Sony (8 mm) VTR.* Sony

LED   Phototransistor

ing a voltage to a comparator that shapes and applies pulses to the control microprocessor, not allowing tape operation. If tape operation began with moisture on the tape heads, the tape and mechanism may be damaged. The dew sensor is often located in the center of the VTR section (FIG. 6-10).

Pentax PV-C850A (8 mm) Condensation Sensor Circuit

The characteristics of the condensation sensor are that its resistance is a few kilohms when the humidity is around 60 percent and rises several hundred kilohms above 80 percent. The voltage drop across this resistance is applied to pin 62 of IC901. If the pin 62 is high, the camcorder is in stop mode with the power indicator flashing and key input inhibited (FIG. 6-11).

RCA CPR100 (VHS-C) Dew Sensor Circuit

The dew sensor circuit in this VHS-C model is the same type of circuit found in RCA CPR300 (VHS) camcorder except a different microprocessor is used with a different input terminal. The dew sensor detects moisture within the VCR section and keeps the unit shut down. The resistance of the dew element increases as moisture increases, and the voltage is applied to a nonin-

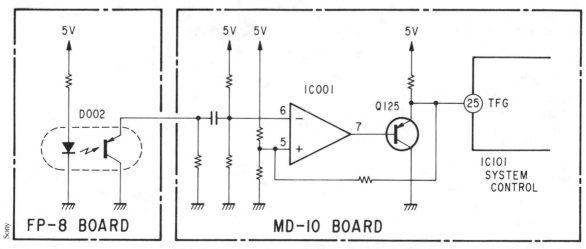

6-9 *Take-up reel rotation check circuit of the Sony CCD-M8E/M8U VTR.*

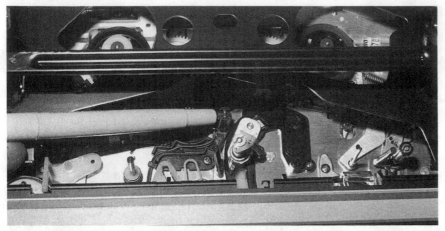

6-10   *The location of the dew sensor in the RCA CPR300 (VHS) VTR.*

verting input of comparator IC902 (FIG. 6-12). When moisture is detected, IC902 goes high and is applied to pin 19 of the control IC901, stopping all VCR operation.

Sony CCD-M8E/M8U (8 mm) Dew Detection Circuit

Sometimes when the camcorder is brought into a warm house from a cold place, condensation may appear upon the drum surface. The tape may stick to the drum surface, causing the drum to stop or jam the take-up reel and capstan assemblies. Tape may pull out or wrap around the capstan and pressure rollers. The purpose of the dew detection circuit is to detect condensation and place VTR in stop mode.

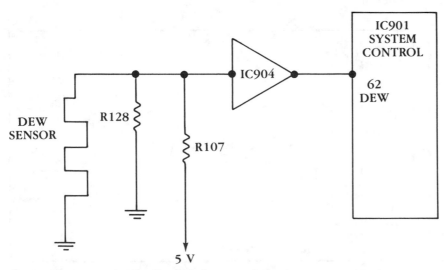

6-11   *Pentax PV-C850A (8 mm) dew condensation sensor circuit.*

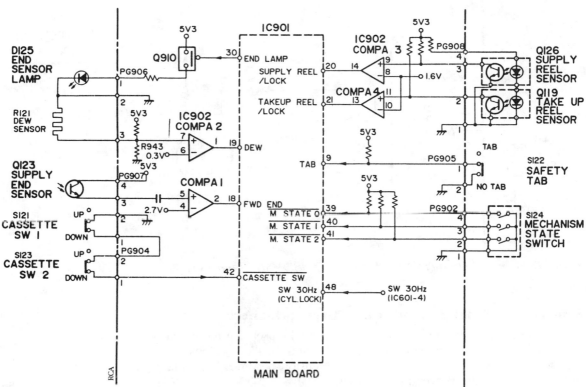

6-12 *RCA CPR100 (VHS-C) trouble detection circuit.*

During the excess condensation period, the dew sensor has a higher resistance value (from a few kilohms to tens of kilohms). The higher voltage is applied to IC102 (FIG. 6-13). Although the dew signal is low when condensation is detected, the dew state is accepted when the signal is low for 100 ms due to the chattering cancel period.

Pentax PV-C850A (8 mm) Cylinder Lock Circuit

The speed/phase control IC601 compares the cylinder speed circuits voltage with the cylinder lock voltage. It sets the unit to stop mode when pin 14 turns low on the system control microprocessor IC901 (see FIG. 6-5).

Realistic 150 (VHS-C) Cylinder Lock Circuit

The cylinder lock (IC601) detects pulse width of SW30 Hz signal obtained by the servo circuit for detecting drop in cylinder motor speed. If the pulse width is less than the rated value, the microprocessor IC901 judges the cylinder lock (SW 30 Hz Cyl. Lock).

Detection is made in the VTR mode and enters the stop mode. In camera mode, it enters the stop mode and will not go to any other mode except eject or off.

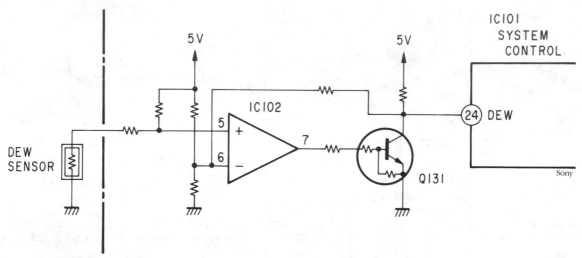

6-13   *The dew detection circuit of Sony's CCD-M8E/M8U (8 mm) VTR.*

Sony CCD-M8E/M8U (8 mm) Drum Phase Lock Check

The purpose of the drum phase lock is to inform the user that recording is prohibited. Drum servo phase unlocking causes abnormal recordings. If the tape tends to stick to the drum or the tape tension becomes high, phase unlocking may occur, preventing recording.

Drum phase lock check is accomplished with IC CX 20035. It has a wide and narrow range (wide is V/2 cycle sampling; narrow is FG/2 cycle sampling). CX20035 determines that the drum lock becomes effective and sends a drum lock signal to the system control IC when the band changes from a wide to narrow range.

There are two types of drum phase lock checks. The first is a phase lock check during a mode transition from the READY mode to standby (STBY) mode. The second is a phase lock check in the record (REC) mode and the standby (STBY) mode.

In the READY-STBY mode, the drum rotates during transition from the READY mode to the STBY mode. If the phase lock does not become effective within five seconds, the mode returns to the READY mode. With the process, there are no limitations of the key acceptance and the keys may be accepted a number of times.

The drum phase lock becomes effective when the loading motor starts and the mode changes to the STBY mode. The lock signal detection (PAL) does not begin for four seconds to avoid missing detection due to drum hunting.

In the REC and the STBY modes, the drum phase detection is executed. The mode changes to READY mode if an out-of-phase state is detected in three seconds. The sampling cycle is set to 12 ms. After the mode changes to READY mode, the recording can be done freely because the key limitation is not applied.

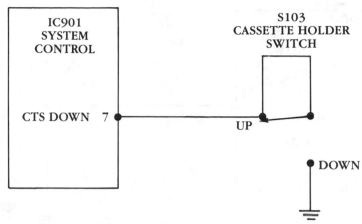

6-14 *Pentax PV-C850A (8 mm) cassette holder sensor.*

Pentax PV-C850A (8 mm) Cassette Holder Sensor

The cassette holder sensor (S103) detects the cassette holder status. The output is applied to pin 7 of IC901. IC901 drives the loading motor to change the mechanism from the eject mode to stop mode with a high signal at pin 7 (FIG. 6-14).

Realistic 150 (VHS-C) Cassette Switch

The object of the cassette switch (S121) is to decide if the cassette holder is up or down. If the cassette holder is up, no function of switches other than power or eject are accepted. When "up" is detected during operation, the system goes into stop mode.

Pentax PV-C850A (8 mm) Tape Thickness Sensor

The tape thickness sensor switch (S102) detects a tab indicating the correct tape thickness. The output is applied to pin 61 of IC901 (FIG. 6-15). It judges the tape thickness to be 13 μm when pin 61 is high and 10 μm when it is low and calculates the length of tape remaining time using this data.

Pentax PV-C850A (8 mm) Safety Tab Sensor Circuit

The safety tab switch (S101) detects the write-protect tab (safety tab) on the back of the cassette. This output is applied to pin 60 of IC901. It prohibits recording when the input is HI, (FIG. 6-16).

Realistic 150 (VHS-C) Safety Tab Switch Circuit

The safety tab switch (S122) detects whether the tab is present to prevent accidental erasure of the cassette. It will not enter the record mode even if the lens door switch (S182) (VTR/CAMERA) is opened (OPEN-CAMERA MODE). The unit will enter camera stop mode (refer to FIG. 6-17).

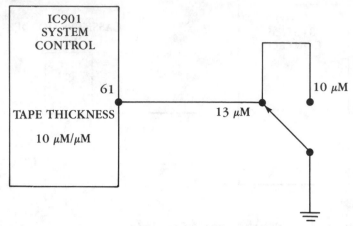

6-15   *Pentax PV-C850A (8 mm) tape thickness sensor circuit.*

MODE SWITCH

The mode or mechanism state switch applies signal to the system control IC microprocessor. At the end of the unloading operation, the loading is stopped with a signal applied to the microprocessor. Also, the mechanism state switch provides signals to the microprocessor to indicate state of the mechanism. These signals are used to determine if the mechanism and mechanical state function switches agree. The VTR is placed in stop mode if they do not agree. The mechanism state switch is used in loading and unloading of the cassette.

RCA CPR100 (VHS-C) Mechanism State (Mode Sense) Switch

Signals from the mechanism mode switch control the system microprocessor (IC901). The instrument is placed in stop mode at the end of the

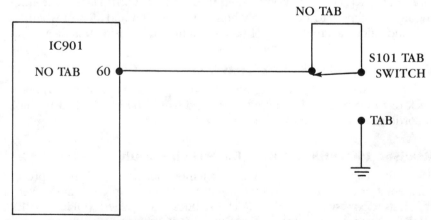

6-16   *Pentax safety tab sensor circuit.*

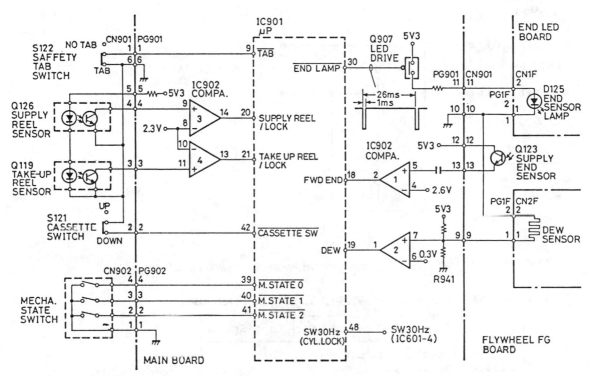

6-17 *Realistic 150 (VHS-C) safety tab switch in the main detection circuits.*
Radio Shack

unloading operation. The mechanism switch (S124) also applies input signals to IC901 to indicate the mechanical state of the VTR mechanism. These signals determine if both agree, and if not, the VTR is placed in stop mode (FIG. 6-18).

Realistic 150 (VHS-C) Mechanism State Switch Circuit

The system control (IC901) inputs mechanism mode data from the mechanism state switch to decide whether to select mode and mechanism mode are the same. If they do not become the same in 10 seconds, IC901 judges the mechanism to be locked (M. STATE 0 to M. STATE 3). Refer to FIG. 6-17 for mechanism state switch circuit.

Radio Shack 150 (VHS-C) Tape Detection Circuit

The system control (IC901) inputs the FLW.FG pulse at pin 49 and the CTL pulse at pin 50 from the servo circuit and counts the FLW.FG pulses within one period of the CTL pulse to detect the playback tape speed (SP or EP) according to the formula in TABLE 6-1. The tape speed detection circuit is shown in (FIG. 6-19).

When the play/pause mode continues for more than 5 minutes, the stop mode is entered to protect the tape with the 5-minute timer control. When

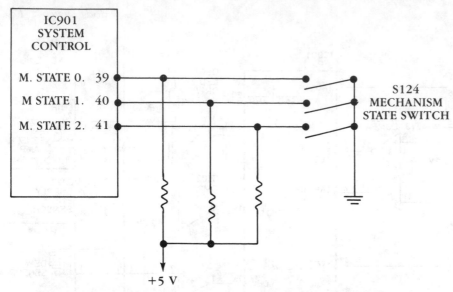

6-18 *RCA CPR100 (VHS-C) mechanism state (mode sense) switch circuits.*

Table 6-1. Radio Shack 150 (VHS-C) Tape Speed Detection

Number of Pulses Counted (N)	Tape Speed
N $\leq$ 7 (detected within 3 periods of CTL pulse)	EP
N $\geq$ 8 (detected within 3 periods of CTL pulse)	SP

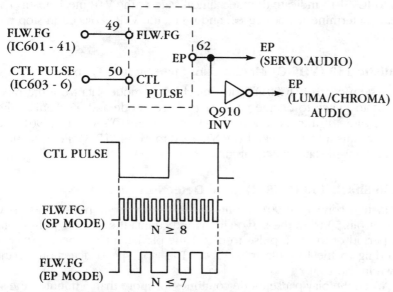

6-19 *Realistic 150 tape speed detection circuit.* Radio Shack

the record pause mode continues for more than 5 minutes, the REC LOCK mode is entered to protect the tape.

RCA CPR100 Tape Speed Detection Circuit

The capstan flywheel with the Hall-effect device produces the flywheel FG signal (FLW.FG). To detect tape speed, this signal is applied to pin 49 of the system control microprocessor IC901 (FIG. 6-20). By counting the number of FLW.FG pulses within three periods of the CTL pulse, the correct speed is detected. With tape speed set at SLP, the number of FLW FG pulses that occur within three periods of the control (CTL) pulse are equal to or less than seven. If the number is eight or greater, the speed is SP.

LOADING MOTOR DRIVE CIRCUITS

The loading and capstan motors are not considered to be in the servo circuits but are controlled by the system control microprocessor. In some camcorders, the capstan motor is driven with the cylinder motor circuits. The output terminals of the system control IC control the loading motor drive circuits, which drives the loading motor that ejects and loads the cassette and loads and unloads the tape. In the RCA CPR300 VHS camcorder, the system control microprocessor controls the loading motor drive with signals from pins 54 and 55 (pin 54 provides the loading signal and pin 55 the unloading signal) (FIG. 6-21). The main brake disengages at the start of the

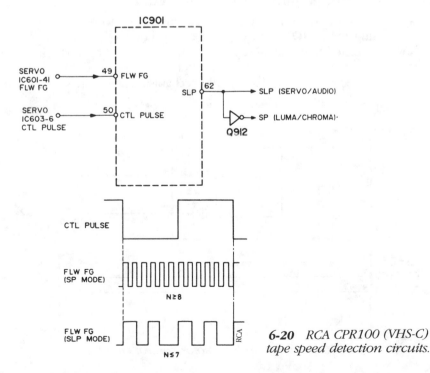

6-20 *RCA CPR100 (VHS-C) tape speed detection circuits.*

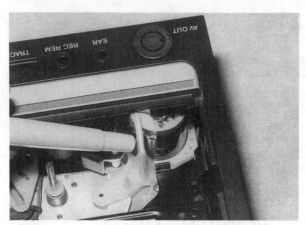

6-21   *The pen points to the loading motor in the VHS RCA CPR300 camcorder.*

loading to release both take-up and supply reels when loading takes place. The pressure roller is pressed against the capstan when loading is completed. During unloading, the pressure roller is released. The take-up brake is applied to prevent tape from spilling out of the take-up reel. The guide roller unloads as the supply reel disk rewinds the tape into the cassette.

Pentax PV-C850A (8 mm) Loading Motor Control Circuit

The system control (IC901) controls the loading motor to set the mechanism operating mode. IC901 drives the loading motor out of terminals 2 and 3 which are fed to the loading motor driver IC102 (FIG. 6-22). The motor continues to run until the mechanism enters the instructed mode. The mode of the mechanism detected by the mechanism state switch (S104) is

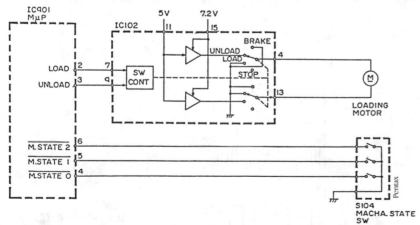

6-22   *Pentax PV-C850A (8 mm) loading motor control circuits.*

**Table 6-2. Loading Motor Drive Signals
(Pentax PV-C850A)**

Input		Output		Mode
Pin 4	Pin 6	Pin 7	Pin 3	
1	1	0	0	Brake
1	0	0	1	Unloading
0	1	1	0	Loading
0	0	-	-	Stop

Pentax

applied to pins 4, 5, and 6 of IC901. Table 6-2 shows the output signals of IC901 and IC102 in relation to the motor mode, while TABLE 6-3 shows the mechanism state switch outputs in relation to the mechanism mode.

RCA CPR100 (VHS-C) Loading Motor Drive Circuits

The system control microprocessor (IC901) controls the loading and unloading of the cassette. Loading signal from pin 22 of IC-901 controls the loading motor driver IC903 to load the cassette (FIG. 6-23). During loading,

**Table 6-3. Mechanism State Switch Outputs and Modes
(Pentax PV-C850A)**

Mechanism state switch	M. STATE			Mode
	2	1	0	
Eject	0	0	0	Eject
Unloading/stop	0	0	1	Unloading/stop
Loading/ unloading	1	0	1	Loading/ unloading
Fast forward/ rewind	1	0	0	Fast forward/ rewind
Loading stop	1	1	0	Unloading stop
Record/play	0	1	0	Record/play/play pause/forward search
Reverse	0	1	1	Reverse search/ record pause

Pentax

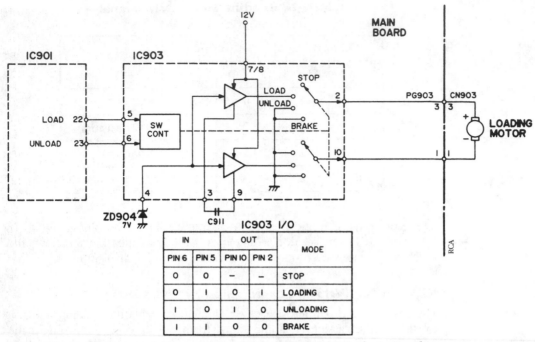

6-23 *The loading motor drive circuit of RCA CPR100 (VHS-C) camcorder.*

IN		OUT		MODE
PIN 6	PIN 5	PIN 10	PIN 2	
O	O	−	−	STOP
O	I	O	I	LOADING
I	O	I	O	UNLOADING
I	I	O	O	BRAKE

pin 22 is high and pin 23 is low. The unloading signal is sent from pin 23 to the driver IC903 to unload the cassette. During unloading, pin 23 is high and pin 22 is low.

CAPSTAN MOTOR DRIVE CIRCUITS

In many of the small VHS-C camcorders, the capstan motor is driven by the control microprocessor, while in other VHS and 8 mm camcorders the capstan motor is with the cylinder motor circuits. Within the RCA CPR 300 camcorder, the capstan motor is controlled by the servo IC601 while in the RCA CPR100 camcorder the system control microprocessor controls the capstan motor in record, fast forward, and rewind (FIG. 6-24). The capstan motor rotates the capstan flywheel to pull the tape from the cassette.

RCA CPR100 (VHS-C) Capstan Motor Circuits

The system control microprocessor (IC901) controls the direction of the capstan motor. Control signal from pin 36 provides the forward (FWD) rotation with pin 37 controlling the reverse capstan motor rotation (FIG. 6-25). The control signals are fed to pin 5 and 6 of the capstan motor driver IC604.

In playback mode, the speed of the capstan motor is controlled by the servo output pin 54 of IC601. While in record, fast forward, and rewind, the speed is controlled by the system control microprocessor IC901. The capstan switch (terminal 35) of IC901 determines which system controls the

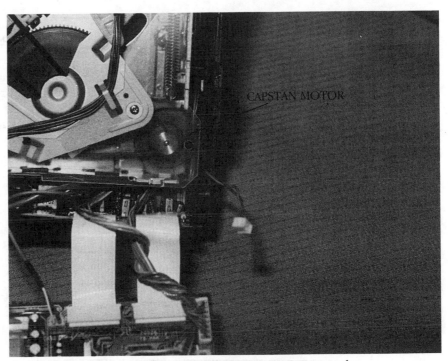

CAPSTAN MOTOR

6-24 *The capstan motor in the RCA CPR300 VHS camcorder.*

capstan motor. Since the capstan and cylinder motors are controlled by the servo signals, they will be discussed in the servo section. Additional motor information is in Chapter 7, Motor Circuits.

SERVO CIRCUITS

During recording, the servo circuits control the tape speed. The tape speed may be 1800 rpm with 8 mm and 2700 rpm in VHS-C camcorder servo circuits. During playback, it ensures the same accurate tape speed, aligning the video track with the scanning of the video heads. Speed and phase control of the capstan and cylinder or drum motor are found in the servo circuits. This tape speed control is to keep the speed of the video head track constant, while phase control is performed by the tracking control system.

Pentax PV-C850A (8 mm) Servo Circuits

While recording, the servo circuits control the tape speed accurately at 1.4345 cm/s to keep the video track ptich at 20.5 μm, it controls the rotary video head speed accurately at 1800 rpm to keep the video track length constant, and it adjusts the rotary video head position accurately with the vertical sync signal in the video signal being recorded to move the beginning of each video track 6H before the location of the vertical sync signal (FIG. 6-26).

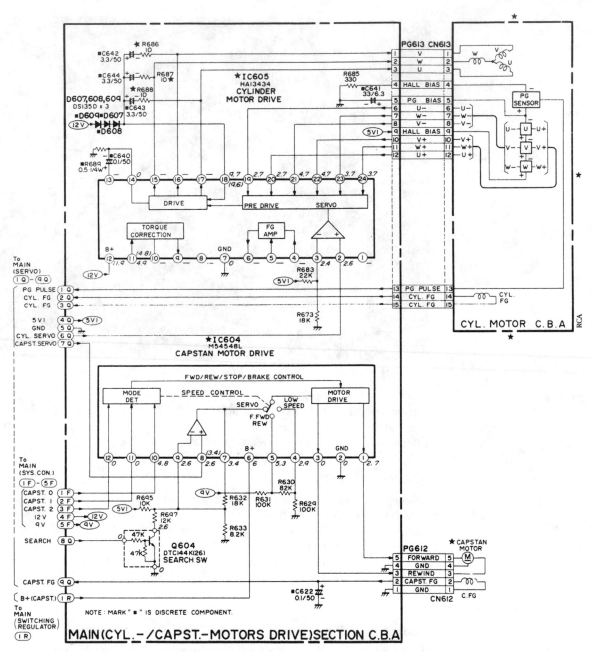

6-25   *Capstan motor drive circuits of the RCA CPR100 (VHS-C) VCR section.*

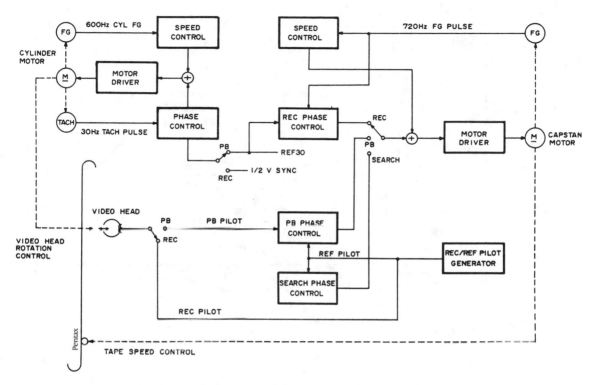

6-26 *Block diagram of the servo circuits in the Pentax PV-C850A camcorder.*

During playback, the servo circuits ensure the same accurate horizontal time axis and continuity as during recording by controlling the video head speed accurately at 1800 rpm and aligning the video track accurately with the scanning of the rotary video head.

Speed control and phase control are exercised respectively for the capstan motor that controls tape running and the cylinder motor that controls the rotary video head. Speed control is to keep the speed of the video head to the video track constant to minimize time axis variations. Phase control is performed by the tracking control (FIG. 6-27). The servo block diagram of Sony CCD-M8E/M8U VTR is in FIG. 6-28.

RCA CPR100 (VHS-C) Servo Circuits

The magnetic tape must run at a fixed speed of 3.34 cm/s during recording in the RCA VHS-C VCR section. The upper cylinder must rotate accurately around 2700 rpm (FIG. 6-29). During playback, the tape must maintain the same speed (2700 rpm) and trace the recorded video cassette. This is done by controlling the phase and speed of the capstan and cylinder motors.

Large fluctuations are controlled by the speed control circuits. Small fluctuations are controlled by the phase control. These speed fluctuations

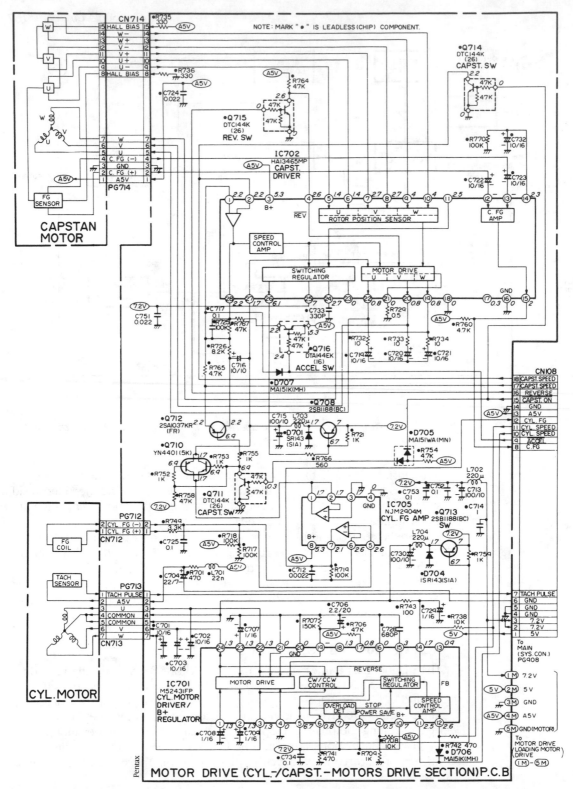

6-27 *The complete cylinder motor drive and capstan motor circuits in the Pentax PV-C850A (8 mm) camcorder.*

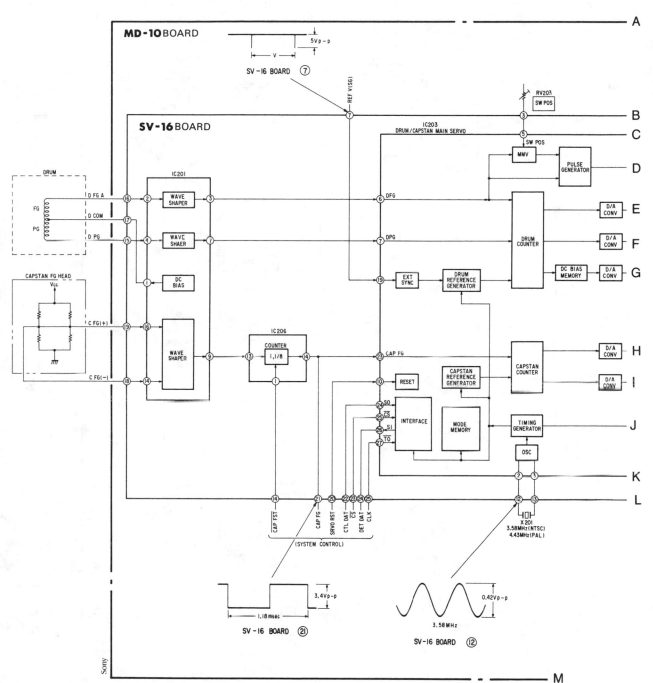

6-28 *Block diagram of the servo system in the Sony CCD-M8E/M8U camcorder.*

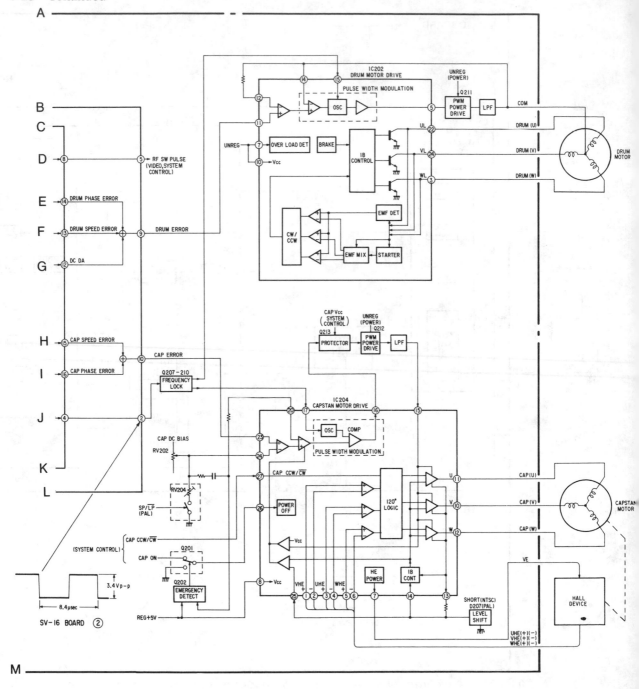

SV-16 BOARD ②

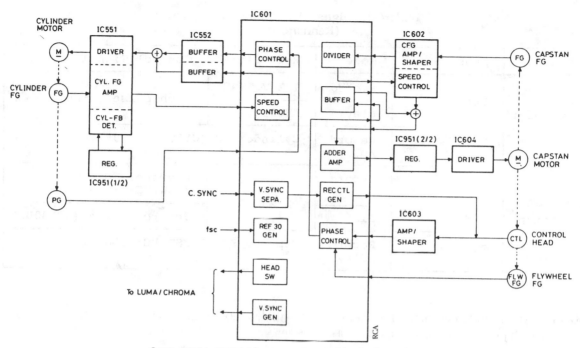

6-29 *RCA CPR100 servo circuit block diagram.*

must be controlled so the capstan and cylinder motors maintain a constant speed for correct recording and playback of the video cassette.

Realistic 150 (VHS-C) Servo Circuits

During recording, the servo system controls the VTR to obtain the VHS track format. The tape speed is controlled at 33.35 mm/s (SP) or 11.1 mm/s (EP) so that the video track pitch is 58 μm (SP) or 19 μm (EP).

The video heads rotate accurately at 2700 rpm so that the length of the video track is fixed at 97.4 mm. The rotating video heads are synchronized with the vertical sync signal of the incoming video signal so that the video track begins at 6.5H + alpha before the vertical sync signal. During play, continuity and exactly the same speed used in recording are maintained by controlling the speed of the video heads accurately at 2700 rpm and by keeping the phased fixed, thereby causing the video heads to trace the video tracks accurately. Actually, the speed and phase of the capstan motor that drives the tape and the cylinder motor that drives the video head are controlled (TABLE 6-4). Speed control is exercised over the relative speed of the video head and the video track. Phase control is done for correct tracking.

RCA CPR300 (VHS) Servo System

During recording, the tape runs at a fixed speed of 3.34 cm/s. The upper cylinder rotates at 2700 rpm speed. The same speed (2700) is maintained in

**Table 6-4.   Signal Used in Servo Control
(Realistic 150)**

Motor	Phase/Speed	Mode	Ref. Signal	Control Signal
Cylinder	Phase	Record	1/2 V.SYNC	Tach pulse (45Hz)
		Play	REF30Hz	
	Speed	Record /play	Cylinder FG (CYL.FG: 720Hz)	
Capstan	Phase	Record	REF30Hz	Flywheel FG (FLW.FG: 360Hz)
		Play		Control pulse (CTL30Hz)
	Speed	Record /Play	Capstan FG (CAPST.FG: 1704Hz)	

both playback and recording. The capstan and cylinder motors are controlled with phase and speed servo circuits (FIG. 6-30).

SERVO CONTROL SIGNALS

The servo control signals are quite common to all VCR or VTR systems. The ½ V sync reference signal is found in most camcorders. It is the reference signal for the cylinder phase control during recording. This is obtained by dividing the V SYNC extracted from the video signal.

The play reference signal (REF 30 Hz) is common to all VCR or VTR systems. It is the reference signal for cylinder phase control during play and for the capstan phase during recording. This is obtained by dividing the 3.58, MHz color subcarrier extracted in the chroma processing circuit down to 30 Hz.

The TACH (PG) pulse is the signal used for cylinder phase control. A magnetic sensor fitted to the lower cylinder generates the signal when it detects the passage of a magnet fitted ahead of the CH1 rotary video head in the upper cylinder TABLE 6-5.

The TACH (PG) pulse is used also for cylinder phase control in the VHS and VHS-C servo circuits. The magnetic sensor that generates this signal detects the passing of the N-pole of a magnet fitted approximately 6.3 degrees before the CH3 video head on the upper cylinder. When the video head is rotating at 2700 rpm, the frequency of the TACH (PG) PULSE is 45 Hz with its phase advanced by approximately 186.3 degrees from the CH1 video head position in the VHS-C camcorder. The cylinder phase control loop times the division of the cylinder FG PULSE using this TACH (PG) pulse to convert it to tach (PG) pulses with three frequencies (15 Hz, 30 Hz, and 60 Hz).

6-30 *Location of the cylinder motor in the RCA CPR300 camcorder.*

Table 6-5. Servo Control Signals (Pentax PV-C850A)

Motor	Control	Mode	Reference Signal	Feedback Signal
Cylinder	Phase	Record	½ V.SYNC	Tach Pulse
	Speed	Play	REF30Hz	
	Speed	Both	Cylinder FG (CYL FG 600Hz)	
Capstan	Phase	Record	REF30Hz	Capstan FG (CFG -720Hz)
	Speed	Both	Capstan FG (CFG -720 Hz)	

Pentax PV-C850A (8 mm) Cylinder FG Pulse

The cylinder FG pulse is the signal indicating the rotation speed of the DD cylinder motor. A magnetic sensor fitted on the chassis generates the signal when it detects the passage of a magnet fitted to the rotor of the DD cylinder motor. Its frequency must be 600 Hz when the rotation is in the rated 1800 rpm. The cylinder head in the 8 mm VTR rotates at 1800 rpm.

RCA CPR300 (VHS) Cylinder FG (CYL FG) Pulse

The signal is used to detect the speed of the cylinder motor. Here the FG pulse is a 360 Hz pulse generated by a stator coil and a 16-pole magnet attached to the rotor on the cylinder motor. This FG pulse controls the speed of the cylinder motor during playback and record operations.

Realistic 150 (VHS-C) Cylinder FG Pulse (CYL FG)

This signal is used to detect the speed of the DD cylinder motor. It is generated from a printed pattern magnetic sensor included on the motor body that detects the passing of a rotary magnet with 32 poles fitted to the rotor of the DD cylinder motor. When the video head speed of 2700 rpm is maintained, the frequency of the cylinder FG pulse is 720 Hz.

Pentax PV-C850A (8 mm) Capstan FG Pulses

The capstan FG pulse signal indicates the rotation speed of the DD capstan motor. The feedback signal for capstan phase control during recording is obtained by dividing this signal by 24. A magnetic sensor fitted to the chassis generates the signal when it detects the passage of a magnet fitted to the rotor of the DD capstan motor. The frequency of the cylinder FG pulse is 720 Hz.

RCA CPR100 (VHS-C) Capstan FG (CFG) Pulse

A 28-pole magnet attached to the rotor on the capstan motor generates the FG pulse. To control the phase of the capstan motor, the REF 30 Hz signal and the CFG pulse are compared. Also, the CFG pulse controls the speed of the capstan motor during record and playback operations (FIG. 6-31). In the RCA CPR300 (VHS) servo circuits, the capstan FG (CFG) pulse has a 48-pole magnet attached to the rotor of the capstan motor to generate this CFG pulse.

Realistic 150 (VHS-C) Flywheel FG Pulse (FLW.FG)

During record mode, the FG pulse is used for capstan phase control. This is generated with a printed pattern magnetic sensor installed on the chassis that detects the passing of a rotary magnet having 204 poles fitted to the capstan flywheel. When the video head speed is maintained, the frequency of the generated pulse signal is 360 Hz in the SP mode and 120 Hz in the EP mode. The frequency is divided to 30 Hz to obtain the flywheel FG pulse.

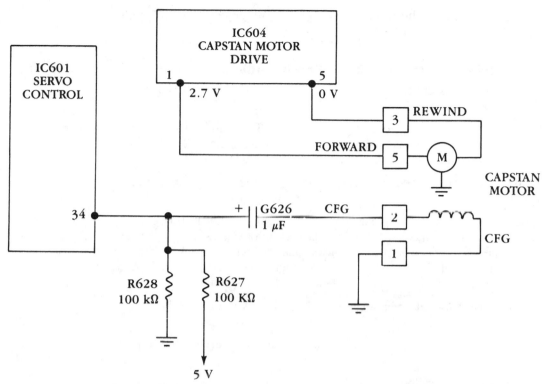

6-31 *RCA CPR100 (VHS-C) servo capstan FG (CFG) pulse circuit.*

RCA CPR100 (VHS-C) Flywheel FG Pulse

During playback, the flywheel FG pulse is used for capstan phase control. A printed magnetic sensor pattern on the chassis is generated with the rotary magnet having 204 poles. The frequency signal in the SP mode is 360 Hz and 120 Hz in the SLP mode. To produce the flywheel FG pulse, the signal is divided down to 30 Hz.

Radio Shack 150 (VHS-C) Control (CTL) Pulse

The signal is used for capstan phase control during play mode. The cylinder phase control reference signal ($\frac{1}{2}$ V CYNC) is shaped into a square wave and recorded on the control track of the tape during recording. The control (CTL) pulse is this signal reproduced during playback. When the rated video head speed is maintained, the frequency of the signal is 30 Hz.

RCA CPR100 (VHS-C) Control (CTL) Pulse

During record, the CTL pulses are derived from the incoming vertical sync. The A/C head applies the CTL pulses to the tape during record mode. In playback operation, the REF 20 Hz and phases of the CTL pulse signals are compared to control the capstan motor phase. The same type of CTL pulse is used in the RCA CPR300 VHS servo system.

Pentax PV-C850A (8 mm) Servo Circuit Configuration

The servo circuits consist of six different IC circuits: IC601, IC602, IC603, IC701, IC702, and IC705 (FIG. 6-32).

IC601   Controls the speed and phase of the cylinder and capstan motors and generates three control signals: head-switching signal (SW30), record inhibit signal (REC INHIBIT), and artificial V sync signal (V DRV).

IC602   Generates speed correction voltage for the cylinder and capstan motors.

IC603   Generates pilot signals during recording. Controls phase (ATF) during playback. Limits bandwidth of playback pilot signals. Controls phase during search. Switches phase control outputs. Smooths PWM cylinder speed error signal. Smooths PWM cylinder phase error signal. Adds smoothed error voltages. Opens and closes cylinder servo loop.

IC701   Drives the DD cylinder motor. Controls power for the cylinder motor.

IC702   Drives the DD capstan motor. Controls power for the capstan driver.

IC705   Amplifies cylinder FG pulse.

Realistic 150 (VHS-C) Configuration of the Servo Circuits

The servo circuit includes seven ICs: IC601, IC602, IC603, IC604, IC551, IC605, and IC951 (FIG. 6-33).

IC601   Controls the speed/phase of the cylinder motor and phase of the capstan motor, generates head-switching signal and aritificial V Sync pulse, and switches capstan motor speed.

IC602   Amplifies and shapes the capstan FG pulse and detects capstan error speed.

IC603   Amplifies and shapes playback control signals.

IC604   Drives the DC capstan motor.

IC551   Drives the DD cylinder motor, controls the power supply, and amplifies the cylinder FG pulse.

IC605   Buffers the control voltage of speed/phase of the cylinder motor.

IC951   Supplies the cylinder and capstan motors with power.

   The speed and phase of the cylinder motor and the phase of the capstan motor are controlled by digital servo systems. The speed of the capstan motor is controlled by an analog servo system. Actually, a cylinder speed self-control system is employed. This regulates the speed automatically

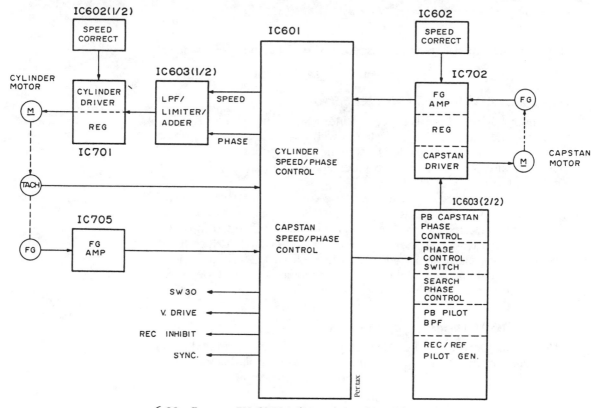

6-32 *Pentax PV-C850A (8 mm) configuration of the servo circuits.*

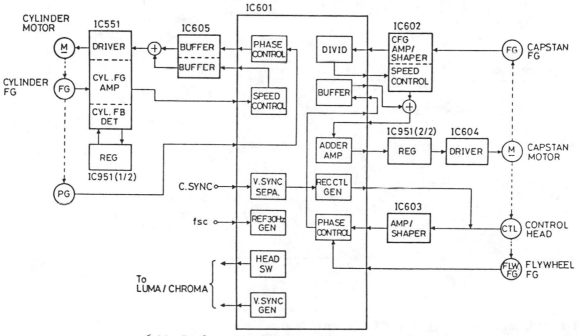

6-33 *Realistic 150 (VHS-C) configuration of the servo circuit.* Radio Shack

when the cylinder motor starts or its speed is out of the speed error detection range.

Pentax PV-C850A (8 mm) Cylinder Servo

The main servo IC601 controls the speed and phase of the cylinder by comparing the speed and phase of the cylinder with reference speed and phase and detecting errors. The signal fed back in the control loops are the 600 Hz cylinder FG pulse of the speed control loop and the 30 Hz tack pulse of the phase control loop.

The reference signals used in the phase control loop are ½ V SYNC during record and REF30 during play (FIG. 6-34). Error signals from the control loops are converted by PWM and then smoothed and added in IC603. The added cylinder servo control signal enters the cylinder driver IC701 and controls the voltage supplied to the three-phase DD cylinder motor drive coil. The system control microprocessor monitors the cylinder servo system for failure and opens and closes the servo loop.

Pentax PV-C850A (8 mm) Capstan Servo

IC601 performs speed control of the capstan servo. Phase control is done in two different ICs (IC601 during record and IC603 during playback).

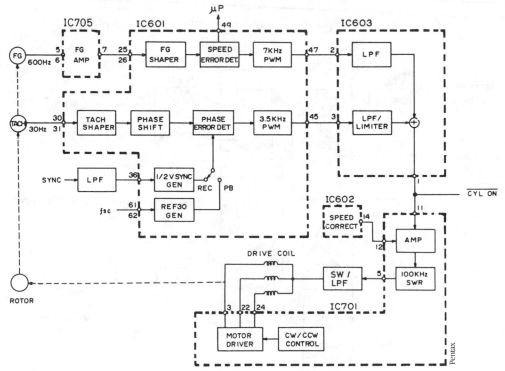

6-34 *Pentax PV-C850A (8 mm) cylinder servo circuits.*

Signals fed back in the control loops are a 720 Hz capstan FG pulse in the speed control loop, capstan FG pulses divided by 24 in the phase control loop during recording. Also, the pilot signals recorded during recording are played back from the tape in the phase control loop during play and search (FIG. 6-35).

Speed and phase error signals are smoothed and added and the sum signal is supplied to the capstan driver IC702. It controls the drive current and power voltages of the three-phase motor drive coil to keep the motor speed at the rated value.

Failure of the capstan servo system is detected by the system control IC as it monitors the rotation of the reel disk. The capstan servo loop is opened and closed by the system control IC as it controls the power voltage of the motor driver. During fast forward/rewind, the tape is released from the capstan, and with the speed set at nine times the normal speed, the capstan driver is driven by the speed error voltage.

CONCLUSION

There are many trouble detection circuits in the camcorder. The larger and expensive camcorders have more trouble detection circuits. These detection circuits are placed in the camcorder to protect components in the unit and to warn the operator of what is happening and why the camcorder might

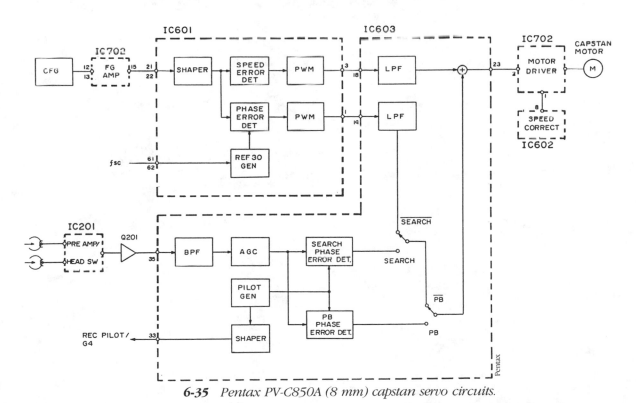

6-35 *Pentax PV-C850A (8 mm) capstan servo circuits.*

not not operate. Often, the control system microprocessor controls the detection circuits.

In the servo circuits, the capstan motor drives the tape operation and the cylinder motor drives the video heads. The capstan motor may be belt-driven and the cylinder motor directly driven (DD) with the motor shaft. Speed controls the relative speed of the video heads and trade system phase control is done for correct tracking. Check Chapter 7 for speed, phase, and drive motor circuits.

Chapter **7**

Motor Circuits

*T*he large camcorder may contain several small motors, including the drum or cylinder, capstan, loading, auto focus, iris, and zoom motors. The small or inexpensive camcorder may operate with only a loading, capstan, and drum motor. These small motors operate from a dc source. Most motors are controlled from the main, system control, servo, and motor drive IC (FIG. 7-1).

These small motors may be checked with voltage or resistance measurements. A continuity check with the low range of the ohmmeter may determine if the motor winding is open. Measuring the voltage at the motor terminals determines if the motor or drive IC is defective. Applying a small external dc voltage to the motor terminals may determine if the motor is intermittent or slow in rotation.

In this chapter, a brief description is given on how the motors are controlled and operated. Several brief descriptions are given of different motors' operation in the different camcorders. Removing and replacing the defective motor is given in each motor section. Servicing and troubleshooting the various motors is given in Chapter 13.

LOADING MOTORS

The loading motor may eject, load, and unload the video cassette, releasing brakes, engaging the fast forward/rewind idler gear and playback gear. Simply press the eject button on most camcorders and the loading door opens to receive the cassette. After loading the cassette, the door may be manually or electrically closed. The motor may be located off to the side of the main chassis. Usually, the loading motor is controlled from the system control IC and a motor drive IC (FIG. 7-2). The load or mode motor may be one of the same.

RCA CPR 100 Loading Motor Drive The loading and capstan motors are controlled by microprocessor IC901 (FIG. 7-3). Here the load signal is

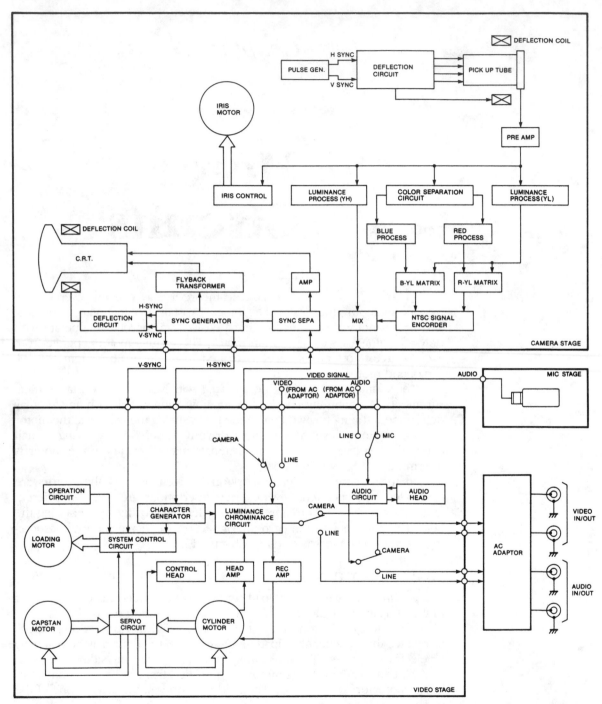

7-1 *Block diagram of the various motor circuits tied to the system and servo control components.*

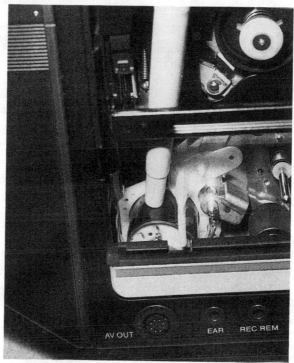

7-2 *The loading motor in the RCA CPR300 camcorder.*

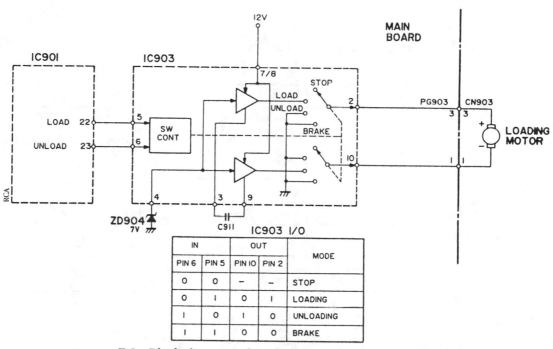

IN		OUT		
PIN 6	PIN 5	PIN 10	PIN 2	MODE
O	O	−	−	STOP
O	1	O	1	LOADING
1	O	1	O	UNLOADING
1	1	O	O	BRAKE

7-3 *Block diagram of RCA's CPR100 loading motor drive circuits.*

applied at pin 22 and the unloading signal at pin 23 of IC901. During loading, pin 22 is high and pin 23 is low, while in the unloading process, pin 23 is high and pin 22 is low.

The controlled signal is applied to the motor drive IC903. In stop mode, zero voltage is at pins 5 and 6. In loading, a signal is at pin 5 and voltage is applied at pin 2 of IC903. When unloading, a signal is at pin 6 and applied voltage is at pin 10 to the loading motor. Zero voltage is at both pins 2 and 10 in the brake mode.

Realistic 150 Loading Motor Drive   The outputs from the system control microprocessor (IC901) pin 22 (load) and pin 23 (unload) control the motor driver IC903. The motor drive (IC903) drives the loading motor, which ejects and loads the cassette and loads and unloads the tape.

The load signal (pin 22) and unload signal (pin 23) from system UP (IC901) controls the loading motor as shown in TABLE 7-1. ZD904 determines the supply voltage (approximately 9 V) applied to the loading motor.

The mechanism state switch detects how much the mechanism moves during loading and unloading. The mechanism state switch changes according to the condition of the mechanism. The detected data is fed back to the system control (IC901) at pins 39 to 41 (FIG. 7-4). The loading and unloading motor drive signals continue to be output until the assigned mode and mechanism state switch detection mode are the same. If the two modes do not become the same in 10 seconds, a mechanism lock is determined. Once mechanism lock is determined during loading, the unloading mode is entered. During unloading, the power-off mode is entered.

Table 7-1. Loading Motor Control (Realistic 150)

Mode	Present Mode	Button Operation	Loading Motor
VTR	Stop	PLAY	Loading
	Stop	F.FWD/REW	Unloading
	Rewind	F.FWD	Loading ➔ Unloading
	Fast forward	STOP	Loading
	Play	PAUSE	Stop
	Still/Forward search	PLAY	Stop
	Forward search	REW	Unloading
	Stop	VTR ➔ CAMERA	Loading
Camera	Record pause	PAUSE	Stop
	Record pause	REW	Unloading
	Record pause	Over 5 minutes/Power	Unloading
	Record pause	EJECT/CAMERA ➔ VTR	Unloading

Radio Shack

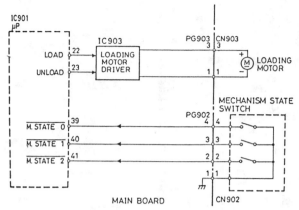

INPUT / SWITCH POSITION	M.STATE 2 (PIN 41)	M.STATE 1 (PIN 40)	M.STATE 0 (PIN 39)	MODE
EJECT	0	1	1	EJECT
FF/REW	0	0	1	F. FWD/REW
STOP	1	0	1	STOP
	1	1	1	
LOADING MID POINT	1	1	0	LOADING
REC LOCK	1	1	0	REC LOCK
REC/PLAY	1	0	0	REC/PLAY/REC PAUSE/FF SEARCH
	0	0	0	
REW SEARCH	0	1	0	REW SEARCH

Radio Shack

7-4 *Realistic 150 loading motor circuits with the mechanical state switch assembly.*

Canon VM-E2 Loading Brake Module Most camcorders use an IC motor drive circuit, except the loading motor brake module in a Canon VM-E2 is made up of transistors. Q1 and Q3 are used for unloading while Q4 and Q2 are the loading transistors (FIG. 7-5). These four loading motor transistors are mounted on a separate brake module board.

Loading Motor Removal

Often the loading motor can be removed very easily with only one or two screws and without removing a lot of other nearby components. The loading motor hookup cable may be unplugged in some models or terminal leads unsoldered for removal. Always replace the loading motor with the exact manufacturer's part number.

Minolta C3300 Loading Motor Removal Disconnect the connector CN15, the plug to the motor cable. Remove the two screws holding the motor to the base chassis (FIG. 7-6). Now remove the loading motor from the chassis. Replace in reverse procedure.

Mitsubishi HS-C20U After the main chassis is free, locate the load-control motor on the chassis (FIG. 7-7). Unplug the motor cable. Remove two mounting screws. Lift the gear-driven motor assembly out of the chassis. Replace the new motor with reverse procedures.

SONY CCD-M8E/M8U The loading motor in this Sony camcorder is located under a cover assembly. First, remove the MD-10 board that covers the bottom section of the chassis. Remove screws (1), (2), and (3), and remove the LM motor assembly (4), (5), and (8) (FIG. 7-8). Disassemble the motor under the cover assembly (4) and dc motor (8), which is attached by magnetic force. Remove loading gear A (5) from shaft (7). Melt the two soldered points as shown in the upper right corner of the illustration. Then remove flexible board FR-14 (6).

LOADING MOTOR
BRAKE MODULE

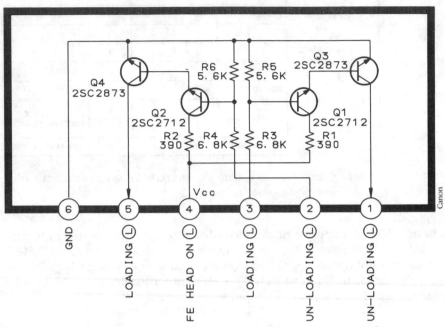

7-5 *Canon VM-E2 loading motor brake module.*

To install the new motor, reverse the procedure. Resolder the two point connections as in the insert and install the FP-14 flexible board (6). Apply ⅓ drop of oil into shaft (7) and install loading gear A (5). Apply Sony grease about the size of one rice grain to the worm gear (9). Install LM under cover assembly (4) and dc motor (8). Install LM under cover assembly (4) to pin (10) of the mechanical chassis by matching the notch of it. Finally, install screws (1), (2), and (3) rather loosely and then tighten in successive order of (1), (2), and (3).

CAPSTAN MOTORS

The capstan motor may be belt or gear driven to various mechanical assemblies, providing tape movement in play, record, rewind, fast forward, and search modes. Since these different modes operate at different speeds, the dc voltage must be controlled by a servo, capstan speed, and phase control system. The system or servo IC may control the capstan motor through a capstan motor drive IC (FIG. 7-9). Often, the capstan and cylinder motors are fed from the same signal source.

Radio Shack 150 The system UP (IC901) controls the rotating direction of the capstan motor by CAPSTAN FWD (pin 36) and Capstan REV (pin 37) signals supplied to pin 5 and 6 of capstan motor driver (IC604). The rotation speed of the capstan motor is controlled in two different ways (FIG. 7-10).

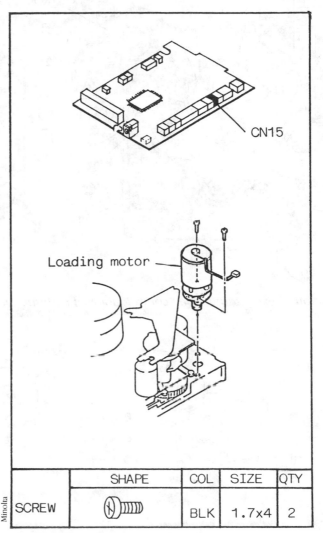

	SHAPE	COL	SIZE	QTY
SCREW		BLK	1.7x4	2

7-6 *Removal of Minolta C3300 loading motor assembly.*

During playback (forward and reverse) mode, it is controlled by the servo control output (IC601, pin 54). In other modes, it is controlled by the system UP's CAPSTAN 0 to CAPSTAN 2 (pins 32 to 34) output. The CAPSTAN SW (IC901, pin 35) selects one of these two. In the low (Lo) output period, switching transistor (Q608, a capstan switch) is off, so the servo control output is fed to the SWR (Capstan servo signal). According to the level of this signal, the SWR outputs B + capstan and supplies it to the capstan motor driver (IC604), pin 8. Then the capstan motor rotating speed is controlled by IC604 according to this B + capstan voltage level.

In the high (Hi) output periods of Capstan SW, Q608 turns on and obstructs the servo control output. Instead of this signal, a three-digit control signal from the system UP (IC901) determines the capstan servo signal.

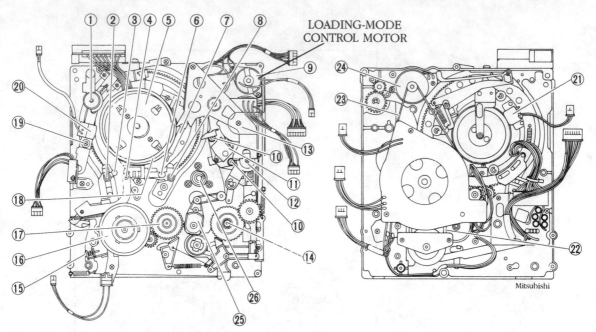

7-7 *Location of the loading mode control motor of a Mitsubishi HS-C20U camcorder chassis.*

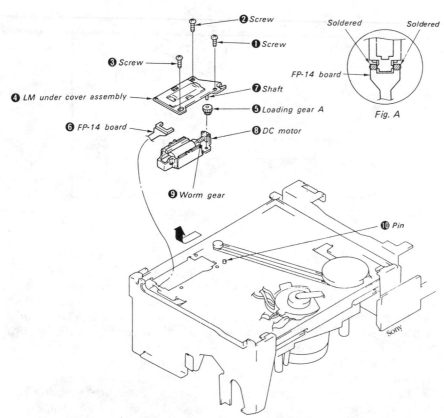

7-8 *Removing the loading motor in a Sony CCD-M8E/M8U camcorder.*

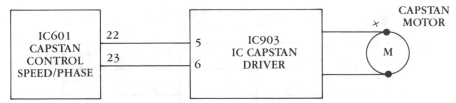

7-9 *Block diagram of the capstan motor with a control IC.*

The truth table of Capstan 0 to Capstan 2 and digital-to-analog-converted capstan REF signal is shown in TABLE 7-2. Simply measuring the capstan reference voltage at pin 8 of IC602 in the different modes indicates the correct signal voltage from the system control IC901.

Especially, a fine speed control during the F. FWD and REW modes is newly provided. Looking at TABLE 7-2, with F.FWD at the tape start and REW at tape end, the capstan REF voltage is at a maximum (4.6 V). But after that, the capstan REF voltage is gradually reduced in 7 steps from 4.3 V to 2 V. Finally, with F.FWD at the tape end and REW at the tape start, the capstan REF voltage is a minimum of 2 volts to reduce the shock at F. FWD end and REW end. This control is provided by counting the reel disc rotating rate that indicates the remaining tape.

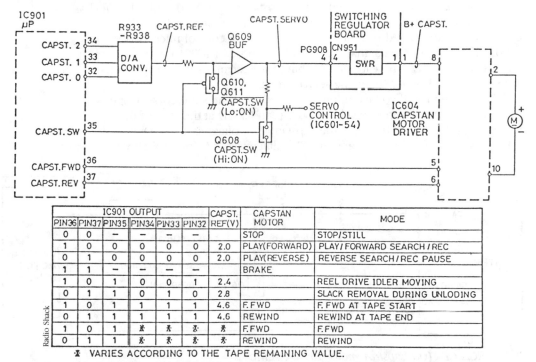

IC901 OUTPUT						CAPST.	CAPSTAN	MODE
PIN36	PIN37	PIN35	PIN34	PIN33	PIN32	REF(V)	MOTOR	
0	0	–	–	–	–		STOP	STOP/STILL
1	0	0	0	0	0	2.0	PLAY(FORWARD)	PLAY/FORWARD SEARCH/REC
0	1	0	0	0	0	2.0	PLAY(REVERSE)	REVERSE SEARCH/REC PAUSE
1	1	–	–	–	–		BRAKE	
1	0	1	0	0	1	2.4		REEL DRIVE IDLER MOVING
0	1	1	1	1	0	2.8		SLACK REMOVAL DURING UNLOADING
1	0	1	1	1	1	4.6	F.FWD	F. FWD AT TAPE START
0	1	1	1	1	1	4.6	REWIND	REWIND AT TAPE END
1	0	1	𝕏	𝕏	𝕏	𝕏	F.FWD	F.FWD
0	1	1	𝕏	𝕏	𝕏	𝕏	REWIND	REWIND

𝕏 VARIES ACCORDING TO THE TAPE REMAINING VALUE.

7-10 *The capstan motor drive circuit of a Realistic 150 camcorder.*

Table 7-2. Capstan Reference
(Realistic 150)

PIN 34	PIN 33	PIN 32	CAPST.REF (V)
0	0	0	2.0
0	0	1	2.4
0	1	0	2.8
0	1	1	3.1
1	0	0	3.5
1	0	1	3.8
1	1	0	4.3
1	1	1	4.6

Radio Shack

RCA CPR100 Capstan Motor Drive Circuit   IC901 controls the direction
of rotation of the capstan motor with a capstan forward signal from pin 36
and a capstan reverse signal at pin 37 (FIG. 7-11). The capstan FWD signal is
fed to pin 5 and capstan REV signal to pin 6 of the capstan motor drive IC
(IC604).

In playback mode, the speed of the capstan motor is controlled by the
servo output from IC601, pin 54. In the record, fast forward, rewind and
other modes, the speed is controlled by the system control microprocessor
IC901. The capstan feed signal is at pins 0, 1, and 2 of IC901 or pins 32, 33,
and 34 respectively. The capstan SW (pin 35) determines if the capstan motor is controlled by IC901 or the servo circuit.

The capstan REF voltage at pin 8 of IC604 indicates the correct operating voltage in the different modes (TABLE 7-3). In F.FWD at the start of the tape
and REW at the end of the tape, the capstan REV voltage is 4.6 V. During the
other operating modes, the capstan REF voltage varies from 2 to 2.8 volts.

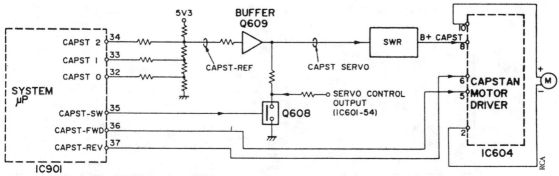

7-11   *RCA CPR100 capstan motor drive circuit.*

Table 7-3. Capstan Motor Drive voltage chart.
(RCA CPR100)

PIN 36	PIN 37	PIN 35	PIN 34	PIN 33	PIN 32	CAPST-REF (V)	CAPSTAN MOTOR	MODE
O	O	—	—	—	—		STOP	STOP/STILL
I	O	O	O	O	O	2.0	PLAY (FORWARD)	PLAY/FORWARD SEARCH/REC
O	I	O	O	O	O	2.0	PLAY (REVERSE)	REVERSE SEARCH/REC PAUSE
I	I	—	—	—	—		BRAKE	
I	O	I	O	O	I	2.4		REEL DRIVE IDLER MOVING
O	I	I	O	I	O	2.8		SLACK REMOVAL DURING UNLOADING
I	O	I	I	I	I	4.6	F. FWD	F. FWD AT TAPE START
O	I	I	I	I	I	4.6	REWIND	REWIND AT TAPE END
I	O	I	X	X	X	X	F. FWD	F. FWD
O	I	I	X	X	X	X	REWIND	REWIND

Column group header: IC901 OUTPUT (PIN 36, PIN 37, PIN 35, PIN 34, PIN 33, PIN 32)

X VARIES ACCORDING TO THE TAPE REMAINING VALUE.

Zenith VM6150 Capstan Servo System In this camcorder, capstan recording servo circuits are the recording speed control, recording phase control, and capstan motor control. Within the recording speed control, the capstan frequency generator output is 2113 Hz (2.113 kHz) in the SP mode and 704 Hz in the EP mode. The FG signal goes via main control board CN401, pins 3 and 4, to IC407, pins 2 and 13 (FIG. 7-12).

The amplified signal appears at TP402 and goes to pins 10 and 11 of the comparator (IC407). This shaped waveform applies to pin 21 of IC401.

The capstan FG is divided to 1,408 Hz (SP) and is supplied to the capstan speed detector where it is converted into a PWM pulse corresponding to the frequency. The LPF converts the pulse from pin 34 to an error voltage.

This error voltage is sent through the voltage follower (IC404) circuit to the capstan gain control circuit of IC401. This connects the capstan motor rotating speed voltage according to the mode. The IC404 mixing amplifier combines the voltage with the phase system error voltage. TRAP-2 removes the 704 Hz component. The resulting voltage is supplied to the capstan motor control circuit. Right here, the mechacon IC301 pin 47 capstan control command circuit selects between servo and mechacon control of the motor.

The reference voltage selected by the mechacon is supplied to the capstan power switching regulator of the servo circuit. The switching regulator output from pin 9 goes via MDA board CN401 (pin 8) to the emitters of Q601, Q602, and Q603 (FIG. 7-13). The collector of these three transistors are connected to the three motor coils.

Hall elements respond to the magnets embedded in the rotor to produce the coil switching pulse. The Hall amp and three-phase logic circuit of IC601 sequentially selects the capstan motor rotation. The MDA rotates the capstan motor in order to transport the tape at a stable speed. Rotational frequency is regulated by the capstan servo control circuit.

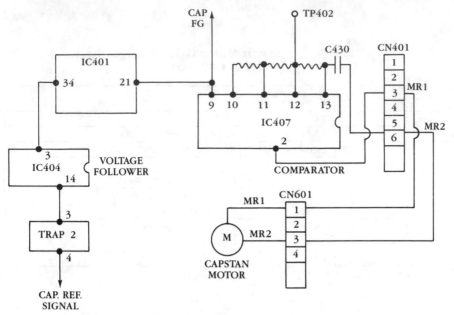

7-12 *Zenith VM6150 capstan servo signal path of CN401, IC407, IC401, and IC404.*

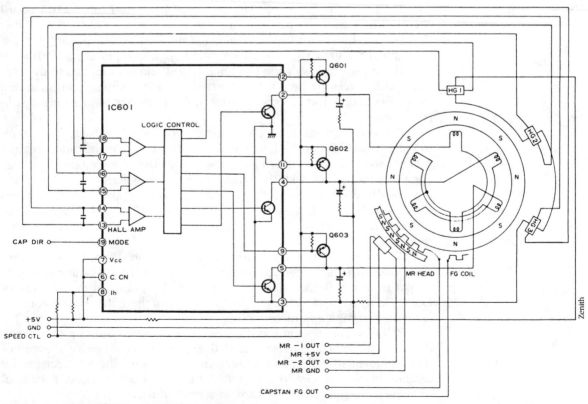

7-13 *Zenith VM6150 capstan MDA drive circuit.*

The recording phase control reference signal generator signal is derived from a 3.58 MHz crystal oscillator connected to pins 42 and 43 of IC401. This is counted down to 30 Hz and sent to the capstan phase comparator.

The comparison signal generator of the capstan FG signal (SP-2, 113 Hz) is supplied to pin 21 of IC402, where it is counted down to 30 Hz and sent to the capstan phase comparator. The comparator uses an FSC/8 clock pulse to count the phase difference between the reference and comparison signals. The result is converted into a PWM pulse and appears at pin 35. After integration by the low power filter (LPF), the signal is supplied to the IC404 mixing amplifier.

The capstan motor speed control error voltage increases with faster capstan motor rotation and decreases with slower rotation. In the phase control system, the error voltage decreases with advanced phase and increases with a delayed pulse. The speed error voltage is applied to the minus (−) side of an op-amp, and the phase error voltage goes to the plus (+) side. As the voltage at the minus side decreases, the inverted output increases, thus increasing the current in the capstan motor. At the plus (+) side, reduced input results in a reduced output, thereby delaying the capstan motor phase.

Capstan Motor Removal

Most capstan motors are easy to remove and replace. Remove the capstan belt from the motor pulley. Then remove screws holding the motor in place and pull the motor from the chassis. You may find a few motors are more difficult to remove, as explained subsequently.

Minolta C3300   Remove the main pc board (FIG. 7-14). Remove the capstan belt from the capstan motor. Remove the two screws holding the capstan motor. Pull the capstan motor from the chassis. Reverse the procedure when replacing a new motor.

Olympus VX-801U   Lift point A and hold it, then draw point B slightly for manual eject (FIG. 7-15). Remove two screws at the left side and two screws at the right side of the cassette compartment. Now remove the cassette compartment. Remove two screws holding the capstan motor. Reverse the same procedure when installing a new capstan motor.

RCA CPR 100   Disconnect connector CN603 from the main circuit board (FIG. 7-16). Remove the belt from the capstan motor. Now remove two screws holding the capstan motor. The motor will drop out of the bottom side.

DRUM MOTORS

Usually, the cylinder or drum motor is controlled by the servo circuits like the capstan motor. The cylinder or drum is located at the top of the motor assembly. The drum or cylinder may consist of an upper and lower drum assembly. Operation of the cylinder or drum motor is quite complex and contains the cylinder or drum speed control, recording phase control, and drum motor.

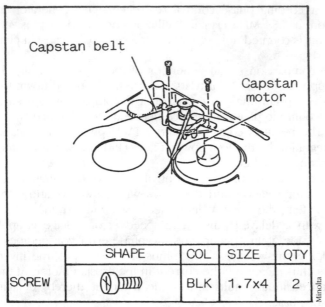

	SHAPE	COL	SIZE	QTY
SCREW		BLK	1.7x4	2

7-14   *Capstan motor removal from a Minolta C3300 camcorder.*

RCA CPR100 Cylinder Motor Servo Circuits   Both the cylinder and capstan motors are controlled by the servo circuits. IC601 controls the phase and speed of the cylinder motor (FIG. 7-17). The two control signals from pins 61 and 64 (IC601) are added in the buffer IC552 and then applied to the motor driver IC551.

By comparing the 720 Hz cylinder FG pulse and the 45 Hz PG pulse to the reference signals (½ V sync) during record and REF (30 Hz) during

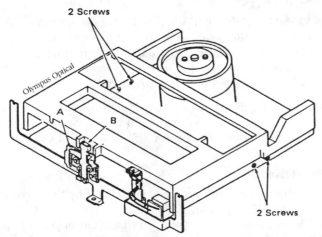

7-15   *How to remove the capstan motor from the Olympus VX-801U camcorder.*

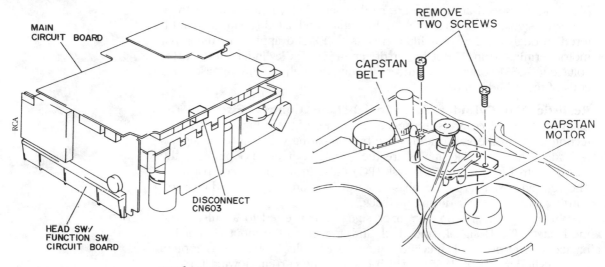

7-16 *Removing the capstan motor from the RCA CPR100 camcorder.*

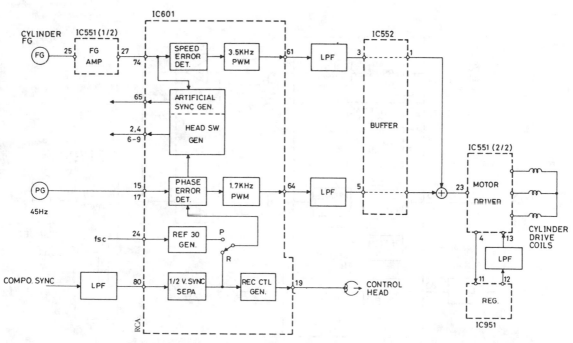

7-17 *RCA's CPR100 cylinder speed/phase control circuits.*

playback, the speed and phase are easily controlled. In each control loop, the error signal is converted to a pulse-width modulated (PWM) signal, filtered through the low-pass filter circuits (LPF), and applied to the input motor terminal (pin 23) of motor driver IC551. The cylinder motor drive voltage to IC551 controls the current flowing through the three-phase drive coils of the cylinder motor.

Realistic 150 Cylinder Servo-Speed-Phase Control Circuits The main servo IC601 controls the speed and phase of the cylinder motor, detecting error in the speed and phase by comparing with reference signals (FIG. 7-18). The feedback signals are the 720 Hz cylinder FG pulse in the speed control loop and 45 Hz tack (PG) pulse in the phase control loop. The reference signals in the phase control loop are ½ V. sync during recording and REF 30 Hz during playback.

In each control loop, the error signal is converted to a pulse-width modulated (PWM) signal, smoothed, and applied to the input after it has passed a buffer IC605. The cylinder motor drive voltage obtained is applied to the cylinder driver (IC551), which controls the current flowing through the three-phase DD cylinder motor drive coils. The system control (IC601) watches for any failure in the cylinder servo system and works to open or close the servo loop.

The cylinder speed control circuit consists of IC551 which amplifies the cylinder FG pulse and drives the cylinder motor (FIG. 7-19). IC601 shapes the cylinder FG pulse, detects speed errors, opens and closes the cylinder servo loop, and converts the speed error signal to a pulse-width-modulated signal.

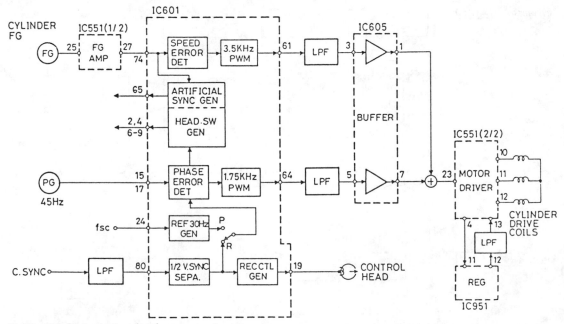

7-18 *Realistic 150 cylinder servo circuits.* Radio Shack

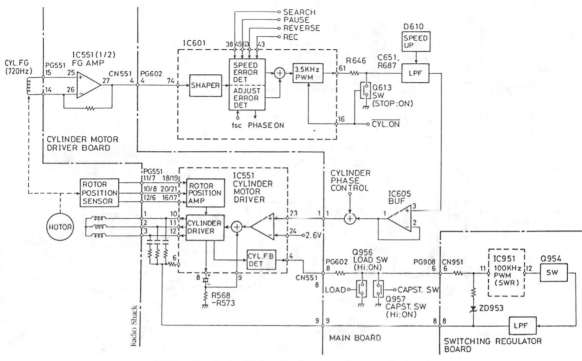

7-19 *Realistic 150 cylinder speed control circuit.*

IC605 smooths out the speed error signal and buffers the control voltage of speed/phase of the cylinder motor. IC951 supplies power to the motor driven IC551.

The cylinder FG pulse signal is generated by a cylinder frequency generator (FG) located inside the cylinder. A printed pattern magnetic sensor, fitted to the lower cylinder, detects the passing magnet with 32 poles, which is fitted to the rotor. When the rated video head speed of 2700 rpm is maintained, the frequency of the cylinder FG pulse is 720 Hz. The cylinder FG pulse enters the FG amplifier in IC551 (FG amp) through pins 25 and 26, and this amplifies the signal for the following stage in IC601.

IC551 is the three-phase DD motor driver IC. Three-phase current supplied to the drive coils connected to pins 10 and 12 are controlled according to the three-phase rotor position data applied to pins 16 and 21 so that a rotating magnetic field that repels the rotary magnet is developed. The speed rotation of the magnetic field is determined by speed/phase error voltage applied to pin 23.

The cylinder phase control circuits include IC601 which amplifies the feedback signal (FG pulse) used in phase control, generates references signals (½ V Sync and REF 30 Hz) and supplies one of them selectively, detects phase error, and generates record-mode control signals and head-switching signals with artificial vertical sync (FIG. 7-20). Buffer IC605 smooths out the speed and phase error voltages.

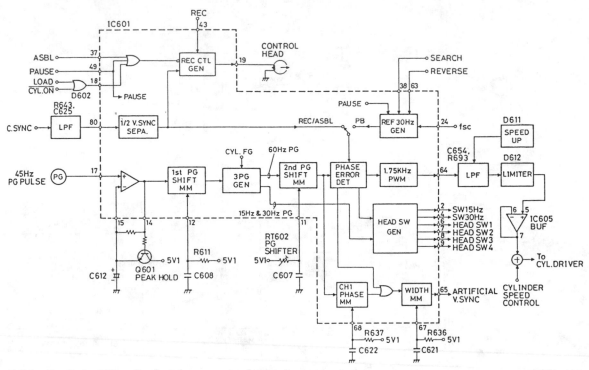

7-20 *Realistic 150 cylinder phase control circuit.* Radio Shack

Sony CCD-M8E/M8U Drum Driving Circuit　The drum motor is a sensorless three-phase unidirectional brushless current motor. The drum motor drive IC202 activates CX20114. The drum motor speed error signal and phase error signals detected by IC203 are fed to the drive motor drive IC202 (pin 11) as a drum servo error signal after it has been mixed by MC-4 board resistors, capacitors, and diodes (R205, R245, R246, R251, R214, C214, and D206) (FIG. 7-21). The error signal is converted into a PWM signal at output pin 5. Q211 is driven by this power PWM signal from pin 5.

Direct current voltage results from the PWM signal after removing the carrier component by means of the filter of L203 and C225 and is added to the drum motor COM terminal. From the motor terminals U, V, and W, phase coil switching is accomplished by the drum motor at drive pins 3, 22, and 24. The switching timing is determined by detection of motor reverse voltage (pin 14).

A motor-starting circuit is needed because the drum motor coil phase switching is a carried-out system detection of the reverse voltage. C214 and R233 provide the start timing circuit. Sometimes the motor may rotate slightly in reverse direction. When unadjusted, the drum servo adjustment can only be made by SW position adjustment. The alignment tape is required for this adjustment.

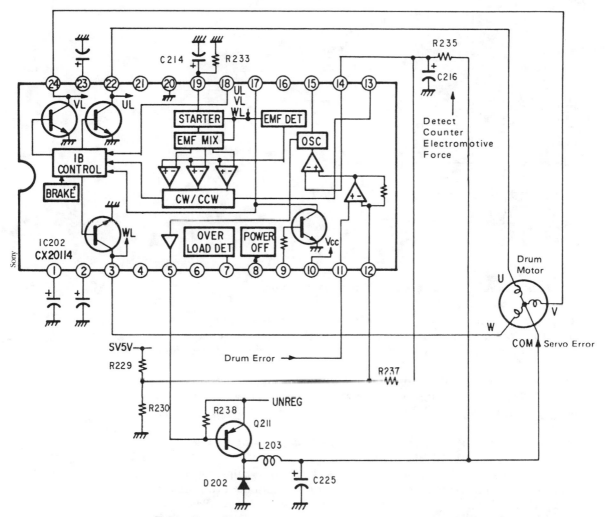

7-21 *Drum motor driving circuit of Sony CCD-M8E/M8U camcorder.*

Zenith VM6150 Drom Motor Circuits The drum servo system consists of the recording speed control, recording phase control, and drum MDA control. The drum motor frequency generator (FG) output signal is converted into a PWM (pulse-width-modulated) pulse and applied to an integrator circuit for detecting the error voltage.

Each rotation of the drum motor yields 40 pulses, which at 45 Hz rotation results in a 1800 Hz drum FG output signal. This signal goes via MDA board Cn501 pins 8 and 11 to IC501 pins 18 and 19 (FIG. 7-22). The signal is amplified and applied to a Schmitt trigger for a waveform shaping and sent down from pin 21 to the main board CN401 pin 12 and IC401 pin 17.

IC401 produces a PWM pulse corresponding to the frequencies' differ-

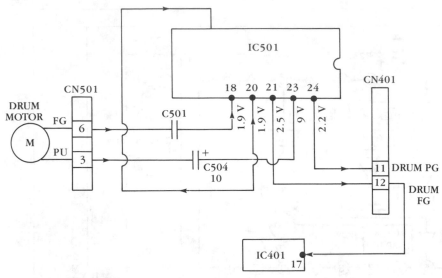

7-22   *Drum motor circuits of Zenith VM6150 camcorder.*

ence due to irregularities in drum motor rotation with the output at pin 37. If the drum motor speed is excessive, the FG pulse frequency increases and the PWM pulse widens. Insufficient speed results in a lower frequency and narrower PWM pulse.

A low-pass filter (LPF) integrates the IC401 pin 37 output to produce an error voltage corresponding to the motor rotation frequency. The error voltage goes through a voltage-follower circuit to a mixing amp for mixing with the error voltage from the phase system. TRAP-1 removes the 45 Hz component, after which the error voltage is sent from pin 5 of CN401 to MCA board and pin 10 of IC501.

IC501 functions to control the magnetic field for rotating the drum motor. The IC output voltage is added or subtracted from the drum motor power supply voltage produced by the drum power switching regulator circuit.

The recording phase control reference signal generator for the drum servo during recording is derived from the vertical synchronization (V Sync) component of the input video signal applied to pin 5 of IC401. With IC401, the V SYNC is separated and counted down $\frac{1}{2}$ to a 30 Hz pulse, which resets the reference counter. The 30 Hz reference signal is supplied to the drum phase comparator.

The drum MDA control consists of the error voltage from the drum speed control system, which increases with a faster rotation and decreases with slower rotation. From the phase control system, the error voltage decreases with phase advance and increases with phase delay.

These error voltages are applied to IC406 (operational amplifier). When the phase error voltage at pin 10 plus (+) input increases, the op-amp output voltage increases. The motor drive amplifier then increases the current to accelerate the drum motor. The speed error voltage at the minus

(−) side is inverted. An increase in speed decreases the voltage at the op-amp and reduces the drum motor current.

The Zenith drum motor is a three-phase direct-drive (DD) motor, featuring high efficiency for producing the torque required by the 270-degree tape wrap while minimizing power consumption. The 80 FG magnet poles produce a 1800 Hz signal at normal 45 Hz rotation (FIG. 7-23). The three-phase stator coils are at 90 degrees with 30-degree spacing between coils. Three Hall elements are located at 120-degree positions for detecting the rotor position. The motor is driven by eight magnetic poles. The four rotary transformers are distributed with CH1 innermost and CH4 outermost.

The Zenith VM6150 motor drive circuits are shown in FIG. 7-24. The power transistors are switched for supplying current to drive coils 1, 2, and 3. The motor drive start position is detected by IC501 from Hall elements located between stator coils. These supply 120-degree phase signals to the three-phase logic circuit. The logic circuit sends switching signals to the power transistors for supplying coil current at the optimum positions for driving the rotary magnet.

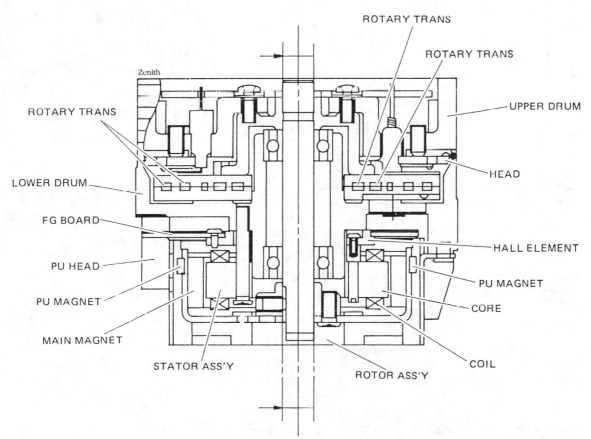

7-23 *Zenith's VM6150 drum motor. Notice the upper and lower drum location.*

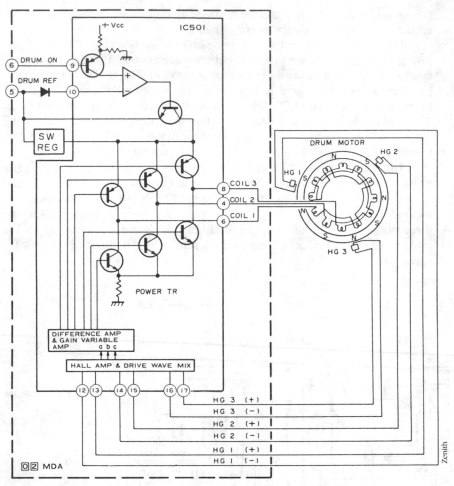

7-24   *The drum motor drive circuits of Zenith VM6150 camcorder.*

Rotational control is performed by adding to or subtracting from the voltage supplied from the switching regulator. The servo error voltage (drum reference) is supplied via the switching regulator to the power transistors, thereby controlling the voltage applied to the motor.

Drum Motor Removal

The drum or cylinder may have top and bottom replacement components. Sometimes the top half must be removed before the bottom half. In other camcorders, the whole cylinder or drum unit is replaced. Make sure the cylinder or drum motor is defective before trying to remove it, as several parts may have to be removed before getting to the motor unit.

General Electric 9-9605 D.D. Cylinder Replacement   Work with extreme care when removing or replacing the D.D. (direct drive) cylinder unit. Remove the tape cover (B) over the upper cylinder (FIG. 7-25A). Open

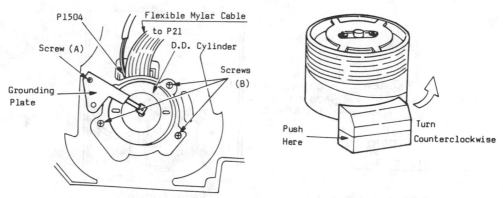

7-25 *Replacing the direct-drive cylinder of the General Electric 9-9605 camcorder.* Thomson Consumer Electronics

the main C.B.A. and battery case unit. Remove screw (A) to remove grounding plate. Remove three screws (B) and then lift the D.D. cylinder unit slightly from the top side. Unlock connector P21 on the main C.B.A. before disconnecting the flexible mylar cable. Disconnect connector P1504 on cylinder unit and then remove the unit.

Be careful and do not pull on the flexible mylar cable coming from the D.D. cylinder unit. Do not try to remove or pull on the flexible wires that connect cylinder unit to P21 on the main C.B.A. Since there is very little clearance around the cylinder unit, raise gently and carefully. Remove the upper cylinder unit from the unit in order to install a new motor.

Reverse the procedure when installing the new D.D. cylinder unit. Reinstall the cylinder so that the two projections on chassis meet the two holes on lower surface cylinder and then fit the cylinder to the chassis turning it counter-clockwise (FIG. 7-25B). If needed, use the alignment tape VFM5001H6 for tape path adjustments.

Olympus VX-801U Cylinder Unit Replacement   Remove the cover of the unit. Remove one screw on the main C.B.A. board under the chassis (FIG. 7-26A). Open up the main C.B.A. Disconnect the connectors P1001, P6002, P2003, P2004, P6003, and P6004. Remove the shield case cover on the main C.B.A. and disconnect the connector P5001. Slide up the connectors P6001, P2002, P2001 and P2004. Then remove the flexible cables.

Remove the three screws from the bottom side of the chassis (FIG. 7-26B). Now remove the three screws and pull out the cylinder unit (FIG. 7-26C). Install the new cylinder unit. Assemble the unit subject to the reverse steps. Confirm the playback picture and sound is good, and if not, clean the video head and adjust post height adjustments.

RCA CPR100 Cylinder Motor Removal   First remove the cassette holder. Remove the upper cylinder. Remove the dew sensor. Disconnect the flat ribbon cable CN51 (FIG. 7-27A). Now remove three screws holding the cylinder base (FIG. 7-27B). Remove the three screws holding the lower cylinder and cylinder base (FIG. 7-27C).

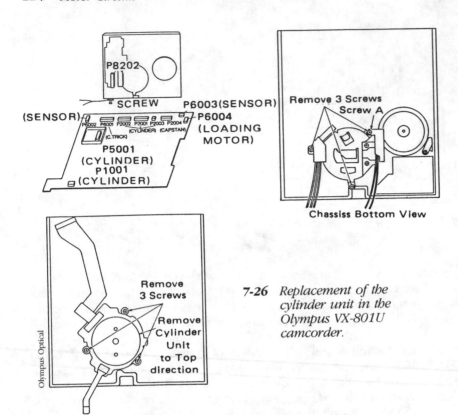

7-26 *Replacement of the cylinder unit in the Olympus VX-801U camcorder.*

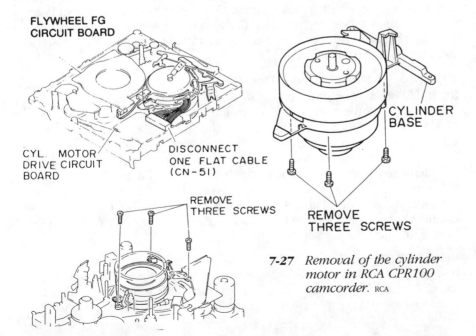

7-27 *Removal of the cylinder motor in RCA CPR100 camcorder.* RCA

AUTO FOCUS MOTORS

Many camcorders use infrared rays to provide automatic focus control. The auto focus motor is located on the camera lens assembly. The automatic focus control system is an external focusing system operating on the principle of triangulation, using the reflection of infrared rays (around 870 nm).

Infrared rays emitted by the infrared LED pass through a projection lens and reach the object. The infrared rays are reflected from the object and back to the sensor via the receiving lens (FIG. 7-28). The receiving lens (sensor) contains two photodiodes. The focus lens is moved until the two photodiodes receive an equal amount of light. The two photodiodes detect the infrared rays reflected back from the object and convert them to current values. The current signals are converted to voltages and are output.

RCA CPR100 Auto Focus Block Diagram

When the focus which is in AUTO position, the 5-volt B+ source is applied to the auto focus control circuits (FIG. 7-29). The auto focus circuit generates an 8 kHz infrared signal applied to the infrared circuit (Q3). This infrared signal is transmitted to the subject, reflected back, and picked up by the two photodiodes (A and B). The reflected signal is rectified by the diodes and produces electrical current in proportion to the amount of infrared light received by each diode. IC2 amplifies the two signals. The signals are synchronized and detected by the 8 kHz clock signal in IC2. The signals are now compared with a reference signal. The correction signal data is applied to microprocessor IC3. This signal is applied to the motor drive circuit (Q4-Q12) to control the auto focus motor.

Realistic 150 Auto Focus Motor Drive Circuit

The auto focus motor drive circuit consists of IC2, Q7, and Q6 (FIG. 7-30). The auto focus motor is driven automatically with the motor drive signal and manually with the power switch. The auto focus motor is driven when the transistors Q1 and Q2 and switching transistors SW1 through SW4 in the

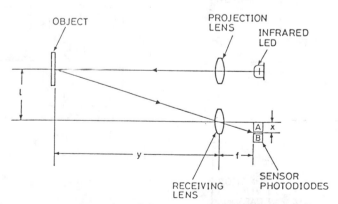

7-28 *Measurement principles of the automatic focusing system.*

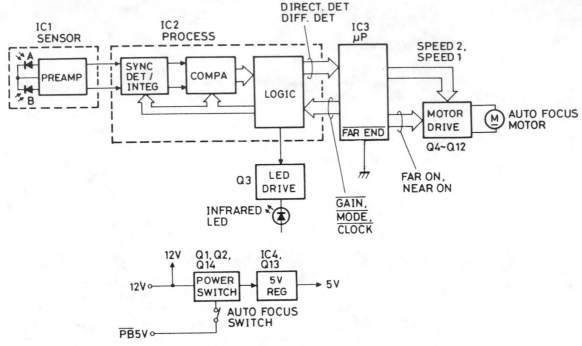

7-29 *Block diagram of RCA CPR100 auto focus circuits.* RCA

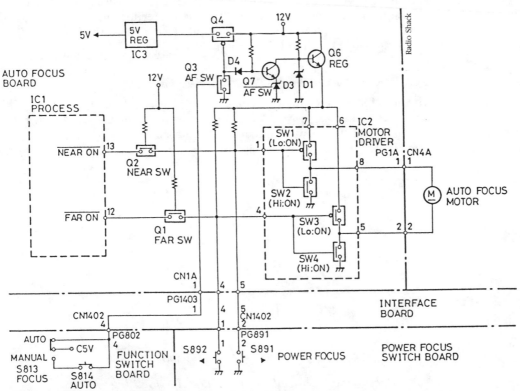

7-30 *Realistic 150 auto focus motor drive circuits.*

motor drive circuit (IC2) are switched according to the NEAR ON signal (pin 13) and FAR ON signal (pin 12) is produced by the process IC1. The duty of the motor drive signals (NEAR ON and FAR ON) is controlled by the distance of the object.

When the power focus switches (S891 and S892) are on, the input of the motor drive circuit (IC2) is grounded and the motor will be driven with manual focusing.

The motor speed control circuit (Q6) generates the motor drive voltage. When the switching circuit (Q7) turns on and off, the base bias varies Q6, controlling the motor drive current.

When auto focus switch (S813) is set to auto or to manual with S814 pressed, C5V is supplied to the switching circuits (Q3) and the AF 8W turns on. D4 is grounded and Q7 is turned off. As a result, the base bias of Q6 is set with a zener diode (D1 at 6.2 V) and approximately 5.5 V is applied to the motor drive circuit (IC2).

In the power focus mode, the auto focus switch (S814) is not operated, so the C5V is not applied. Now Q3 is off and Q7 remains on and a zener diode (D3 at 4.7 V) is connected to the base of Q6. As a result, the voltage supplied to the motor drive circuit (IC2) falls to about 4 V to reduce the motor speed and facilitate focusing operation.

Auto Focus Motor Removal

In some camcorders, the whole lens unit assembly must be removed before getting to the AF motor, while in others, the auto focus motor is held with just two mounting screws. The auto focus motor is located on the lens assembly of all camcorders.

General Electric 9-9605   The lens unit, auto focus C.B.A. and angle must be removed before the auto focus motor can be removed in this camcorder (TABLE 7-4). Remove the processor C.B.A. and then remove the lens unit from chassis by removing three screws (A) (FIG. 7-31A). Remove two screws at the bottom of the assembly. Release the metal fasteners. Remove two screws (D) fixing the angle (PCB) holder (FIG. 7- 31B). Remove the auto focus C.B.A. by unlocking the tabs. Now remove two screws to pull out the motor assembly (FIG. 7-31C).

Minolta C3300   After the outside covers have been removed, the auto focus motor is easily removed. Remove the two screws holding the motor (FIG. 7- 32). Pull out the motor. Reverse the procedure when replacing the new motor.

IRIS MOTOR DRIVES

In the early VHS iris mechanism, a meter system was used to mechanically connect brake and drive coils. This iris mechanism worked somewhat like the camera aperture. Today, besides this iris mechanical system you will encounter an iris motor with an AIC (auto iris circuit).

The auto iris circuit operates the lens iris in order to maintain the optimum average video signal level (FIG. 7-33). The luminance (YE) and wide

Table 7-4. Disassembly Flowchart
(General Electric 9-9605)

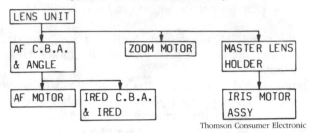

Thomson Consumer Electronic

blanking (W.BLK) signals control the auto iris circuit. The luminance signal level declines with reduced scene brightness. This increases the Q13 bias and the Q13 emitter voltage declines. The reduced Q14 gate voltage reduces the Q14 drain current, decreasing the voltage at pin 6 of IC7.

The op-amp output from pin 7 of IC7 increases and the current flows in the iris driver coil in the direction from pin 2 to pin 4. Now the iris opens to increase the incoming light. Voltage is produced in the iris damper coil with the speed at which the iris operates. As the iris opens, positive voltage appears at pin 3, which tends to increase the voltage at pin 6 of IC7. This damping action provides smooth iris operation.

An increase in scene illumination yields the opposite generation. D7, in

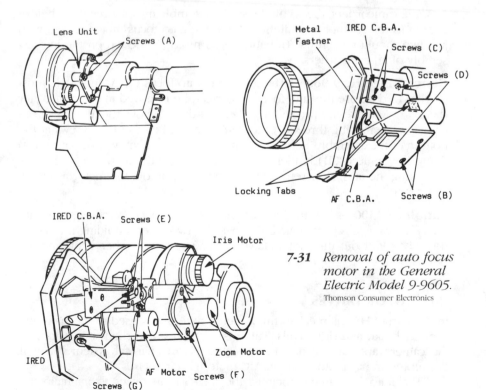

7-31 *Removal of auto focus motor in the General Electric Model 9-9605.*
Thomson Consumer Electronics

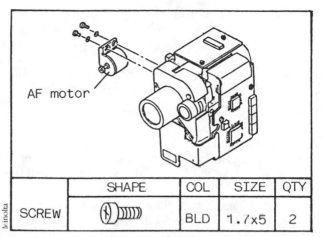

	SHAPE	COL	SIZE	QTY
SCREW		BLD	1.7x5	2

7-32 *Removing the auto focus (AF) motor in the Minolta C3300 camcorder.*

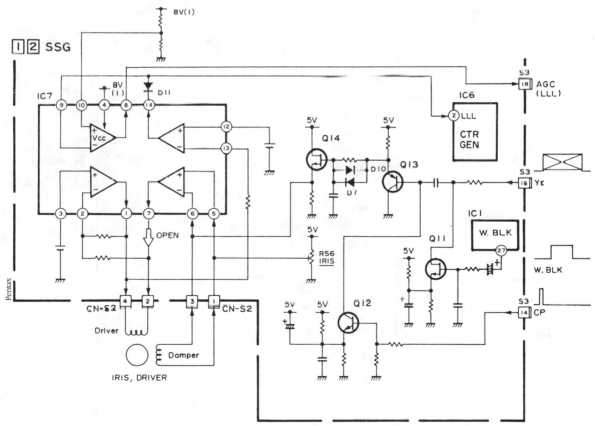

7-33 *Block diagram of the auto iris circuit (AIC).*

the Q14 gate resistance circuit, provides quick iris response to rapid increase in incident light. If the scene brightness declines to where the iris is completely open and pin 13 of IC7 voltage becomes lower than that of pin 12, pin 14 of IC7 comparator output goes high. Then the AGC circuit functions. Spring force is applied to the iris driver in the "close" direction. With the power turned off, the 5 V power supply is low and the iris is closed.

RCA CPR100 AIC (Automatic Iris Circuit)   This circuit controls the lens iris according to the object brightness. It contains the AIC circuit IC1402, iris motor AGC, and the iris control (FIG. 7-34). The output level from the video signals are controlled by the AIC circuit. This circuit controls the iris opening, depending on the level of the iris detect signal from the processing IC1102.

The generated voltage is the difference between the reference voltage at the differential amplifier circuit and the comparison voltage at the noninverting input. The comparison voltage input is the iris detect signal filtered by the capacitor connected to pin 9. RT1103 adjusts the reference voltage and RV1601 the iris control. When the average lighting of the scene viewed by the camera decreases, the comparison voltage input decreases. Likewise, the output of this circuit decreases, and when the average light increases, the output also increases.

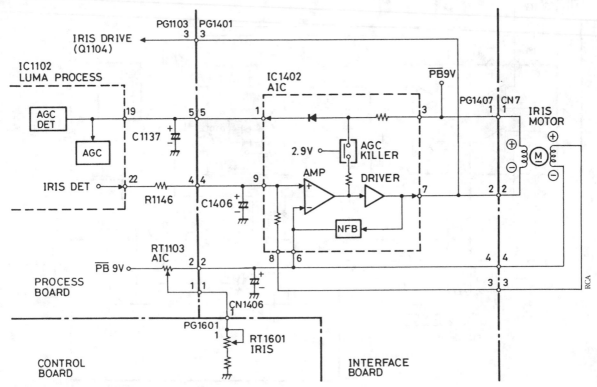

7-34 *RCA CPR100 automatic iris circuit (AIC).*

REMOVE
THREE SCREWS

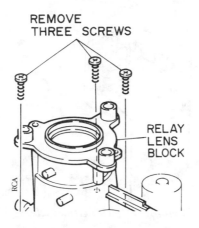

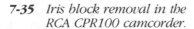

RELAY
LENS
BLOCK

REMOVE
TWO SCREWS

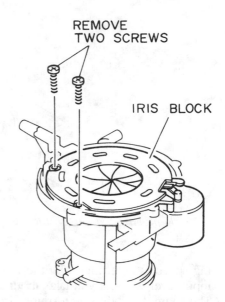

IRIS BLOCK

7-35 *Iris block removal in the RCA CPR100 camcorder.*

The video output level is controlled by a combination of AIC and AGC circuits. RT1401 controls the crossover point for the auto iris control and automatic gain control. RT1401 is adjusted during setup of video output level procedures.

RCA CPR100 Iris Block Removal   Remove the lens block assembly. Remove one screw from the auto focus circuit board and open the auto focus circuit board. Now remove the focus motor. Remove three screws (3) holding the relay lens block (FIG. 7-35A). After the relay lens block is removed, remove two screws holding the iris block assembly (FIG. 7-35B). Reverse the procedure when replacing the iris block assembly. Keep finger marks off of iris assembly and wipe off all dirt and dust.

Zenith VM6150 Lens Shutter Removal   Take out two screws (A) to remove the lens shutter, with power switch board (FIG. 7-36). Reverse the procedure for installation. To install, set the shutter to OPEN position and the front panel power switch to the ON position. When installing the lens to the front panel, set the close-up switch lever to the normal position.

ZOOM MOTORS

The zoom motor brings the image close or far away from the lens. In some camcorders, the zoom motor is called a PZ (power zoom) motor. The zoom motor is on the lens board assembly. In the early camcorders, the zoom motor was controlled by transistors (FIG. 7-37). The zoom motor drive circuits are controlled by voltage in the zoom motor circuits.

Radio Shack 150 Zoom Motor Drive Circuits   The zoom motor driver (IC1403), located on the interface board, drives the zoom motor. The zoom-

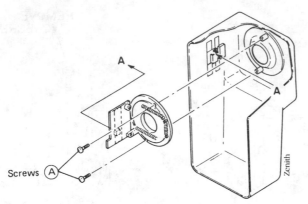

7-36 *Removing the lens shutter assembly of Zenith's VM6150 camcorder.*

ing speed is determined by the level applied to pin 9 (FIG. 7-38). When the input level is 1 V, it will take about 8 seconds to zoom the lens all the way. The zoom direction is determined from the level applied to pin 2 of IC1403. With the TELE switch (S1101) on, the lens assembly is zoomed all the way in with an input voltage (0.3 V). When S1102 (wide) is on, the motor will zoom the lens way out with approximately 6.4 V applied to the input voltage terminal.

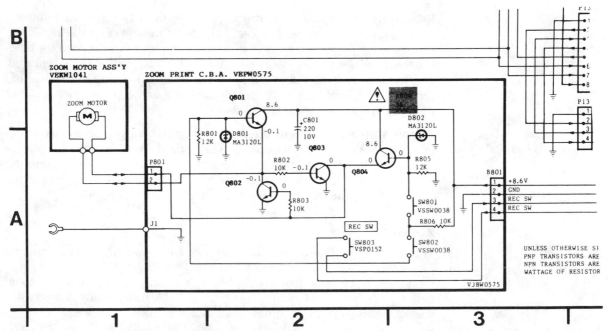

7-37 *Transistors control the zoom motor within the General Electric 9-9605 VHS camcorder.* Thomson Consumer Electronics

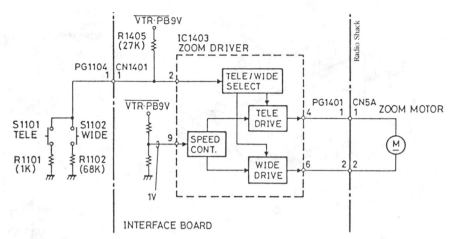

7-38 *Realistic 150 zoom motor drive circuits.*

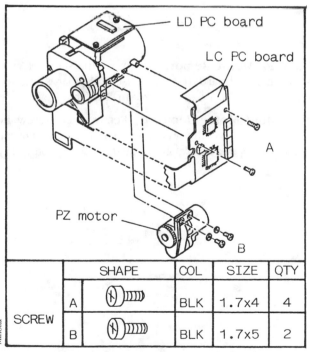

		SHAPE	COL	SIZE	QTY
SCREW	A	🔩	BLK	1.7x4	4
	B	🔩	BLK	1.7x5	2

7-39 *Removal of PZ motor (power zoom) in the Minolta C3300 camcorder.*

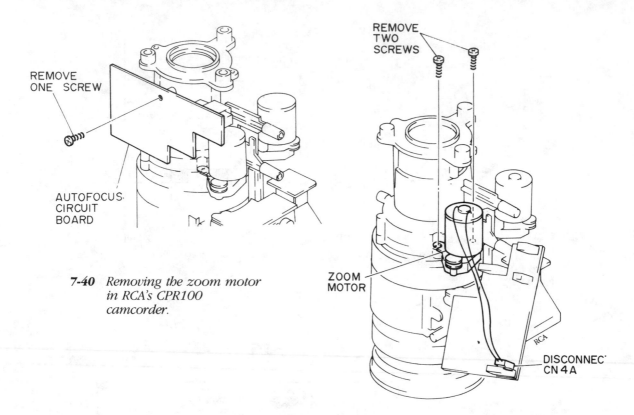

REMOVE
ONE SCREW

AUTOFOCUS
CIRCUIT
BOARD

REMOVE
TWO
SCREWS

ZOOM
MOTOR

DISCONNEC
CN 4 A

7-40   *Removing the zoom motor
in RCA's CPR100
camcorder.*

Minolta C3300 PZ Motor Removal   Remove the screws (A) holding the
LD pc board and L.C. pc board (FIG. 7-39). Raise both boards, and then remove
the screws (B) holding the PZ (power zoom) motor.

RCA CPR100 Zoom Motor Removal   Remove one screw holding the
auto focus board and open the auto focus circuit board. Disconnect connector CN4A. Remove the screws holding the zoom motor (FIG. 7-40A and
7-40B).

Chapter **8**

Audio
Circuits

The audio circuits are quite simple compared to the video or color circuits. The VHS and VHS-C audio circuits are quite similar in operation. The audio control head (a/c) is in both circuits, while in the 8 Mm camcorders, frequency-modulated audio signals can be recorded by multiplexing them with video signals. PCM recording is also possible, or a conventional fixed head may be used to record audio signals near the edge of the tape. Most 8 mm camcorders employ the multiplexing FM audio signals with the video signals, which is called FM audio signal recording.

VARIOUS MODELS

The following models' audio circuits are discussed in this section: GE 9-9605, RCA CPR100, Realistic 150, Pentax PV-C850A, and the Sony M8E/M8U.

General Electric 9-9605 VHS Audio Circuits

The audio circuits consists of three IC components, line-mic-amp, audio REC/PB process, and switching IC., There are six transistors, which include mic amp, switching line-on, bias oscillator, inverter, switching audio delay rec-on, and ripple filter transistor (FIG. 8-1). Provisions are made for earphone operation, external microphone, and external audio line input.

The signal path in record mode starts at the microphone input (3) and feeds to the mic amp (Q4001). Here the amplified audio is capacitor-coupled to the line-mic input IC4001 (pin 2) (FIG. 8-2). If the audio is to be recorded through the line input terminal of P4002, it is capacitor-coupled to pin 7 of IC4001. The signal of both line or mic input is switched here and amplified with the output on terminal 5.

The amplified signal is fed to pin 18 of IC4002, which acts as the audio REC/PB processing IC. In REC mode, the signal is again amplified by IC4002,

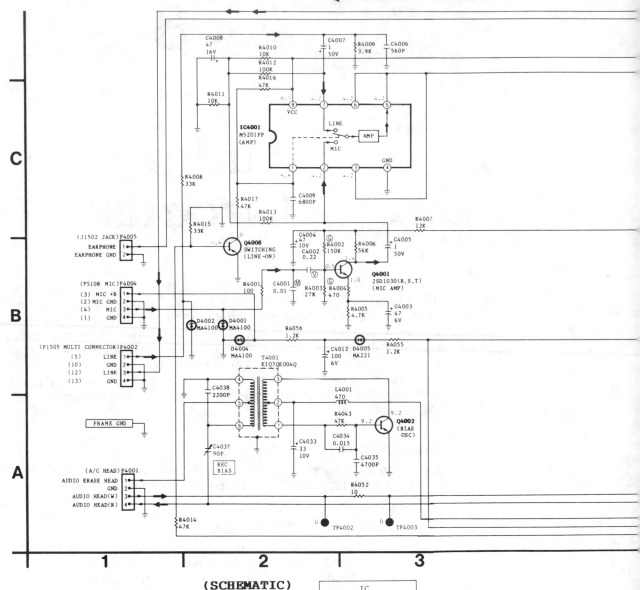

CALLOUTS NEXT TO WIRING PLUGS INDICATE
CONNECTIONS TO OTHER SCHEMATIC DIAGRAM.

← SIGNAL PATH IN REC MODE

← SIGNAL PATH IN PLAYBACK MODE

(SCHEMATIC)

AUDIO	
TRANSISTOR	
Q4001	3-B
Q4002	3-A
Q4003	5-B
Q4006	5-A
Q4007	5-A
Q4008	2-B

IC	
IC4001	2-C
IC4002	3-C
IC4003	3-B
CONNECTOR	
P4001	1-A
P4002	1-B
P4003	6-A
P4004	1-B
P4005	1-B

8-1 *The audio schematic of General Electric 9-9605 (VHS) camcorder.*
Thomson Consumer Electronics

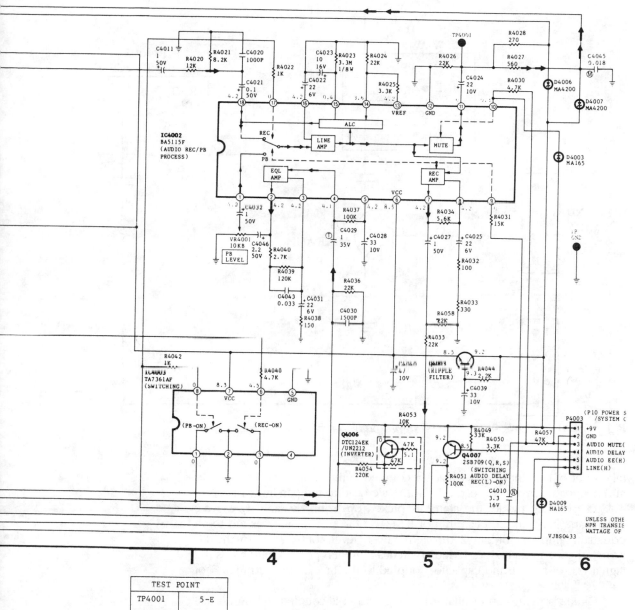

TEST POINT	
TP4001	5-E
TP4002	2-A
TP4003	3-A
GND	6-B
ADJUSTMENT	
VR4001	4-B
C4037	2-A

4 5 6

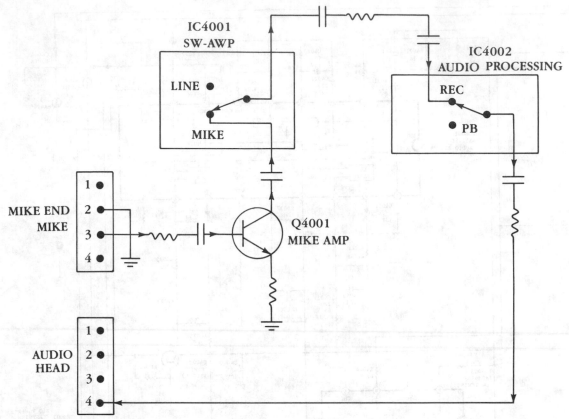

8-2 *General Electric 9-9605 (VHS) signal path in record mode.*

taken out of terminal 7 and capacitor-coupled to the audio head at pin 4. In audio signal is then transferred from the a/c head to the passing tape.

In playback mode, the signal is picked up from the tape by the a/c audio tape head and fed to pin 4 of IC4002 (FIG. 8-3). The signal is fed to an equalizer amp out of pin 2 through the PB level control and to the PB switch through pin 1. Here IC4002 switches to the PB position and feeds the signal out of pin 11 and capacitor-coupled to the line output terminal 3 of P4002.

Q4002 provides an oscillator bias signal and is coupled through transformer T4001 to erase the previous recording. The bias signal from pin 5 of T4001 is fed to pin 1 of P4001 to excite the erase head like all cassette audio erase heads (FIG. 8- 4).

RCA CPR100 VHS-C Audio Circuits

The VHS audio circuit in the RCA CPR300 camcorder is quite similar to the CPR 100 VHS-C model except for differently numbered components. The audio signal enters the input circuit with the built-in microphone or the

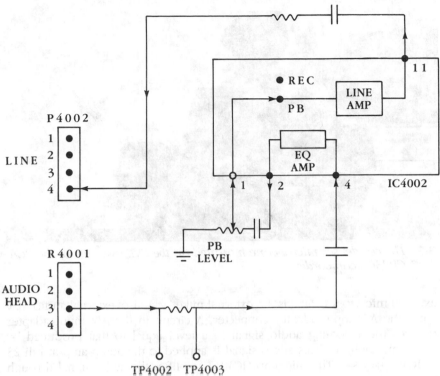

8-3 *Playback (PB) signal path in the General Electric 9-9605 VHS camcorder.*

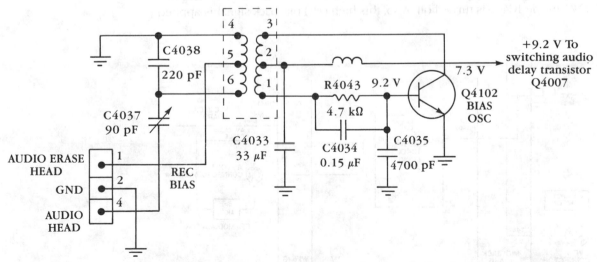

8-4 *The oscillator bias erase head circuit in the General Electric 9-9605 camcorder.*

8-5 *The condenser microphone mounted on the EVF assembly of the RCA CPR300 camcorder.*

external mic (FIG. 8-5). J452 is the external mike jack. Also, external audio may enter the A/V input adapter connecter. A circuit in the A/V input adapter reduces the incoming audio signal to a level equal to that produced by either microphone. This audio signal is applied to the audio amp at pin 23 of IC401 (FIG. 8-6). The mic amp (IC401) amplifies the audio signal through the ALC circuit and output at pin 10 of IC401. The picked-up E-E signal may be heard in the earphone to the A/V output connector.

The record/playback audio heads are switched by the playback (PB) signal by the system control microprocessor (IC901). When the playback signal is high (Hi), Q401 is turned on and IC402 is low (Lo) at pin 5 (FIG. 8-7). SW1 inside IC402 is turned off. Also, this high (Hi) playback signal is applied

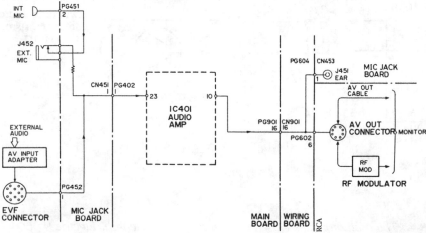

8-6 *RCA CPR100 (VHS-C) audio/input circuits.*

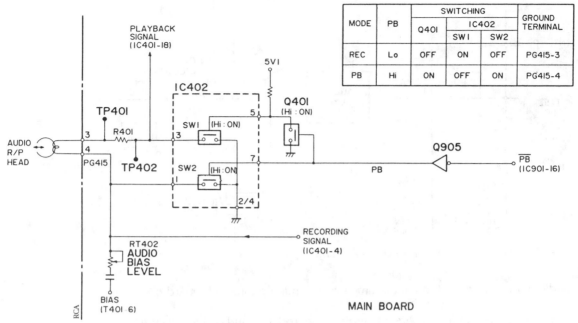

MODE	PB	SWITCHING			GROUND TERMINAL
		Q401	IC402		
			SW1	SW2	
REC	Lo	OFF	ON	OFF	PG415-3
PB	Hi	ON	OFF	ON	PG415-4

8-7 *RCA CPR100 (VHS-C) audio head-switching circuits.*

to pin 7 of IC402 which turns SW2 on. This switching grounds the record terminal of the audio head and allows the playback signal to be picked up by the audio head with outputs through IC401 and R401.

In record position, the playback (PB) signal is low (Lo) and turns off SW2 and Q401. Now SW1 is on, which grounds out the playback terminal through R401. Now the record signal is applied to the audio head to record. The bias oscillator is controlled by system control IC902. The oscillator is turned on when the OSC on signal is high (Hi) and supplied by IC901.

IC401 is placed in the playback mode by a high (Hi) signal applied to pin 2 and a low (Lo) mute signal at pin 3, during playback operation. IC901 provides the playback signal. The playback head audio signal is sent to the playback amplifier. This amplified audio signal passes through a PB equalizer. The audio signal is equalized to produce a flat response. The signal passes through a 15750 Hz trap to the line amplifier. This amplified audio signal is picked up by the earphone jack and A/V output jack.

The playback signal is applied to pin 2 of IC401. The mute signal goes low (Lo) and is applied to pin 3 of IC401 in record operation. The input audio signal is applied at pin 23 of IC401 and amplified by the mike amp. This amplified signal goes through a 15750 Hz trap to the record amplifier. This signal is then applied to the audio record head.

Realistic 150 Audio Input/Output Circuits

The audio input signal comes from the built-in microphone (INT.MIC) or an external microphone plugged into the microphone jack (J452 MIC) to the

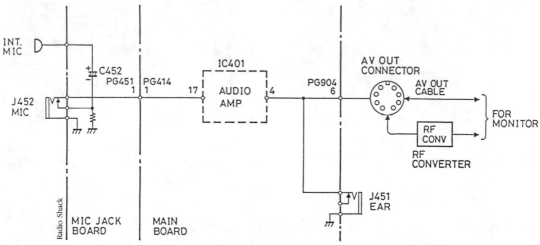

8-8 *Realistic 150 audio input/output circuits.*

audio amplifier (IC 401, an audio amp) via the microphone jack board (FIG. 8-8).

The audio output supplies EE audio or reproduced audio signal to the earphone jack (J451-EAR) or AV OUT connector. To monitor the audio signal through the AV OUT connecter, connect the AV output cable or RF converter to the AV OUT connector.

Head switching is provided by IC402 in the head-switching circuits (FIG. 8-9). The playback signal comes from pin 24 of the system control IC901 to

MODE	PB5V	PB̄	IC402		GROUND
			SW1	SW2	TERMINAL
REC	Lo	Hi	OFF	ON	PG415-3
PB	Hi	Lo	ON	OFF	PG415-4

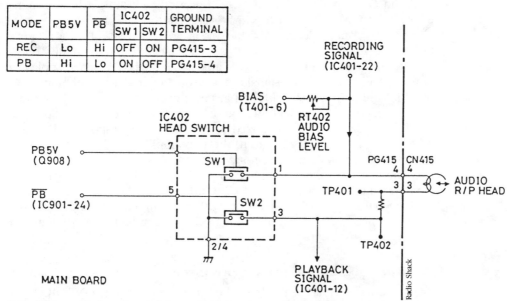

8-9 *The audio head-switching circuit in the Realistic 150 camcorder.*

pin 5 of the head-switching circuit (IC402, HEAD SWITCH) and to Q908 (PB5V switch) to generate PB5V. PB5V is also supplied to IC402 (HEAD SWITCH) to switch the record/play heads between the record and play modes.

The audio amp (IC401) includes recording and playback (PB) circuits, and either of them is selected by PB5V (pin 20) and AUDIO MUTE (pin 21), supplied from the system control IC901 (FIG. 8-10).

The recording circuit consists of a 15.75 kHz trap, ALC, recording amplifier, and recording equalizer. The 15.75 kHz trap circuit (L401, C410) connected to pins 7, 1, and 23 removes the 15.75 kHz component (buzz sounds) from the audio signal. The ALC circuit detects the input level and keeps the output level constant. The output controls the gain of the line amplifier (LINE AMP).

In the recording amplifier, the microphone amplifies (MIC AMP) and line amplifier (LINE AMP) amplifies the audio signal (FIG. 8-11). In the recording amplifier (REC AMP) and recording equalizer, the series resonance circuit (SP MODE: L402, C417, R432; EP-MODE: L402, C417, R432, C445, R446) boosts high-frequency components of the audio signal and makes the frequency response as shown in TABLE 8-1. In the EP mode, the EP signal causes Q408 to turn on in order to raise the amount of compensation to about 15

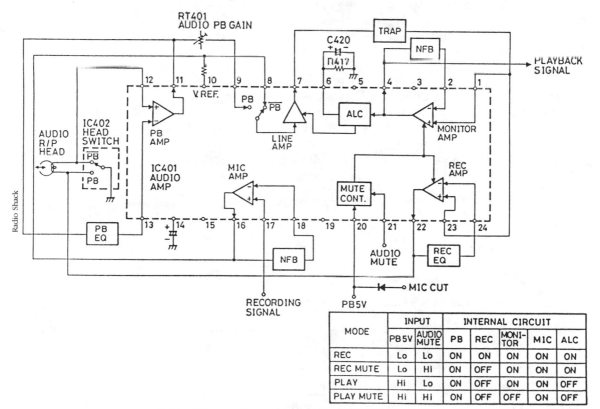

MODE	INPUT		INTERNAL CIRCUIT				
	PB5V	AUDIO MUTE	PB	REC	MONITOR	MIC	ALC
REC	Lo	Lo	ON	ON	ON	ON	ON
REC MUTE	Lo	Hi	ON	OFF	ON	ON	ON
PLAY	Hi	Lo	ON	OFF	ON	ON	OFF
PLAY MUTE	Hi	Hi	ON	OFF	OFF	ON	OFF

8-10 *The audio amplifier circuit (IC401) of the Realistic 150 camcorder.*

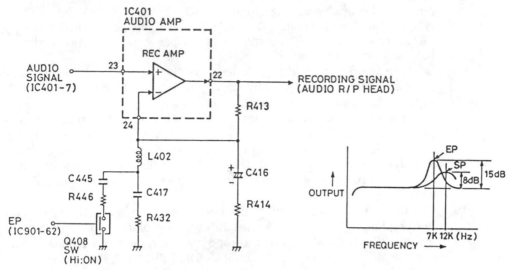

8-11 *The audio recording equalizer circuits in the Realistic 150 camcorder.* Radio Shack

dB and compensate for deterioration of response at high frequency due to a fall in tape speed.

The audio cutoff signal circuit operates during eject operation. A MIC CUT signal (Hi) comes from pin 64 of the system UP (IC901) to cut off the output signal and inhibit it from being recorded (FIG. 8-12). When the MIC CUT signal (Hi) comes to pin 20 (PB5V INPUT), a muting control circuit (MUTE CONT) operates to disable the recording amplifier (REC AMP) and monitor amplifier (MONITOR AMP). The low-pass filter (R422 and C424) connected to pin 16 (OUTPUT OF MIC AMP) removes the component, including the bias signal frequency.

In the playback equalizer circuit, the play head has a frequency response boosted by a 6 dB/octave at high frequencies. The playback equalizer is given a frequency response boosted by −6 dB/octave at low frequencies to flatten the frequency response. In the EP mode, the head peaking frequency and high frequency time constant of NAB equalization is given in TABLE 8-2 to compensate for deterioration of response at high frequencies due to the fall in the tape speed.

Table 8-1.   Characteristics of the Recording Equalizer (Realistic 150)

Tape speed	Resonant Frequency	Compensation
SP	Approx. 12kHz	Approx. 8dB
EP	Approx. 7kHz	Approx. 15dB

Radio Shack

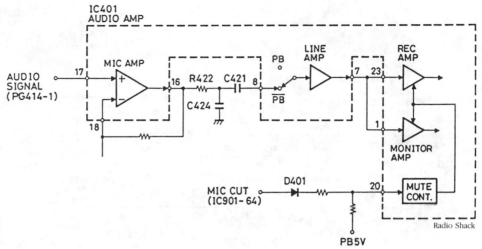

8-12 *The audio signal cutoff circuit in the Realistic 150 camcorder.*

The EP mode signal from the system control (IC901) turns on a switch (Q403, EP SW), grounding C466 to switch the head-peaking frequency from 14 kHz (SP MODE) to 8 kHz (EP MODE). Q407 (EP SW) turns off, triggered by the EP signal and inverted by an inverter (Q910) (FIG. 8-13). This grounds C442, to switch the high frequency time constant of NAB equalization from about 100 μs (SP MODE) to about 120 μs (SP MODE).

The bias oscillator operates during the record mode with an OSC ON signal high (Hi), which comes from pin 58 of the system control IC901 to the bias oscillator Q404 (FIG. 8-14). The bias oscillator exits the audio record/play head, audio erase head, and full-erase head with a bias current of about 70 kHz generated by a Hartley oscillator circuit.

Pentax PV-C850A (8 mm) Audio Circuits

The Pentaz 8 mm camcorder employs the multiplexing FM audio signals with the video signals (called FM audio signal recording) the FM audio signal recording provides single-channel monaural sound. The FM carrier frequency is 1.5 MHz and frequency deviation of ± 100 kHz. A noise reduc-

Table 8-2. Characteristics of the Playback Equalizer (Realistic 150)

Tape Speed	Head Peaking Frequency	Higher Time Constant
SP	Approx. 14kHz	Approx. 100μsec
EP	Approx. 8kHz	Approx. 120μsec

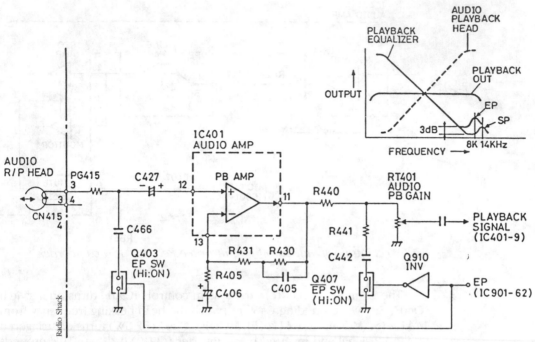

8-13   *The playback equalizer circuit of the Realistic 150 camcorder.*

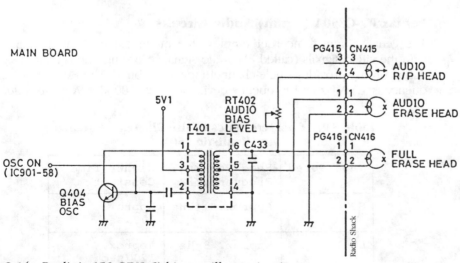

8-14   *Realistic 150 (VHS-C) bias oscillator circuits.*

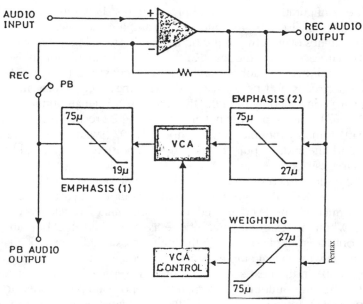

8-15 *Block diagram of the FM audio noise reduction circuit in the Pentax PV-C850A camcorder.*

tion system is employed like that in a hi-fi VTR. It is 2:1 compression-expansion type noise reduction, which is basically the same as in VHS hi-fi (FIG. 8-15). The audio signal is compressed to one-half (in decibels) during recording and expanded two times in playback. At the same time, fixed emphasis is applied to reduce high-frequency noise (FIG. 8-16).

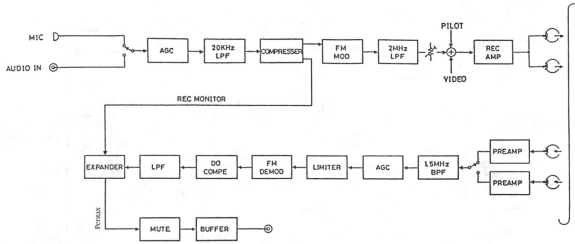

8-16 *Block diagram of Pentax PV-C850A audio recording/playback circuits.*

The configuration audio signal processing is shown in FIG. 8-17. The audio circuits consist of Q403 and Q404 (amplify the microphone input), IC402 (switches over between the built-in and external microphone), IC401, and AGC (in record/play modes), FM modulator/demodulation, noise reduction, preemphasis/ deemphasis and muting circuits, and IC201 (included in the video circuits and performs head switching). Record/play modes and muting are controlled by the PB, MUTE, and SW30 signals applied to IC401.

The audio signal-processing circuits during EE/record consists of Q403 and Q404 (amplify the microphone input), IC402 (switches over the microphone and line audio inputs, IC401, the AGC, noise reduction, and FM modulator circuits.

The built-in microphone is a condenser microphone to which power is supplied from R424 through the microphone output line (FIG. 8-18). When an external microphone is connected, the built-in mike is switched out of the circuit. When no external microphone is connected, the built-in microphone output is supplied to Q403 through the external mike jack. Q403 and Q404 amplify the signal amplitude so it is enough for the audio signal processing IC401 in the next stage. The output is supplied to pin 4 of IC402. It selects either the built-in or external microphone output applied to pin 4, the line signal applied to pin 4, or the line signal applied to pin 8, controlled by the CAMERA/VTR and CAMERA/VTR signals from Q405. The selected output comes out to pin 9 or 3. CAMERA/VTR applied to Q405 is high when the CAMERA/VTR switch on the side of the unit is set to CAMERA (VTR). CAMERA/VTR, inverted by Q405-1, controls S2 through pin 6. After inversion again by Q405-2, it controls S3 through pin 5. Thus, the built-in or

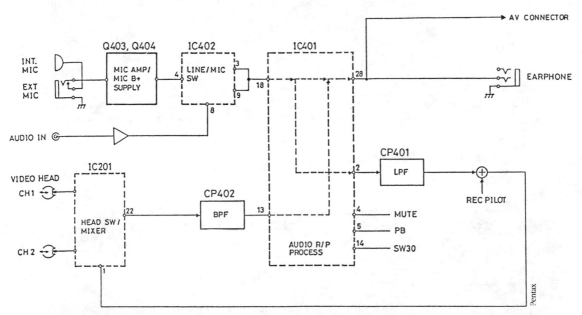

8-17 *Pentax PV-C850A block diagram configuration of audio signal-processing circuits.*

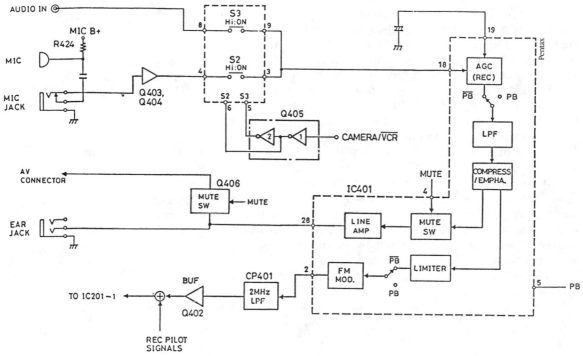

8-18 *Audio EE/record signal-processing circuit of the Pentax PV-C850A camcorder.*

external microphone output is selected in the camera mode and the audio signal coming in through the AV connecter is selected in the VTR mode.

The selected signal comes to pin 18 of IC 401. Its mode depends on the PB signal applied to pin 5. When PB is low, IC401 is in the record mode. The audio signal comes from pin 18 to the AGC circuit. It detects the mean value of the input and controls the gain to fix the audio output according to the detected voltage averaged by the capacitor connected to pin 19.

After passing through the AGC circuits, the audio signal comes to a low-pass filter (LPF). This extracts audio signal components under 20 kHz. Next, the output passes through a compressor/preemphasis circuit (compressor/emphasis), which compresses the signal to one-half over the entire frequency range and then applies emphasis. The output passes a muting circuit (MUTE) and a limiter (LIMITER). During the record mode, the muting circuit permits the input signal to simply pass through. The signal comes out pin 28 through the line amplifier (LINE AMP).

The limiter limits the audio signal amplitude to under the maximum frequency deviation before FM modulation to prevent over modulation. It also removes AM noise. The limited audio signal enters the FM modulator (FM MOD), which frequency modulates the input with a frequency deviation of within ± 100 kHz and a carrier of 1.5 MHz. The output comes out to pin 2.

From pin 2 of IC401, the FM audio signal is supplied to a low-pass filter (CP401), which limits the signal to 1.5 MHz ± 100 kHz. After this, it is supplied to the pilot signal mixer through buffer Q402.

The audio signal-processing circuits during playback are shown in FIG. 8-19. They consist of IC201, which amplifies the mixed RF playback signals and produces a continuous signal from the mixed RF signals of CH1 and CH2 supplied alternately, IC401, performing AGC, FM demodulation, muting, noise reduction, and deemphasis of the playback FM audio signal.

The mixed RF signal from Q201 (described in the video circuits) passes a bandpass filter (CP402), which extracts the FM audio signal of 1.5 MHz ± 100 kHz. The output is supplied to pin 13 of IC401 through a buffer Q401.

IC401, set in the play mode by the PB (playback) signal applied to pin 5, supplies the FM audio signal to the AGC circuit. It detects the AGC voltage by synchronous detection, rectifies the voltage, and controls gain in order to fix the output by examining the voltage (stored in a capacitor in the IC). The gain of the AGC circuit is controlled by the output of the playback FM signal level detection.

The playback (PB) FM signal, with its output level fixed, is supplied to the playback FM signal level detector (AM DETECTOR) and limiter (LIMITER). The playback FM signal level detector detects the playback FM signal

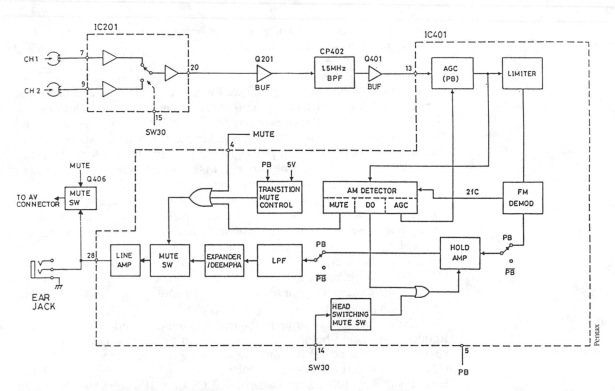

8-19   *Audio playback signal-processing circuits of Pentax PV-C850A camcorder.*

level by multiplying the doubled FM audio signal carrier from the PLL FM demodulator by the FM audio signal.

The output is used to control the AGC circuit gain, compensate for dropout, and control muting. The limiter limits the FM audio signal amplitude before demodulation to remove the AM noise. The limited FM audio signal is supplied to the FM demodulator (FM DEMOD). In this PLL FM demodulator, when the VCO's output frequency is locked at twice the input FM audio signal frequency, the voltage controlling the oscillation frequency is taken as the audio output. The oscillator frequency of the VCO (equal to double the FM audio signal frequency) is also used as a timing signal of the playback FM signal level detector. The demodulated audio signal then enters a hold amplifier. This holds the signal amplitude before dropout with a width of about 1 ms or less or before head switching to compensate for the dropout or prevent switching noise. The FM signal level detector detects dropout. On head switching, an edge of the head-switching signal applied to pin 14 is detected. A pulse about 10 μs wide is generated according to the detection output and the hold time of the audio signal, which is determined from the pulse.

Having passed through the hold amplifier, the audio signal passes through a low-pass filter (LPF) that cuts off its components over 20 kHz. The output enters the expander/deemphasis circuit (EXPANDER/DE-EMPHA). This has characteristics opposite to those of the compressor/emphasis circuit during recording. The audio signal compressed to one half (in decibels) during recording is expanded two times in order to expand the dynamic range, improve the S/N, and prevent deterioration of high-frequency components.

The expanded audio signal enters the muting circuit (MUTE SW). This mutes the audio signal (controlled by the mute signal applied to pin 4), the output of the mode transition detector (TRANSITION MUTE CONTROL) in the IC, and the output of the playback FM signal level detector. The MUTE signal remains high at power-on time for about 0.5 seconds after transition from stop to play mode and until the track play mode is released. While the MUTE is high, the output of the expander/deemphasis circuit is grounded to mute the audio signal. The mode transition detector remains high, for about 0.5 seconds after the play mode changes to the stop mode, generating a muting signal.

The playback FM signal level detector generates a muting signal when dropout continues for 1.1 ms or more. In these cases, the audio signal is muted as when MUTE turns to high (Hi). The audio signal having passed through the muting circuit comes out to pin 28 and is supplied to the circuits described for the recording mode.

Sony CCD-M8E/M8U (8 mm) Audio Circuits

The whole audio circuit in the Sony camcorder revolves around IC401 (FIG. 8-20). The microphone feeds into the mike amp Q401 and Q402 and has a high-pass filter that cuts off frequencies below 200 Hz. The mike amp has a

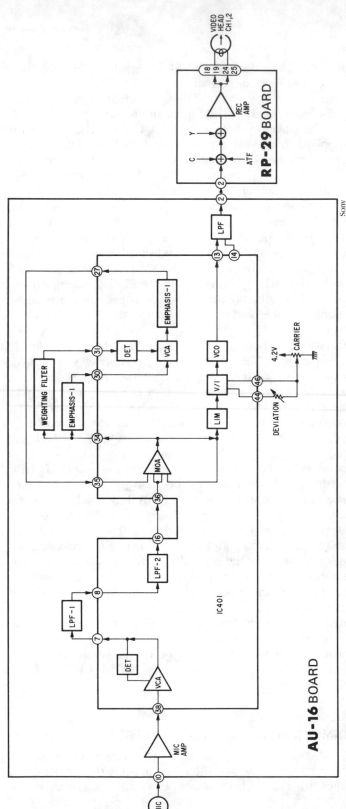

8-20 *Audio block diagram of Sony CCD-M8E/M8U camcorder.*

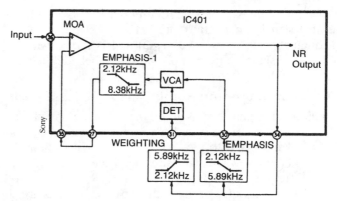

8-21 *Sony CCD-M8E/M8U noise reduction (NR) block diagram.*

gain of 31 dB. The high-pass filter network removes wind noises, input noise, and low-frequency noises.

The audio signal is detected after passing through the voltage-controlled amp (VCA). A dc voltage in proportion to the input signal is obtained in the detector circuit. This voltage controls the gain of the VCA with AGC action. The AGC time constant is determined by the CR at pin 23 of IC401.

The audio signal output at pin 7 (IC401) is fed to the buffer amplifier pins 8 and 9 with the tertiary active low-pass filter (LPF-1), which is composed of R401 through R406 and C403 through C405. LPF-1 prevents malfunctions of the NR circuit by cutting off unwanted frequencies above 20 kHz. The audio signal from LPF-1 passes through LPF-2 and out pin 16. The noise reduction (NR) circuit input begins at pin 36 with the attack, recording, and hold time of the NR circuit determined by capacitors at pins 32 and 33 (FIG. 8-21).

The audio signal of the overmodulation prevention limiter (LIM) is converted into current by the V/I converter and then fed to the voltage-controlled oscillator (VCO). RV401 controls the V/I converter output current and sets the carrier wave frequency of the AFM signal to 1.5 MHz (FIG. 8-22). RV402 controls the conversion gain of V/I at pin 44 and controls the fre-

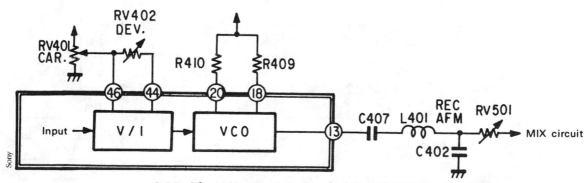

8-22 *The VCO circuit in Sony's CCD-M8E/M8U camcorder.*

quency deviation of the voltage-controlled oscillator so as to become ± 60 kHz. The AFM signal is converted into FM signal at pin 13. This FM signal passes through the LPF (L401 and C402) and is mixed with the chroma signal, ATF, and Y signals and then passed on to the video head.

SONY CCD-M8E/M8U 8 mm Audio Tape Path

The 8 mm audio tape path begins at the mike unit and is fed into pin 10 of the AV-16 board (FIG. 8- 23). In sound record the audio comes from pin 2 of the AV-16 board and is fed to pin 2 of the RP-29 board assembly. The REC audio signal and the video Y/C signal are found at terminals 24 and 19 of the RP-29 board. Here the recording signals are sent to pin 2 of video head CH1 and pin 5 of video head CH2. Many of the tape path circuits are shown with arrows in different color showing the record and playback routes.

MICROPHONES

Most of the microphones used within the camcorder are the unidirectional condenser or electret types. These small mikes must have from 2 to 10 dc voltages applied to the terminals to make them work. In a Pentax PV-C850A microphone circuit, dc voltage is applied to pin 2 from R424 of the + 5-volt source (FIG. 8-24). The audio signal is capacitor-coupled (C420) through the external mike jack shorting terminals to the base of Q403. Q404 and Q403 amplify the audio mike signal and feed it to the line/mic Switch (IC402). Some mike circuits contain a low-pass filter to eliminate wind and low-frequency noises.

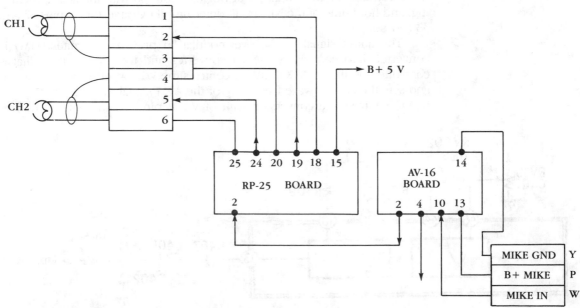

8-23 *Sony 8 mm audio board recording tape path.*

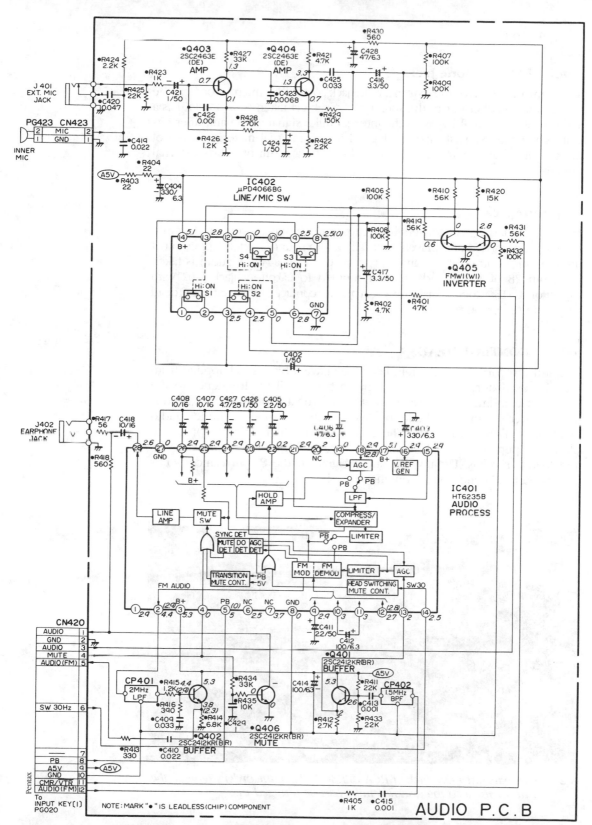

8-24 *Complete audio circuits of Pentax PV-C850A camcorder.*

External Microphone Jack

Most camcorders have the external mike jack so another microphone can be plugged in to get closer to the sound of the subject taken (FIG. 8-25). J401 is a self-shorting jack that bypasses the internal mike signal to the amplifier circuit. When the external mike is plugged in, the internal mike is cut out of the circuit. Erratic or intermittent sound may be a result of a dirty external mike jack.

Earphone Jack

Many of the larger camcorders have earphone circuits so you can listen to the sound recorded and played back. The audio sound is often tapped off at the line amp output of the audio process IC. In FIG. 8-24, the audio is taken from pin 28 of IC401 and capacitor-coupled to earphone jack J402 with capacitor C418. Check for a dirty earphone contact with erratic or dead earphone reception.

AUDIO CONTROL HEADS

The audio record/playback (R/P) head may have a bias signal applied from the bias oscillator, which also supplies a bias oscillator frequency to the audio erase and the full erase heads (FIG. 8-26). The audio A/C control head is located after the upper cylinder or drum assembly (FIG. 8-27). The R/P audio head terminals are switched by the head switch IC when either recording or playback operation is used. The audio A/C control head is found in the VHS and VHS-C models. Usually, the audio signal in the 8 mm camcorder is processed to FM and mixed with the video heads.

8-25   *The external mike jack of RCA CPR300 VHS camcorder. Remove the built-in mike so the external mike can be plugged in.*

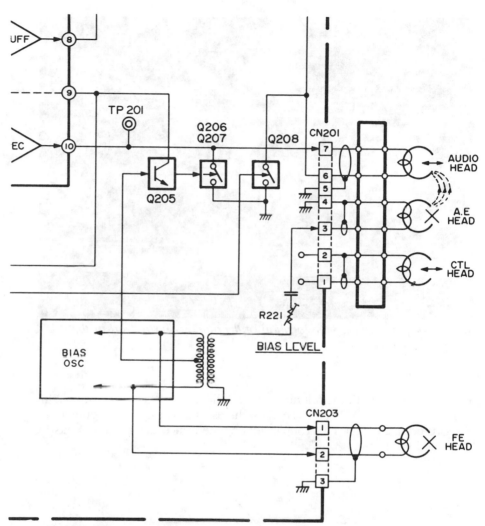

8-26 *The bias oscillator excites the audio, audio erase (AE), and full erase (FE) heads.* Sony

The video and audio signals are applied to the tape with the REC/PB drum and A/C tape head in the helical scan format. Of course, the video signal is recorded in the center of the tape with the drum or cylinder head and the audio track at the edge of the tape in the VHS and VHS-C tape formats (FIG. 8-28). The control track keeps the picture and sound synchronized with a CTL head.

Audio Erase Head

Often, the audio head is excited from the bias oscillator circuit and is used to erase the audio portion from the tape. The full-erase head erases the

8-27   *The pen points to the location of the audio control head in the RCA CPR300 camcorder.*

entire tape path. Both the full erase and A/C heads are located on the VTR in the tape path of the VHS and VHS-C machines. Audio tape head alignment is discovered in Chapter 11. Troubleshooting the camcorder audio circuits is discussed in Chapter 13.

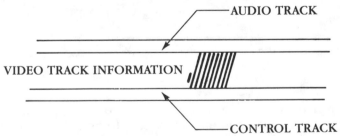

8-28   *The audio track is located at the edge of the tape in the VHS and VHS-C formats.*

Chapter 9

Mechanical Tape Operations

*T*he mechanical VTR or VCR section of the cam-corder contains components that provide tape movement. Most of these mechanical components are located in the main chassis. Each part may be outlined or located upon the chassis (FIG. 9-1). To service the mechanical section, the VTR main chassis should be removed. The main components are described in this chapter with its mode of operation along the tape run path. The audio heads and capstan motor operations are given in Chapters 8 and 7 respectively.

GENERAL HEAD DESCRIPTION

The video tape head, upper cylinder, or drum assembly may pick up the recording from the tape in playback and record upon the tape in record mode. The conventional tape head (VHS) has two video heads 180 degrees apart on a 62 mm cylinder. The VHS-C camcorder uses the same size tape as the VHS units, except a smaller video head is found with a 41.33 mm cylinder or drum assembly (FIG. 9-2). The 8 mm camcorder has a smaller tape width (8 mm) with a 40 mm diameter drum or cylinder. The video head assembly is rotated with a cylinder or drum motor.

To reduce the camcorder overall size, the cylinder or drum assembly was reduced with a smaller size cassette. To maintain compatibility with the standard VHS system, the tape head cylinder diameter was reduced by two-thirds in the VHS-C camcorder. To get the same length of tape around the head surface, greater tape wrap must be made around the small cylinder or drum assembly. The same tape track length is recorded on the video tape with the same length of tape wrapped around the cylinder or drum. With a smaller diameter tape head, the speed rotation is increased to maintain relative head-to-tape speed compatibility.

Pentax PV-C850A (8 mm) Video Head Cylinder   The cylinder is 180 degrees + wind (without PCM recording). The track width is 20 microns

9-1   *The video head may be called upper cylinder or drum assembly. The pen points to the video head in the RCA CPR300 VHS camcorder.*

(in SP) on a 40-degree cylinder diameter for a tape speed of 14.345 mm/s, which is slower than VHS. The relative speed of the cylinder and tape is 3.8 m/s (FIG. 9-3).

Two video heads (CH1 and CH2) are separated and attached to the cylinder 180 degrees apart. The angle of azimuth for CH1 is – 10 degrees, for CH2 + 10 degrees (as seen from the front surface of the head. The

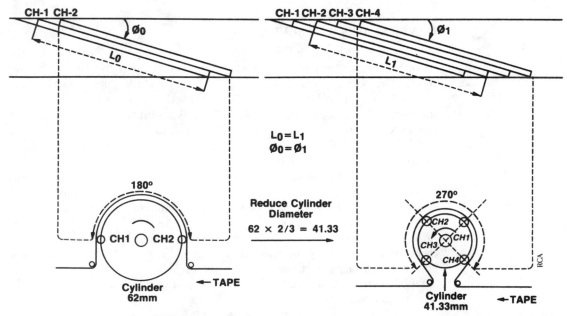

9-2   *The VHS cylinder is 62 mm in diameter and has a tape wrap of 180 degrees while the VHS-C video head has a diameter of 41.33 mm with a 270-degree tape wrap.*

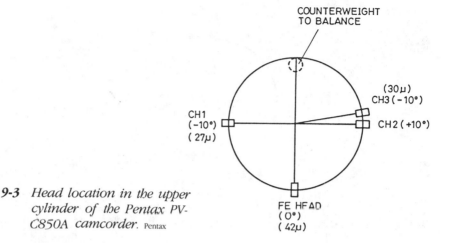

COUNTERWEIGHT
TO BALANCE

(30μ)
CH3 (-10°)

CH1
(-10°)
(27μ)

CH2 (+10°)

FE HEAD
(0°)
(42μ)

9-3 *Head location in the upper cylinder of the Pentax PV-C850A camcorder.* Pentax

upper cylinder has another CH3 head, which is ahead of the CH2 by 1.7 degrees (2.5H). This head is used for trick play with the azimuth angle at −10 degrees.

Between the Ch1 and CH2 video heads, 90 degrees counterclockwise from CH1 head, is a rotating erase head. Opposite to the rotating (flying) erase head is a counterweight to maintain balance (FIG. 9-4). The rotating erase head is 42 microns wide so that it can erase two tracks at the same time. The video tape runs in the same direction as the rotating cylinder rotates.

Sony CCD-M8E/M8A (8 mm) Tape Head Format   The tape width is 8 mm wide with two rotary heads and helical scanning FM signal. The drum diameter is 40 mm that travels at 37.5 m/s in standard play, 3.12 m/s in SP (short play) and 3.13 m/s in LP (long play). Besides CH1 and CH2, there is a flying erase head (FE) (FIG. 9-5).

Realistic 150 (VHS-C) Video Head Assembly   The VHS-C VTR uses the same recording format as the standard VHS system for compatibility. The cassette is compact (C-20) and a cassette adapter is needed to use it in the ordinary VTR or VCR. The size of the head is reduced to 41.33 mm. Four video heads are mounted on the cylinder (FIG. 9-6). The tape contacts the cylinder surface over 270 degrees, with the cylinder rotating at 45 revolutions per second (2700 rpm).

Recording is possible in the SP and EP modes. In SP mode, 20 minutes of recording and playback is possible, while in the EP mode, it is 60 minutes. The video head has a track width of 30 μm so that recording is done with guard bands of 28 μm in the SP mode and overwritten for 10 μm in the EP mode.

MECHANICAL OPERATIONS

Most of the mechanical parts found in the VHS, VHS-C, and 8 mm camcorders are the same except they may be called by another name. Of

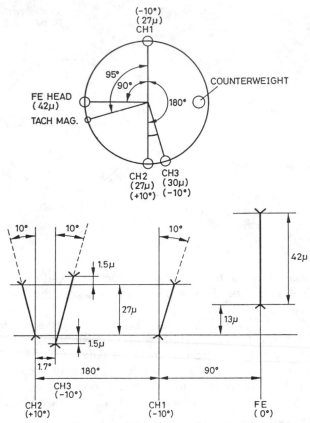

9-4 *Pentax PV-C850A (8 mm) video flying erase head.* Pentax

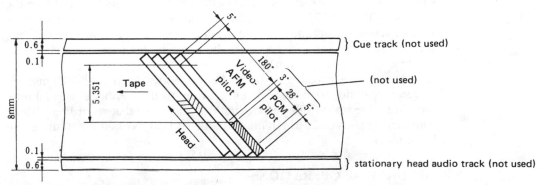

9-5 *The 8 mm tape format in the Sony CCD-M8E/M8U camcorder.* Sony

	Conventional VHS	VHS Movie
Cylinder diameter(mm)	62ø	41.33ø
Tape wrap–around angle (°)	180	270
Cylinder rotation(rpm)	1,800	2,700
Number of heads	2	4

9-6 *The video head configuration and tape pattern in the Realistic 150 (VHS-C) camcorder.* Radio Shack

course, the VHS camcorder's main tape transport assembly is much larger than the VHS-C or the 8 mm (FIG. 9-7). The bottom side of the VHS-C camcorder is shown in FIG. 9-8.

Pentax PV-C850A (8 mm) Supply Reel Disk The supply reel disk has a slip mechanism inside, which is used for tape take-up during reverse visual search and unloading. At the bottom of the reel disk is a reflective plate used in indicating the amount of tape remaining. It emits an eight-pulse sinewave every time the disk rotates. The periphery of the reel disk is a gear that accurately transmits torque. A tension band wound around the side of the reel disk controls tension on the supplied tape. See TABLE 9-1.

Realistic 150 (VHS-C) Supply Reel Disk The supply reel disk is molded of plastic with a reflector on the bottom (three pulses per revolution) with no slip mechanism. A tension band is wound around the reel disk at its bottom and controls tape tension. Inside the cassette, the tab that links with the supply reel hub is inclined, and when the cassette has been loaded, the supply reel disk rotates counterclockwise and removes tape slack (FIG. 9-9).

Realistic 150 (VHS-C) Tension Band The tension band controls the tension of the tape that comes from the supply reel. No means to vary the spring force for tape tension adjustment is provided. If the tension band is dirty or worn so that tape tension falls below the specified range, the tension band must be replaced to adjust the tension to within specifications.

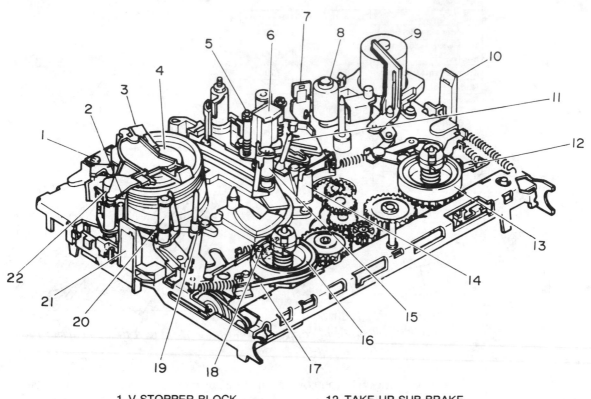

1 V-STOPPER BLOCK
2 FULL ERASE HEAD
3 STATIC DISCHARGE BRUSH
4 UPPER CYLINDER (VIDEO HEAD)
5 GUIDE POST
6 A/C (AUDIO/CONTROL) HEAD
7 DEW SENSOR
8 PRESSURE ROLLER ARM
9 CAPSTAN MOTOR
10 TAKE-UP END SENSOR
11 GUIDE ARM ASSEMBLY

12 TAKE-UP SUB BRAKE
13 TAKE-UP REEL TABLE
14 END LAMP
15 TAKE-UP GUIDE ROLLER
16 SUPPLY REEL TABLE
17 TENSION BAND
18 SUPPLY SUB BRAKE
19 TENSION ARM
20 SUPPLY GUIDE ROLLER
21 SUPPLY END SENSOR
22 IMPEDANCE ROLLER

9-7 *Top view of the tape transport mechanism in the RCA CPR300 camcorder.* RCA

The angle at which the tension band runs over the tension pole is adjustable by rotating the adjustment screw provided at the end of the tension band. During unloading, the tension arm will be forced to return to the stop position by the tension arm operation lever.

Pentax PV-C850A (8 mm) Tension Arm Assembly   The tape winds around the tension pin standing on the tension arm. The force and balance of the spring attached to the opposite edge of the arm controls tape tension. Changing the strength of the spring is the way to adjust tape tension. The

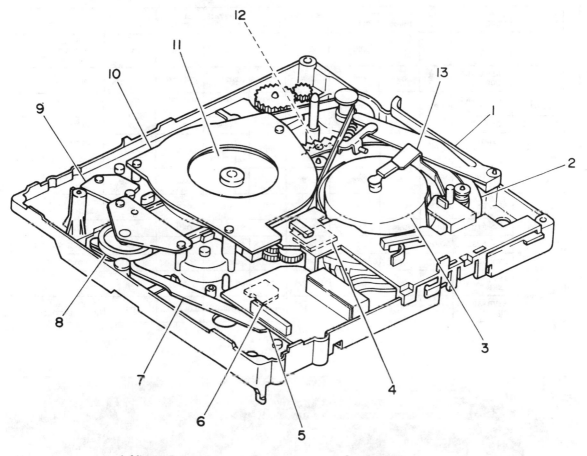

1 Middle Pole Lever
2 Supply Loading Ring
3 Lower Cylinder
4 End Lamp
5 Cylindor Motor Drive Circuit Board
6 Supply Reel Sensor
7 Tension Control Plate

8 Center Pulley
9 Take-up Reel Sensor
10 Flywheel FG Circuit Board
11 Capstan Flywheel
12 Take-up Loading Ring
13 Static Discharge Brush

9-8 *The bottom view of RCA CPR100 (VHS-C) tape transport mechanism.* RCA

other end of the tension band is attached to the tension arm so that it can freely rotate the arm. The other end of the band is rigidly attached to the adjustment plate on the chassis. Adjusting the position of this fixed plate changes the angle of the wind in relation to the tension pole and changes the tension servo's gain.

Realistic 150 (VHS-C) Impedance Roller   This consists of a body of polyacetal resin and a brass ring fitted around the body. Jitter is reduced by raising the moment of inertia. This is a precision-made roller. Be careful not to damage the surface. If it is damaged, jitter will occur, synchronized with

Table 9-1. Mechanism Modes
(Pentax PV-C850A)

	MODE SW POSITION	OPERATION MODE	MAIN BRAKE	T. BRAKE	PRESSURE ROLLER	TENSION ARM	GUIDE POLE	CAPSTAN MOTOR	SUB-CHASSIS	CYLINDER MOTOR	REMARKS
1	EJECT	EJECT	OFF	ON	OFF	OFF	OFF	STOP	UNLOAD	STOP	CASSETTE UP POWER OFF MODE: UL STOP
2	UL STOP	UNLOADING STOP	OFF	ON	OFF	OFF	OFF	STOP	UNLOAD	STOP	POWER OFF
3	UN-LOADING	UNLOADING	OFF	ON	OFF	OFF	OFF ↓	ON (REV) ↓	UNLOAD ↓	STOP ↓	
	LOADING	LOADING					ON	ON (FWD)	LOAD	ON	C.MOTOR: M
4	FF	F.FWD	OFF	OFF	OFF	OFF	ON	ON (FWD)	LOAD	ON	C.MOTOR: Hi
	REW	REW						ON (REV)			CLATCH TORQUE: Hi
5	L.STOP	LOADING STOP	ON	ON	OFF	OFF	ON	STOP	LOAD	STOP	POWER OFF CLATCH TORQUE: L
6	REC PLAY	REC/PB	OFF	OFF	ON	ON	ON	ON	LOAD	ON	C.MOTOR: L CLATCH TORQUE: L
		REC-PAUSE	OFF	ON	ON	OFF	ON	STOP	LOAD	ON	C.MOTOR:STOP
		PB-PAUSE	OFF	OFF	ON	ON	ON	STOP	LOAD	ON	CLATCH TORQUE: L
		FWD SEARCH	OFF	OFF	ON	ON	ON	ON	LOAD	ON	C.MOTOR: M
7	REVERSE	REV. SEARCH	OFF	ON	ON	OFF	ON	ON (REV)	LOAD	ON	C.MOTOR: M CLATCH TORQUE: L
		REVERSE PB	OFF	ON	ON	OFF	ON	ON (REV)	LOAD	ON	C.MOTOR: L CLATCH TORQUE: L

Pentax

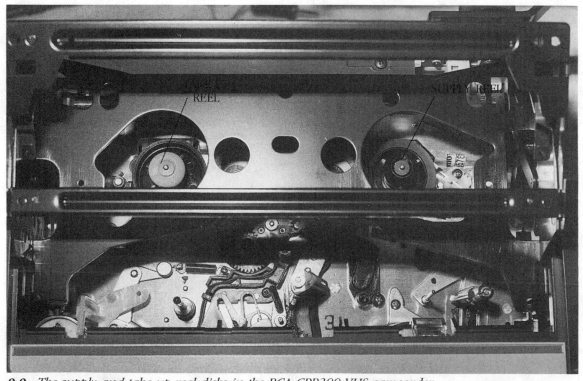

9-9 *The supply and take-up reel disks in the RCA CPR300 VHS camcorder.*

the rollers rotation. Light oil is applied slightly to the bearing. Felt rings (oil barriers) are attached to the top and bottom of the roller to prevent oil from leaking and adhering to the tape. Be sure and replace the felt washers when replacing the impedance roller.

Pentax PV-C850A (8 mm) Impedance Roller Assembly   This roller clamps vibrations in the tape's running direction to reduce jitter during play. The fixed flanges on the top and bottom regulate the tape's running height. The roller rotates around another roller of polyacetal resin at the center. A compressor spring set at the bottom of the impedance roller allows the impedance rollers height to be changed by rotating the nut on the top. This is used in adjusting the height of the running tape (FIG. 9-10).

Pentax PV-C850A Guide Roller   This guide roller has the same structure as previously used guide rollers, and it works to control changes in tape run direction and height direction. The bottom of the guide roller shaft is held by a screw, and the height of the top cover section can be adjusted by turning it with a special screwdriver (FIG. 9-11). There is also a lock screw at the bottom of the roller.

Realistic 150 Guide Rollers   These have the same construction as conventional guide rollers and are precision-made rollers molded of polyacetal resin. These rollers change the direction of the tape transport and control tape height. One is provided on the supply side and the other is on the take-up side (FIG. 9-12). The guide rollers are adjusted so that the bottom edge of the tape runs along a reference line called the lead.

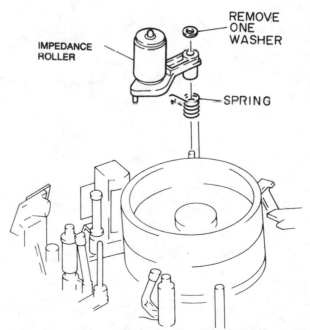

9-10 *The impedance roller assembly of the RCA CPR100 camcorder.* RCA

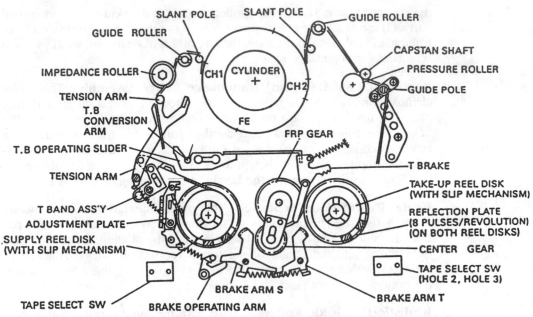

9-11 *Layout of the chassis main components in the Pentax PV-C850A camcorder.* Pentax

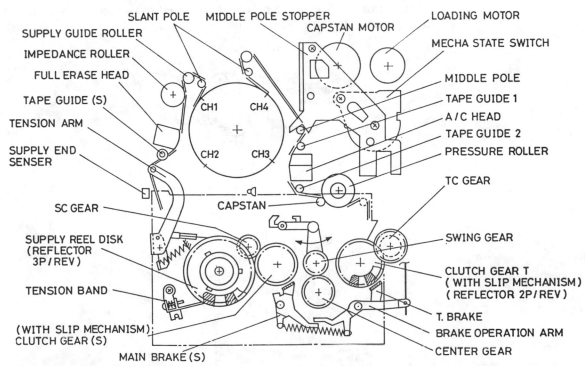

9-12 *Main chassis component layout in the Radio Shack 150 (VHS-C) camcorder.* Radio Shack

Pentax PV-C850A Cylinder   The cylinder is attached to the pedestal with two screws. Signals from the video heads go to the upper rotary transformer, which is attached by the converter to the pedestal (FIG. 9-13). Below this is attached a fixed transformer that transfers the video signals and sends them to the circuit board. The center shaft is supported by two ball bearings at the top and bottom. Mounted in the upper cylinder are the video heads with azimuths of ± 10 degrees and the FE head with azimuth of 0 degrees. Channels (1 and 2) heads are 27 microns wide, channel 3's head is 30 microns wide, and the FE head is 42 microns wide. At the opposite edge of the FE head is a counterweight to balance the FE head.

Since the track pitch of an 8 mm VTR is 20 microns, the overlapped write during recording is 7 microns. Since the width of the FE head is 42 microns and it is placed at a point 90 degrees ahead of the CH1 video head, after erasure by the FE head the video signals are first recorded by CH1 and then CH2 head. There is a 13-micron gap between the video heads and the FE head in view of the various errors that can occur. The tach magnet is attached at a position 95 degrees ahead of the CH1 head. This allows the creation of a the SW30Hz signal for switching. An FG magnet, which is magnetized in about 40 places, is attached to the bottom of the rotary transformer. A signal of 600 Hz is generated for the cylinder FG.

Realistic 150 (VHS-C) Cylinder Assembly   This cylinder has the same construction as the four-head small diameter cylinder. The four video heads always contact the tape and are switched during recording and playback. A damper fitted to the upper cylinder absorbs vibrations of the cylinder occurring due to torque ripples of the motor to reduce jitter. The lower cylinder has a bulge at around 270 degrees to reduce picture bending in the vertical direction caused by the projection of the head tapes subject to a small diameter cylinder.

Realistic 150 (VHS-C) Middle Pole and Stopper   After leaving the cylinder and the slant pole, the tape runs around another pole before it reaches

9-13 *The cylinder structure in the Pentax PV-C850A (8 mm) camcorder.*

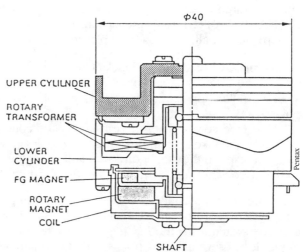

φ40

UPPER CYLILNDER

ROTARY TRANSFORMER

LOWER CYLINDER

FG MAGNET

ROTARY MAGNET

COIL

SHAFT

Pentax

the A/C head. The middle pole is horizontal inside the take-up side guide rail before the tape is loaded. It becomes erect as the tape loading proceeds, and on completion of loading, the middle pole is positioned by the middle pole stopper over the capstan motor and is locked by the arm on the A/C head plate. Adjust the inclination of the middle pole by loosening three screws and move the stopper correctly. Adjust so that the FM output becomes maximum and flat.

Pentax PV-C850A (8 mm) Capstan Assembly   A two-degree-diameter direct drive capstan motor and six-pole motor drive coil drives the capstan assembly. At the bottom, a magnetic ring for CFG on the flywheel periphery has 632 magnetic poles that allow the flywheel to generate 316 pulses in one revolution. The tape speed of 14.345 mm/s generates 720 CFG/s for the capstan CFG.

The capstan shaft is held in place by the pressure roller and supported by oil-less metal at two places on top and bottom. The metal gives the comparatively thin shaft an adequately strong structure. The entire shaft holder is attached to the chassis by three screws, giving it a structure that makes replacement easy. The capstan motor torque drives a gear and a square belt to the center gear that is placed between two reel disks and is then routed through the RFP gear to drive both reel disks.

Realistic 150 (VHS-C) Capstan Assembly   The capstan has a diameter of 3 mm, and its speed is 3.5 revolutions per second. The capstan FG detection coil generates 102 pulses per rotation, and therefore the capstan FG is 360 Hz in the SP mode and 120 Hz in the EP mode. The flywheel is supported by two ball bearings (FIG. 9-14).

Pentax PV-C850A (8 mm) Pressure Roller   Most pressure rollers operate the same in most camcorders. This pressure roller has the same construction as the conventional table-top VCRs. It has one ball bearing in the center and uses ball bearing chatter to push it parallel to the capstan shaft. This structure moves the tape in an even line without pulling it up or down. The pressure roller pushes the tape against the metal capstan shaft to move the tape, like in all audio cassette players.

Slant and Guide Poles   The slant poles guide the tape so that it winds around the cylinder at an angle. They do not control the tape height. The angle of inclination cannot be varied. Do not try to straighten these slanted poles.

The tape comes from the capstan shaft through the guide pole to be wound by the take-up reel disk. The guide pole allows a neat wind by regulating the tape in the height direction and letting the reel disk wind the tape so that it does not touch the inside walls of the cassette.

Realistic 150 Mechanism State Switch Operation   The mechanism state switch is located in VHS and VHS-C camcorders. In the Realistic 150 unit, the switch turns the loading motor on or off according to the current mode. It has seven contact points and is normally set to the third position.

9-14 *The pen points to the capstan shaft in the RCA CPR300 VHS camcorder. The pressure roller and capstan rotate the tape.*

The seven positions are 1—EJECT, 2—FF/REW, 3—STOP, 4—LOADING MID POINT, 5—REC LOCK, 6—REC, PLAY, RECORD PAUSE, and FF SEARCH, and 7— REW SEARCH.

The REC LOCK mode is entered after the REC PAUSE mode has continued for more than 5 minutes. In the REC LOCK mode, the VTR stands by as the loading motor unloads the tape so that the mechanism state switch moves from position 6 to 5, and the pressure roller comes apart from the capstan. At this time, the tension arm returns in the STOP direction to reduce tape tension and to protect the tape from damage and the head from wear.

Adjust the timing of the mechanism state switch and the mechanism in state (3) STOP. Position the mechanism state switch so that the projection on the A/C head drive arm becomes parallel with the chassis and in line with the groove in the mechanism state switch. Check Chapter 11 for proper mechanical adjustment of the state switch.

Pentax PV-C850A (8 mm) Center Gear and FRP Gear The capstan motor with a square belt drives the center gear. The center gear meshes with the FRP gear and oscillates the FRP gear to left and right in line with the center gear's direction of rotation. If the capstan shaft is rotating counterclockwise (normal winding direction), the center gear rotates clockwise, which oscillates the FRP gear to the take-up side. This allows the take-up reel disk to rotate clockwise, which takes up the tape and enters play (record) or search mode. When the capstan motor is rotating clockwise, all rotation is in reverse, and the supply reel disk rotates counterclockwise to take up the tape in the rewind or unloading modes.

Realistic 150 (VHS-C) Center Gear The torque produced by the capstan motor is transmitted to the center gear through the flywheel. The swing gear is engaged with the center gear, which swings to the left and right according to the direction of rotation of the center gear, to drive the take-up or supply clutch gear assembly.

Realistic 150 (VHS-C) Clutch Gear   The clutch T gear has a slip mechanism where the capstan motor rotates the take-up reel hub and permits slipping, to take up the tape. The slip mechanism controls the amount of torque transmitted. This clutch also operates during the fast-forward mode. A reflector (two pulses per revolution) fitted on the bottom is used to detect rotation of the take-up reel hub. The clutch T gear stops rotating when rewinding is complete. The T brake pressed against the bottom of the clutch T gear applies reverse torque to the tape at the take-up side during loading and reverse search.

The clutch S gear like the T gear, has a slip mechanism that applies capstan motor torque to the supply reel disk, permitting slippage, to take up the loose tape.

Pentax PV-C850A (8 mm) Take-Up Reel Disk   The take-up reel disk operates the same way as the supply reel disk slip mechanism slipping during take-up, fast forward and visual search. At the bottom of the take-up reel disk is the reflecting plate for outputting a sinewave at eight pulses per revolution, which is used to indicate the amount of tape remaining and to detect rpm. The gears on the periphery of the take-up reel disk are the same as those on the supply reel disk—they provide sure transmission of torque.

Realistic 150 (VHS-C) Main S Brake   The main brake applies braking to clutch gear S when driven by the B-cam lever linked with the groove provided at the top of the control cam.

The T brake pressed against the bottom of the clutch gear T applies reverse torque (weak brake) to the take-up reel hub.

Pentax PV-C850A (8 mm) Main Brake   This brake method uses the coupling torque from both the reel disks to apply the main brake. The brake arm's S and T teeth sections are applied, which is equivalent to the coupling torque from both reel disks. When the loading motor turns in the loading direction, the mechanism changes from REC or PLAY to STOP. The main brake engages and the rotation of the drive gear engages the brake at normal speed.

The T brake weakly brakes the take-up side during loading and reverse run (reverse visual search and reverse run in recording pause) to prevent tape slack. It also brakes to make the next tape run easier. Applying the T brake to the take-up reel disk during loading allows the tape to be almost pulled out from the supply reel disk. Since the tape winds on the supply reel disk during unloading, there will be no large dislocation of tape position even in constant repeats of loading and unloading.

LOADING AND DRIVE MECHANISMS

The loading and drive mechanism components are usually found on the bottom side of the main chassis (FIG. 9-15). The top of the main chassis contains the take-up and supply reel, braking mechanism and tension arms. Under the main chassis are the loading worm and cam gears, lower cylinder motor, loading motor, capstan flywheel, main brake arm, and supply loading and take-up loading cam gears.

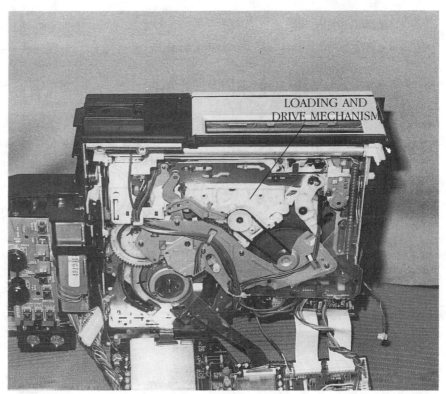

9-15 *The inside view of the loading and drive mechanism in RCA's CPR300 VHS camcorder.*

Pentax PV-C850A (8 mm) Subchassis Layout Components   The main components in the subchassis are the supply and take-up reels, tension arm and pin, T brake, guide pole, T band, operating TB slider, brake arm T and the tape select switches (FIG. 9-16).

When the cassette moves down, the subchassis slides forward and the chassis loading mechanism loads the cassette and winds the tape around the cylinder. The loading motor at the left rear of the chassis slides the subchassis to the front and loads. The subchassis drive pin slides the subchassis forward as the loading motor rotates to load the tape.

Pentax PV-C850A (8 mm) Main Chassis Components   The main components shown in the chassis are the loading mechanism and the main brake drive mechanism. The loading mechanism is located on the left side of the chassis (FIG. 9-17). Power from the loading motor, located on the chassis, rotates the drive gear, which is on the left bottom corner, to the L gear to pull the guide roller assembly, which is coupled to the L ring 1 and the L ring 0.

A cam gear is placed in front of the chassis and the pin at the left tip of this arm is connected to the cam groove, which is located behind the drive gear. This cam performs the following operations:

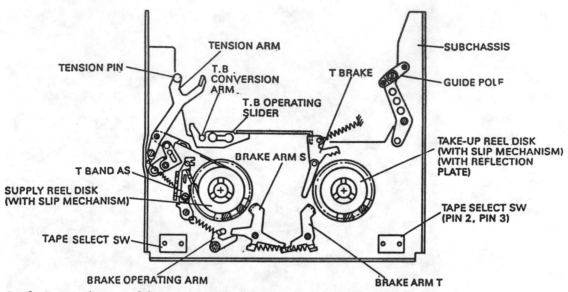

9-16 *Pentax layout of the main components in the subchassis.* Pentax

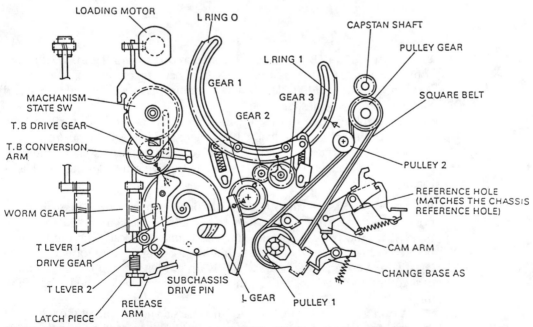

9-17 *Layout of components in main chassis of Pentax camcorder.* Pentax

- Slides the center gear up and down and switches between the transmission of weak and strong (Hi and Lo) torque on both reel disks.
- Turns the pressure roller on and off.
- Runs the brake mechanism.

The square belt transmits torque from the capstan motor through the pulley gear to pulley 1 to drive both reel disks.

Pentax PV-C850A (8 mm) Reel Disk Drive Mechanism The supply reel disks' slip mechanisms generate the torque necessary to eleminate tape slack and take up the tape during reverse visual search and unloading (FIG. 9-18). The take-up reel disk's slip mechanism works in the same way to eliminate tape slack and take up the tape during the take-up modes and visual search. This allows the slip torque on the take-up and supply sides to be independently controlled.

Loading motor force that moves the change base assembly plate up and down passes the capstan motor torque through the FRP and to the both reel disks. If the center gear assembly is set in the high position at this time, the capstan motor torque will pass through the slip mechanisms in both reel disks, causing the torque to become weak (FIG. 9-19). Setting the center gear assembly in the low position transmits torque directly to both reel disks.

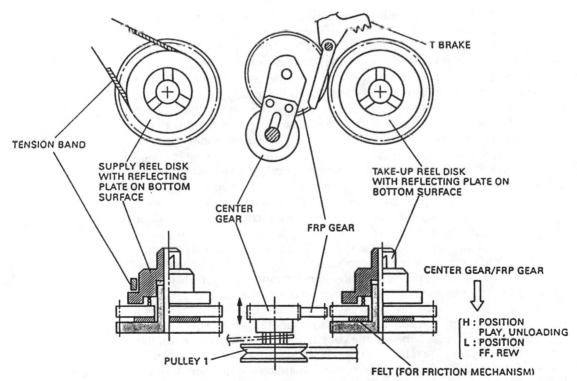

9-18 *Pentax PV-C850A (8 mm) reel disk drive mechanism.* Pentax

9-19   *Loading motor and mechanism in the RCA CPR300 VHS camcorder.*

Realistic 150 (VHS-C) Loading Mechanism   The loading motor provided on the right side of the chassis is the source of power for loading operations. During loading, the tape is drawn from the supply reel disk and wound around the cylinder (FIG. 9-20). The rotation of the loading motor is reduced by two worm gears and transmitted to the control cam gear. The rotation of the control cam gear is conveyed to the adjacent cam gear, the ring gear, and the lower supply loading ring, which is one of the loading rings located around the cylinder. The supply loading ring is fitted with the supply guide roller assembly, which will be set in the supply arm stopper (V block) along the guiding groove on the chassis as the loading ring rotates.

The supply loading ring is linked with ring gears 0 and 1, which transmit torque from the supply loading ring to the upper take-up loading ring. The take-up loading ring is fitted with the take-up guide roller assembly, which will advance along the guiding groove in the chassis as the loading ring rotates until it is set in the take-up arm stopper.

During loading, clutch gear S and the SC gear are linked with the supply reel disk to apply weak reverse torque to the supply reel disk to prevent slack tape. The T-brake pressing against the bottom of the clutch gear T applies brake so that the tape does not come out of the take-up reel. The middle pole is horizontal on the chassis before the tape is loaded. A pin provided in the supply loading ring lifts the middle pole as tape loading proceeds, and immediately before the completion of loading, it is set on the middle pole stopper. Then the middle pole holder provided on the arm of the A/C head locks the middle pole with the middle pole stopper. The A/C head is initially located under the mechanism state switch. As loading pro-

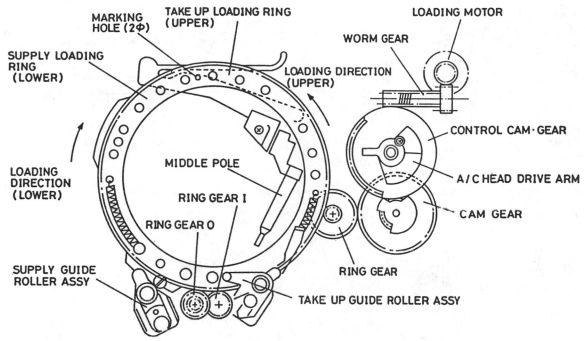

9-20 *Loading mechanism in the Realistic 150 (VHS-C) camcorder.* Radio Shack

ceeds, the AC head drive arm screwed to the control cam gear moves the A/C head to the play position. The pressure roller comes into contact with the capstan shaft, driven by the P-operation lever, which is linked with a groove provided under the control cam gear.

When loading is completed, the mechanism state switch detects the sixth position so that the loading motor stops and the VTR enters the play or record mode. The control cam gear driven by the loading motor has two cam grooves in the top surface and one cam groove in the bottom surface (FIG. 9-21). The B cam lever is linked with the outer of the two top-side cam grooves and drives main brake S. The TE lever is linked with the inner groove and drives the T-brake and eject arm on the take-up side through a rod.

Pentax PV-C850A (8 mm) Loading Mechanism   The loading motor located in the upper left hand side rotates the worm gear at the left front of the chassis. There are cam grooves in both the top and bottom surface of the drive gear, which is meshed with the worm gear (FIG. 9-22). The pin of the L gear fits into the groove on the top side and the force from the L gear goes through gears 1, 2, and 3, to the L rings 1 and 0. The pins of the guide roller assemblies for the supplied side and take-up side are inserted into the L rings 1 and 0, and when the L ring 1 moves counterclockwise and L ring 0 moves clockwise, the pins are pulled in the loading direction and placed into the catchers on the supply and take-up sides. The compression force at this time is applied by the tension spring, which is attached to the guide

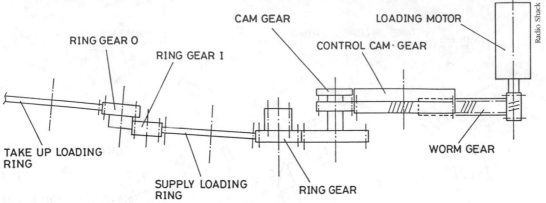

9-21 *Side view of the Realistic 150 (VHS-C) loading mechanism.*

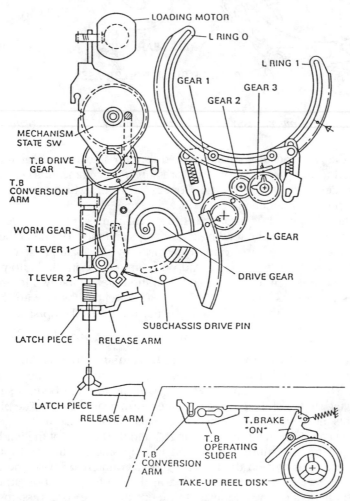

9-22 *Loading mechanism of Pentax (8 mm) VTR unit.* Pentax

roller assembly tension mechanism built into the tips of the L ring 1 and L ring 0.

At the moment that loading ends, the T.B. drive gear (take-up reel disk T-brake drive arm), which meshes with the drive gear, drives the mechanism state switch, which stops the rotation of the loading motor when it detects the PLAY mode position.

Realistic 150 (VHS) T-Brake Drive Mechanism   The TE lever is linked with the upper cam groove in the control gear. The TE operation arm is linked with the TE lever at its end through the TE operation rod (FIG. 9-23). The TE operation arm has a projection on the left side, which contacts one end of the T-brake. When the control cam gear rotates counterclockwise, the TE lever pin moves counterclockwise, driven by the cam groove of the control gear. In the TE operation, the rod is pulled upward and the TE operation arm turns counterclockwise so that the T-brake presses against the clutch gear T to weaken or stop (brake) the rotation of the take-up reel disk. The eject lever, linked with the TE operation arm through a rod, unlocks and lifts the cassette holder when the TE operation arm has turned counterclockwise completely.

Pentax PV-C850A (8 mm) Main Brake Drive Mechanism   The main brake engages the reel disks only in L. STOP mode. Since L. STOP mode is in the standby status in CAMERA mode, turn power off when stopped in this mode for a long period of time during camera recording to engage and hold the main brake on both reel disks (FIG. 9-24).

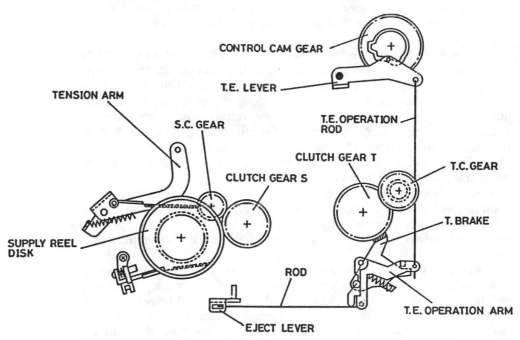

9-23   *T brake drive mechanism of the Realistic 150 (VHS-C) VTR.* Radio Shack

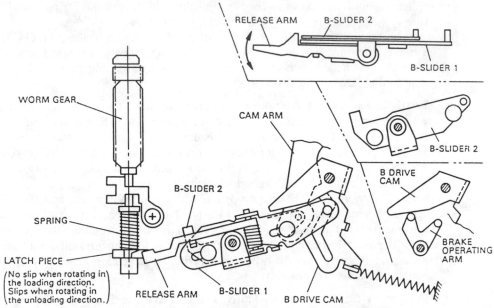

9-24 *Pentax PV-C850A (8 mm) main brake drive mechanism.* Pentax

When switching from the fast forward or rewind mode to the L. STOP mode, the main brake is applied in quick operation. Braking must be applied quickly in the fast-forward and rewind modes. Braking is applied at the normal speed in the record and play modes while the cam arm is turning.

In switching from the fast-forward or rewind mode to the L. STOP mode, the latch piece turns and the release arm lifts up simultaneously. This operation disengages the release arm and B-slider 2 and the force of the spring at the right-hand side of the chart rapidly pulls the release arm and B-slider 1, which is the pedestal for the release arm. Because the pin caulked to the right edge of B-slider 1 fits into the groove in the B drive cam, the B drive cam turns counterclockwise when B-slider 1 moves to the right. This operation turns the brake operating arm clockwise to engage the main brake on both reel disks.

Now when the loading motor turns in the loading direction, the mechanism moves from L.STOP mode to PLAY (REC) mode, the drive gear turns, and the cam arm turns clockwise, pushing B-slider 1 to the left. This operation turns the B drive cam clockwise and disengages the main brakes from both reel disks.

When in the PLAY mode and the STOP button is pressed, the loading motor will turn in the unloading direction to turn the cam arm clockwise and turn the B-slider counterclockwise, which turns the B drive cam counterclockwise and turns the brake operating arm clockwise to engage the main brake on both reel disks. When in the L.STOP mode and the FF or REW button is pressed, the cam arm and the B drive cam both turn clockwise to release the main brake.

Realistic 150 (VHS-C) Tension Arm Operation   The lower cam groove of the control cam gear is linked with the pin provided at an end of the P-operation lever (PRESSURE ROLLER OPERATION LEVER). The other end of the P-operation lever has teeth that engage with the teeth at the end of the adjacent gear arm (FIG. 9-25). The gear arm pin at the end of the gear arm is linked with the U-groove which is at the end of the T-operation lever (TENSION ARM OPERATION LEVER). The T-operation lever drives the tension arm as the left end of the lever applies force for a pin staked on the tension arm.

Pentax PV-C850A (8 mm) Tension Band and Reel Disk Drive Mechanism   The capstan motor rotates the center gear. The FRP gear oscillates to right and left in line with the center gear direction of rotation. This action is conveyed to the left and right reel disks to drive both disks (FIG. 9-26).

A tension band is wound around the supply reel disk and attached to the tension arm. As the S-guide roller pulls out during loading, the force from the spring sets the tension arm to play position. During unloading, the S-guide roller pushes the flat plate on the side opposite the tension pole to return that section to the STOP position. Adjusting the position of the stopper adjustment plate allows the angle at which the tape winds to be adjusted.

Realistic 150 (VHS-C) Pressure Roller Drive Mechanism   The lower groove of the control cam gear is linked with the pin of the P-operation lever (PRESSURE ROLLER OPERATION LEVER). As the control cam gear rotates counterclockwise, the P operation lever also turns counterclockwise (FIG. 9-27). The lower end of the P-operation lever has teeth that engage with the teeth in the adjacent gear arm. When the P-operation lever turns counterclockwise, the gear arm rotates clockwise to cause the pressure roller lever to turn counterclockwise. This moves the pressure roller near the

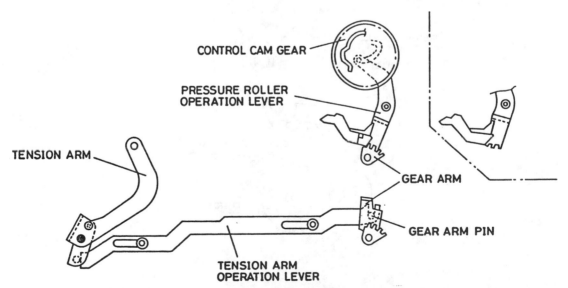

9-25   *Realistic 150 (VHS-C) tension arm drive mechanism.* Radio Shack

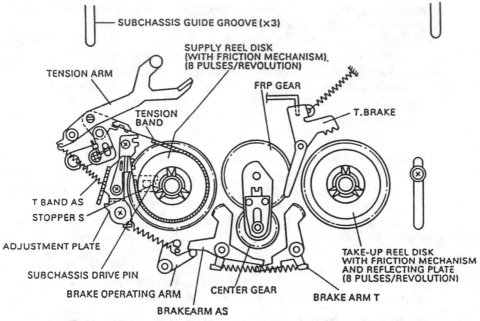

SUBCHASSIS GUIDE GROOVE (x3)

SUPPLY REEL DISK
(WITH FRICTION MECHANISM),
(8 PULSES/REVOLUTION)

TENSION ARM

FRP GEAR

T.BRAKE

TENSION
BAND

T BAND AS

STOPPER S

ADJUSTMENT PLATE

SUBCHASSIS DRIVE PIN

BRAKE OPERATING ARM

BRAKEARM AS

CENTER GEAR

TAKE-UP REEL DISK
WITH FRICTION MECHANISM
AND REFLECTING PLATE
(8 PULSES/REVOLUTION)

BRAKE ARM T

9-26   *Pentax PV-C850A (8 mm) tension band and reel drive mechanism.* Pentax

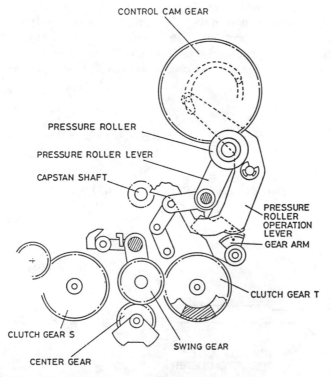

CONTROL CAM GEAR

PRESSURE ROLLER

PRESSURE ROLLER LEVER

CAPSTAN SHAFT

PRESSURE
ROLLER
OPERATION
LEVER

GEAR ARM

CLUTCH GEAR T

CLUTCH GEAR S

CENTER GEAR

SWING GEAR

9-27   *Realistic 150 (VHS-C) pressure roller drive mechanism.* Radio Shack

capstan shaft and the toggle mechanism brings the roller into contact with the shaft.

Pentax PV-C850A (8 mm) Pressure Roller Guide Mechanism The pin at the left tip of the cam arm connects with the cam groove in the drive gear and moves in line with the drive gear rotation. This movement causes the other tip of the cam arm to drive the pressure roller and to turn the pressure roller on and off (FIG. 9-28).

After the pressure roller is compressed against the capstan shaft, the turning of the arm, which was directly driving the pressure arm, stops. But since the cam arm continues to rotate, the pressure roller spring stretches to provide pressure force.

Pentax PV-C850A (8 mm) Record Pause Mode Pressing the PAUSE button during record moves the loading motor from the 6th to the 7th mode. This operation causes T lever 2 to move the T band AS, slacken the tension band, and aid the tape's reverse run. The capstan motor is operating in the reverse direction at this time to wind the tape on the supply reel disk.

The capstan motor is in stop state in either the record pause mode or the loading stop mode. When the pause mode is released during recording pause, the loading motor starts to rotate and performs the assemble operation while moving from the 7th to 6th mode.

The capstan motor turns in the forward direction in the assemble mode. Now the tape is played to match the phases between the new track and previously recorded track. However, monitor cut is performed and an EE picture appears in this period. The next record mode will be entered at one field before pause is turned on.

Sony CCD-M8E/M8U (8 mm) Ready-Rec Mode The drum will begin to rotate when the REC button is pressed. The loading motor is turned on and rotates M-SW clockwise (FIG. 9-29). When lever A moves in the direction of the

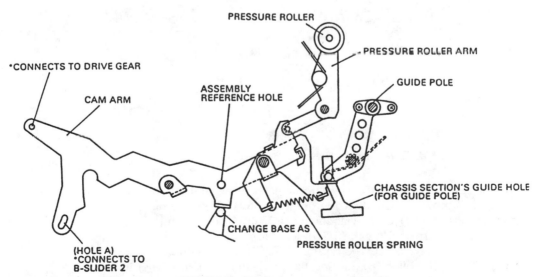

9-28 *Pentax PV-C850A (8 mm) pressure roller drive mechanism.* Pentax

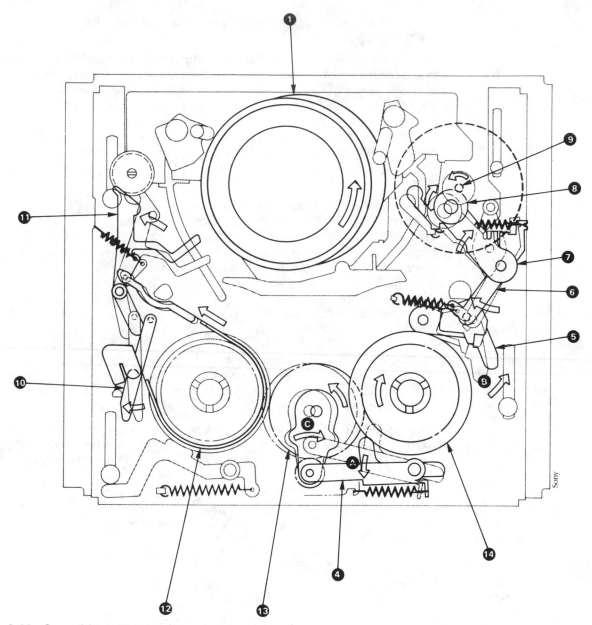

9-29 *Sony CCD-M8E/M8U (8 mm)* READY-REC *mode.*

arrow, it releases the cassette reel lock mechanism. Simultaneously, the pinch arm B moves in the direction of the arrow to press the pinch roller against the capstan (9), by moving the pinch arm (C) and pinch lever in the direction of the arrow. Now the TG1 release arm (10) moves the TG1 arm (11) to pull the TG1 band. The capstan shaft (9) rotates counterclockwise, turning the pinch roller (8), moving the pendulum gear arm (13) in the direction of the arrow (C) and rotating the take-up (T) reel (14).

CONCLUSION

Since the VHS-C camcorder operates somewhat like the VHS modes, the Realistic 150 and the Pentax PV-C850A camcorders were chosen to illustrate operation of the VTR mechanism. Although the operation description may be lengthy in some areas, you should have some idea how the VTR or VCR section operates. Always check with the manufacturer's service literature for detailed assembly charts and part location, especially when ordering the exact replacements.

Chapter **10**

Remove and Replace

*B*efore you attempt to repair the camcorder, you must get inside and locate the defective component. Cleaning and small-part removal may be done by first removing the cassette compartment cover. Sometimes you can locate the small parts on top of the VTR assembly. Try to locate the manufacturer's service manual on the camcorder you are servicing. This will save you a lot of time because most have different disassembly procedures.

Disassembly flowcharts provide certain steps to take in getting to the defective section of the camcorder (FLOWCHART 10-1). If you do not follow some type of procedure, you may lose a lot of time and remove parts that are not necessary. Of course, after replacing the defective component, reverse the disassembly procedure. Remove the cabinet plastic covers, camera section, and VCR deck in that order.

WRITE IT DOWN

If you do not have any method of removing the cabinet and components or no service literature, make drawings of components removed in step procedures. In step one, write down what you removed (covers and panels) and make rough drawings. Likewise, use the same procedure when removing any components. You may be called away from the bench and then forget where each part goes.

When removing the outside cabinet, place a cloth or soft material under the plastic cabinet so it does not get scratched. Lay cabinets out of the way after they are removed. Keep a cloth under the removed cabinet side to prevent pc board or component damage. Be careful not to break locking tabs or plastic inserts in removal. Remember where certain cable and wires lay if they stick to the cabinet panels.

When installing the new part or component, follow the manufacturers cleanup and lubrication of the moving part. Clean off all around the area for

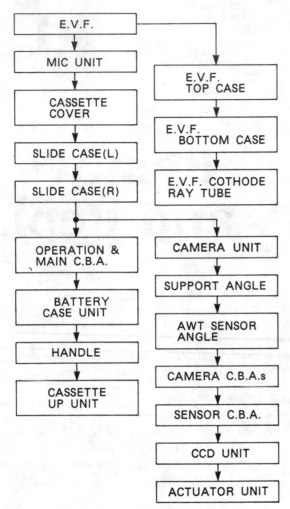

Flowchart 10-1   *A typical disassembly flowchart.* Minolta

loose dust or dirt. Do it very carefully, so not to disturb other components. Make sure that all connectors and electrical connections are made with correct polarity. Push the connectors and plugs in tight. Do not apply power or insert the battery while removing or replacing defective parts. Check for wires that may be misplaced keeping the covers from closing.

TOO MANY SCREWS

There seems to be several hundred different sizes of screws in the camcorder. Place the screws in a certain area or write down the length and where they belong. In the service literature, many manufacturers list the size, color, and length of the screw that hold the components in position. Be especially careful with the cabinet screws. Keep the correct pressure on such screws so not to strip or scar the top surface. If one or two are difficult to remove and replace, place black enamel paint over the screw head after the camcorder is fully tested. Make sure no loose screws are left over.

General Electric 9-9605 (VHS) Disassembly Flowchart This flowchart indicates disassembly steps for the cabinet parts and the pc boards in order to find the items necessary for servicing (FLOWCHART 10-2). When reassembling, perform the steps in the reverse order.

Follow the following proedures to prevent breakage:

- When removing the cabinet, work with care so as not to break the locking tabs.
- Place a cloth or some soft material under the pc boards or unit to prevent damage.
- When reinstalling, ensure that the connectors are connected and electrical components have not been damaged.
- Do not supply power to the unit during disassembly.
- Use a wrist strap to prevent ESD protection while disassembling and when operating the unit while disassembled.

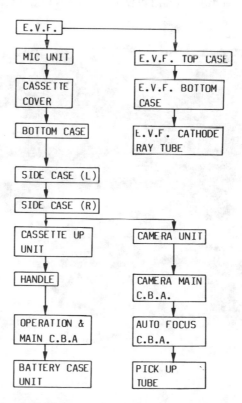

Flowchart 10-2 *General Electric 9-9605 (VHS) camcorder flowchart.*
Thomson Consumer Electronics

CASSETTE COVER REMOVAL

In some models, you can easily remove the cassette cover to clean or re-move any tape stuck. Remove two rubber inserts (one white and one black) and the two screws under the inserts to remove the cassette panel from the VHS RCA CPR300 camcorder (FIG. 10-1). While in others, the two top screws holding the cassette cover are removed and the cassette comes off. In many smaller camcorders, the side cabinet must be removed to get at the front components.

Pentax PV-C850A (8 mm) Cassette Lid Removal   When the camcorder is in the eject state, push in the cassette holder without inserting a cassette (FIG. 10-2). Remove the two top screws and tilt the cassette lid forward to remove it in the direction of the arrow.

Sony CCD-M8E/M8U (8 mm) Cassette Compartment and LS Cover Removal   Turn the eject knob to ON and put the cassette compartment in the "up" state (FIG. 10-3). Remove the cassette lid screws (2). Remove the cassette cover (3) by sliding in the direction of the arrow (A). When reinstalling, make sure the lid claws (4) fit into the two positions (5). While inserting thin flat blade screwdriver or other instrument, push on spring (6) in the direction of the arrows (C). When installing, make sure and set the claw (8) where it comes to the slot and claw (10) comes to the rear of the claw (11).

10-1 *Only two small screws hold the cassette door in the RCA CPR300 camcorder.*

10-2 *Remove two screws at the top to remove the cassette door in a Pentax PV-C850A model (8 mm).*

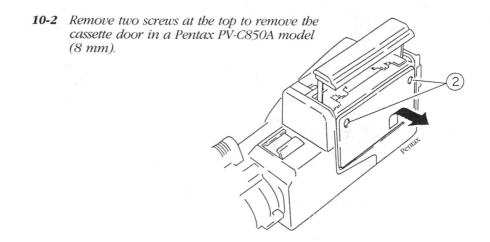

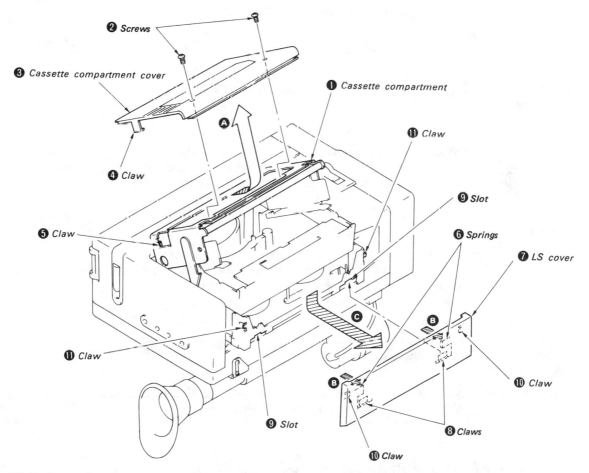

10-3 *Removing the cassette compartment in a Sony (8 mm) CCD-M8E/M8U camcorder.* Sony

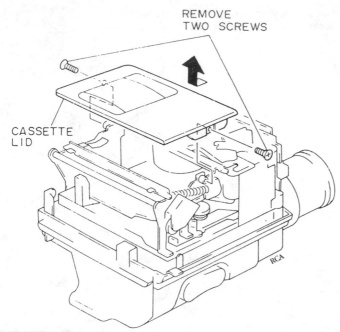

REMOVE
TWO SCREWS

CASSETTE
LID

RCA

10-4   *Take out two side screws to remove the cassette cover in the RCA CPR100 model.*

RCA CPR300 (VHS) Cassette Cover Removal   First remove the electronic viewfinder (EVF). Remove the microphone. Now, remove the left case. Remove two screws holding the cassette cover at each end (FIG. 10-4). Remove the cassette cover in the direction of the arrow.

CASE REMOVAL

To remove the outside plastic case to get at the components, simply remove the cassette lid. If the battery case is in the way, remove the cover. Now remove the left case or cover and then the right case or cover (FIG. 10-5). Remove the VTR block or chassis if trouble exists in the movement of tape.

General Electric 9-9605 (VHS) Left Case Removal   Remove four screws (D) (FIG. 10-6). Remove screw E (FIG. 10-7). Release the locking tab and lift the side case (L) unit slightly. Now disconnect the connectors on the left side (L) unit.

Minolta VHS-C C3300 Right Cover Removal   First remove the front cover (FIG. 10-8). Now remove the upper cover. Take out nine screws holding the right cover. Disconnect the connector CN105 on the LC pc board. Now the right cover is free and can be removed.

Pentax PV-C850A (8 mm) Right Case Removal   Remove the cassette lid and battery cover. Remove the eight screws at the top of the camcorder case (3) (FIG. 10-9). Remove the microphone in the direction of the arrow and

10-5 *Often, both side case covers must be removed for mechanical and electronic servicing. Here the right cover is removed in the RCA CPR300 camcorder.*

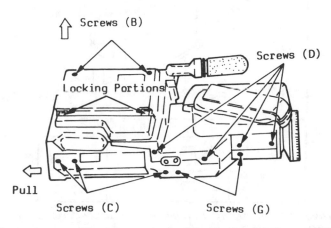

10-6 *Take out ten screws to remove the left case in the General Electric 9-9605 (VHS) model.* Thomson Consumer Electronics

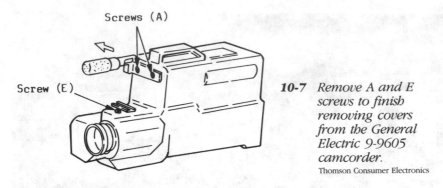

10-7 *Remove A and E screws to finish removing covers from the General Electric 9-9605 camcorder.*
Thomson Consumer Electronics

disconnect the mike cable connector. Remove the right case in the direction of the arrow. Remove the three remaining screws (3). Now pull the lid away from the camcorder.

VCR SECTION REMOVAL

To repair or replace any component in the tape path, the video cassette record and playback assembly must be removed from the cabinet. In some camcorders, a lot of components must be removed, while in others it's a breeze to remove the cabinet and VCR section. The cassette-up unit may be

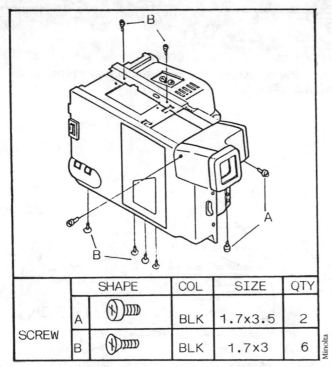

	SHAPE	COL	SIZE	QTY
SCREW A	🔩	BLK	1.7x3.5	2
SCREW B	🔩	BLK	1.7x3	6

10-8 *Take out nine screws to remove the outside covers in the Minolta (VHS-C) C3300 camcorder.*

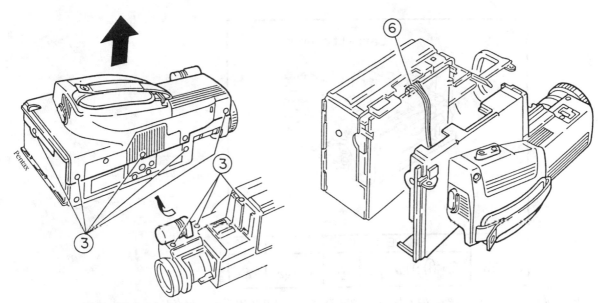

10-9 *Take out eight screws to remove the right case in Pentax (8 mm) PV-C850A model.*

removed in some VHS camcorders to get at the VCR components, while in the smaller units, the whole VCR section is removed. Keep all loose screws in a separate container. Check off the removed components.

Minolta C3300 (VHS-C) Cassette Housing Removal   Remove the four screws holding the cassette housing (FIG. 10-10). Now pull out the cassette housing from the deck block.

NEC V500 (VHS) Cassette Compartment Removal   After all side panels are removed, the cassette compartment may be pulled up after removing four corner screws (M) (FIG. 10-11). Now remove the cassette-up unit. When installing the cassette-up unit, make sure the cassette is in the closed (down) position. Check for correct seating of the cassette unit before replacing the screws.

Pentax PV-C850A (8 mm) VTR Block Removal   There are several different components to remove before the VTR block is free. Remove the cassette lid and battery cover. Remove eight screws holding the cabinet case together. Remove the microphone. Remove the left camera case and disconnect the cable connector. Remove three screws holding the body of the VTR block to the plastic case (6) (FIG. 10-12). Disconnect the two connectors (7). Now open the case in the direction of the arrow and remove the VTR block.

CAMERA SECTION REMOVAL

The camera section often comes out with one side of the cabinet. Then the camera unit must be separated from the cabinet. The EVF, microphone, and small accessories must be removed before the cabinet or case screws are

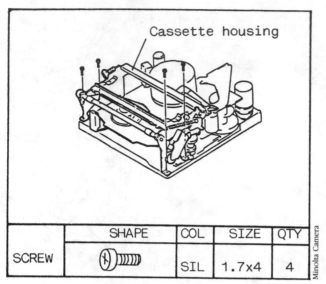

	SHAPE	COL	SIZE	QTY
SCREW		SIL	1.7x4	4

Minolta Camera

10-10   *Remove four screws to take out the cassette housing in the Minolta C3300 (VHS-C) camcorder.*

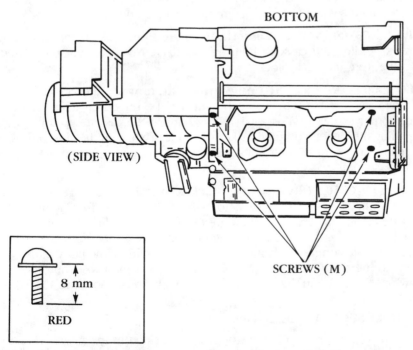

10-11   *In some camcorders, you need only to take out four screws to remove the cassette compartment.*

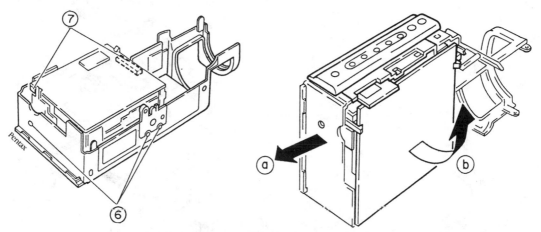

10-12 *Several different components must be removed before the VTR block can be removed in a Pentax PV-C850A (8 mm) camcorder.*

removed. In smaller camcorders, the camera (front section) is removed from the camcorder body. A full size view of all cabinet parts of a small Zenith VM6150 camcorder is shown in FIG. 10-13.

Olympus VX-801U (8 mm) Camera Disassembly Method Remove two gold screws holding camera and frame (FIG. 10-14). Remove two black screws holding the camera block to the plastic cabinet. Separate the camera unit from the frame and disconnect P1506 (start/stop) three-pin connector. In this condition, the camera part and the VTR part works if the 14-pin connector (P1001) is connected to the VTR and power is applied. The VTR is set in REC PAUSE condition when the tape is inserted because the start/stop switch is separated.

RCA CPR100 (VHS-C) Camera Section Removal First remove the electronic viewfinder (EVF) microphone, left case, cassette cover, left cover, and the VCR section. Now remove two screws holding the right case. Notice the camera section is attached to the right plastic cabinet (FIG. 10-15A). Disconnect the two connectors (CN1402) and CN214). Remove two screws holding the zoom switch circuit board holder (FIG. 10-15B). Pull out the camera section in the direction of the arrow. Disconnect connector CN52 (FIG. 10-15C).

Zenith VM6150 (VHS-C) Camera Section Disassembly Before the camera section can be repaired, the camera section must be removed from the deck section. Take out one screw (J) and one screw (K) on each side of the camera section holding the unit to the deck (FIG. 10-16). Carefully pull out the camera section in the direction of the arrow. Disconnect connectors (M), (N) and (O).

After the camera section is removed from the deck section, the camera is easily disassembled. Take out two screws (T) and two screws (U) to remove the camera lens section and circuit boards from the front panel (FIG. 10-17).

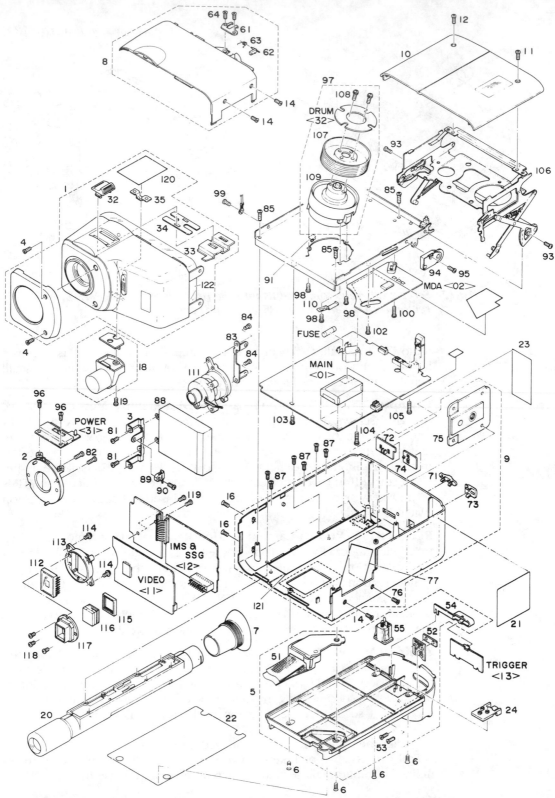

10-13 *The cabinet assembly component layout in the Zenith VM6150 camcorder.* Zenith

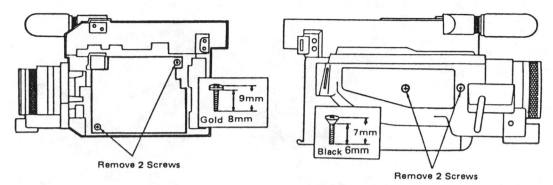

10-14 *Remove two gold and two black screws to take out the camera section in the Olympus VX-801U (8 mm) camcorder.* Olympus

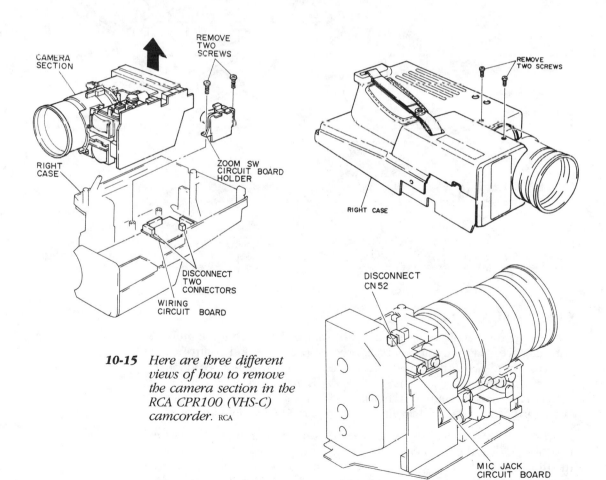

10-15 *Here are three different views of how to remove the camera section in the RCA CPR100 (VHS-C) camcorder.* RCA

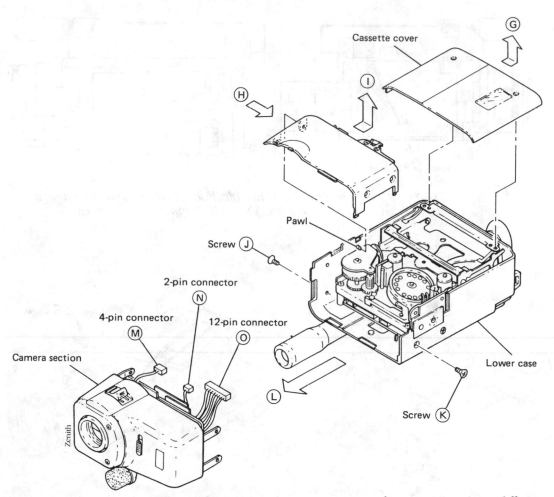

10-16 *Disassemble Zenith's VM6150 (VHS-C) camera section by removing three different sections.*

CIRCUIT BOARD REMOVAL

You may find several circuit boards in the camcorder called the luminance/chrominance, main circuit, interface process, regulator, and control circuit boards. These are little boards connected to the operating components throughout the camcorder. The smaller boards may consist of the input key, fuse circuit, sensor, autofocus, function switch, motor drive and audio circuit board (FIG. 10-18). You may find only two large boards in some units.

Pentax PV-C850A (8 mm) Main Circuit Board Removal   Release the two tabs holding the main circuit board (FIG. 10-19). Open the circuit board in the direction of the arrow. Disconnect the connector (1a). Disconnect four connectors (2). Now release the two tabs holding the circuit board.

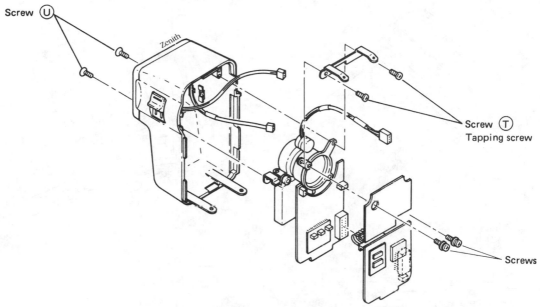

10-17 *Remove four screws to disassemble the camera section in a Zenith VM6150 (VHS-C) camcorder.*

10-18 *The main, sensor, and switch boards are shown in the RCA CPR300 camcorder.*

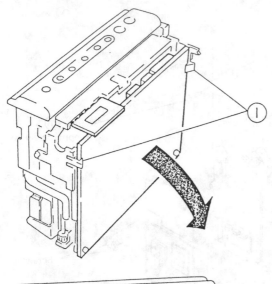

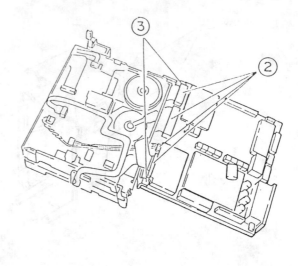

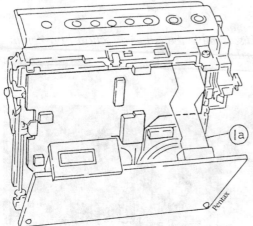

10-19   *Release the two tabs to let the main circuit board fold down in the Pentax PV-C850A (8 mm) camcorder.*

RCA CPR100 (VHS-C) Main Circuit Board Removal   See FIG. 10-20.

- Remove the EVF, microphone, left case, cassette cover, left cover, VCR section, and luminance/chrominance circuit boards.
- Remove one screw (1) holding the VCR board and the main circuit board.
- Remove one tab on the VCR board holder.
- Disconnect eight connectors (CN16, CN603, CN604, CN902, CN903, CN904, CN906, and CN908).
- Disconnect the following four connectors (CN16, CN551, CN905, and CN214).
- Remove the main circuit board from the head switch and function switch circuit board in the direction of the arrow.

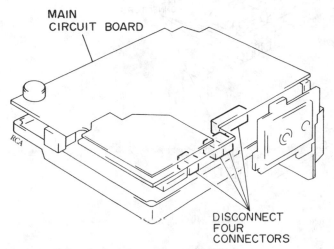

MAIN
CIRCUIT BOARD

DISCONNECT
FOUR
CONNECTORS

10-20 *Disconnect four connectors to remove the main circuit board in the RCA CPR100 model.*

Realistic 150 (VHS-C) Main Circuit Board and Switching Regular Removal Remove the VCR section. Remove the focus switch circuit board. Now remove the function switch circuit board. Remove the luma/chroma circuit board. Disconnect five connectors (CN415, CN416, CN603, CN903, and CN2) (FIG. 10-21). Disconnect the two flat cables (CN551 and CN901). Now remove one screw holding the main circuit board. Remove two screws holding the switching regulator. Disconnect connector CN951.

Sony CCD-M8E/M8U (8 mm) Camera Circuit Boards (VC-4, VC-5, and VC-6) To remove or open camera board VC-6, remove one screw holding the tripod plate (1). Remove the tripod plate (2). Bend claws (3) at two positions in the direction of the arrow (A). Now pull out the VC-6 board (4) in the direction of the arrow (B) (FIG. 10-22).

To open the VC-4 and VC-5 camera circuit boards, remove screw (1), screw (2), and screw (3). Open the VC-4 board (4) in the direction of the arrow (FIG. 10-22). Slide the VC-5 board (5) in the direction of the arrow (B). Now remove from the C board holder (6). Remove the VC-5 board (5) from the claw (7) and open in the direction of the arrow (C).

Pentax PV-C850A (8 mm) Process Board Removal Remove three screws (1) holding the process circuit board in place (FIG. 10-23). Lift up the process board in the direction of the arrows. Now disconnect ten connectors.

Realistic 150 (VHS-C) Luma/Chroma Circuit Board Removal

- Remove the VCR section.
- Remove the focus circuit board.
- Remove the function switch circuit board.

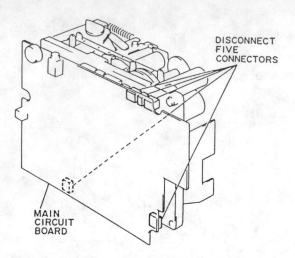

DISCONNECT
FIVE
CONNECTORS

MAIN
CIRCUIT
BOARD

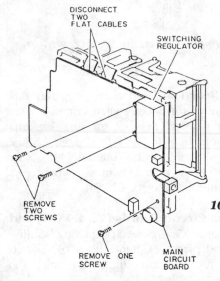

DISCONNECT
TWO
FLAT CABLES

SWITCHING
REGULATOR

REMOVE
TWO
SCREWS

REMOVE ONE
SCREW

MAIN
CIRCUIT
BOARD

10-21 *Three different views on how to remove the main and switching regulator boards in the Realistic 150 (VHS-C) unit.* Radio Shack

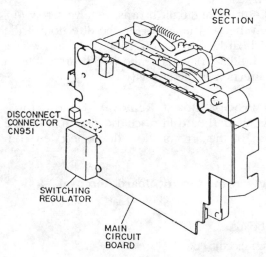

VCR
SECTION

DISCONNECT
CONNECTOR
CN951

SWITCHING
REGULATOR

MAIN
CIRCUIT
BOARD

1) Remove 1 screw **❶**.
2) Remove tripod plate **❷**.
3) Bend claws **❸** at 2 positions in the direction of arrow **Ⓐ**, and remove from VC-6 board **❹**.
4) Open VC-6 board **❹** in the direction of arrow **Ⓑ**.

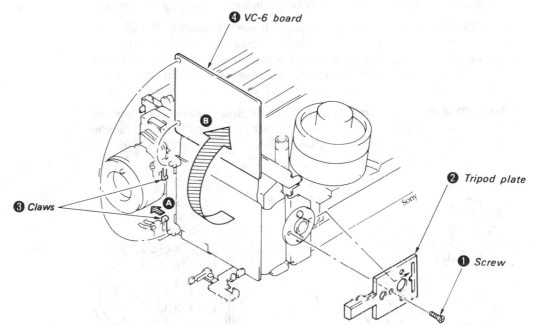

10-22 *Removing the VC-4, VC-5, and VC-6 boards in the Sony CCD-M8E/ M8U (8 mm) camera section.*

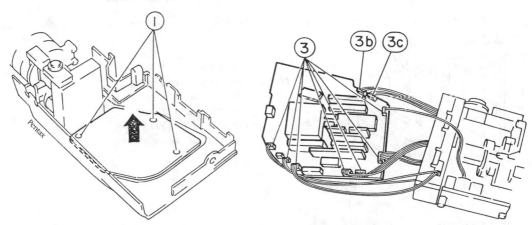

10-23 *Removing the process board from a Pentax PV-C850A (8 mm) camcorder.*

- Release the two tabs and remove the shield cover on the luma/chroma circuit board (FIG. 10-24A).
- Disconnect the flat cable (CN1) (FIG. 10-24B).
- Remove one screw holding the luma/chroma circuit board (FIG. 10-24C).
- Remove the luma/chroma circuit board in the direction of the arrow.

RCA CPR100 (VHS-C) Process Circuit Board Removal   Remove the electronic viewfinder, microphone, left case, cassette cover, left cover, VCR section and camera section. Remove two screws holding the process circuit board (FIG. 10-25). Open the process circuit board in the direction of the arrow. Now disconnect three connectors (CN1001, CN1002, and CN1103).

Pentax PV-C850A (8 mm) Sensor Circuit Board Removal   Remove one screw and take out the sensor shield cover in the direction of the arrow (FIG. 10-26). Remove two screws and take out the sensor circuit board. Now the sensor circuit board is free.

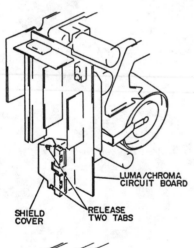

LUMA/CHROMA
CIRCUIT BOARD

SHIELD
COVER

RELEASE
TWO TABS

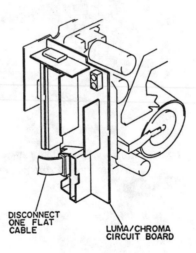

DISCONNECT
ONE FLAT
CABLE

LUMA/CHROMA
CIRCUIT BOARD

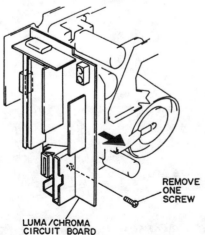

REMOVE
ONE
SCREW

LUMA/CHROMA
CIRCUIT BOARD

10-24   *Three views of how to remove the process circuit board in the Realistic 150 (VHS-C) camcorder.* Radio Shack

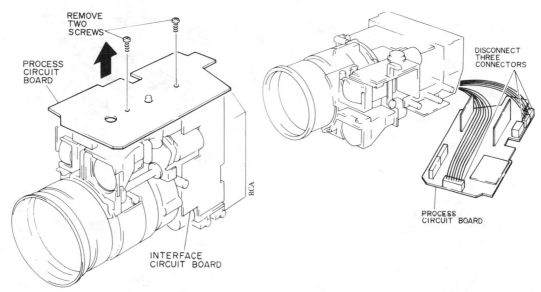

10-25　*Removing the process circuit board in the RCA CPR100 unit.*

Realistic 150 (VHS-C) Interface Circuit Board Removal　First remove the camera section. Disconnect two connectors (CN 907 and CN1401) (FIG. 10-27A). Release two tabs and open the interface circuit board in the direction of the arrow (FIG. 10-27B). Now disconnect three connectors (CN1A, CN5A, and CN6A) (FIG. 10-27C).

RCA CPR100 (VHS-C) Control Circuit Board Removal　Remove the electronic viewfinder, microphone, left case, cassette cover, left cover, VCR section and the camera section. Unsolder four points (CN1406) (FIG. 10-28).

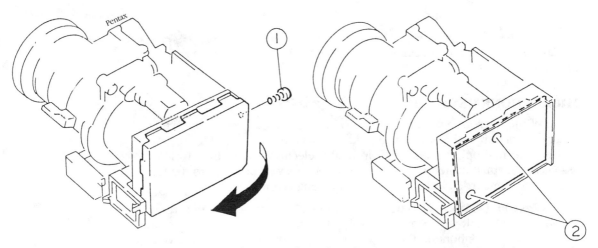

10-26　*Remove three screws to remove the sensor board in the Pentax PV-C850A (8 mm) camcorder.*

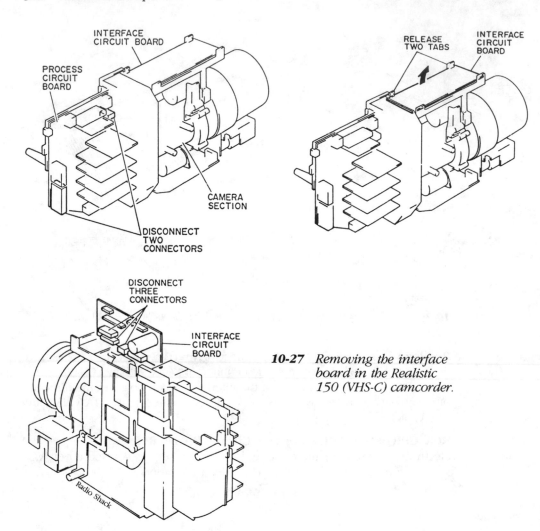

10-27 *Removing the interface board in the Realistic 150 (VHS-C) camcorder.*

Release one tab and then remove the control board in the direction of the arrow.

MICROPHONE REMOVAL

Some of the microphones are screwed to one side of the plastic case while others simply unplug from a mike jack (FIG. 10-29). In the RCA CPR300 camcorder, the microphone unscrews from the electronic view finder (EVF) assembly. In small camcorders, the microphone may be screwed to the top side of the camcorder with one or two mounting screws.

RCF CPR100 (VHS-C) Microphone Removal   Remove the electronic viewfinder (EVF). Remove one screw holding the microphone (FIG. 10-30). Remove the microphone in the direction of the arrow. Disconnect the connector CN51.

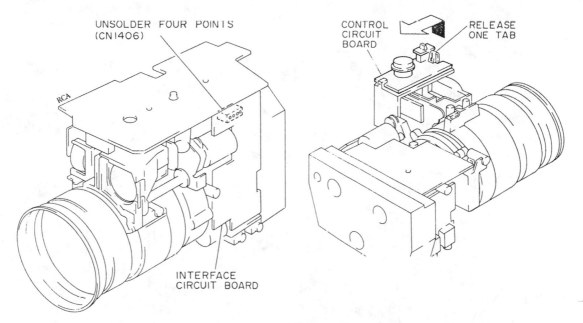

UNSOLDER FOUR POINTS
(CN1406)

RCA

INTERFACE
CIRCUIT BOARD

CONTROL
CIRCUIT
BOARD

RELEASE
ONE TAB

10-28 Unsolder four points and release one tab to remove the control circuit board in the RCA CPR100 (VHS-C) model.

10-29 Here in the RCA CPR300 camcorder, the microphone unplugs from the electronic viewfinder (EVF).

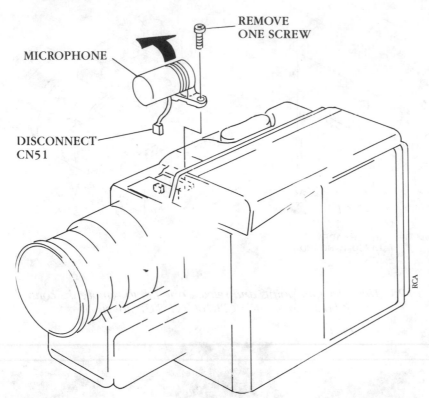

MICROPHONE

REMOVE
ONE SCREW

DISCONNECT
CN51

RCA

10-30   *Remove one screw to remove the microphone in the RCA CPR100 camcorder.*

Sony CCD-M8E/M8U (8 mm) Removal of Built-in Microphone
Remove screw (1). Remove optical viewfinder (OVF) in the direction of the arrow (A) (FIG. 10-31). Now remove two more screws (3) and remove the built-in microphone (4) in the direction of the arrow (B).

RCA CPR100 (VHS-C) Mike Jack Board Removal   Remove the electronic viewfinder, microphone, left case, cassette cover, left cover, VCR section, and camera section. Remove one screw holding the mike jack circuit board (FIG. 10-32). Release the tab and remove the mic jack circuit board assembly.

ELECTRONIC VIEWFINDER REMOVAL

Most camcorders have an electronic viewfinder (EVF). Smaller cameras may not have one, or you may find the optical viewfinder (OVF) as in regular cameras. Often, the viewfinder is mounted on top of the camcorder. In the RCA CPR300 model, the EVF locks in and slides off to the side (FIG. 10-33). Just unplug the cable and the EVF unit is free. In FIG. 10-34, the Canon VM-E2NA camera and EVF unit is laid out, showing the various breakdown of components.

1) Remove 1 screw ❶.
2) Remove OVF ❷ in the direction of arrow Ⓐ.
3) Remove 2 screws ❸, and remove the built-in microphone ❹ in the direction of arrow Ⓑ.

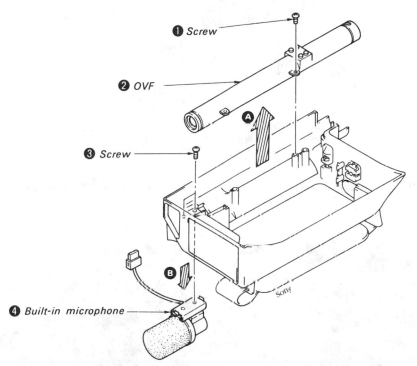

10-31 *Remove one screw to take off the built-in microphone in a Sony CCD-M8E/M8U (8 mm) camcorder.*

General Electric 9-9605 (VHS) EVF Unit Removal Remove three screws (N) on the bottom of the EVF unit and then remove the bottom case (FIG. 10-35). Remove CRT case (B) by separating the CRT case A and B. Lift the CRT assembly up to remove it from the CRT case. Pull the CRT socket assembly in the direction of the arrows.

Reverse the procedure for installing a new EVF unit. Be careful when installing the DY assembly (FIG. 10-36). Reinstall the CRT masking by sliding it onto the face of the CRT. Adjust the position of the DY assembly so that the V-shaped portion of the coil meets the projections of the CRT masking. This will align when the CRT masking is installed on the CRT case A properly. Confirm the display after installation.

Minolta C3300 (VHS-C) EVF Cover and Block Removal First remove the eye hood. Notice the top of the hood is smaller than the bottom when installing. Remove one screw (A) in the left cover and screw (B) in the CRT holder (FIG. 10-37). Remove the EVF cover opening of the right cover slightly

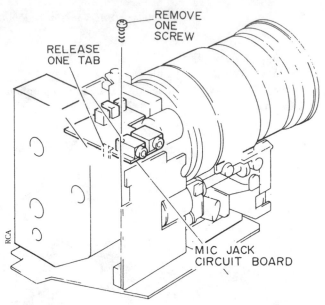

10-32 *Remove one screw and release one tab to remove the mike jack circuit board in the RCA CPR100 unit.*

10-33 *In the RCA CPR300 model, release the slide lock to remove the electronic viewfinder (EVF). Then unplug the EVF cable.*

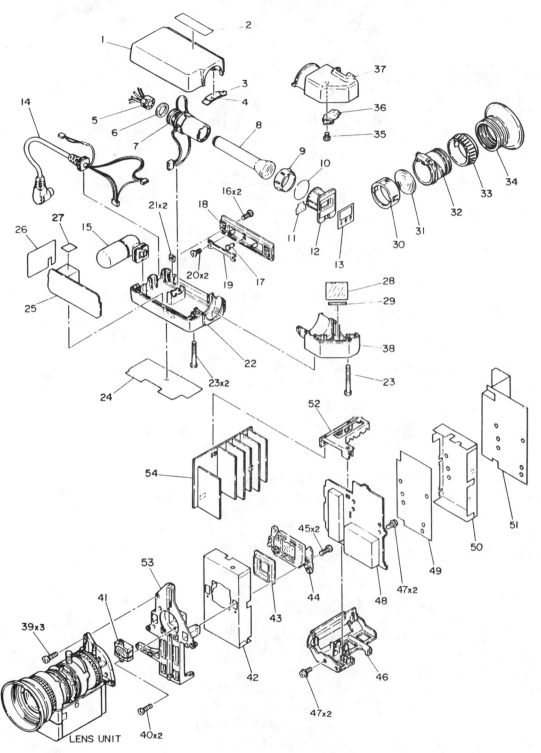

10-34 *The electronic viewfinder (EVF) and camera lens assembly is broken down into separate components of a Canon VM-E2NA camcorder.* Canon

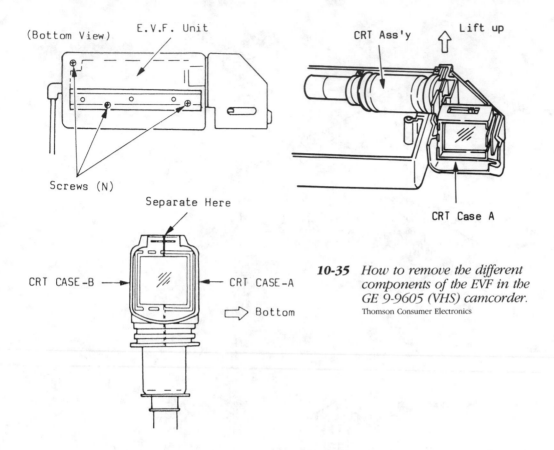

(Bottom View)   E.V.F. Unit

Screws (N)

CRT Ass'y   Lift up

CRT Case A

Separate Here

CRT CASE-B →   ← CRT CASE-A

⇒ Bottom

10-35   *How to remove the different components of the EVF in the GE 9-9605 (VHS) camcorder.*
Thomson Consumer Electronics

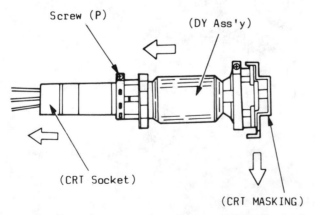

Screw (P)   (DY Ass'y)

(CRT Socket)

(CRT MASKING)

10-36   *Reverse the procedure to replace the new EVF tube in the General Electric 9-9605 (VHS) unit.* Thomson Consumer Electronics

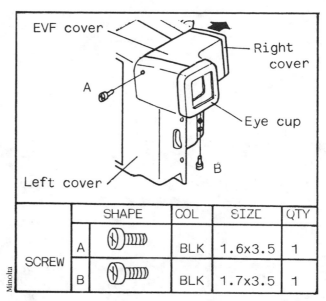

		SHAPE	COL	SIZE	QTY
SCREW	A		BLK	1.6x3.5	1
	B		BLK	1.7x3.5	1

10-37 *Removal of the EVF cover in the Minolta C3300 (VHS-C) camcorder.*

in the direction of the arrow. To remove the EVF block assembly, disconnect the two connectors, one is on the pw pc board and the other is on the VF pc board. Remove screw (A) holding the pw pc board, and then remove the pw pc board. Disconnect the lead wires in the battery terminal from the connector CN1 on the main pc board in the deck. Remove the screw (B) holding the EVF board. Now pull out the EVF board assembly.

Pentax PV-C850A (8 mm) EVF Removal Stand the viewfinder up. Remove the screw (2) underneath and take out the EVF in the direction of the arrow (FIG. 10-38). Disconnect the connector (3) and lift the EVF unit upward.

CCD SENSOR REMOVAL

The charge-coupled device (CCD) is in the latest camcorders, where the early models have small pickup tubes. The CCD sensor is subject to electrostatic breakdown like other C-MOS devices. Use extreme care when removing and installing the CCD sensor. Proper storage, handling and soldering must be performed to prevent damage.

Be careful not to soil the optical surface of the CCD image sensor with fingerprints or scratches. If soiled, wipe off and clean gently with a silicon lens tissue, chamois, etc. Sometimes a shield is placed over the CCD image sensor and should not be removed until ready to install. Quickly solder the sensor terminals. The optical filter of the CCD sensor can be discolored by excessive heat.

Minolta C3300 (VHS-C) CCD PC Board Removal Loosen the two screws (A) holding the sensor block assembly (FIG. 10-39). Remove the sensor

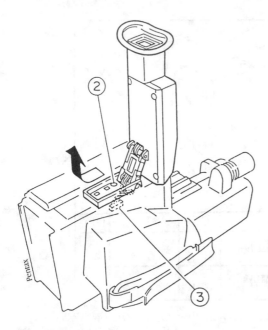

10-38 *Removal of the electronic viewfinder (EVF) in the Pentax PV-C850A (8 mm) camcorder.*

block from the lens block. Unsolder the CCD Pin on the CCD pc board. Always use a conductive mat and take precautions against static electricity. Now remove the screws (B) holding the CCD pc board.

Mitsubishi HS-C20U (VHS-C) CCD Image Sensor Removal   Take out two screws (A) and separate the optical block and imager board (FIG. 10-40). Remove three screws (B) from the filter holder (C) and remove the filter holder, filter (D) and rubber spacer (E). Take out two screws (F) from the image holder (C). Unsolder and remove the image sensor (H).

To install the CCD component, remove the protective seal from the CCD image sensor and place it on the imager holder (C). Then atop these,

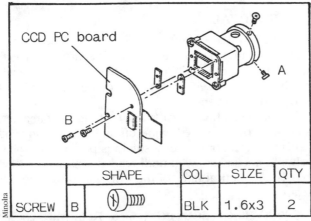

10-39   *Removing the CCD pc board in the Minolta C3300 unit.*

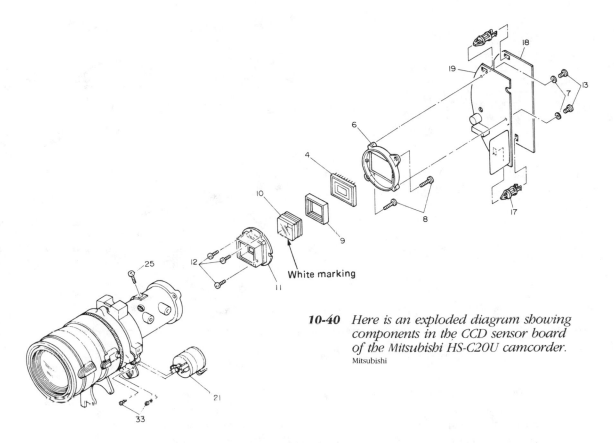

10-40 *Here is an exploded diagram showing components in the CCD sensor board of the Mitsubishi HS-C20U camcorder.*
Mitsubishi

White marking

place the rubber spacer, optical filter (D), and filter holder (C). Notice if the CCD image sensor is correctly oriented with respect to the imager holder board. Also, check that the masking of the optical filter is positioned at the lower front. Secure the filter holder to the imager holder with three screws (B). Now install the filter holder to the optical block with the two screws (A). Carefully insert the CCD image sensor pins protruding from the imager holder into the holes of the imager board and secure with two screws (F). Be careful when soldering the CCD image sensor pins.

PICKUP TUBE ASSEMBLY REMOVAL

In the early video cameras and camcorders, the Vidicon, Newvicon, and Saticon tubes used image pickup tubes in the VHS camcorder. These tubes may be removed from the front, rear or with the yoke assembly. The lens and filter assemblies must be removed if it comes out of the front of the camcorder. Most of the pickup tubes in the camcorder come out with the yoke assembly attached. Often, the front lens assembly is attached to the pickup tube holder.

General Electric 9-9605 (VHS) Pickup Tube Removal   After outside plastic cases are removed, take out the three screws (D) holding the coil holder (FIG. 10-41). Unsolder the target (H) lead. Now unsolder the tube

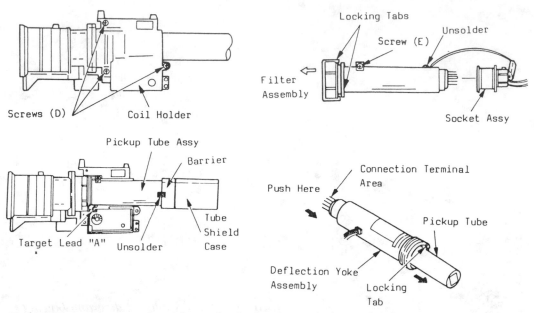

10-41 *How to remove the pickup tube in the General Electric 9-9605 (VHS) camcorder.*
Thomson Consumer Electronics

shield case to remove it and the barrier. Unsolder the lead on the pickup tube assembly and remove the socket assembly. Remove the filter assembly by unsnapping the locking tabs. Loosen screw (E) and remove the pickup tube from the deflection yoke assembly by pushing the tube at the connection terminal while unsnapping the locking tab on the face of the tube. Try not to touch the pickup tube surface when removing it.

To install the new pickup tube in the deflection yoke assembly, simply insert the tube through the yoke assembly (FIG. 10-42). Line up the two arrow marks on the face of the pickup tube with the two projections on the deflec-

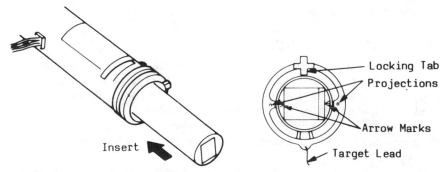

10-42 *Reverse the procedure to replace the new pickup tube in the General Electric 9-9605 (VHS) camcorder.* Thomson Consumer Electronics

tion yoke assembly. Now push the pickup tube into the deflection yoke assembly. Reverse the previous steps to reassembly the unit.

After replacement of the pickup tube, the following readjustments should be made. a slight touch-up may be needed on some adjustments:

- Target voltage adjustment
- Beam current adjustment
- Focus adjustment
- Rotation adjustment
- Back focus adjustment
- Beam alignment adjustment
- Vertical size/centering
- Horizontal size/linearity
- Bias light adjustment
- Horizontal centering adjustment
- Bias light shading adjustment
- R/B separation adjustment
- Dynamic focus adjustment
- Color shading adjustment
- R/B gamma adjustment

AUTO FOCUS AND POWER ZOOM ASSEMBLY

Before leaving the camera section, a few words should be noted about the AF zoom lens assembly. (The auto focus and power zoom motors are discussed in Chapter 7.) These two motors are on the lens assembly. The auto focus (AF) is controlled by the AF motor. The power zoom of extending a wide or close up scene is done with the zoom motor. The Macio lens may have a manual setting on most camcorders. Here in a Canon VM-E2NA camcorder is a breakdown of the various components found upon the lens section (FIG. 10-43).

TAPE TRANSPORT MECHANISM REMOVAL

Most of the mechanical problems are caused by the loading and tape transport mechanism. The VCR or VTR transport must often be removed from the camcorder for normal component removal and replacement. The tape heads and guide assemblies are fixed components found on the VCR transport. Replacement of the cyclinder, mode, loading, and capstan motors are discussed in Chapter 7. The many components found in the VTR and VCR assembly are shown in FIG. 10-44.

VIDEO HEAD REMOVAL

The video head (upper cylinder or drum) found in most camcorders is removed from the bottom section in replacement. The lower cylinder or

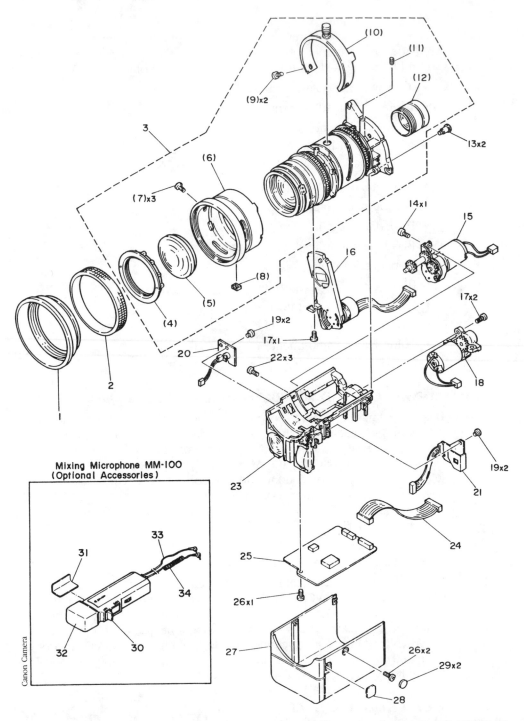

10-43   *The different components in the AF zoom lens unit of the Canon VM-E2NA camcorder.*

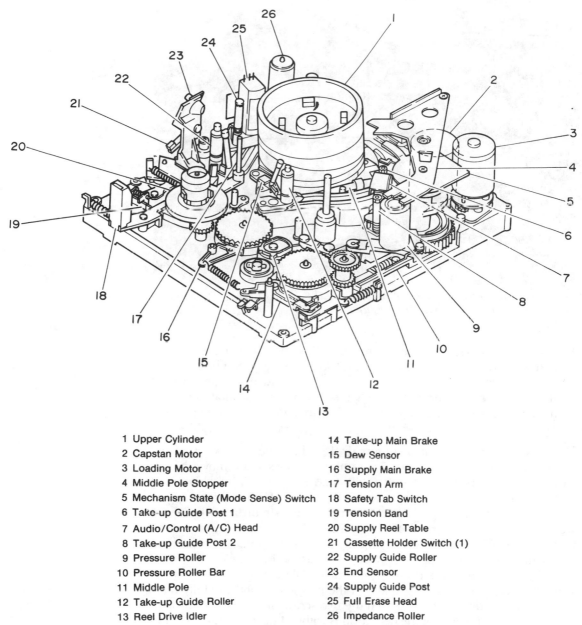

1 Upper Cylinder
2 Capstan Motor
3 Loading Motor
4 Middle Pole Stopper
5 Mechanism State (Mode Sense) Switch
6 Take-up Guide Post 1
7 Audio/Control (A/C) Head
8 Take-up Guide Post 2
9 Pressure Roller
10 Pressure Roller Bar
11 Middle Pole
12 Take-up Guide Roller
13 Reel Drive Idler

14 Take-up Main Brake
15 Dew Sensor
16 Supply Main Brake
17 Tension Arm
18 Safety Tab Switch
19 Tension Band
20 Supply Reel Table
21 Cassette Holder Switch (1)
22 Supply Guide Roller
23 End Sensor
24 Supply Guide Post
25 Full Erase Head
26 Impedance Roller

10-44 *The top view of the tape transport mechanism in the RCA CPR100 camcorder.* RCA

drum is with the motor assembly. The drum or cylinder (video head) leads must be removed from the upper drum assembly. Be careful not to touch the video heads with your fingers. Often, drum adjustments are required after installing a new upper head assembly (FIG. 10-45).

10-45 *With the cassette door removed on the RCA CPR300 camcorder, you can see the drum or cylinder assembly.*

Minolta C3300 (VHS-C) Drum Removal   Unsolder the eight lead wires of the upper drum assembly. Remove the two screws and then take out the upper drum (FIG. 10-46). Be careful not to touch the video heads with your fingers or tools. Alternately fasten the two screws when installing the upper drum. Always conduct the adjustments after exchanging the upper drum assembly.

Mitsubishi HS-C20U Drum Removal   Unsolder the lead wires of the upper drum relay pins (FIG. 10-47). Take out two screws and remove the upper drum in the upward direction. Install the new upper drum while using care not to touch the head tips or scratch the drum. After installing the new drum, use the micro-checker with its probe 2 to 5 mm from the upper circumference of the upper drum. Point the probe toward the center of the drum. At the point the probe just contacts the upper drum, set the scale to zero. While taking care not to apply pressure, use a drinking straw or similar tool to slowly turn the drum. Check for needle deflection within 4 microns. If greater than 4 microns, loosen the two screws and carefully readjust the upper drum position. Tighten the two screws in a balanced manner. Repeat this adjustment until the deflection is within 4 microns. After replacement, perform checks and adjustments for the playback switching point and FM waveform.

Pentax PV-C850A (8 mm) Upper Cylinder Removal   Remove the two top screws on the cylinder head (FIG. 10-48). Lift up the upper cylinder in the direction of the arrow. Do not touch the head tips (video head) with fingers or tools during removal and installation. Match the white point marking on the lower cylinder and the balance weight of the upper cylinder when in-

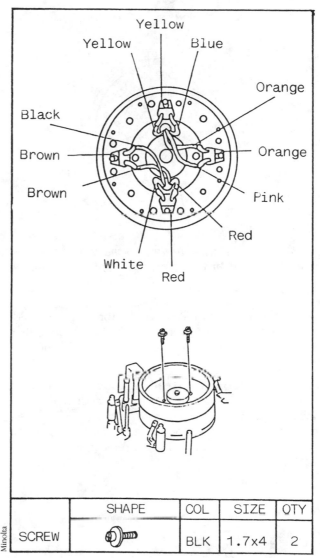

	SHAPE	COL	SIZE	QTY
SCREW		BLK	1.7x4	2

10-46 *Unsolder the drum wires before the upper drum assembly can be removed in the Minolta C3300.*

stalling. Now wipe the upper cylinder with a clean cloth. After reinstalling, perform adjustments necessary after the cylinder is replaced.

OTHER TRANSPORT PARTS REMOVAL

This section covers the miscellaneous tape transport parts in the various models.

Minolta C3300 Audio/Control (A/C) Head Removal Remove the cassette housing. Disconnect connector CN13. Move the A/C head to the load-

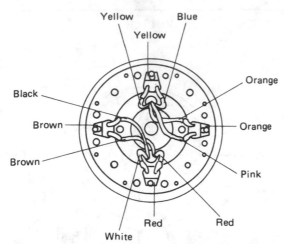

10-47 *Unsolder eight lead wires in the upper drum assembly before removing it in the Mitsubishi HS-C20U camcorder.* Mitsubishi

ing position (to the drum side). Remove the three screws holding the A/C head (FIG. 10-49). Take out the A/C head from the base mount. Be careful with the head spring in removing the A/C head. Adjust the A/C head after installation.

RCA CPR100 Audio/Control Head Removal Remove the cassette holder. Disconnect connector CN15. Move the audio/control head toward the upper cylinder (operation position). Remove three screws holding the A/C head (FIG. 10-50). Now remove the A/C head from the base. The A/C head height adjustment spring is removed when removing the head. Perform the

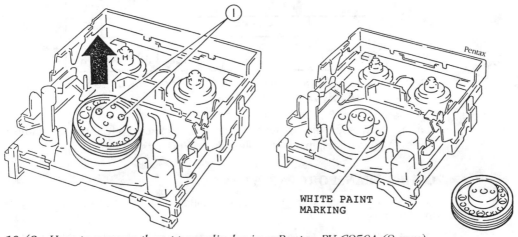

10-48 *How to remove the upper cylinder in a Pentax PV-C850A (8 mm) camcorder.*

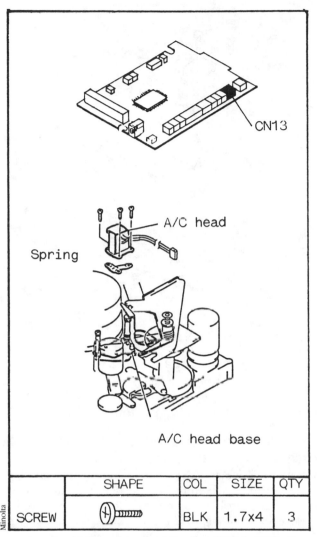

CN13

A/C head

Spring

A/C head base

	SHAPE	COL	SIZE	QTY
SCREW		BLK	1.7x4	3

Minolta

10-49 *Removing the A/C head in the Minolta C3300 (VHS-C) camcorder.*

audio/control head rough, height/tilt/azimuth, and horizontal position adjustments after installing A/C head.

Mitsubishi HS-C20U Full-erase Head (FE) Removal The full-erase head is replaced without removing the supply guide pole. Remove the slit washer and spring, and then remove the roller arm in the upward direction (FIG. 10-51). Gently press the erase head arm in the outward direction and remove the screw from the erase head arm and replace. Install the new full erase head in the proper position. Use a spare cassette tape and observe the tape running in the area of the supply guide pole. If tape curling or wrinkling occurs, perform supply guide pole height and interchangeability adjustments.

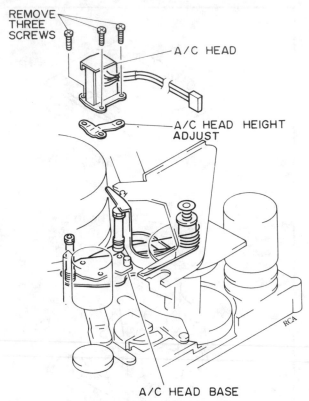

REMOVE
THREE
SCREWS

A/C HEAD

A/C HEAD HEIGHT
ADJUST

A/C HEAD BASE

10-50　*How to remove the audio/control head in the RCA CPR100
camcorder.*

RCA CPR100 Full-erase Head (FE) Removal　Remove the cassette
holder. Disconnect connector CN16. Remove the washer holding the impedance roller and spring between the impedance roller and chassis (FIG. 10-52).
Lift up the impedance roller and remove. Remove one screw holding the
full-erase head.

Pentax PV-C850A (8 mm) Supply End Sensor Removal　Unsolder two
points on the sensor (FIG. 10-53). Remove the screw holding the supply-end
sensor.

RCA CPR100 (VHS-C) Supply End Sensor Removal　Remove the cassette holder. Disconnect connector CN907 (FIG. 10-54). Remove one screw
holding the end sensor and cassette holder switch. Take out one screw
holding the switch to the end sensor.

Pentax PV-C850A (8 mm) Dew Sensor Removal　Remove the lower
cylinder (FIG. 10-55). Remove one screw holding the dew sensor. Disconnect
the connector on the motor drive circuit board.

RCA CPR100 (VHS-C) Dew Sensor Removal　Release the dew sensor
cables from the wire clamp plate. Disconnect one connector (CNPF) on the

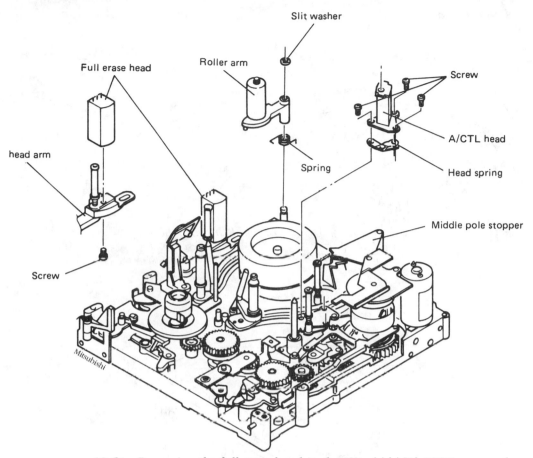

10-51 *Removing the full-erase head in the Mitsubishi HS-C20U camcorder.*

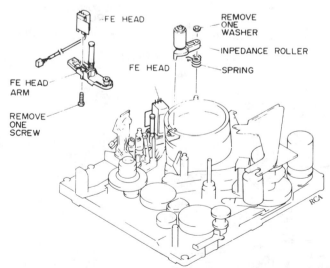

10-52 *How to remove the full-erase head (FE) in the RCA CPR100 model.*

10-53 *Removing the supply end sensor in the Pentax PV-C850A (8 mm) camcorder.*

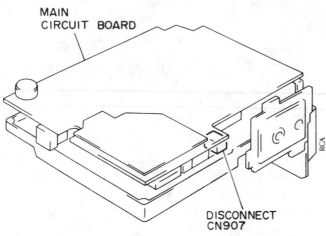

MAIN
CIRCUIT BOARD

DISCONNECT
CN907

10-54 *How to remove the supply end sensor assembly in the RCA CPR100 camcorder.*

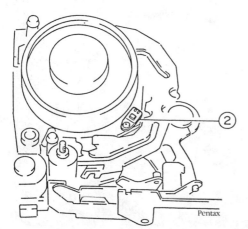

10-55 *Removing the dew sensor in the Pentax PV-C850A (8 mm) model.*

flywheel (FG) circuit board. Remove one screw holding the dew sensor (FIG. 10-56).

Minolta C3300 (VHS-C) Supply and Take-up Reel Sensor Removal
Remove the main pc board. Disconnect the connector CN-M1 on the MDA pc board. Remove two screws holding the MDA pc board (FIG. 10-57). Now remove the MDA pc board from the chassis. Remove the two screws—one holds the supply reel sensor and the other holds the take-up reel sensor. Lift up both sensors from the chassis.

Pentax PV-C850A Supply/Take-up Reel Sensors Removal   Refer to FIG. 10-58.

- Remove the cassette holder.
- Remove the sub chassis.
- Unsolder four points on each sensor.
- Remove sensors from the board.

Minolta C3300 Safety Tab Switch Removal   Refer to FIG. 10-59.

- Remove the cassette housing.
- Disconnect connector CN3.
- Remove the screw holding the Tab switch.
- Remove tab switch from chassis.

RCA CPR100 Safety Tab Switch Removal   Remove the cassette holder. Disconnect connector CN905 (FIG. 10-60). Remove one screw holding tab switch.

RCA CPR100 Mechanism State (Mode Sensor) Switch Removal
Remove the cassette holder. Remove three screws holding the middle pole

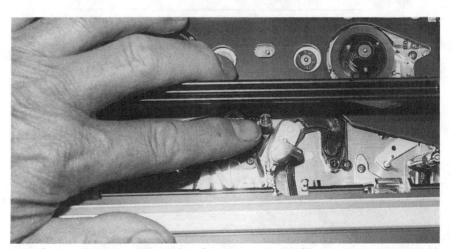

10-56   *The finger points at the dew sensor assembly in the RCA CPR300 (VHS) camcorder.*

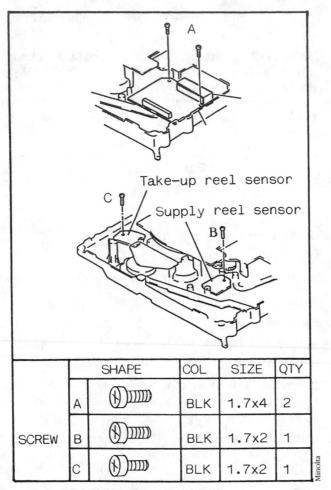

		SHAPE	COL	SIZE	QTY
SCREW	A		BLK	1.7x4	2
	B		BLK	1.7x2	1
	C		BLK	1.7x2	1

10-57 *Removal of the supply and take-up reel sensor in the Minolta C3300 (VHS-C) camcorder.*

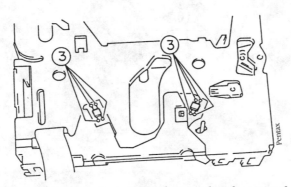

10-58 *Unsolder eight points to remove the supply/take-up reel sensors in the Pentax PV-C850A (8 mm) unit.*

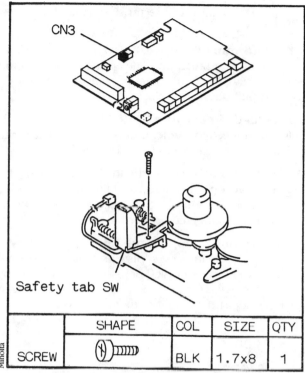

CN3

Safety tab SW

	SHAPE	COL	SIZE	QTY
SCREW	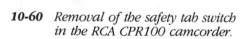	BLK	1.7x8	1

Minolta

10-59 *Removal of the safety tab switch in the Minolta C3300 (VHS-C) camcorder.*

10-60 *Removal of the safety tab switch in the RCA CPR100 camcorder.*

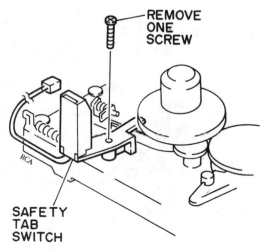

REMOVE
ONE
SCREW

RCA

SAFETY
TAB
SWITCH

stopper (FIG. 10-61). Disconnect connector CN902 and remove the state switch.

Pentax PV-C850A (8 mm) Pressure Roller Arm Assembly Removal
Remove the E ring (FIG. 10-62). Remove the spring hooked to the pressure roller. Lift the pressure roller arm assembly, taking care that it does not hit the guide pole, and pull out (FIG. 10-63).

Minolta C3300 (VHS-C) Impedance Roller Arm Removal   Remove the washer holding the impedance roller arm (FIG. 10-64). Release the torsion spring. Remove the impedance roller from the chassis.

RCA CPR100 (VHS-C) Take-up Guide Roller Removal   Remove the cassette holder. Remove one hex screw holding the take-up guide roller (FIG. 10-65). Turn the upper section of the take-up roller using the hex wrench to remove the roller from the guide roller base assembly.

Pentax PV-C850A (8 mm) Supply and Take-up Reel Disk Removal
Remove the two screws on the cover plate (FIG. 10-66). Take out the plate cover to remove the take-up reel disk. Remove top washer and pull up reel disk. The tension band assembly must be removed to get at the supply reel disk. After installing, adjust the height of the reel disks (FIG. 10-67).

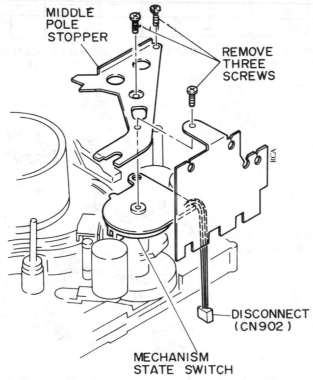

MIDDLE
POLE
STOPPER

REMOVE
THREE
SCREWS

RCA

DISCONNECT
(CN902)

MECHANISM
STATE SWITCH

10-61   *How to remove the mechanism state switch in the RCA CPR100 (VHS-C) model.*

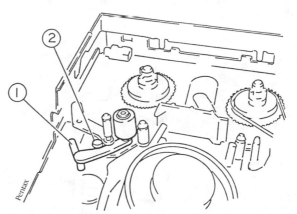

10-62 *How to remove the pressure roller arm assembly in the Pentax PV-C850A (8 mm) camcorder.*

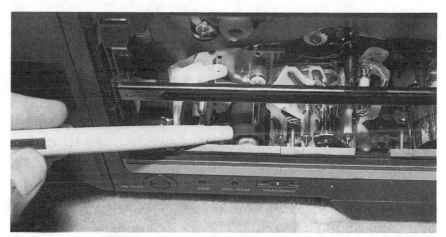

10-63 *The pen points to the pressure roller assembly in the RCA CPR300 camcorder.*

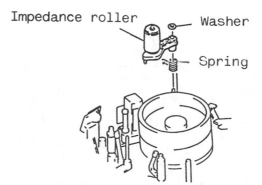

10-64 *How to remove the impedance roller in the Minolta C3300 (VHS-C) tape transport.* <small>Minolta</small>

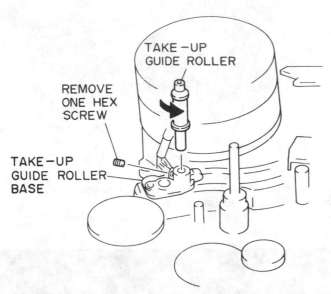

10-65 *Removing the take-up guide roller in the RCA CPR100 camcorder.* RCA

Olympus VX-801U (8 mm) Tension Band Replacement Method
Remove the top ring supply reel table and then remove the supply reel table (FIG. 10-68). Remove the spring. Remove the top ring of the tension unit and remove the tension band unit. Install the new tension band unit and assemble the unit subject to the reverse steps. Adjust tension adjustment procedures.

Mitsubishi HS-C20U (VHS-C) Supply Guide Pole Removal
The guide poles serves to improve tape transport stability between the cassette output and drum input by maintaining the required height. Adjust the supply guide rollers for smooth tape movement (FIG. 10-69). Remove the screw at the top of assembly and pull off the guide pole.

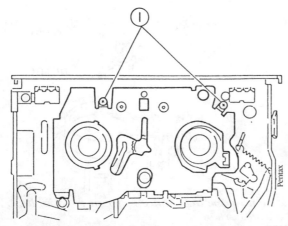

10-66 *How to remove the supply and take-up reel disks in the Pentax PV-C850A (8 mm) camcorder.*

10-67 *A close-up view of the supply and take-up reels in the RCA CPR300 (VHS) camcorder.*

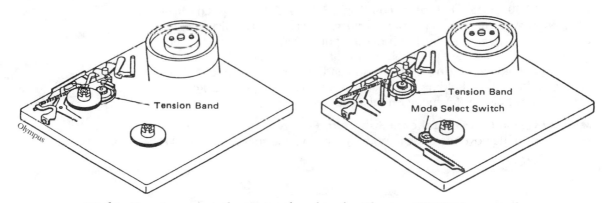

10-68 *How to remove the tension band in the Olympus VX-801U camcorder.*

10-69 *How to remove the guide poles in the Mitsubishi HS-C20U (VHS-C) tape path.* Mitsubishi

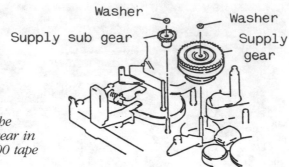

10-70 *How to remove the supply and sub gear in the Minolta C3300 tape chassis.* Minolta

Minolta C3300 (VHS-C) Supply Gear and Subgear Removal   Remove the cassette housing (FIG. 10-70). Remove the supply reel disk. Remove the washer holding the supply subgear. Take out the washer holding the supply gear. Now remove the supply gear and subgear from the chassis.

Pentax PV-C850A (8 mm) Loading Cam Gear Removal   Remove the cassette holder (FIG. 10-71). Remove the subchassis. Remove the loading drive gear. Lift up the loading cam gear in the direction of the arrow. After reinstalling, adjust the mechanism state switch position.

RCA CPR100 (VHS-C) Supply Loading Ring and Take-up Loading Ring Removal   Remove the lower cylinder, wire clamp plate, flywheel FG circuit board, capstan flywheel, and middle pole lever. Remove one washer (1) holding the loading (4) and pull out loading gear (FIG. 10-72). Remove one washer (1) holding the ring idler gear (1) and pull out the ring idler gear. Take out the washer holding the ring idler gear (2) and pull off. Remove three E rings holding the supply and take-up loading ring.

Minolta C3300 (VHS-C) Take-up Subbrake Removal   Remove the cassette housing. Remove the cassette housing. remove the supply main brake

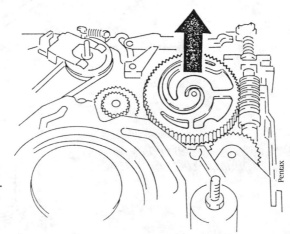

10-71 *Removing the loading cam gear in the Pentax PV-C850A (8 mm) camcorder.*

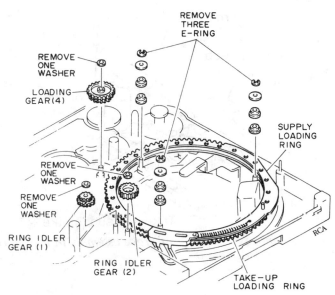

10-72 *Removing the supply loading and take-up loading rings in the RCA CPR100 (VHS-C) transport.*

and take-up main brake. Remove the take-up reel gear (FIG. 10-73). Remove the E ring holding the control plate (2).

Now remove the subbrake arm. Remove the spring that is between the take-up subbrake and the chassis. Remove the screw holding the take-up subbrake. Remove the take-up subbrake from the chassis.

RCA CPR100 (VHS-C) Supply Guide Roller Base Removal Remove the cassette holder, lower cylinder, wire clamp plate, cylinder motor drive circuit board, flywheel FG circuit board and the capstan flywheel. Now remove (1) screw holding the supply guide roller base (FIG. 10-74).

Minolta C3300 (VHS-C) Take-up Guide Roller Base Removal Remove the main pc board, cassette housing, lower drum, wire clamp, MDA pc board, FG pc board, and flywheel. Remove the screw holding the take-up guide roller base (FIG. 10-75). Now remove the take-up guide roller base from the take-up loading ring.

RCA CPR100 (VHS-C) Capstan Flywheel Removal Remove the cassette holder and flywheel FG circuit board. Remove three (3) screws holding the capstan flywheel (FIG. 10-76). Now take off capstan and pulley belt. Pull out the capstan flywheel.

Although removing all of the components in the camcorder can not be shown here, at least one has the idea how to remove and what is involved in replacement. Always follow the manufacturer's service manual, if handy. If not, write down or draw a rough sketch of where each part goes. Correct removal and replacement of the component is just as important as locating it.

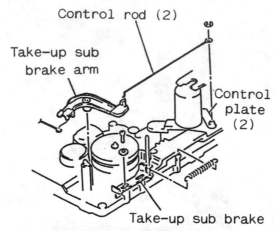

Control rod (2)

Take-up sub
brake arm

Control
plate
(2)

Take-up sub brake

10-73 *How to remove the take-up subbrake assembly in the Minolta C3300 camcorder.* Minolta

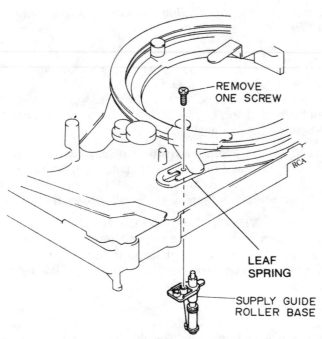

REMOVE
ONE SCREW

RCA

LEAF
SPRING

SUPPLY GUIDE
ROLLER BASE

10-74 *Removing the supply guide roller base in the RCA CPR100 camcorder.*

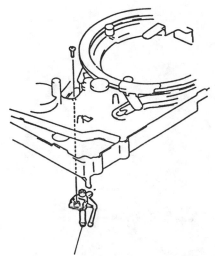

Take-up guide roller base

10-75 *Remove one screw to remove the take-up roller base in the Minolta C3300 tape transport.* Minolta Camera

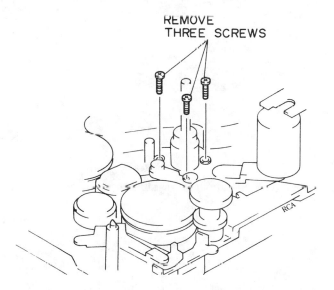

REMOVE
THREE SCREWS

10-76 *Remove three screws to take out the capstan flywheel assembly in the RCA CPR100 camcorder.*

Chapter **11**

Mechanical Adjustments

*T*here are from 10 to 20 mechanical adjustments to be made in the camcorder after replacing certain parts and for better play/record operation. In the smaller camera there are less mechanical adjustments to be made due to size. Some of the adjustments may be made with visual means, while in others, alignment tapes, operation fixtures, and critical test equipment must be used. Besides test equipment, several small special hand tools are required.

IMPORTANT PRECAUTIONS

Always disconnect the camcorder from the power (battery or ac adaptor) before removing or soldering components. Be careful when removing small screws, bolts, or washers so not to drop them inside the unit's mechanical areas. Retrieve all loose parts. When removing a component, be careful not to damage or dislodge other parts (FIG. 11-1). Be careful when working around the tape guides and video head drum to prevent breaking or scratching the video head surface. Do not try to make important mechanical adjustments without the correct test equipment and alignment tapes. Always follow the manufacturer's alignment procedures. Remember, some manufacturers have made precise adjustment at the factory, like the tape transport mechanism, that ordinarily do not require adjustment.

TEST EQUIPMENT

Most manufacturers require the alignment and torque meter cassettes (FIG. 11-2). Some manufacturers require certain patch cords, adjustment plates, and fixtures. Besides the regular bench tools, special head drivers, torque gauge adapter tools, height jigs, and special screwdrivers are needed for certain adjustments. Check the manufacturer's servicing tool list before attempting any electrical or mechanical adjustments (FIG. 11-3).

11-1   *The mechanical transport section of the RCA CPR300 camcorder.*

PRELIMINARY ADJUSTMENT STEPS

After replacing or adjusting the tape guide posts, check the coarse adjustment of the guide posts' height to confirm the linearity envelope output on the scope.

When repairing or installing a new upper drum or complete cylinder unit, confirm the envelope output with the scope and make fine adjustments of the A/C head in the horizonal position (VHS and VHS-C models). Do not change the position of P1 and P4, tape transport posts (FIG. 11-4).

Alighnment tape MH–C1 7982–8012–01	Cassette torque meter 7982–8010–01	Patch cord 2705–0005–75	A/C head pre-set driver 2705–0001–75

Mirolta

11-2   *Minolta C3300 (VHS-C) jigs and adjustment equipment.*

Ref No.	Name	Part No.	Jig	Usage and Others
J1	Cleaning fluid	Y-2031-001-0		
J2	Chamois cloth	2-034-697-00		
J3	Head degausser	Widely available		
J4	Small adjustment mirror	J-6080-028-A	SL5052	Tape path
	Spare mirror	J-6080-030-1		
J5	Alignment tape (WR5-1N)	8-967-995-01		Tape path
J6	Dial tension gauge	J-6080-827-A		Various torque measurement
J7	Tension measurement reel	J-6080-831-A		With φ30 tape
J8	Tension measurement reel	J-6080-832-A		With φ16 string
J9	FWD and RVS winding torque cassette	J-6080-624-A	GD-2086	
J10	Rotary drum jig	(Packed with the repair rotary upper drum)		
J11	Screwdriver for tape path	J-6080-811-A		For tape guide adjustment
J12	Mode selector II panel	J-6080-844-A		
J13	Mode selector	J-6080-825-A		For all models
J14	Mode selector II conversion connector	J-6080-845-A		
J15	Tape end detecting filter	J-6080-848-A		Tape end detecting adjustment

Other equipment
- Oscilloscope
- Analog tester (20 kΩ)

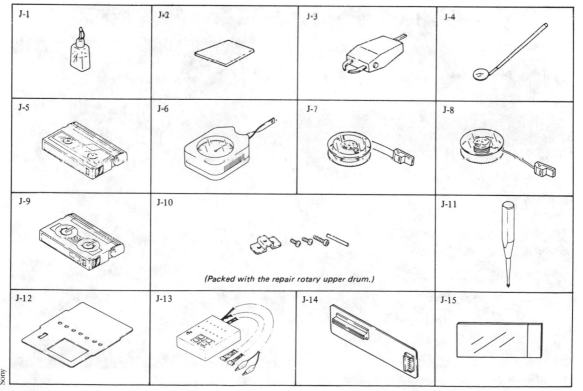

11-3 *List of service jigs and alignment equipment for Sony CCD-M8E/M8U (8 mm) camcorder.*

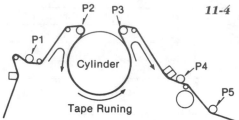

11-4 *The loading post location with a VHS cylinder and tape running path.*

After reinstalling all new posts or if any adjustments have been made to the tape guide posts, make coarse adjustments of each tape guide post's height, confirm the tape transport, readjust the pullout post (P5) height, confirm the A/C head tilt (VHS and VHS-C), and confirm the envelope output with the scope (FIG. 11-5).

When installing the A/C head (VHS and VHS-C), confirm the A/C head tilt. Do not change height of P4 post. Adjust the A/C head coarse height, the A/C head height and azimuth, horizontal course adjustment of the A/C head, and fine horizontal adjustment of the A/C head position.

After installing or adjusting the P4 Post, make the coarse adjustment of the tape guide post heights (only P4 post), confirm the tape transport, confirm the A/C head tilt, and confirm the envelope linearity output on the

11-5 *Guide post positions in the RCA CPR300 VTR section.*

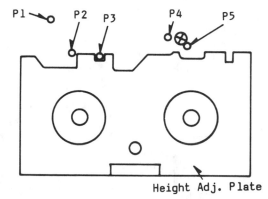

11-6　*Height adjustment plate of General Electric 9-9605 (VHS) chassis.*
Thomson Consumer Electronics

scope. When installing the pullout post (P5) readjust the pullout post position. Do not readjust any other post after the P5 post. After making several of these post adjustments, you may need to only touch up one or two post heights for accurate running of the tape.

General Electric 9-9605 (VHS) Tape Posts Height Adjustment　The required adjustment tools consist of a hex wrench, post adjustment plate, reel table height fixture, nut driver, and post adjustment screwdriver. The steps are as follows,

- Remove the cassette compartment from the mechanical chassis and cylinder barrier.
- Put the post adjustment plate on the chassis (FIG. 11-6).
- Install the post adjustment plate and move all posts if required so that they are in the exact position for STOP mode. (Lower end of post and tape guide should be lower than foot scraper of fixture.) Loosen the hex screw located on the lower portion of post P2 and P3 and turn the top of the posts with the post adjustment screwdriver. (Remove the plastic piece on the slanted loading pin of P2 to make the adjustment and replace after adjustment.) (FIG. 11-7).
- Place the height fixture on the adjustment plate and place the foot scraper guage next to the post.
- Set the height fixture to zero, and slowly raise the post until it touches the foot scraper of fixture. Use a nut driver on P1, P4, and P5 (FIG. 11-8). (Upon completion of adjustment, tighten hex screws on P2 and P3.)
- Reinstall the cassette compartment. Now play back a normal video cassette tape and make sure that the edges of the tape are not curling against the edge of any of the posts (FIG. 11-9). If curling appears, readjust each post.

Olympus VX 801 (8 mm) Tape Deck Mechanism Adjustment　This adjustment is necessary following the replacement of major parts in the tape running path, such as cylinder motor, posts, etc. The main purpose of this

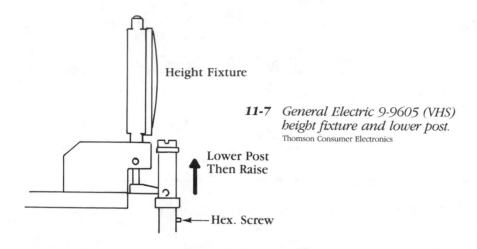

Height Fixture

Lower Post
Then Raise

Hex. Screw

11-7   *General Electric 9-9605 (VHS)
height fixture and lower post.*
Thomson Consumer Electronics

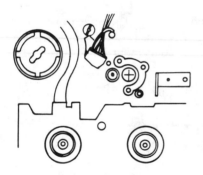

11-8   *Height fixture of General Electric
9-9605 (VHS) post adjustment.*
Thomson Consumer Electronics

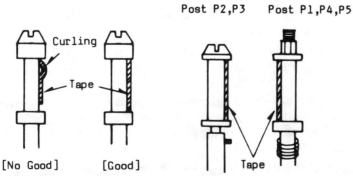

Post P2,P3   Post P1,P4,P5

Curling

Tape

Tape

[No Good]   [Good]

11-9   *Check for curling of tape on posts of the General Electric 9-9605
(VHS).* Thomson Consumer Electronics

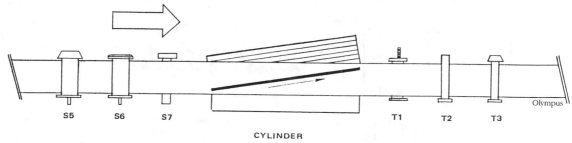

11-10 *Olympus VX-801 (8 mm) tape deck mechanism post and cylinder with respect to the tape path.*

adjustment is to compensate for the large deviation in the components, which, taken together, constitute the tape drive mechanism. You may use a regular record/play test for this adjustment.

The adjustment points are posts T1, T2, T3, S6, and S7 (FIG. 11-10). The measurement points are the posts and cylinder. No tape warp or spillover should be noted on any of the posts. Place the VTR in playback mode. Use a driver post adjustment tool.

Playback a conventional record/play test tape. Check that the tape makes firm contact with the cylinder tape guide. If a gap exists between the tape and the cylinder head or tape spillover occurs, correct by adjusting S6 or T1, respectively. Visually inspect and check the tape is not warped and no spillover occurs at posts S1 or S7 and T1 to T3. If warping and spillover occur, adjust S6, S7, T1, T2, and T3 (FIG. 11-11).

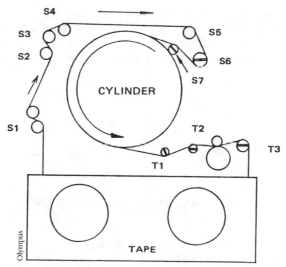

11-11 *Location of posts with the Olympus VX-801 tape deck mechanism (8 mm).*

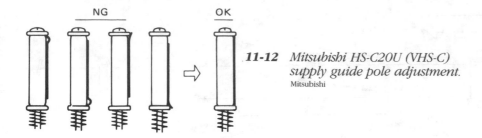

11-12 *Mitsubishi HS-C20U (VHS-C) supply guide pole adjustment.*
Mitsubishi

Mitsubishi HS-C20U (VHS-C) Supply Guide Pole Adjustment   The guide supply poles serve to improve tape transport stability between the cassette output and drum input by maintaining the correct height. Adjust the supply guide roller to obtain smooth tape transport at the lower flange of the guide poles (FIG. 11-12).

Pentax PV-C850A (8 mm) Guide Pole Height Adjustment   Place the master plane on the cassette holder and lower the holder (FIG. 11-13). Mount the reel disk height jig on the master plane and fit it to the guide pole. Adjust the guide pole height adjustment nut so the lower flange of the guide pole is 0.2 to 0.3 mm from the bottom edge of the reel disk height jig.

RCA CPR100 (VHS-C) Mechanism State (Mode Sense Switch)   Always make this adjustment after replacing the mechanism state switch. Make sure that the control cam gear is in the unloaded state. The T-shape is parallel with the top edge of the chassis. Install the mechanism state switch so the markings on the state switch circuit board and the triangular marking on the rotor are aligned. Make sure the control cam T-shape is within the A section (FIG. 11-14).

Pentax PV-C850A (8 mm) Mechanism State Switch Adjustment   After replacing the new state switch assembly, align the marking on the mechanism state switch gear and the recess of the mechanism state switch holder (FIG. 11-15). Align the marking (A) on the mode transmission gear and mark-

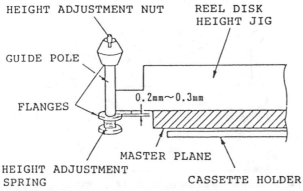

11-13   *Pentax PV-C850A (8 mm) guide pole height adjustment.* Pentax

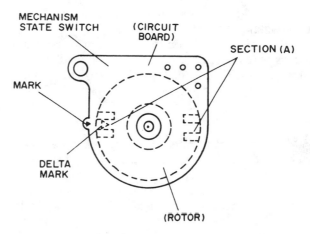

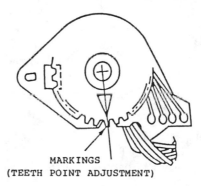

11-14   *RCA CPR100 (VHS-C) mechanism state mode switch adjustment.* RCA

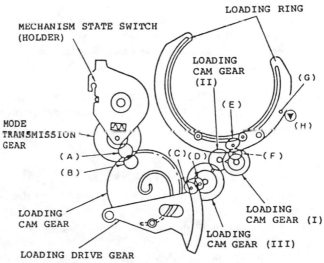

11-15   *Pentax PV-C850A (8 mm) mechanism state switch adjustment.*
Pentax

ing (B) on the loading cam gear in the STOP mode. Reassemble the mechanism state switch holder into the chassis.

Now align marking (C) on the loading drive gear and marking (D) on loading gear (111). Align marking (E) on the loading ring and marking (F) on loading cam gear (1). Finish by aligning mark (G) on the loading ring and mark (H) on the chassis.

TAPE INTERCHANGE ABILITY ADJUSTMENT

A quick check should be made after any service operation is performed that could adversely affect the tape such as replacement of the cylinder or drum motor, tape guide, audio/control head, or any component in the tape path. Usually this adjustment is performed only after the tracking preset adjustment is completed. Often, no tape guide adjustments are needed if the unit passes this check.

General Electric 9-9605 (VHS) Tape Interchange Ability Adjustment   Before making these adjustments, make sure the tracking control is set into the detent (fixed) position. Connect CH1 input of the scope to TP3501 and CH2 to TP2005, the head amp output (FIG. 11-16).

Loosen the hex screws on P2 and P3. Playback the monoscope portion of the alignment tape (VFKS 001H6) and adjust the height of posts P2 and P3 while watching the scope display so that the RF envelope on the scope becomes flat as possible. Now tighten the hex screws. (Remove the plastic piece on the slanted loading pin of P2 to make this adjustment. Replace after adjustment.)

If the scope display is as shown in Figure A, (FIG. 11-17), adjust the height of P2. Now adjust the height of P3 (B). If P2 and P3 posts are adjusted correctly, the scope display will become flat (C). Recheck post for normal tape travel (FIG. 11-18).

RCA CPR100 (VHS-C) Tape Interchange Ability Confirmation   With a dual-trace scope, connect CH1 probe to TP205. Connect CH1 probe to TP209. Insert monoscope test tape and place in play mode. The tracking control should be set at the center of the FM envelope. Adjust the vertical gain for four divisions on the scope. Likewise, set the tracking control for amplitude of three divisions (FIG. 11-19). Confirm that the minimum envelope is 1.6 divisions or more. If the following adjustments are good, tape guide adjustment is not needed.

AUDIO/CONTROL HEAD ADJUSTMENT

Incorrect position of the audio/control (A/C) head reduces the playback audio output, has poor signal-to-noise ratio (S/N) and may interfere with servo stability when the head cannot pick up the control signal. The audio/control coarse adjustment should be made before head height, tilt, azimuth, or horizontal position adjustments. The A/C control head is only in the VHS and VHS-C camcorders (FIG. 11-20).

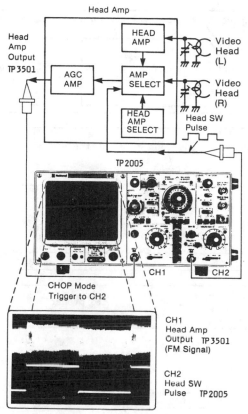

11-16 *General Electric 9-9605 (VHS) tape interchange ability adjustment hookup.* Thomson Consumer Electronics

Minolta C3300 (VHS-C) A/C Head Slant and Height Adjustment For the rough adjustment, run the tape and then adjust the slant of the A/C head with screw B so that the tape runs smoothly along the bottom flange of take-up guide pole.

Connect the scope to TP302 on the main pc board (FIG. 22-21). Insert the stairstep signal on alignment tape MH-C1. Turn the azimuth screw C for maximum and flat by turning screws A, B, and C in the same direction. (Turn screws A, B, and C with the same angle for height adjustment.)

Minolta C3300 (VHS-C) Audio/Control (A/C) Head X Value Adjustment Connect the scope to TP6 of (PB FM) on the Y/C pc board. Trigger the scope with the TP13 (Drum FF) on the Y/C pc board (FIG. 11-22). Insert alignment tape MH-C1 and play the stairstep wave signal. Check if the FM waveform is maximum in the center position and also if the FM signal output signal drops with the same angle from the center position to the right and left sides when turning the tracking dial from the center (detent) position to the right and left side. If this situation remains, X value is okay. If the

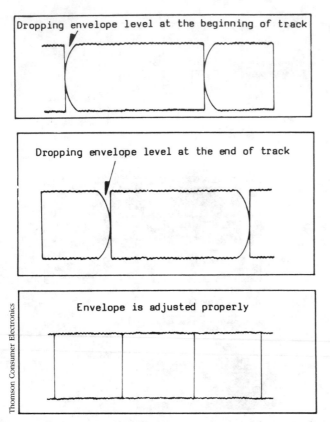

11-17   *General Electric 9-9605 (VHS) scope display of parts adjustments.*

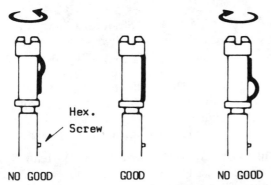

11-18   *General Electric 9-9605 (VHS) correct post adjustment of the tape path.* Thomson Consumer Electronics

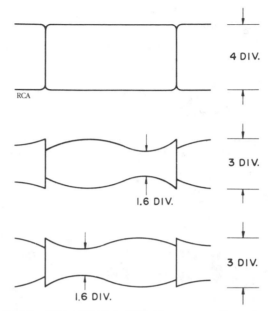

4 DIV.

3 DIV.

1.6 DIV.

3 DIV.

1.6 DIV.

11-19 *RCA CPR100 (VHS-C) tape confirmation.*

AUDIO/CONTROL HEAD

11-20 *The location of audio/control (A/C) head in RCA CPR300 camcorder.*

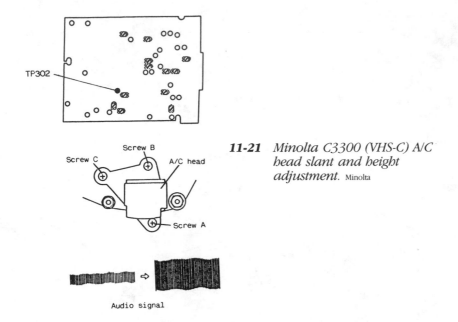

11-21 *Minolta C3300 (VHS-C) A/C head slant and height adjustment.* Minolta

X value is not adjusted properly, set the tracking dial to center (detent) position, slightly loosen screws D and E of the A/C head. Place the head-positioning tool over screw D with the pin of the tool inserted in the adjustment hole near the screw. Now check the FM waveform for maximum. (After adjusting the A/C head X value adjustment, adjust the play level in the audio circuit and bias level.)

General Electric 9-9605 (VHS) A/C Head Height Adjustment Do not make this adjustment unless the A/C head has been replaced or tampered with. Looking at the lower edge of the control head with the tape running, ensure that the lower edge of the tape runs along the lower edge of the control head. If it does not, slightly turn the nut (A) in either direction (FIG. 11-23). Counterclockwise raises the head and clockwise lowers it.

Confirming A/C Head Tilt

Make this adjustment after height adjustment of P4. Play back the tape and make sure the tape runs between the lower and top limits of post P4 (FIG. 11-24). Notice the tape movement. If adjustment is needed, turn screw (C) clockwise so that the curling is apparent with the lower edge of P4. Now turn the screw (C) counterclockwise so the curling of tape smooths out.

Adjustment of A/C Head Height and Azimuth

Connect the scope to TP4001 on the audio CBA board. Playback the mono-scope portion (6 kHz) of the alignment tape (VFM50001H6). Adjust screw (B) on the A/C head for maximum output (FIG. 11-25).

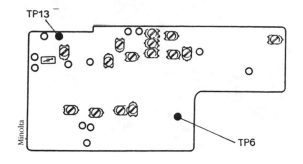

TP13

Minolta

TP6

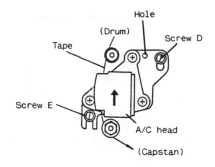

Hole
(Drum)
Tape
Screw D
Screw E
A/C head
(Capstan)

FM output
level

A—B—B—C

A B C

Tracking button

Clockwise ——Click—— counterclockwise

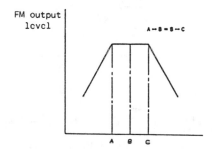

FM output

Tracking button

Click point

Beging to drop
FM output signal
with the same angle
of right and left
sides.

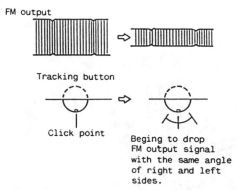

11-22 *Minolta C3300 (VHS-C) audio/control head X value adjustment.*

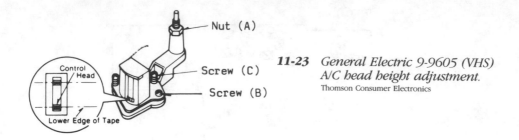

— Nut (A)

Control
Head

— Screw (C)

— Screw (B)

Lower Edge of Tape

11-23 *General Electric 9-9605 (VHS)*
A/C head height adjustment.
Thomson Consumer Electronics

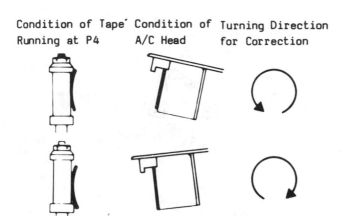

Condition of Tape   Condition of   Turning Direction
Running at P4   A/C Head   for Correction

11-24 *General Electric 9-9605 (VHS) A/C head tilt adjustment.*

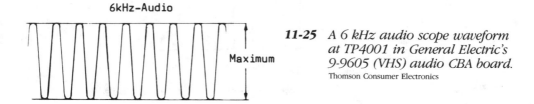

6kHz–Audio

Maximum

11-25 *A 6 kHz audio scope waveform*
at TP4001 in General Electric's
9-9605 (VHS) audio CBA board.
Thomson Consumer Electronics

Adjustment Nut

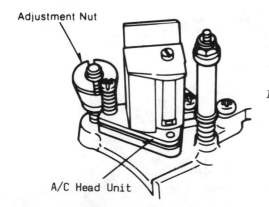

A/C Head Unit

11-26 *General Electric 9-9605 (VHS)*
A/C head horizontal adjustment.
Thomson Consumer Electronics

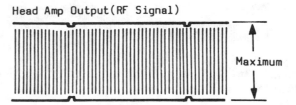

Head Amp Output(RF Signal)

Maximum

11-27 *General Electric 9-9605 (VHS) scope waveform of horizontal head adjustment.* Thomson Consumer Electronics

Horizontal Position Adjustment of A/C Head

Set the tracking control to the detent (fixed) position. Connect the scope to TP3501 on the head amp section. Play back the monoscope portion of the alignment tape (VFM50001H6) and note the envelope that corresponds to the high period of the head switching signal at TP2005 (FIG. 11-26). Use this envelope for the following adjustments. Slowly turn the azimuth nut so the envelope is at maximum. Before finding the center of the maximum period of the envelope, rotate the adjustment nut back and forth slightly to confirm the limits on either side of the maximum period (FIG. 11-27). Now determine the center point. Confirmation of the correct adjustment can be made by turning the tracking control to the right and left to correspond with the envelope. The adjustment is okay when the envelope changes symmetrically.

Zenith VM6150 (VHS-C) Audio/Control Head Adjustment Since this is a record-only camcorder, all tapes made with this unit are played back on another machine. Of course, the AC/CTL head must be correctly adjusted to ensure adequate audio output and S/N in addition to correct pickup of the control signal for servo operation.

Start by inserting play stairstep (audio, 7 kHz) section of the MY-C1 alignment tape. Turn screw 3 for maximum output on the scope (FIG. 11-28). Turn screws 1, 2, and 3 by a small amount (about 45 degrees) in equal increments to adjust the head height for maximum audio signal (FIG. 11-29).

The control head phase (X value) effects the playback synchronization between sound and picture. It is more delicate in the EP mode than the SP mode. Use the operation fixture and set for observing the FM waveform with the scope. Set the tracking control to the OFF position. Now play the

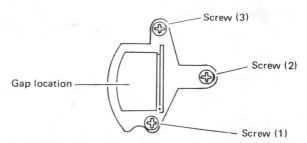

Screw (3)

Screw (2)

Gap location

Screw (1)

11-28 *Zenith VM6150 (VHS-C) audio/control head adjustment.* Zenith

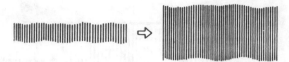

11-29   *Zenith VM6150 (VHS-C) audio signal A/CTL head adjustment waveform.* Zenith

stairstep signal of MY-C1 alignment tape. Slightly loosen screws 4 and 5 (FIG. 11-30). Insert one prong of the tweezers into the notch (A) and the other prong into the hole (B). Twist to shift the head fully forward towards the capstan. Carefully shift the head in the opposite direction while observing

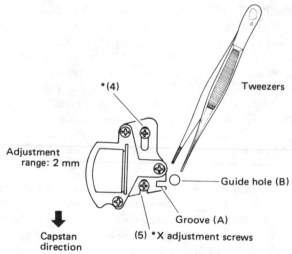

11-30   *Zenith VM6150 (VHS-C) X value head adjustment.* Zenith

the CH1 FM waveform and set to the maximum peak position. Now tighten screws 4 and 5. Check for maximum FM waveform.

For the final check, record a signal and confirm that the playback FM waveform meets the required performance in both SP and EP modes (FIG. 11-31). Now complete the different checks and adjustments in the electrical adjustment section, if needed.

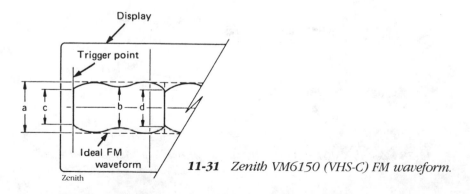

11-31   *Zenith VM6150 (VHS-C) FM waveform.*

11-32 *Close-up of the take-up and supply reels on the loading platform of RCA CPR300 camcorder.*

REEL TABLE HEIGHT ADJUSTMENTS

The supply and take-up reel tables should be the same height. Often the reel table heights are adjusted by changing the stack of washers under the reel assembly within the VHS camcorder (FIG. 11-32). A height fixture or reel jig is used for the correct height adjustment. If one of the reels is lower than the other, the adjustment is made by adding another washer. Usually, reel table height adjustment is only required when a new reel table is installed. If only one reel is replaced, compare the height with the original.

NEC V50U (VHS) Reel Table Height Adjustment   A post adjustment plate and reel table height gauge is needed for this adjustment. Place the post adjustment plate on the reels and put the gauge on the plate. Set the gauge to zero with the foot scraper of the gauge touching the cut-out portion of the plate (FIG. 11-33). Then measure the height of the reel table. Confirm the difference just performed in the former step (A). Do the same for

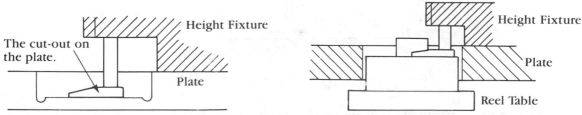

11-33 *Example of VHS reel table height adjustment.*

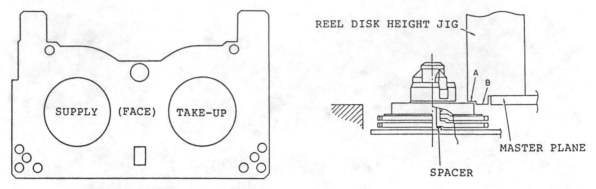

11-34   *Pentax PV-C850A (8 mm) reel disk height adjustment.* Pentax

the other reel table (B). If the height difference in measurements between the cut-out portion of the plate and reel tables are not 0 to 0.15 mm (higher or lower), adjust the height of the reel to obtain the specified height. Just add or reduce a washer.

Pentax PV-C850A (8 mm) Reel Disk Height Adjustment   (Take-up side only.) Place the master plane on the cassette holder and lower the holder. Mount the reel disk height jig on the master plane and fit it to the reel disk (FIG. 11-34). Make sure that the top of the reel disk pedestal is positioned between sections A and B of the reel disk height jig. If the top of the reel disk pedestal is not positioned between actions A and B, adjust the number of the spacers at the bottom of the reel disk. (Use a spacer of 0.25 mm thick. If the disk is still low, place a spacer of 0.13 mm thick on it.)

Sony CCD-M8E/M8U (8 mm) Reel Table Height Check   Make sure the height of the LS chassis to the supply reel table receptacle plate surface (2) and from the LS chassis to the take-up reel receptacle plate surface (3) should be the same as 6.85 ± 0.15 mm. Both A and B heights should be the same. If a case washer (T = 0.13) is inserted under the take-up reel table, it becomes 6.98 ± 0.15 mm (FIG. 11-35).

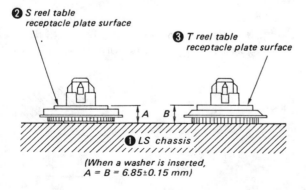

11-35   *Sony CCD-M8E/M8U (8 mm) reel table height check.* Sony

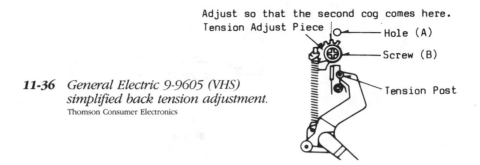

11-36 *General Electric 9-9605 (VHS) simplified back tension adjustment.*
Thomson Consumer Electronics

BACK TENSION ADJUSTMENT

The back tension is done in play mode to take up tape slack and slippage with correct tension. Some manufacturers use a back tension meter (Tentelometer), while others use a video cassette torque meter, which includes back tension and take-up in one cassette. This adjustment can be made with a regular video cassette, small screwdriver, and tension meter.

General Electric 9-9605 (VHS) Simplified Back Tension Adjustment Place the camcorder in PLAY mode. Loosen screw (B) slightly and adjust the tension piece so that the second cog of the tension adjust piece comes straight on its vertical axis (FIG. 11-36). Now tighten screw (B). With this simplified adjustment, back tension may come into the required specifications in spite of parts tolerances.

For complete back tension adjustment, play back the video cassette recorded in SP mode from the start and wait until the tape has rotated for one minute. Make sure the back tension is within specifications with the back tension meter. Be careful not to touch other parts that keep the meter from adding tension to the tape while measuring. Loosen screw B and insert fine screwdriver blade into small hole A. Turn the tension adjust piece in either direction until the specification is reached. Now tighten screw B (FIG. 11-37).

Minolta C3300 (VHS-C) Tension Adjustment A back tension torque and take-up torque cassette is used in this adjustment. Set the video cassette torque meter, and then place the deck in play mode. Make sure the take-up torque meter is 40 to 75 GF CM and the back tension torque meter is 15 to 24 GF CM (FIG. 11-38). In case the measurement value is out of standard value, clean the supply reel disk and exchange the tension band after seeing the tension pole position. Paint the screw (1) after adjustment.

11-37 *General Electric 9-9605 (VHS) point of measurement in back tension adjustment.*
Thomson Consumer Electronics

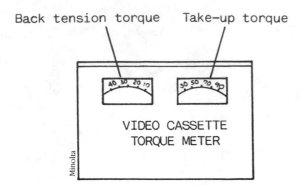

11-38   *Minolta C3300 (VHS-C) tension adjustment meters.*

Sony CCD-M8E/M8U Forward Back Tension Adjustment   Set the camcorder in record (REC) mode. Measure the tension with dial tension gauge of tension measuring exclusive reel (FIG. 11-39). At this step, the measurement should be done by pulling the tape at a speed of 14 mm/s. Move the spring backing position (4) of tension regulating spring 3 so that the tension applied becomes with the 7.9 to 8.9 G (FIG. 11-40).

RCA CPR100 (VHS-C) Back Tension Confirmation   The service test tape will play back with a minimum skew error (picture tension is properly

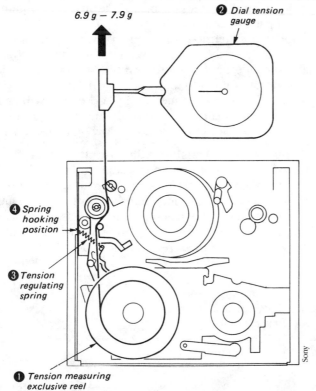

11-39   *Sony CCD-M8E/M8U (8 mm) forward back tension adjustment.*

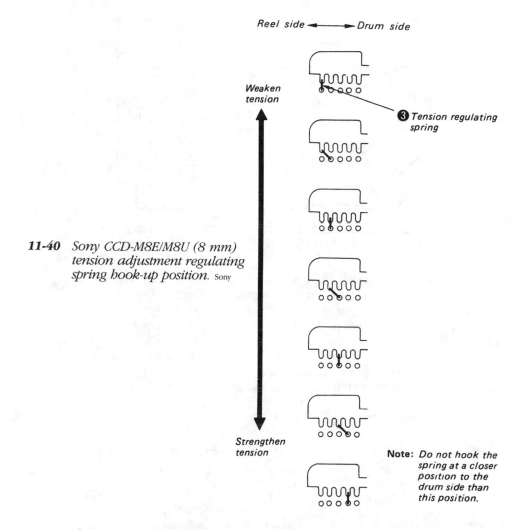

11-40 *Sony CCD-M8E/M8U (8 mm) tension adjustment regulating spring hook-up position.* Sony

adjusted) (FIG. 11-41). Usually, the back tension is adjusted at the factory and may not require additional adjustments. If adjustment is needed, insert the back tension cassette. Place camcorder in SP play mode. Check the measurement (12 to 28). If the reading is not within these limits, make tension arm adjustments.

To adjust the tension arm position, load the camcorder with a blank tape. Rewind the blank tape. Place instrument in PLAY mode. After loading, adjust screw (A) so that the outermost line of the four lines on the EE head arm is aligned with the point of the tension pole flange (FIG. 11-42).

Pentax PV-C850A (8 mm) Tension Pole Position and Tension Adjustments These adjustments should be made after the subchassis sliding mount adjustment is made. Check the position and tension and adjust the tension pole position simultaneously.

For position adjustment, hook the tension spring to position (B) of the tension spring stopper (FIG. 11-43). Cover the supply end sensor light with

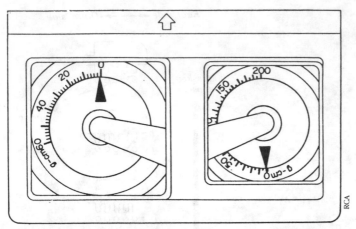

11-41   *RCA CPR100 (VHS-C) back tension confirmation.*

paper so it does not pass light. Press the PLAY button without loading a cassette. Adjust the position of the tension torque adjustment plate so that the holes in the supply-side guide plate and tension arm are aligned. After adjustment, set the unit to the play and record modes and recheck tension arm position.

Now for tension adjustment, hook the tension spring to position B of the tension spring stopper. Load the tension cassette and play back. The meter should read between 9 and 12 g/cm. If not between these readings,

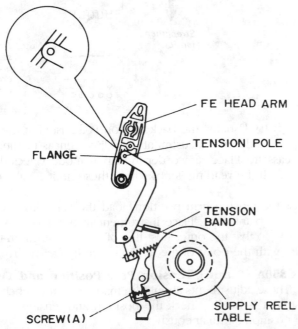

FE HEAD ARM

TENSION POLE

FLANGE

TENSION BAND

SUPPLY REEL TABLE

SCREW (A)

11-42   *RCA CPR100 (VHS-C) tension arm position adjustment.* RCA

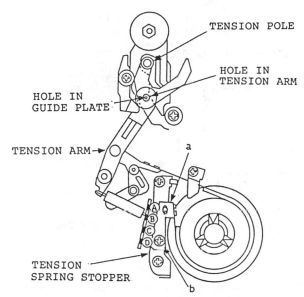

11-43 *Pentax PV-C850A (8 mm) tension pole position adjustment.* Pentax

set the back tension spring to position A if the tension is higher than 12 g/cm. When the tension is lower than 9 g/cm, hook the spring to position C of the tension spring stopper. Perform these measurements with the tape deck in horizontal position.

If the tension value has changed more than 2 g/cm, recheck the tension pole position and readjust if needed. Remove the paper covering after the adjustment is completed.

Pentax PV-C850A (8 mm) Impedance Roller Height Adjustment Place the master plane on the cassette holder and lower the holder. Mount the reel disk height jig on the master plane and fit to the impedance roller (FIG. 11-44). Adjust the impedance roller height adjustment nut (located on top), so the bottom edge of impedance roller flange is 0.1 to 0.2 mm higher than the bottom edge of the reel disk height jig. Load a blank tape and run to check if there is any curling of tape at the lower flange.

RCA CPR100 (VHS-C) Brake Confirmation First remove the cassette holder. Check to see if the take-up main brakes are against the supply and take-up gears in the stop mode. If not, check for a bent control rod or improper setting of the control plate (FIG. 11-45).

Now install the cassette holder and load with a blank tape. Push fast-forward and then quickly press the stop button. Notice if there is any slack in the tape. Clean the brake contact surface of the supply gear and main brake if slack tape appears. Use "Kimwipes" and a mild solvent (FIG. 11-46).

Sony CCD-M8E/M8U (8 mm) Soft Brake Torque Check Remove the cassette arm and L5 cassette compartment assembly. Place unit in USE - STOP mode. Mount the tension measuring exclusive reel on the supply reel

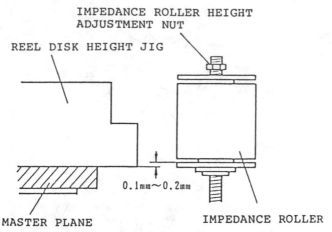

IMPEDANCE ROLLER HEIGHT
ADJUSTMENT NUT

REEL DISK HEIGHT JIG

0.1mm~0.2mm

MASTER PLANE

IMPEDANCE ROLLER

11-44   *Pentax PV-C850A (8 mm) impedance roller height adjustment.* Pentax

table. Pull the dial tension gauge in the direction of the arrow (FIG. 11-47). Notice the specified value with the track shifting and monitoring jig in place. Read the value on the dial tension gauge.

Pentax PV-C850A (8 mm) Tension and Torque Checks   Always check the tension, torque, and compression force of the tape take-up section and moving section to smooth the tape transport and to satisfy the basic performance of the VTR. When the tape speed is abnormal, detect the defective sections by this check. Replace the defective parts with new ones and take another tension check.

11-45   *Close-up of brake assembly in the RCA CPR300 tape deck mechanism.*

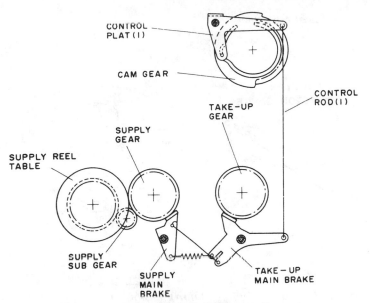

11-46 *RCA CPR100 (VHS-C) brake confirmation.* RCA

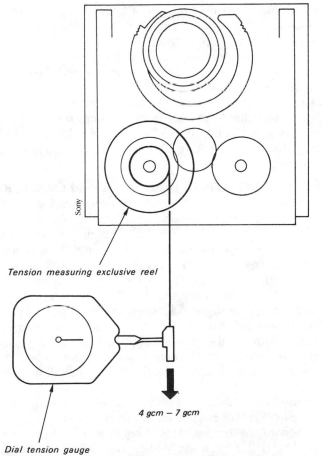

11-47 *Sony CCD-M8E/M8U (8 mm) soft brake torque check.*

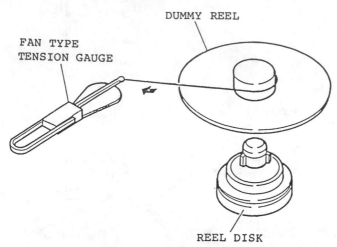

DUMMY REEL

FAN TYPE
TENSION GAUGE

REEL DISK

11-48   *Pentax PV-C850A (8 mm) tension and torque check.* Pentax

Cover up the receiving windows of both supply and take-up end sensors with paper or tape or something that will not pass light. Lower the cassette holder. The VTR can now accept the input of each operation made. However, the rewind operation can be done for only a few seconds in this state because the take-up reel disk is stopped and the reel sensor cannot detect reel pulses (FIG. 11-48).

TABLE 11-1 shows the various adjustments to be made with the measured values. Note 1 are values measured using a dummy reel and fan-type tension gauge while pulling the take-up reel disk counterclockwise and the supply reel disk clockwise at a speed of 50 mm/s. Note 2 are values measured with an NTSC tension cassette.

Mitsubishi HS-C20U (VHS-C) Loading Gear and Locking Ring Adjustment   Set the mechanical STOP mode before removing or replacing the loading gear and loading ring assemblies. Turn the take-up and supply loading rings in the unloading direction. Be careful not to apply excessive force. Adjust to overlap the holes and teeth of the take-up and supply loading rings. Install the rings as shown in FIG. 11-49.

Mount the ring idler gear (1) with its markings at the 12 o'clock position (FIG. 11-50). Now install idler gear (2). If it cannot be installed smoothly, turn the unloading ring slightly clockwise to permit installation.

Adjust the control cam for the STOP position. Set the larger wedge of loading gear (3) toward the loading ring. Make sure the edge of the smaller wedge contacts the edge of the control cam wedge (FIG. 11-51). You may want to turn the mode control motor slightly clockwise to allow easy installation of the loading gear (3).

Install the loading gear (4) with its teeth engaged with loading gear (3) and the take-up loading ring. Now the marked teeth of loading gear (4) should be roughly at the 3 o'clock position and engaged evenly with the take-up loading ring. Repeat the loading and unloading operations several

Table 11-1. Tension and Torque
(Pentax PV-C850A)

Item	VTR Mode	Measured Reel	Measurement value	Remarks
Main brake torque	Stop	Supply	25 g or more	Note 1
		Take-up	7.5 g or more	Note 1
Slack removal torque	Unloading	Supply	20 - 30 g·cm	Note 2
Fast forward torque	Fast forward	Take-up	150 g or more	Note 1
Rewind torque	Rewind	Supply	150 g or more	Note 1
Take-up torque	Play	Take-up	6 - 24 g·cm	Note 2
Back-tension torque	Fast forward	Supply	0.2 - 6.2 g·cm	Note 1
	Rewind	Take-up		
Take-up back-tension	Play	Supply	9 - 12 g·cm	Note 2
Reverse torque	Reverse play (Reverse search)	Supply	20 - 30 g·cm	Note 2
Take-up brake torque	Play to stop	Take-up	6 g·cm or more	Note 2

Note 1:   These are values measured using a dummy reel and fan type tension gauge while pulling the take-up reel disk counterclockwise and the supply reel disk clockwise at the speed of 50 mm/s.

Note 2:   These are values measured using an NTSC tension cassette.

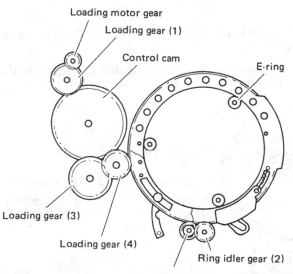

11-49 *Mitsubishi HS-C20U (VHS-C) loading gear and locking ring adjustment.* Mitsubishi

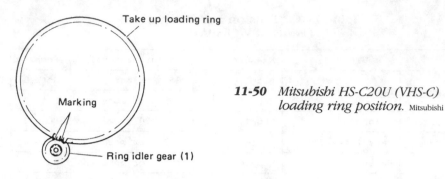

Take up loading ring

Marking

Ring idler gear (1)

11-50   *Mitsubishi HS-C20U (VHS-C) loading ring position.* Mitsubishi

times. Make sure the marked teeth of loading gear (4) comes to correct position with respect to the loading ring and mechanical operation is normal (FIG. 11-52). If the mechanical operation is not correct, assemble it once again.

RCA CPR100 (VHS-C) Loading Ring Adjustment   This adjustment should be made after installing the loading gear, supply loading gear, take-up loading ring, and cam gear. Follow these steps.

- Rotate the take-up and supply loading rings fully in the unloading direction. Gradually turn the take-up and loading rings in the loading direction. Match the inner empty holes of both rings (FIG. 11-53).
- Install "E" ring (A).
- Install ring idler gear (1) with the markings facing the loading gear (FIG. 11-54). Now reinstall the idler gear (2).

RCA CPR100 (VHS-C) Cam Gear Adjustment   This adjustment should be made after installing a new cam gear or mechanism state (mode sense) switch.

- Make sure the loading ring adjustment and the loading rings are in the unloaded state.
- Install the cam gear so the control cam (T-shape) on the cam gear is parallel with the top edge of the chassis (FIG. 11-55A).

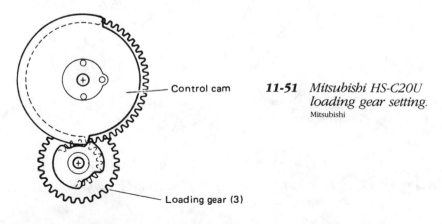

Control cam

Loading gear (3)

11-51   *Mitsubishi HS-C20U loading gear setting.* Mitsubishi

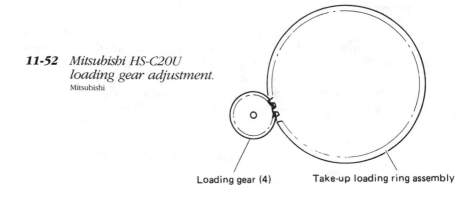

11-52 *Mitsubishi HS-C20U loading gear adjustment.*
Mitsubishi

Loading gear (4)   Take-up loading ring assembly

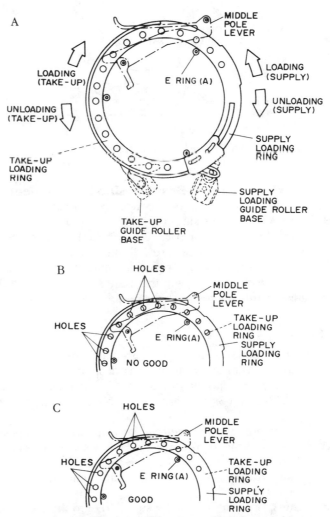

A

MIDDLE POLE LEVER

LOADING (TAKE-UP)

LOADING (SUPPLY)

UNLOADING (SUPPLY)

UNLOADING (TAKE-UP)

E RING (A)

SUPPLY LOADING RING

TAKE-UP LOADING RING

SUPPLY LOADING GUIDE ROLLER BASE

TAKE-UP GUIDE ROLLER BASE

B

HOLES

MIDDLE POLE LEVER

HOLES

TAKE-UP LOADING RING

E RING(A)

SUPPLY LOADING RING

NO GOOD

C

HOLES

MIDDLE POLE LEVER

HOLES

TAKE-UP LOADING RING

E RING(A)

SUPPLY LOADING RING

GOOD

11-53 *RCA CPR100 (VHS-C) loading ring adjustment.* RCA

- Install loading gear (3) (B) and then loading gear (4) (C). Make sure the markings on the ring idler gear (1) and loading gear (4) face the loading ring in the unload state after several loading and unloading operations. Ensure the take-up and loading supply rings do not drift from the positions set during loading ring adjustment.

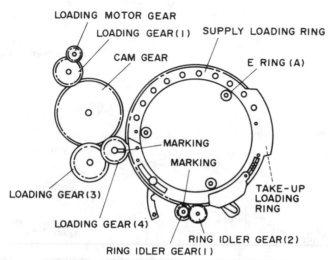

11-54 *RCA CPR100 (VHS-C) loading ring adjustment with ring idler gear.*
RCA

RCA CPR100 (VHS-C) Circuit Board Position Adjustment Perform this adjustment after reinstalling the flywheel FG circuit board. Place the VTR in SLP mode. Move the tracking control to detent position. With a blank tape, make a recording and play it back. Connect CH1 of the scope probe to pin 36 of IC601. Loosen the three screws holding the flywheel FG circuit band and adjust the position of the board for maximum indication on the scope (FIG. 11-56). Now carefully tighten the three screws. Notice if the scope waveform changes while tightening the screws.

CONCLUSION

Most mechanical adjustments are only required after removing, installing or adjusting. Sometimes when the camcorder is dropped, denting or bending components, mechanical adjustments may be needed. Usually, all three tape formats—VHS, VHS-C, and 8 mm—are given within the same type of adjustment.

Many of the manufacturers have their own fixtures, test tapes, and jigs for their own VTR adjustments. You may find a few special tools are needed for the camcorder you are now repairing. Securing the exact service literature for each camcorder helps to make easier and quick mechanical adjustments.

The tape transport system from the supply reel to the take-up reel disk across the video heads is the most crucial section in the VTR (FIG. 11-57). The

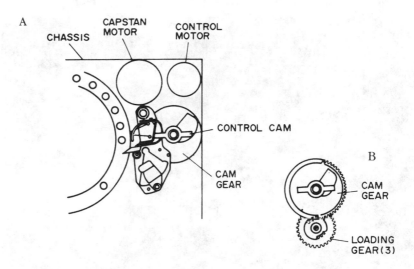

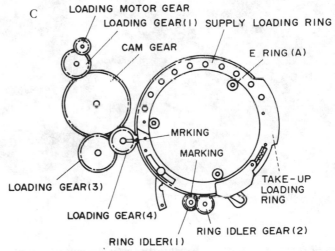

11-55 *RCA CPR100 (VHS-C) cam gear adjustment A, B, and C.* RCA

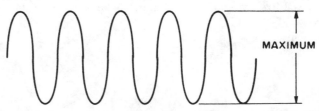

11-56 *Flywheel FG circuit board position adjustment of RCA CPR100 (VHS-C).* RCA

11-57   *Tape path from reel to reel across the tape head in the RCA CPR300 VTR deck.*

tape transport components, especially those that come in contact with the tape should be kept clean. Remove scratches, dust, and oil from these surfaces.

Most transport tape systems are adjusted before it leaves the factory. If the parts are not tampered with or broken, no adjustments are needed. Always make the correct mechanical adjustments after replacing a new component to stablize the transport system. Make sure exact factory replacements are used.

Chapter **12**

Electrical
Adjustments

*E*lectrical adjustments are required after replacing critical components in the camera section. Electronic viewfinder (EVF) adjustments may be needed after the viewfinder has had rough treatment or the camera was accidentally dropped. Sometimes only a touch-up is needed. All electrical adjustments should be followed according to the manufacturer's specifications (FIG. 12-1). You may find basic adjustment charts in the back of the service manuals.

REQUIRED TEST EQUIPMENT

Basically, there are seven or eight (minimum) test instruments that are required for electrical adjustments. Other special tools and servicing jigs may be required by each manufacturer. Many of these test instruments are probably already on your electronic service bench. Basic instruments include:

- Oscilloscope
- Color TV monitor
- Signal generator
- Frequency counter
- Audio tester
- Regulated power supply
- Digital voltmeter (DVM)
- Blank video cassette for recording and playback
- Alignment tape
- Patch cords
- Camera jigs
- Electronic service tools

12-1 *You must remove covers to take voltages and make electrical adjustments.*

Each camcorder manufacturer may have its own list of test instruments and tools for electrical adjustments (FIG. 12-2). Special jigs and harnesses may be required for certain adjustments. Additional test instruments are:

- Vectorscope
- Light meter
- Tripod
- Light box
- Reflection charts and test patterns
- Special screwdrivers
- Camera accessories
- Color temperature conversion filter
- Special camera extension jigs and harnesses

The oscilloscope should be dual-trace with delayed sweep and a minimum bandwidth of 25 MHz. Most electronic technicians servicing the TV chassis already have a dual-trace scope on their work benches. The frequency counter should have a frequency of 20 MHz or greater. Most TV establishments have a digital voltmeter DVM or DMM for critical voltage

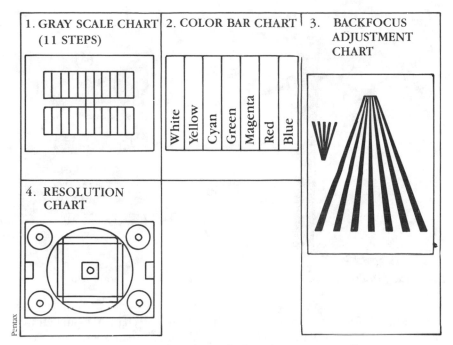

12-2 *Pentax PV-C850A (8 mm) chart for camera adjustments.*

adjustments. If not, choose one that can measure up to 1500 volts dc, because pickup tubes in the older camcorders have a high sweep voltage.

The vector scope is used for TV repairs and adjustments such as burst, black balance, white balance, auto white balance, and chroma balance adjustments. The vector scope may show the color level to be low or off and not show up on the color monitor or charts.

The light meter is to ensure proper light of the camera test patterns while the light box is used instead of the test patterns. The wall charts are inexpensive compared to light boxes. Some manufacturers use both the charts and light boxes in camera adjustments. Secure the wall charts or light box recommended by the camcorder manufacturer on the camcorders you are servicing or selling. Some camcorders' service manuals contain a back focus and gray and white scale chart.

REFLECTION OR WALL CHARTS

There are many different wall charts and test patterns used in different camera tests and alignment. The gray scale chart, color bar and back focus chart are recommended by most. The gray scale chart is used for troubleshooting, testing, and alignment. The gray scale chart is used when waveforms are presented by the service manual if by chart or a gray chart upon the light box. Besides the gray scale chart, there are several others including color bar chart, resolution chart, ball chart, white chart, black and white chart, gray and white chart, and the back focus chart. Since the white/black chart is reflective, a halogen lamp should be used with it.

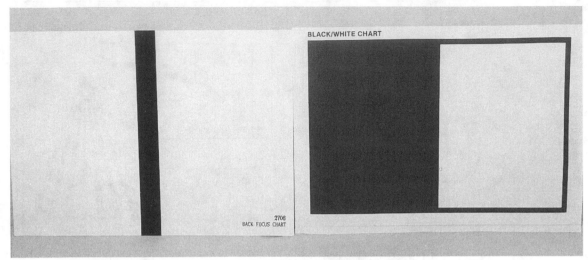

12-3   *Back focus adjustment may be made with a solid black line chart.*

The back focus adjustment using the back focus chart is to match the distance to the object with the index of the distance on the focus ring. Poor back focus adjustment may occur when the distance to the object and the index of the distance on the focus ring do not match. The back focus adjustment chart may be one with lines coming together at the end or a black solid line down the center (FIG. 12-3).

TOOLS AND FIXTURES

Most small tools on the TV service bench are all that is required to make electrical adjustments. A blank video cassette is used for recording and playback operations. The cassette alignment tape is used for color, audio, and servo alignment (TABLE 12-1).

Patch cord, extension cables, and test jig harnesses may be used in auto and back focus adjustments, color adjustments, camera dummy setup, iris extension cable and operation fixtures (FIG. 12-4). Some manufacturers do not have any jig harnesses or external circuit boards for making electrical adjustments. Several camcorders use light balancing, and ND and CCD filters over the lens in making electrical adjustments (FIG. 12-5).

CAMERA SETUP

For camera adjustments, the camcorder should be mounted on a solid work bench or a heavy duty tripod for accurate measurements (FIG. 12-6). In the RCA CPR100 VHS-C camcorder, the unit is operated from the ac power supply with the audio/video (A/V) cable between camcorder and color video monitor. The video output cable must be matched with the RCA-BNC adapter to plug into the color monitor (FIG. 12-7).

Table 12-1. Test Cassette Alignment Tapes

Manufacturer	*Type*	*Alignment Tape*	*Part Number*
Minolta	VHS-C	M+-C1	7892-8012-01
Mitsubishi	VHS-C	MH-C1	859C35909
Olympus	8 mm	Color bar monoscope	VFM9010P9D VFM9000P9N
RCA	VHS-C	3 kHz alignment	156502
Pentax	8 mm	NTSC	20HSC-2
NEC	VHS	Alignment	79V40302
Zenith	VHS-C	Color EP mode	MY-C1 CY-C1L

To make electrical adjustments in the Pentax PV-C850A (8 mm), a light box is used in front of the lens assembly with an RF converter as distribution box. A monitor TV without audio/video jacks may be plugged into the RF converter, or the monitor TV with A/V jacks may also plug into the converter unit. Notice the color bar generator provides a signal to the RF converter (FIG. 12-8).

The standard setup for the Zenith VM 6150 (VHS-C) camcorder is with charts and test patterns at 50 cm from lens of camcorder (FIG. 12-9). A set of patch cords and operation jigs are connected to the camera. A dc power source (VAC401) is plugged into the ac line for long periods of adjustments. The test instruments used for electrical adjustments are a color monitor (TV), oscilloscope, full-size VHS recorder for checking, frequency counter, audio tester, regulated dc power supply, digital voltmeter, and a spare VHS-C video tape (TC-60).

CAMCORDER BREAKDOWN

Often, both plastic sides of the camcorder must be removed for electrical adjustments (FIG. 12-10). Some adjustment boards are located on one side while others are on the other side and behind the camera lens assembly (FIG. 12-11). Here boards 1 through 7 are located on the right side of RCA CPR100 camcorder, and the mike and interface circuit boards at the top of the lens assembly. The process circuit board (10) is at the front and underneath the lens assembly.

Besides containing critical circuits of the camcorder, the service manuals include test points and control board layout (FIG. 12-12). Most camcorder

Ref. No.	Name	Part Code	Purpose
J-1	ND Filter 0.4	J-6080-806-A	LLA Adjustment
	ND Filter 1.0	J-6080-808-A	LLA Adjustment
	ND Filter 0.9	J-6080-833-A	Max. Gain Adjust, LLA Adjust
J-2	PTB-100 Pattern Box	J-6020-490-A	
J-3	Color Chart for Pattern Box	J-6020-250-A	
J-4	M8 Repair Bench	J-6080-847-A	
J-5	Iris Extension Cable (4P)	J-6080-846-A	
J-6	Track Shifting and Monitoring Jig	J-6080-843-A	

Have a below described jig prepared for yourselves.

High Luminance Pattern

Cover Color-bar Chart J-3 with black paper except half the width of its white bar, for shooting in a standard pattern frame.

Black Paper

White Clip Adjustment (2)

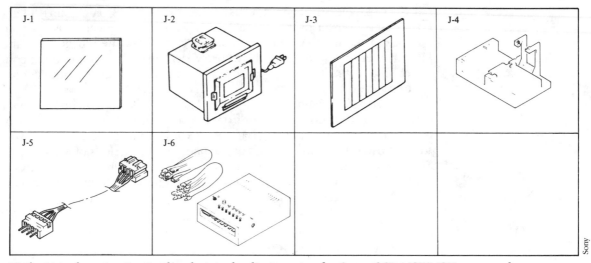

12-4 *List of service jigs in the electrical adjustments of a Sony CCD-M8E/M8U camcorder.*

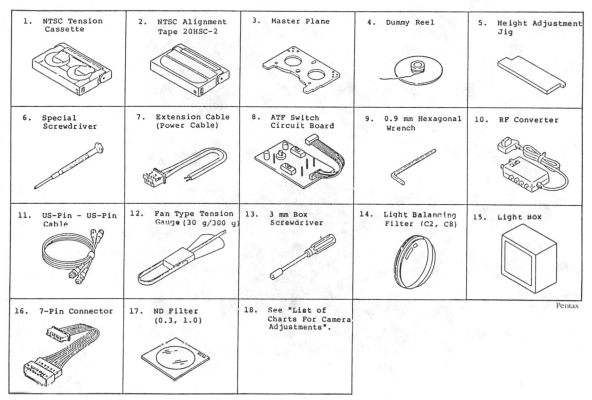

1. NTSC Tension Cassette	2. NTSC Alignment Tape 20HSC-2	3. Master Plane	4. Dummy Reel	5. Height Adjustment Jig
6. Special Screwdriver	7. Extension Cable (Power Cable)	8. ATF Switch Circuit Board	9. 0.9 mm Hexagonal Wrench	10. RF Converter
11. US-Pin – US-Pin Cable	12. Fan Type Tension Gauge (30 g/300 g)	13. 3 mm Box Screwdriver	14. Light Balancing Filter (C2, C8)	15. Light Box
16. 7-Pin Connector	17. ND Filter (0.3, 1.0)	18. See "List of Charts For Camera Adjustments".		

Pentax

12-5 *Besides various jigs and servicing tools, filter lenses are used in Pentax PV-C850A camcorders for electrical adjustments.*

service manuals list the various test points and parts for easy camera adjustments. Like on any electronic product, alignment procedures are difficult at first, but after repairing several camcorders, each one becomes easier.

POWER CIRCUIT ADJUSTMENTS

Before attempting to make electrical adjustments, the output of the power supply voltage must be set correctly (FIG. 12-13). Incomplete adjustments may cause the signal-processing system to operate normally. Most dc power source adjustments are made with a digital voltmeter, blank tape, and dc power supply. These adjustments take only a few minutes but are very critical. Make sure the lens cap is on.

Minolta C3300 (VHS-C) 5 V Adjustment With the dc power supply connected to the camcorder, insert a blank tape and place the unit in the record mode. Locate TP1 and TP2 on the main board (FIG. 12-14). Now connect the digital voltmeter between TP1 and ground. Check for a $\pm$ 5 V at 0.2 V percent. When connecting the digital voltmeter between TP2 and ground, make sure the 5 volts is with $\pm$ 0.25 volts.

12-6 *Place the camcorder on a tripod or work bench for accurate adjustments.*

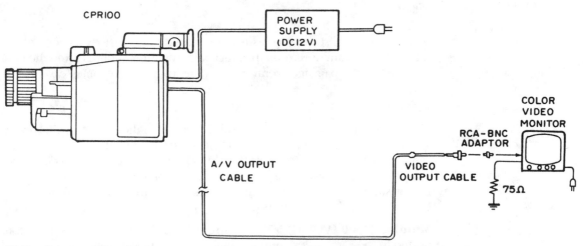

12-7 *Camera adjustment connections in the RCA CPR100 (VHS-C) camcorder.* RCA

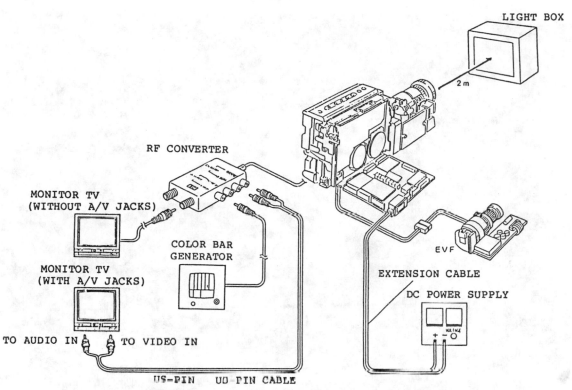

12-8   *Pentax PV-C850A (8 mm) connections for electrical adjustments.* Pentax

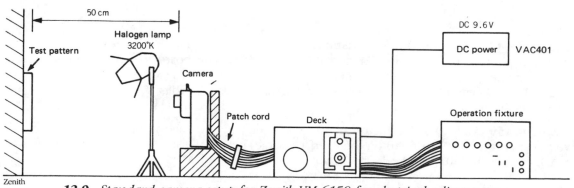

12-9   *Standard camera setup for Zenith VM 6150 for electrical adjustments.*

12-10   *Usually both sides of the camcorder are removed for adjustment in the Quasar VM10 camcorder.*

Pentax PV-C850A (8 mm) 5 V Adjustment   Load the VTR with a blank tape and place in record mode. Connect the ATF switch circuit board to PG621 and turn SW1 and SW2 off. Connect the digital voltmeter to TP4 (5 V) and TP1 (GND) and AFT board (FIG. 12-15). Adjust RT801 to read 5.3 volts ± 0.05 volts on the voltmeter.

Realistic 150 (VHS-C) 9 V Adjustment   To set the dc output voltage to 9 volts, connect the DVM to TP401 on the interface (large) board. Adjust the 9 V ADJ control (RT1402) for 9 volts ± 0.1 volts.

SERVO AND SYSTEM CONTROL ADJUSTMENTS

After adjusting the power supply, check the system control, servo system, video, and audio adjustments, in that order. The system control adjustments may consist of the battery down and tape end adjustments, while the servo system adjustments may contain drum pulse, capstan sampling, pb switching, SP control delay MMV, EP tracking, and tracking preset.

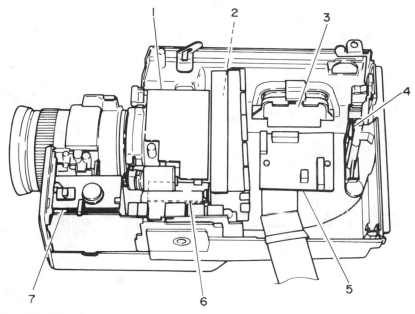

1. Autofocus Circuit Board
2. Sensor Circuit Board
3. Zoom Switch Circuit Board
4. VCR Record Switch Circuit Board
5. Wiring Circuit Board

6. Regulator Circuit Board
7. Control Circuit Board
8. Mic Jack Circuit Board
9. Interface Circuit Board
10. Process Circuit Board

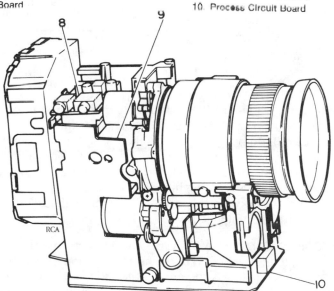

12-11   *Electrical adjustment and circuit boards of the RCA CPR100 (VHS-C) camcorder.*

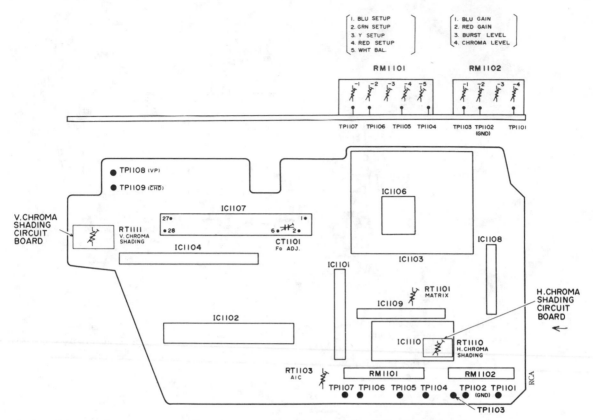

12-12 *Electrical process test adjustments and controls on the RCA CPR100 camera.*

Sony (8 mm) CCD-M8E/M8U Battery Down Adjustment Place camcorder in the stop mode and connect digital voltmeter to the emitter of Q124 on the MD-10 board. Make sure there is 5.78 volts from the dc power supply to the power supply contact point spring. Short pin 6 of IC101 to ground. Rotate RV 102 counterclockwise and stop at the point where the emitter of Q124 goes from high to low. Notice that Q124 changes even if RV102 is turned clockwise, but this is different from the adjustment point, so be sure to turn it counterclockwise.

Sony (8 mm) CCD-M8E/M8U Tape End Detection The scope on CH1 is connected to the base of Q118 on the ac range and CH2 at the collector of Q119 on the dc range. Fix the erase switch so that it is pushed in with the tape (FIG. 12-16A). Without inserting a cassette, lower the cassette compartment and load. Place the tape end detection filter in the space between the cassette compartment and the end sensor light receiving portion (FIG. 12-16B). Now place camcorder in record mode. Adjust RV001 fully clockwise. Adjust RV001 by turning counterclockwise so that the collector voltage of Q119

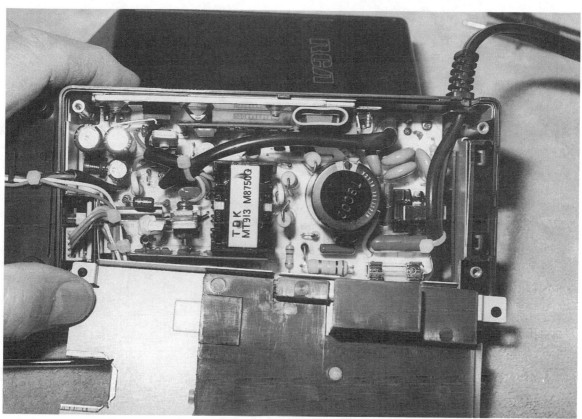

12-13 *Inside view of the RCA CPR100 power supply.*

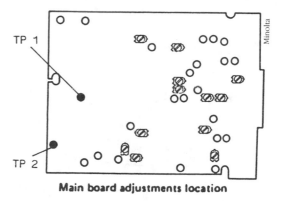

Main board adjustments location

12-14 *Minolta C3300 (VHS-C) 5-volt power source adjustment.*

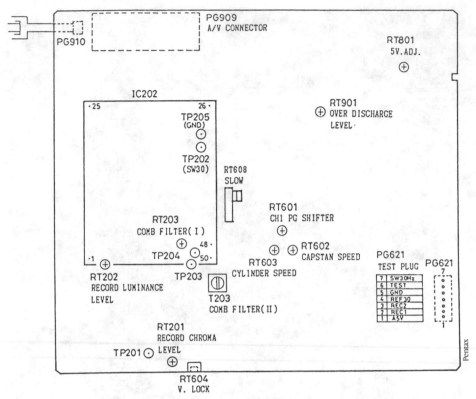

12-15 *Pentax PV-C850A (8 mm) 5-volt adjustment.*

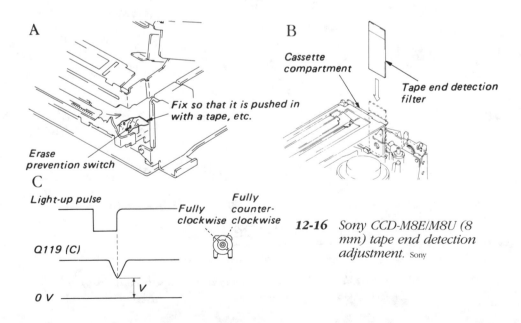

12-16 *Sony CCD-M8E/M8U (8 mm) tape end detection adjustment.* Sony

voltage (dc level) is more than 2 V and less than 3 V at the rising point of the light up pulse (FIG. 12-16C).

If the voltage is less than 2 V at this time, end detection will operate and shut-off occurs, so in this case, turn RV001 slightly counterclockwise and put unit into recording mode again and readjust. Now remove the tape end detection filter and confirm that Q119 collector voltage is less than 0.2 V.

Minolta C3300 (VHS-C) Drum Pulse Adjustment   The purpose of this adjustment is to set the switching signal of CH SW MMV at 0.35 V ± 0.1 V. Connect the scope to TP111 of the main board with VTR in record mode. Adjust R218 so that the positive pulse becomes 0.35 V ± 0.1 V and negative pulses become 0.35 V ± 0.1 V (FIG. 12-17).

Mitsubishi HS-C20U Drum Sampling Position Adjust   Set the VTR in play mode with a MH-C1 cassette. Locate the drum sampling position terminal (TP 101) on the main board. Connect the scope to TP101 and adjust R139 so that the sampling pulse is positioned nearly at center of the failing slope of the trapezoidal waveform (FIG. 12-18). To check for drum phase error, locate TP107 and connect the digital voltmeter to TP107 and ground of the main board. Adjust R139 to obtain 2.5 V ± 0.1 V.

Sony (8 mm) CCD-M8E/M8U Capstan DC Bias Adjust   Place the VTR in playback mode. Locate the capstan dc bias adjustment on the MD-10 board. Playback a blank tape. Connect the frequency counter to pin 21 of SU 16. Adjust RU202 for a reading of 825.5 Hz ± 1 Hz (FIG. 12-19).

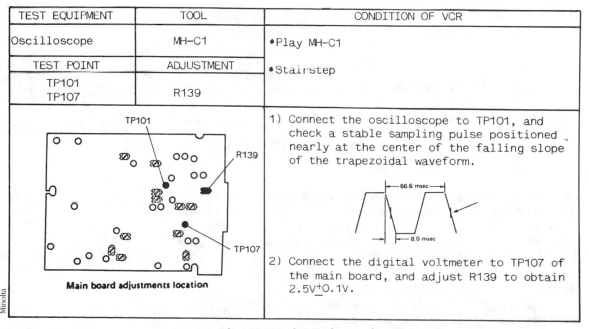

TEST EQUIPMENT	TOOL	CONDITION OF VCR
Oscilloscope	MH-C1	•Play MH-C1
TEST POINT	ADJUSTMENT	•Stairstep
TP101 TP107	R139	

1) Connect the oscilloscope to TP101, and check a stable sampling pulse positioned nearly at the center of the falling slope of the trapezoidal waveform.

2) Connect the digital voltmeter to TP107 of the main board, and adjust R139 to obtain 2.5V±0.1V.

Main board adjustments location

Minolta

12-17 Minolta C3300 drum phase adjustment.

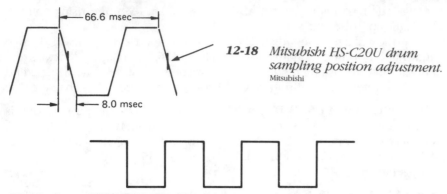

12-18   *Mitsubishi HS-C20U drum sampling position adjustment.* Mitsubishi

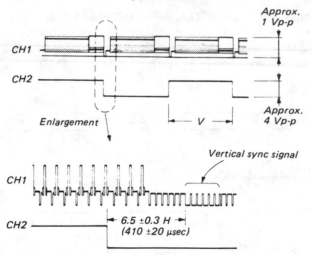

12-19   *Sony CCD-M8E/M8U (8 mm) capstan dc bias adjustment.* Sony

Sony (8 mm) CCD-M8E/M8U RF Switching Position Adjust   Place VTR in record mode. Record the color-bar chart. Play back the recorded tape on VCR. Check the switching position on the playback equipment (FIG. 12-20). If not satisfactory turn RV203 and repeat adjustment.

12-20   *Sony CCD-M8E/M8U (8 mm) RF switching adjustment.* Sony

Zenith VM6150 (VHS-C) PB Switching Point Adjust   Locate test point (TP FM) on main board. Plug the stairstep signal of MY-C1 cassette. Connect the scope to TP-FM and ground. Trigger the scope with external signal of test point FF. Adjust R435 to set the switching portion of the FM waveform to approximately 0.4 ms (FIG. 12-21).

Minolta C3300 (VHS-C) Capstan Sampling Adjust   The purpose is to set the sampling position of the comparison signal in the capstan phase servo circuit and the phase detection voltage at 2.5 ± 0.1 volts. Place VTR in play mode with MY-C1 test cassette. Connect the scope to test point TP104

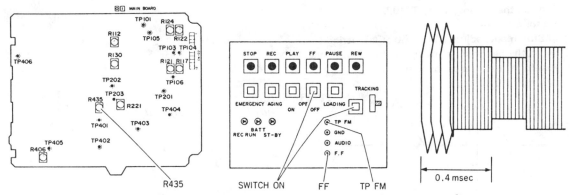

12-21 *Zenith VM 6150 (VHS-C) PB switching point adjustment.* Zenith

and check a stable sampling pulse positioned nearly at the center of the rising slope of the trapezoidal waveform (FIG. 12-22). Now connect the digital voltmeter to TP106 and adjust R187 to obtain 2.5 ± 0.1 volts.

Mitsubishi HS-C20U (VHS-C) SP Control Delay Adjust   Place VTR in stop mode. Connect the scope to TP102 on main board. Now place VTR in SP mode. Short circuit TP1 and TP103. Now adjust R113 so that *a* (period between the beginning of rising and the peak of the waveform) becomes *a* = 10 $^+$ ms (FIG. 12-23).

Mitsubishi HS-C20U EP Control Delay Adjust   Place in stop mode to connect scope to TP102 on main board. Short TP1 and TP103 together. Set for EP mode. Adjust R111 so that the period between the beginning of rising and the peak of the waveform is *a* = 30 ± 0.2 ms. (FIG. 12-24).

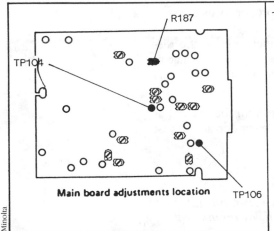

Main board adjustments location

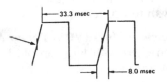

1) Connect the oscilloscope to TP104, and check a stable sampling pulse positioned nearly at the center of the rising slope of the trapezoidal waveform.

2) Connect the digital voltmeter to TP106, and adjust R187 to obtain 2.5V+0.1V.

12-22 *Minolta C3300 (VHS-C) capstan sampling adjustment.*

1) Connect the oscilloscope to TP102.
2) Set for SP mode.
3) In Stop mode, adjust R113 so that (a) (period between the beginning of rising and the peak of the waveform) becomes as follows:

a = 10 ± 0.5 msec

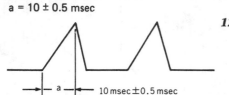

12-23 *Mitsubishi HS-C20U SP control delay adjustment.*
Mitsubishi

Zenith VM 6150 EP Tracking Preset Adjust   Connect the scope to TP401 on the main board. Set tracking control of the fixture to the OFF position. All of Zenith's servo adjustments are made with the operation fixture jig (868-263). Place the VTR in play mode (EP) with a CY-C1L cassette. Observe the FF and CTL pulse waveforms. Adjust R406 to set these waveforms (FIG. 12-25).

CCD DRIVE SECTION

There are four or five important electrical adjustments to be made in the CCD drive section including focus, drive pulse frequency, PLL frequency, V-Sub or OFD, and CCD output adjustments. These adjustments are to ensure proper focus, set proper drive pulse frequency, to prevent blooming, and provide sufficient CCD or MOS outputs. The lens cap is removed with these tests. Be sure and make the FO/Q, VCO-PLL, AFC, and playback (PB) level adjustment after replacing heads or preamplifier.

Back Focus Adjustment

The purpose of the back focus adjustment is to ensure proper focus tracking throughout the zoom range or to match the distance to the object with the index of distance on the focus ring. Improper adjustment means the distance to the object and index of distance on the focus ring do not match. Many camcorder back focus adjustments are made with a back focus chart or light box with test patterns.

General Electric 9-9605 (VHS) Focus Adjustment   Aim the camera at the registration chart with lens cap off. Look in the viewfinder and adjust VR904 for best resolution.

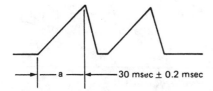

12-24 *Mitsubishi HS-C20U EP control delay adjustment.*
Mitsubishi

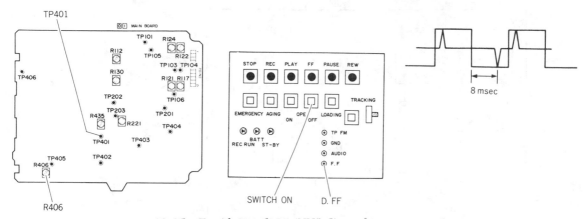

12-25 *Zenith VM 6150 (VHS-C) tracking preset adjustment.* Zenith

Pentax (8 mm) PV-C850A Back Focus Adjustment   Use the back focus adjustment chart and color video monitor in this adjustment. Set the zoom to wide-angle and turn the focus ring to the index of 2 M. Loosen the hexagonal screw holding the relay lens. Insert the back focus adjustment screwdriver into the back focus adjustment hole and turn it clockwise and then counterclockwise to optimize focus (FIG. 12-26).

Set the zoom to telephoto and check if the chart zooms wide-angle and readjust the back focus adjustment. Adjust the back focus adjustment hole using the screwdriver so the subject is approximately in focus at both wide angle and telephoto ends when the focus ring remains set to 2 M. Do not forget after adjustments to tighten the relay holding lens screw and lock it with a dash of paint.

Realistic 150 (VHS-C) Back Focus Adjustment   Observe the back focus adjustment on the color monitor. Position the camera 3 meters (M) from the back focus chart and illuminate the object with approximately 100 lux. Set the zoom ring to the wide-angle position and the focus ring to the three (3) meter position (FIG. 12-27). Loosen the hexagonal screw. Insert the back focus adjustment screwdriver point to adjust for optimum focus. Set the zoom

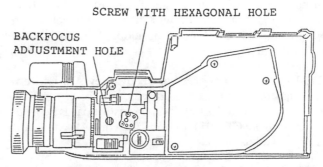

12-26 *Pentax PV-C850A (8 mm) back focus adjustment.* Petnax

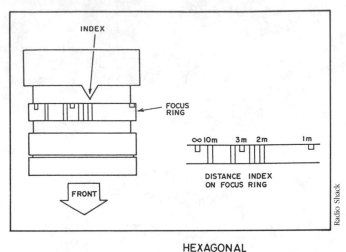

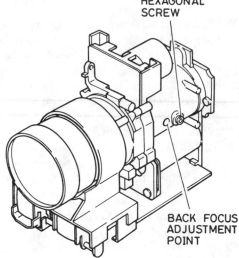

12-27 *Realistic 150 (VHS-C) back focus adjustment.*

ring to telephoto end and confirm that the chart is in focus. If not, return the zoom ring to the wide-angle end and readjust. Confirm that the chart is approximately in focus at both the wide-angle and telephoto ends with the focus ring set to the three (3) meter position. After this adjustment is completed, tighten the hexagonal screw and coat the screw with lock paint.

RCA CPR100 (VHS-C) Drive Pulse Frequency Adjustment The purpose of this adjustment is to set the drive pulse frequency to the specified value. Connect the DVM to TP1002 of the sensor board (FIG. 12-28). Adjust the drive clock to control (CT1001) for 2 ± 0.1 volts. Disconnect the EVF connector during this adjustment.

Olympus VX-801U PLL (VCO) Frequency Adjust Connect the DVM to TP8003. Connect the VF-BA81 to the VX-801 camcorder and set the unit to

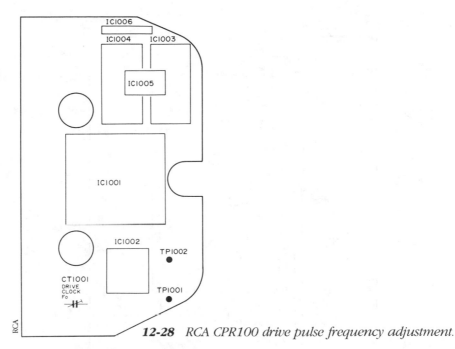

12-28 *RCA CPR100 drive pulse frequency adjustment.*

VTR stop mode. Input the color bar signal through the VF-BA81. Adjust VR8001 to read 2.4 ±0.1 volt on the DVM.

Canon VM-E2NA (8 mm) Blooming (OFD or U-SUB) The purpose is to set the antiblooming level, or blooming is likely to occur. Shoot the halogen lamp (300 W) wide-angled at 2 M and observe monitor TV. Place ND400 or ND800 filter on the camera lens. Adjust VR2002 on the sensor CBA board until blooming disappears (visually on monitor TV) (FIG. 12-29).

When the CCD or the REF module has been replaced, make the following adjustments (FIG. 12-30).

- Ground pin 2 of CN2106 (with iris opened).
- Prepare ND filter according to the type of halogen lamp used (300 V lamp—use ND400; 500 W lamp—use a ND800 filter lens).
- Remember that excessive turning of VR2002 may cause the image to disappear.

Minolta VOG (CCD) Output Adjust The purpose of this adjustment is to set the CCD output to maximum. Display the gray scale chart. Connect the scope to TP101 (FIG. 12-31). Rotate VR032 to counterclockwise to obtain waveform (FIG. 12-32A). Now turn VR032 to clockwise to erase the above A part, and then slightly turn VR032. Do not turn to the right end. The waveform should look like that in FIG. 12-32B.

CAMERA SECTION

The process section adjustments consist of AGC, brightness or luminance, white balance, auto white balance, color, and audio gain adjustments. Within

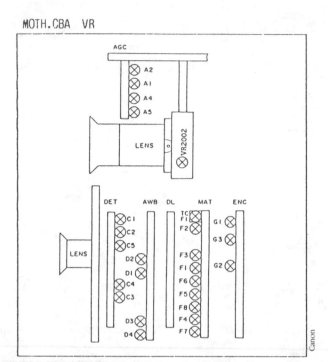

12-29   *Canon VM-E2NA (8 mm) blooming (OFD or V-SUB) adjustment.*

12-30   *Location of the CCD module in the RCA CPR300 camcorder.*

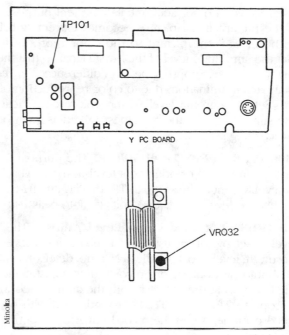

TP101

Y PC BOARD

VRO32

Minolta

12-31 *Minolta C3300 VOG (CCD) output adjustment location.*

1) Connect the oscilloscope to TP101.

2) Turn VRO32 to counter clockwise to obtain the following waveform.

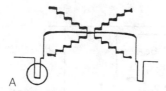

A

3) Turn VRO32 to clockwise to erase the above A part, and then after turning VRO32 slightly, stop turning it.

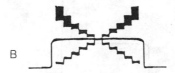

B

NOTE : Do not turn the right end.

12-32 *Minolta C3300 CCD output waveforms.* Minolta

these sections are several other adjustments. The real purpose is to set the brightness of the picture if the picture becomes extremely bright or dim. Set the white balance of the picture so the color reproduction does not deteriorate. Set the amplitude level of the burst signal so that the color does not become light or dense. Suppress the level differences between R, G, and B signals in standard illuminations due to color reproduction of poor white in the picture. Set the chroma level so the color reproduction does not deteriorate. Be sure and make the brightness (Y) adjustment before adjustments of the recording system.

Minolta C3300 (VHS-C) PBY Level Adjust   The purpose of this adjustment is to set the luminance or brightness level in the playback (PB) mode to the correct level. Connect the scope to TP115. Play an MH-C1 test cassette. Adjust R24 so that the level is 2 ± 0.03 volts peak-to-peak (FIG. 12-33).

RCA CPR100 (VHS-C) Record Luma Level Adjust   The best record brightness level is set by this adjustment. If record luma level is too high, video may occur. If level too low, the S/N ratio deteriorates. The record chroma level should be done before record luma adjustment. Apply NTSC color bar signal ($I V_{p-p}$) at the EVF jack with the audio/video input adapter. Connect the scope to TP201 and TP204 ground. Load with blank tape and place in SP record mode. Adjust the record luma level control (TR201) for 120 mV$_{p-p}$, (FIG. 12-34).

GE 9-9605 (VHS) Iris Level (ALC or AGC) Adjust   Aim the camera at the gray scale chart. Remove lens cap. Convert the scope to TP303 (H. rate) (FIG. 12-35). Adjust the ALC control (VR303) so that the signal level is 0.5 ± 0.5 V$_{p-p}$. Now connect the scope to TP304. Adjust AGC control (VR305) so that the signal level is 0.5 ± 0.05 V$_{p-p}$.

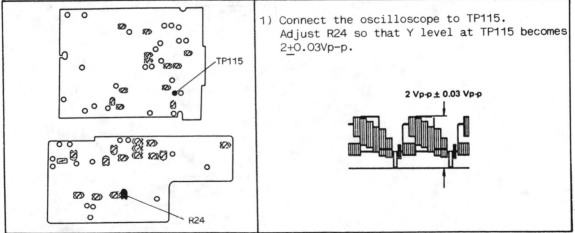

1) Connect the oscilloscope to TP115.
Adjust R24 so that Y level at TP115 becomes
2+0.03Vp-p.

TP115

R24

2 Vp-p ± 0.03 Vp-p

Minolta

12-33   *Minolta C3300 (VHS-C) PB Y level adjustments.*

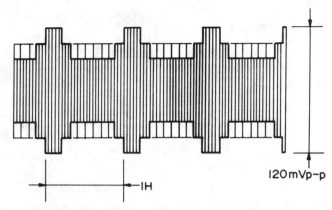

12-34 *RCA CPR100 record luma level adjustments.* RCA

Sony CCD-M8E/M8U (8 mm) Iris Setting Adjust Point camera at the color bar chart (in standard pattern frame). Connect the scope to TP681 on VC-4 board. Rotate RV722 so the signal level is set at 185 ± 5 mV$_\text{p-p}$ (FIG. 12-36).

Olympus VX-801U (8 mm) ALC Adjust Aim the camcorder at the gray scale. Monitor the waveform at TP401 with the scope. Adjust VR704 to set the signal level to 350 ± 20 mV$_\text{p-p}$ (FIG. 12-37). Check the signal level if lights enter after the lenses are shaded. Readjust if the level is not within the standard range. If noise is present in the signal, measure from center to center.

Olympus VX-801U (8 mm) AGC Adjust Aim the camera at the gray scale. Connect the scope to TP410. Adjust VR401 to set the signal level at 400 mV ± 20 mV$_\text{p-p}$ (FIG. 12-38).

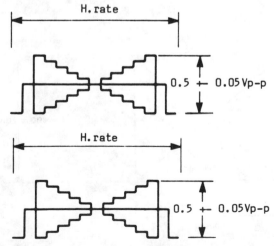

12-35 *GE 9-9605 (VHS) iris level (ALC or AGC) adjustment.*
Thomson Consumer Electronics

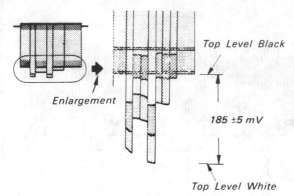

12-36 *Sony CCD-8ME/M8U (8 mm) iris setting adjustment.* Sony

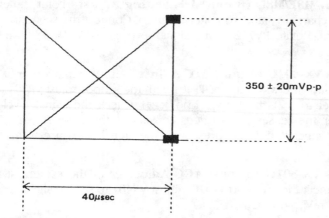

12-37 *Olympus VX-801U (8 mm) ALC adjustment.* Olympus

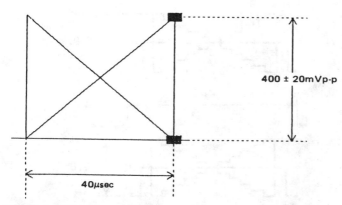

12-38 *Olympus VX-801U (8 mm) AGC adjustment.* Olympus

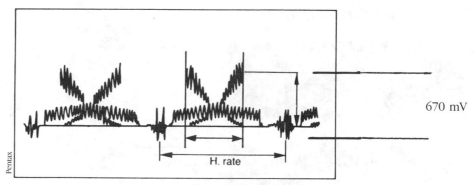

12-39 *Pentax PV-C850A (8 mm) AGC adjustment.*

Pentax PV-C850A (8 mm) Adjust The purpose of adjustment is to set the brightness for low illumination. Improper adjustment makes the picture extremely bright or dim in low illumination. Attach the ND filter over the lens. Connect scope to the video output jack. Synchronize the scope with TP1201-8 (AGC). Adjust TP1201 so that the amplitude of the waveform is 670 $\pm$ 15 mV$_{p-p}$. (FIG. 12-39).

RCA CPR100 (VHS-C) Red/Blue/Green Setup Adjust This adjustment may also be referred to as the *black balance* adjustment in other camcorders. Actually, this adjustment sets the black balance of the picture.

Cap the lens. Short TP1101 to ground terminal (TP1102) on the process board (Refer to FIG. 12-12). Connect the video out to a terminated vectorscope (75-ohm termination). Connect TP1103 and TP1106 to ground terminal (TP1102). Adjust the green setup control (RM1101-2) so that the bright portion of the vector is located as close as possible to the center of the vectorscope screen (FIG. 12-40). Now remove the ground connections from TP1103 and TP1106. Adjust the blue setup control (RM1101-1) and the red setup (RM1101-4) so the bright portion of the vector is positioned in the center of the vectorscope screen.

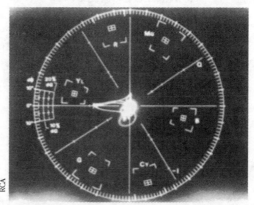

12-40 *RCA CPR100 (VHS-C) red/blue/green setup adjustment.*

MINIMIZE CARRIER

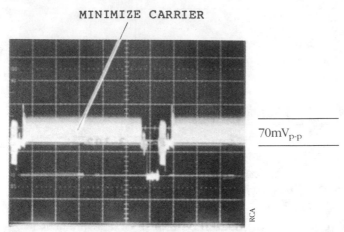

70mV$_{\text{P-P}}$

12-41　*RCA CPR100 Y (luminous) setup control adjustment.*

Connect the VIDEO OUT to the scope (terminate in 75 ohms). Trigger the scope at the horizontal rate (use TP1109 on the process board). Adjust the Y setup control RM1101-3 for 70 mV$_{\text{P-P}}$ from blanking to the center of the waveform (FIG. 12-41).

Realistic 150 (VHS-C) Black Balance/Y Setup Adjust　Cover the lens. Apply 1.4 volts dc to PG 1100-2. Connect video out (A/V out) to a 75-ohm terminated scope. Ground terminals PG1100-3 (blue) and PG1100-4 (red) to ground terminal (PG1100-1). Adjust the green control RM1101-4 for minimum carries in the waveform (FIG. 12-42). Remove ground connections PG1100-3 and PG1100-4. Adjust red setup control (RM1101-3) and blue setup control RM 1101-2 for minimum carries in waveform. Adjust Y setup circuits (RM1101-5) for 70 mV ± 7 mV from blanking to the center of waveform (FIG. 12-43).

MINIMIZE CARRIER

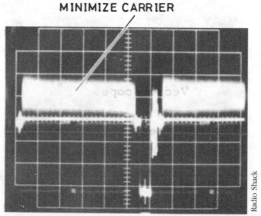

12-42　*Realistic 150 (VHS-C) block balance/Y setup adjustments.*

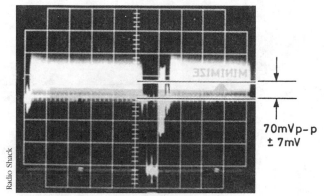

12-43 *Realistic 150 block balance/Y 70 mV$_{p-p}$ adjustment.*

Mitsubishi HS-C20U White and Dark Clip Adjust Set VTR in E-E mode. Connect scope to TP2 and ground. Adjust R5 (white) and R6 (Dark) controls so that the white clip becomes 85 ± 5 percent and the dark clip becomes 50 ± 5 percent respectively (FIG. 12-44).

Zenith VM 6150 White and Dark Clip Adjust Use the gray scale pattern chart. Connect the scope to TP104 (FIG. 12-45). Place camcorder in stop mode. Adjust R117 and R121 to set the white and dark clip components.

Pentax PV-C850A (8 mm) White Balance Adjust Set the white balance of the picture so the color reproduction does not deteriorate. Apply 1.6 V dc to TP1201-1. Connect the vectorscope to the video output jack. Adjust RM1201-6 and RM 1201-7 so that the bright point comes to the center of the waveform (FIG. 12-46).

GE 9-9605 (VHS) Chroma Phase and Color Gain Adjust Connect the vectorscope to the video output. Aim the camera at the color bar chart. Remove lens cap. Adjust the color phase controls (VR 201, VR 202, VR 204, and VR 205) (FIG. 12-47). Adjust the chroma gain control VR 207 so that the red vector is 180 percent ± 10 percent as compared to the burst signal in the vector scope.

Minolta C3300 (VHS-C) PB Burst Level Adjust This adjustment sets the burst level in playback (PB) mode to the best level. Connect the scope to TP 115 (FIG. 12-48). Adjust R33 so that the burst level is 0.6 V$_{p-p}$. Use the color bar chart.

12-44 *Mitsubishi HS-C20U white and dark clip adjustment.*

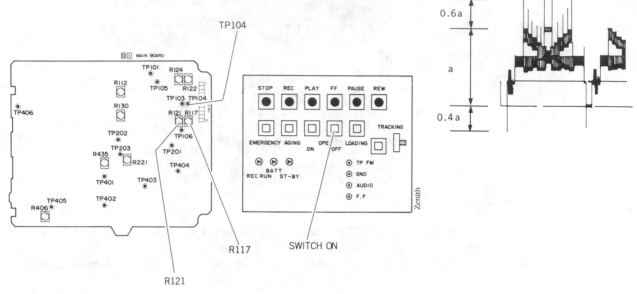

12-45   *Zenith VM 6150 (VHS-C) white and dark clip adjustment.*

Canon VM-E2NA (8 mm) Color Balance Adjust   Use the color bar chart, AWB module, and vectorscope. Adjust VKF1 (R-Y level), VRF5 (B-Y Level), and VRF2 on MAT module. When adjusting VRF2, check and adjust 3 to 13 carrier balance/modulation axis adjustments (FIG. 12-49).

    R: 102 ± 2 degrees
    YE: 166 ± 4 degrees
    G: 234 ± 8 degrees

RCA CPR100 (VHS-C) Record Chroma Level Adjust   This adjustment regulates the recorded color level. Sometimes if the color level is too high, diamond-shaped beats appear in the picture. Color may be degraded if too

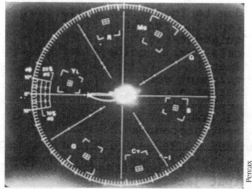

12-46   *Pentax PV-C850A (8 mm) white balance adjustment.*

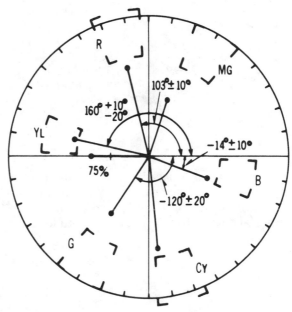

12-47 *General Electric 9-9605 (VHS) chroma phase and color gain adjustment.* Thomson Consumer Electronics

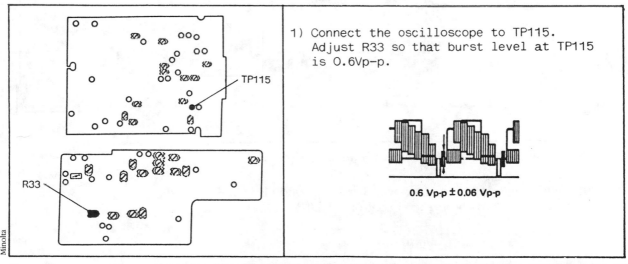

1) Connect the oscilloscope to TP115. Adjust R33 so that burst level at TP115 is 0.6Vp-p.

0.6 Vp-p ±0.06 Vp-p

12-48 *Minolta C3300 play back (PB) burst level adjustment.*

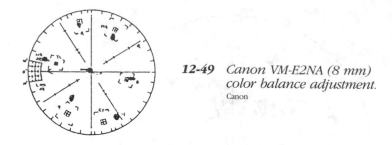

12-49   *Canon VM-E2NA (8 mm)
color balance adjustment.*
Canon

low. Apply the NTSC color bar signal (1 V_{p-p}) to the EVF jack with audio/
video adapter. Connect the scope probe to TP 201 on the head switch/func-
tion switch board (FIG. 12-50). Check the upper cylinder for an identification
number (0 through 4) stamped on top. Rotate record luma level control (RT

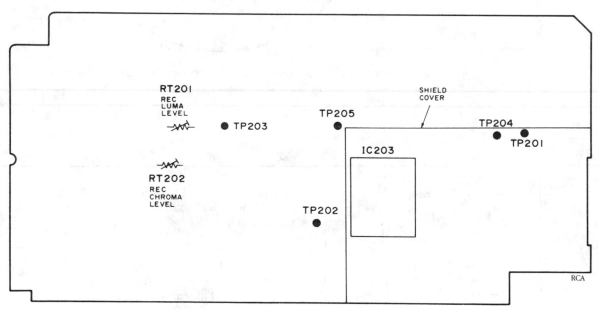

12-50   *RCA CPR100 record chroma level adjustment at TP201.*

201) fully counterclockwise. Load with blank tape and place in SP record
mode. Adjust record chroma level control (RT 202) for correct value (FIG.
12-51):

Mark	Level
0	30 mV$_{p-p}$
2	35 mV$_{p-p}$
4	40 mV$_{p-p}$

RCA CPR100 (VHS-C) Audio Bias Level Adjust   The audio bias adjustment should be made before the playback level adjustment. If the bias is too

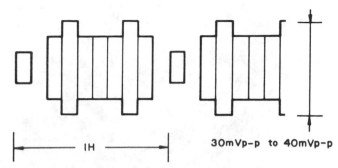

12-51 *RCA CPR100 (VHS-C) record chroma level adjustment.* <small>RCA</small>

low, high frequency increases with distortion. The high frequencies are alternated when bias is too high. Connect a millivoltmeter between TP401 and TP402 (GND). Load with a blank tape in SP record mode. Adjust audio bias level control (RT 402) for 2.2 mV$_{rms}$ ± 0.1 mV.

General Electric (VHS) Audio Back Level Adjust   Insert a blank tape and record a 1 kHz audio signal connected to AUDIO IN with an ac adapter and an audio generator. After a few minutes, play back the portion recorded. With scope connected to TP 4001, adjust the playback level control (VR 4001) so the level of playback waveform is equal to that of the recorded signal.

Sony CCD-M8E/M8U (8 mm) Audio Distortion Check   Input a 400 Hz, −66 dB signal to the microphone connecter pin (3) (white) and record for about one minute. Play back the recorded portion on VCR playback equipment. Make sure the playback distortion at audio output is less than 1 percent.

ELECTRONIC VIEWFINDER (EVF) ADJUSTMENTS

Most of the EVF adjustments are made with the gray and resolution scale for best results (FIG. 12-52). The deflection coil position adjustment is to provide correct tilt of the viewfinder. The centering adjustment is to match center of the TV and EVF pictures. Vertical size adjustment is to set vertical deflection size. Horizontal hold adjustment sets the horizontal frequency. Brightness adjustment optimizes the brightness of the picture, and the focus adjustment makes the EVF picture clear and distinct.

RCA CPR100 EVF Horizontal Hold Adjustment   Set the H. hold control (RT 1801) to its mechanical center. Connect the frequency counter to TP 1801. Connect a 47 μF capacitor between pins 1 and 2 of CN 1801 (FIG. 12-53). Adjust the H. hold control (RF 1801) for 15.75 kHz ± 0.1. Now remove capacitor.

Pentax PV-C850A (8 mm) Horizontal EVF Tilt Adjust   If the picture in the EVF screen is tilted, readjustment of the deflection coil is required. Loosen the deflection coil retaining screw (FIG. 12-54). Turn the deflection coil

12-52   *Photo shows the EVF alignment controls in the bottom side of the electronic viewfinder.*

CN1801

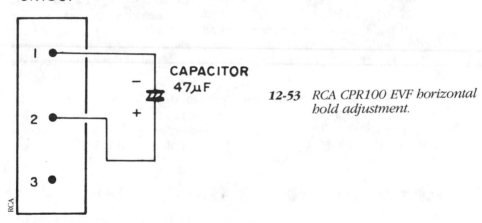

12-53   *RCA CPR100 EVF horizontal hold adjustment.*

12-54   *Pentax PV-C850A horizontal EVF tilt adjustments.*

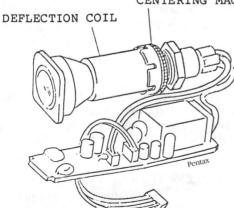

so the picture is parallel. Use a resolution chart and centering magnet to center the picture if off to the side.

Mitsubishi HS-C20U EVF Vertical Scanning Adjust   Aim the camcorder at the gray scale. Check the vertical height in the EVF screen. Adjust VR3 for normal picture amplitude (FIG. 12-55).

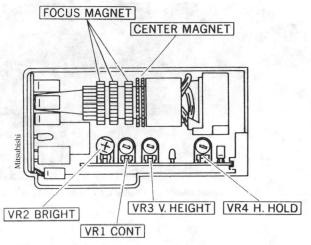

12-55 *Mitsubishi HS-C20U EVF vertical scanning adjustment.*

Pentax PV-C850A (8 mm) EVF Brightness Adjust   Aim the camera at the resolution chart. Adjust RT 1804 (bright) so that the EVF picture is clean (FIG. 12-56).

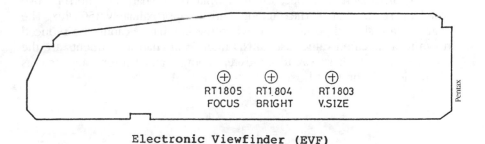

12-56 *Pentax PV-C850A (8 mm) EVF brightness adjustment.*

Realistic 150 (VHS-C) EVF Focus Adjust   This control adjusts for optimum focus of the electronic viewfinder (EVF). Aim the camera at the resolution chart. Adjust the focus control (RT 1803) for maximum resolution of the EVF display (FIG. 12-57).

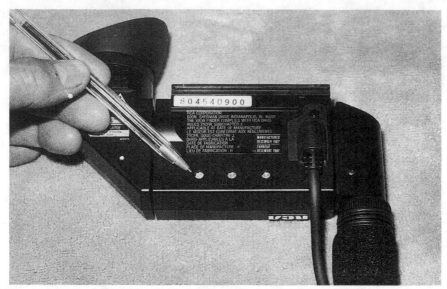

12-57   Bottom control adjustment of RCA's CPR300 (VHS) electronic view-finder.

ADJUSTMENT NOTES

After replacing the heads and preamplifier, make the FO/Q, VCO-PLL, AFC, and playback (PB) level adjustments. If the drum assembly is replaced, the FO/Q adjustment is needed. Adjust the playback system prior to adjusting camera and deviation. Each manufacturer may have their own camcorder adjustment procedures.

Use a halogen lamp because most white/black charts are the reflective type. Adjust the chart surface temperature to approximately 1500 lux. The chart surface should be lit evenly. When the luminance cannot be reduced down to a specified value, use an ND filter. Wall chart adjustments are the cheapest and quickest way to go, except some manufacturers' adjustments are made with the light box.

Chapter 13

Troubleshooting

Troubleshooting the camcorder may not be as difficult as it seems. Try to match the most likely section on the block diagram with the defective symptom. Then, find the defective section on the regular schematic (FIG. 13-1). Most manufacturers have the schematics broken down into the various sections because one large schematic would be impossible to print.

For instance, if the trouble symptom was no color and the camera section was normal in black and white operation, check the chroma circuits. Likewise, if the color picture was normal with no sound, you would check the audio circuits and microphone. If more than one section was defective, check the power source. Although the following camcorder servicing methods on the different circuits may not be the same as the one you are working on, they are serviced in the same manner.

VOLTAGE MEASUREMENTS

Critical voltage measurements with correct waveforms may solve critical service problems in the camcorder circuits. Only a few of the manufacturers place the actual voltage measurements on the schematic. Separate voltage charts are given in the back of the service manual. Several manufacturers break down the voltage charts with the camcorder in the various modes (stop, record, play, rewind, fast forward, review search, and forward search) (TABLE 13-1).

If the loading motor was not operating properly, check the voltage on the loading motor drive IC903. Check the input signal and voltage on pins 5 for loading and 6 for unloading. Measure the dc supply sources of 8.9 volts on pin 4 and 11.8 volts on pins 7 and 8 of IC 903 (FIG. 13-2). Check for correct motor operating voltage on pins 2 and 10. Usually, accurate voltage measurements locate the defective component.

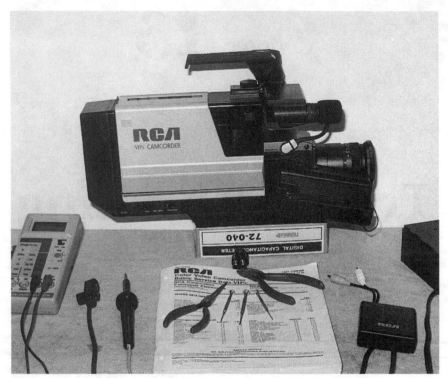

13-1 *Check the block diagram and then the schematic to locate the possibly defective component.*

SCOPE WAVEFORMS

There are many critical waveforms to be taken in the camcorder circuits. Critical waveforms may determine if the circuit is working or not. Waveforms taken throughout the camcorder signal paths may locate the defective section or stage. Often, signal tracing with the scope and critical voltage measurements uncover the defective component. Critical waveforms of the process, servo, sensor, luma/chroma, and the electronic viewfinder (EVF) circuits are given in the manufacturer's literature.

For instance, to determine if the mechacon circuits are performing in the Zenith VM6150 camcorder, critical waveforms taken of the reset, clock, supply reel sensor, and end sensor LED are given (FIG. 13-3). The various test points are shown in FIG. 13-4.

COMMON FAILURES

A "dead" camcorder may result from a blown fuse, or poor battery voltage or ac power supply. Check the battery terminals for poor connections. Test the camcorder in both battery and ac operation to determine if the power source or the camcorder is defective. Sometimes the camera detection circuits shut the camcorder down if the battery is too low, although it's possi-

Table 13-1.   System Control Voltages
(RCA CPR300)

MODE / PIN NO.	IC903						
	STOP	REC	PLAY	REW	F. FWD	REV S.	FWD S.
PIN 1	0	0	0	0	0	0	0
PIN 2	0	–	0	0	0	0	0
PIN 3	0	0	0	0	0	0	0
PIN 4	0	8.9	8.9	8.9	8.9	8.9	8.9
PIN 5	0	0	0	0	0	0	0
PIN 6	0	0	0	0	0	0	0
PIN 7	11.8	11.6	11.8	11.7	11.7	11.8	11.8
PIN 8	11.8	11.6	11.8	11.7	11.7	11.8	11.8
PIN 9	0	0	0	0	0	0	0
PIN 10	0	0	0	0	0	0	0

MODE / PIN NO.	IC904 (Continued)						
	STOP	REC	PLAY	REW	F. FWD	REV S.	FWD S.
PIN 5	0.9	0.8	0	–	–	–	–
PIN 6	2.7	2.7	2.7	–	–	–	–
PIN 7	2.7	2.8	–	–	–	–	–
PIN 8	0	0	0	0	0	0	0

MODE / PIN NO.	IC905						
	STOP	REC	PLAY	REW	F. FWD	REV S.	FWD S.
PIN 1	11.0	10.9	11.0	11.0	11.0	11.0	11.0
PIN 2	0	0	0	0	0	0	0
PIN 3	0	5.5	5.5	0	0	5.5	5.5
PIN 9	5.2	5.2	5.2	–	–	5.2	5.2
PIN 10	0	0	0	–	–	0	0
PIN 11	–	0	–	–	–	0	0
PIN 12	0	0	0	0	0	0	0
PIN 13	0	0	–	–	0	0	0
PIN 14	3.6	0	–	–	–	–	–
PIN 15	–	–	0	–	–	–	–
PIN 16	5.2	5.2	5.2	5.2	5.2	5.2	5.2

MODE / PIN NO.	IC904						
	STOP	REC	PLAY	REW	F. FWD	REV S.	FWD S.
PIN 1	5.2	5.2	5.2	5.2	5.2	5.2	5.2
PIN 2	0	0	0	0	0	0	0
PIN 3	0.5	0.5	0.5	0.5	0.5	0.5	0.5
PIN 4	0	4.7	0	4.7	0	0	0

MODE / Tr No.	STOP			REC			PLAY			REW			F. FWD			REV S.			FWD S.			MODE / Tr No.
	E	C	B	E	C	B	E	C	B	E	C	B	E	C	B	E	C	B	E	C	B	
Q 901	0	11.5	0	0	11.6	0	0	11.8	0	0	11.8	0	0	11.8	0	0	11.8	0	0	11.8	0	Q 901
Q 902	0	0	0	0	11.6	0	0	11.8	0	0	11.8	0	0	11.8	0	0	11.8	0	0	11.8	0	Q 902
Q 903	0	0.6	0	0	0.6	0	0	0.6	0	0	0.6	0	0	0.6	0	0	0.6	0	0	0.6	0	Q 903
Q 904	11.2	11.0	11.8	11.4	10.9	11.6	11.2	11.0	11.8	11.2	11.0	11.8	11.2	11.0	11.8	11.2	11.0	11.8	11.2	11.0	11.8	Q 904
Q 905	5.2	0	5.2	5.2	0	5.2	4.5	5.2	5.2	5.2	0	5.2	5.2	0	5.2	4.4	5.2	5.2	4.4	5.2	5.2	Q 905
Q 908	4.9	0	5.2	5.2	5.2	4.4	4.7	0.1	5.2	4.6	0.1	5.2	4.6	0.1	5.2	0	5.2	4.6	0	5.2	4.6	Q 908
Q 911	4.7	–	–	4.7	–	–	4.7	–	–	4.7	–	–	4.7	–	–	4.7	–	–	4.7	–	–	Q 911
Q 912	4.4	3.9	4.7	0	3.9	0	4.4	3.9	4.7	–	–	4.7	–	–	4.7	–	–	4.7	–	–	4.7	Q 912
Q 913	0	0	0	0	0	0	4.2	4.7	4.7	0	0	4.7	4.2	4.6	4.6	4.2	4.6	4.6	4.2	4.6	4.6	Q 913
Q 914	0	0	0	0	0	0	0	0	0	0	0	0	0	0	0	0	0	0	0	0	0	Q 914
Q 915	0	–	0	0	–	0	0	–	0	0	–	0	0	–	0	0	–	0	0	–	0	Q 915
Q 916	0	–	0	0	–	0	0	–	0	0	–	0	0	–	0	0	–	0	0	–	0	Q 916
Q 918	–	–	–	–	–	–	–	–	–	–	–	–	–	–	–	–	–	–	–	–	–	Q 918
Q 919	–	–	–	–	–	–	–	–	–	–	–	–	–	–	–	–	–	–	–	–	–	Q 919

RCA

ble that the tape movement could continue to operate. Monitor the battery voltage with the camcorder operating to determine if the battery breaks down under load. In some models, the cassette must be loaded before any power comes on.

The fuse may be blown or intermittent. The intermittent operation may be caused with a loose fuse in the connector. Sometimes the fuse's metal ends have arced and cause a poor contact, resulting in intermittent operation. When checking the fuse in place, measure the voltage from metal clip to clip to determine if the fuse is open or has poor contact.

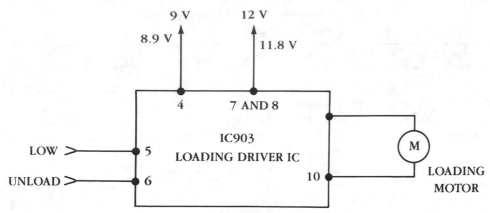

13-2 *Check the supply voltage on IC903 to troubleshoot no loading motor rotation.*

No Picture

This may be caused with the lens cap on, showing nothing in the viewfinder. Check the white switch setting and brightness control. Recheck the manual iris setting. Determine if the tape is moving. Connect the camcorder to the TV set or monitor to determine if viewfinder is defective.

No Picture in Viewfinder

May be caused by a defective or improper setting of the camera/playback switch. Make sure the switch is in playback mode. Make sure the EVF cable is plugged in tight. Check the EVF connection for bent or misaligned prongs. If no picture in the viewfinder, connect camcorder to TV set monitor to make sure EVF is not operating.

No Picture or Sound

Make sure camera/playback switch is in playback mode. Check the power distribution source for a common defective power source.

No Audio

May result from a defective microphone or cables. Most of these microphones plug directly into the EVF assembly or camera. Clean mike controls. Make sure the ring tightner is snug. Try another external microphone. Next, check the VCR sound circuits.

No or Improper Color

This may be caused by poor or insufficient lighting. Check the camera with proper white setup adjustments. Sometimes extreme light from the bright sun outdoors coming through the living room picture window causes poor color pictures. Check color temperature switch setting.

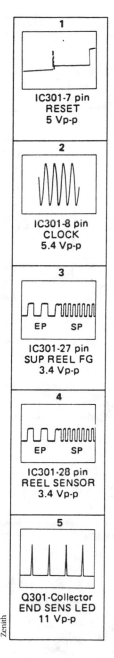

13-3 *Critical waveforms are taken of the Zenith VM6150 mechancon circuits.*

Fuzzy or Out of Focus

This may result from improper focus of the zoom lens. When the zoom motor is operating the picture may naturally be out of focus for a few seconds. Sometimes changing quickly from scene far away to a close-up shot may be out of focus. Poor lighting may result in fuzzy pictures.

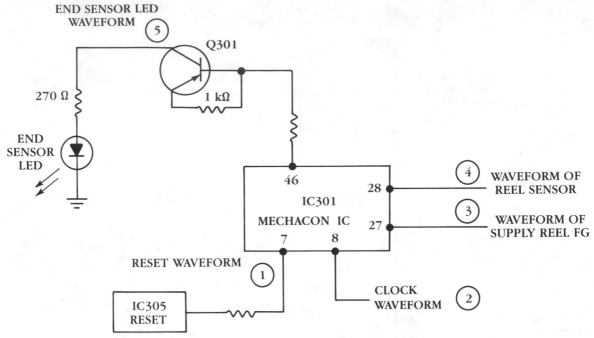

13-4 *The various test points correspond with the waveforms in Fig. 13-3.*

Damaged Parts

Damage to parts is usually caused by the operator dropping the camcorder or rough treatment. If the camcorder uses a pickup tube as sensor, the glass tube may be broken. You can hear the rattling of pieces of glass, indicating pickup tube damage.

Cracked or Broken Boards

Cracked boards may produce dead or intermittent camcorder operation. Make sure all board sockets are firmly pushed down. Look for heavy objects mounted on the pc board for the cracked areas. Sometimes the pc wiring can be repaired. Try to splice the cracked area. Do not run long wire leads. Be careful around multilead microprocessors and ICs because the leads are close together and may be difficult to repair. Replace cracked boards.

Poor Soldered Joints

Poor soldering may cause intermittent or dead operations. Push down and pry up on a board at different areas to uncover a badly soldered connection. Sometimes the poorly soldered connection may be solved by soldering all joints in that area. Be very careful not to apply too much solder so that it doesn't run into another circuit.

You may find a lot of poor joints or broken boards in the camcorder. This is due to the fact it is carried around in many different places. Check for large parts or shields for poorly soldered connections. Sometimes cooling these joints with cooling solution helps to make it act up to aid in pinpointing the problem. A Zenith VM6150 symptom and checkpoint chart is given in TABLE 13-2.

TROUBLESHOOTING THE VARIOUS CIRCUITS

Many of the manufacturer's provide a troubleshooting flow chart of what components to check in the proper order. Besides critical waveform and voltage measurements, camera electrical adjustments may determine if that particular circuit is defective. Do not overlook doing accurate resistance measurements in difficult circuits.

No Power

With no VCR or camera operation, go to the power input circuits. Try the camcorder in both battery and ac operation. A blinking green LED in the viewfinder may indicate a weak battery. If nothing, plug in the ac power supply. Check the fuse. Make sure battery or external jack is normal. If okay, measure the voltage at the fuse terminals. Proceed into the circuit and do not overlook an isolation polarity diode in the dc power line. Check the voltage going into the power circuits (FIG. 13-5). If it comes on and then shuts off, it could be that the end-of-reel detection circuit has activated.

Table 13-2.   Symptoms and Checkpoints (Zenith VM6150)

	Symptom	Checkpoint	Remark
1	No power ON	Cassette absent. Cassette switch (sensor) and REC safety switch must be ON before power is supplied.	
2	Cassette present, but power not supplied	Erase protector tab of the cassette missing or REC safety switch is defective. In this case, when the DC jack is connected, the power LED lights and loading motor sound can be heard. However, operating the power switch does not supply power.	Power ON obtained in Test (emergency OFF) mode.
3	Occasionally in recording, REC Lock mode, then power OFF. Again setting power ON produces the REC Pause mode, after which recording is enabled.	Check REC safety switch for faulty contacts (replace if necessary).	
4	While recording, unloading, then power OFF. Afterwards, no power ON.	Tape end or defective type.	When end of tape is detected, power is switched OFF. Afterwards, only Eject is enabled.
5	During service with external covers removed, inserting a cassette starts loading, but immediately, unloading and power OFF. Afterwards, no power ON.	End sensor activated. Check for following possibilities. 1) Cassette at end of tape. 2) Tape not engaged with SP guide pole. 3) Nearby infrared light source.	
6	At power ON, POWER LED lights briefly and loading motor sound can be heard, but immediatly power OFF.	Cassette switch OFF (light strikes sensor). If during service, cassette housing light not blocked by lever. Also check PHS303.	With both mode sensors A and B Low, and cassette switch OFF, loading motor turns to Stop position.
7	Dew sensor activated.	Check MDA board CN701 contacts. Observe that pin plug and jack are firmly mated. Also check CN401.	

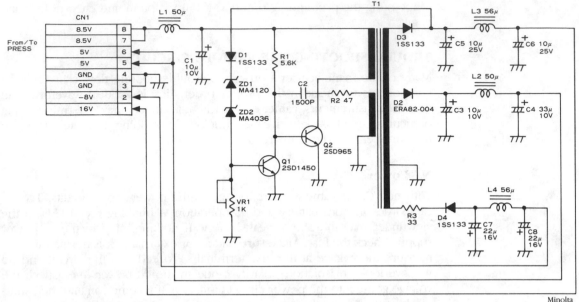

13-5 *Minolta C3300 power circuits.*

Measure the 5-volt source at pins 5 and 6. Check for a −8 volts at pin 2 and −16 volts at pin 1. If no voltage, check D2, D3, and D4 with the diode tester. Very low output voltage may be caused by a burned resistor, leaky diode, or open filter capacitor. Check the diodes and transistors in the primary circuits with a transistor tester. Measure the primary and secondary windings' continuity with the low range of the ohmmeter.

In other camcorders, the power circuit may consist of transistor switching, power on, and power off circuits (FIG. 13-6). Check fuse FQ70. Measure the voltage at the fuse terminals. Check the external jack and D970 if no voltage is at the fuse. Measure the voltage at the emitter and collector of Q904. No collector voltage may indicate leaky or open Q904 transistor. Proceed to IC 905, the 5.6-volt regulator (if no 5-volt source). Suspect D914 if there is voltage at pin 1 of IC905 (no 5 V2 or 5 V3).

Notice if RL901 is energizing. Check the coils for continuity. Measure the voltage at pin 14 of the power switch IC901 (4.6 V). Check ZD901 for leakage. If no 5-volt output, check each regulator circuit (Q909 and Q908) and switching regulators IC951 and Q52.

No Power Supply to Camera

Set the select switch to CAMERA mode and check the picture in the viewfinder. Try the camcorder with the ac power supply and required battery. If the camera or VCR do not operate, go directly to the power distribution circuits. Check the 9- and 12-volt sources. If there is no or low voltage on pin 2 of IC 1401, check switch Q1401, Q1403, and diode D-1401 (FIG. 13-7). Check the 9-volt regulator (IC1401) and 5-volt regulators (IC1402)for leak-

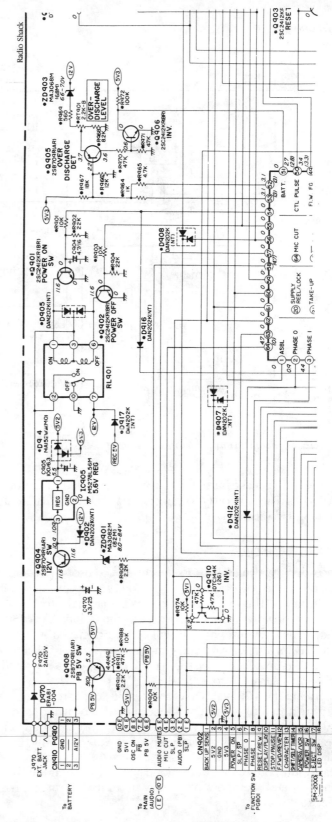

13-6 *Realistic 150 power circuits.*

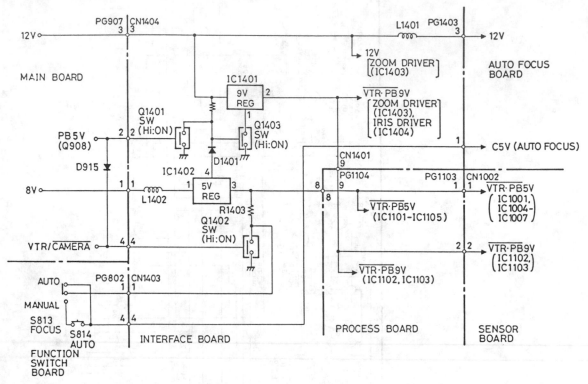

13-7   *Realistic 150 power supply distribution board.* Radio Shack

age or open conditions. Make sure the 12-volt source is fed to the distribution board at P6907. The no-power-to-camera flowchart of the RCA CPR100 power distribution circuits is given FLOWCHART 13-1.

DEACTIVATING SENSORS

In some camcorders, you may have to deactivate a sensor in order to use the EMERGENCY ON mode for observing operation, waveforms, and locating the source of trouble. The REC safety left switch may have to be shorted together to supply power to the camcorder. In the Zenith VM 6150 VCR, cover the photosensor with tape so it will not be damaged with cassette switch on. Construct a jumper wire and connect it to pin 1 of CN1 and pin 3 of PH S301, the take-up reel sensor (FIG. 13-8 and FIG. 13-9). Use a small, stiff wire in the clip for inserting into PHS301 pin 3.

When operating the VCR without a cassette, the supply reel sensor must be deactivated in order to avoid emergency shutdown in the Zenith VM 6150 camcorder (FIG. 13-10 and FIG. 13-11). This type of shorting arrangement is made to defeat both the supply and take-up reels. Sometimes the "tape remaining" indicator appears, but it does not affect the operation. Double-check the deactivating of sensors when not using a cassette in the machine. If power comes on and then goes off, it may mean that a battery charge is nearly completed.

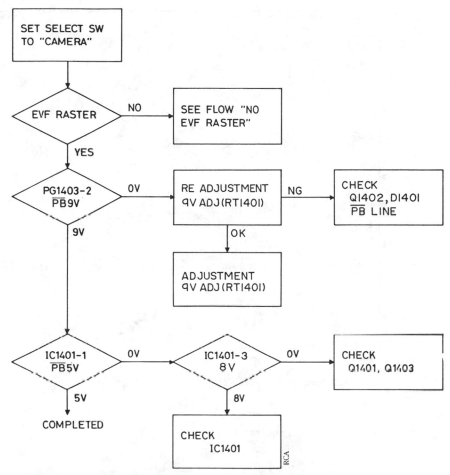

Flowchart 13-1   *RCA CPR100 "No Power to Camera" troubleshooting flowchart.*

NO AUTO FOCUS

Try shifting the camera to different scenes to determine if the lens is changing back and forth in auto focus operation. Often the camera section must be torn down to get at the focus motor and circuits (FIG. 13-12). If not, check the regulated voltage at the outer focus circuit. Here 5 volts should be applied to the auto focus circuits (FIG. 13-13). Check the infrared D5 with infrared tester. Test IC3 with no voltage at pin 1. Next check on switches Q4 and Q3. Measure the 5 volts applied to the process IC1. The controlling

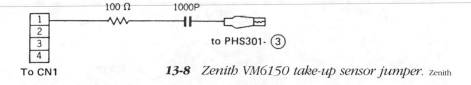

To CN1   **13-8**   *Zenith VM6150 take-up sensor jumper.* Zenith

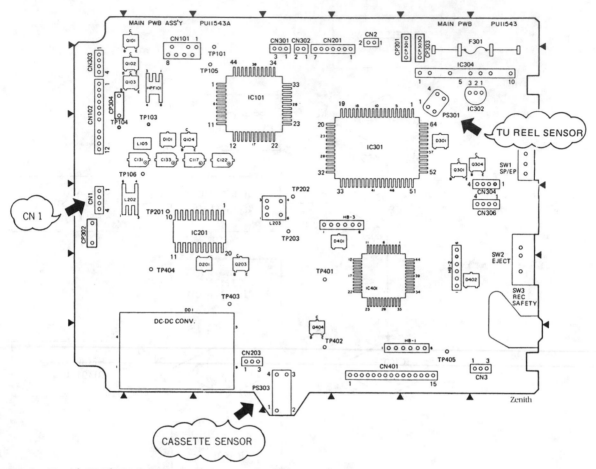

13-9 *Zenith VM6150 location of CN1 and take-up reel sensor on the chassis.*

focus motor signal is found at pins 12 and 13 of IC1. Measure the supply voltage applied to the motor drive IC2. Check the voltage across the motor terminals at pins 1 and 2 of the focus motor. Remove motor plug and check motor continuity if no motor rotation. It's possible to have a leaky infrared diode (D5), process (IC1), or IC2. The focus motor should be replaced with original part number.

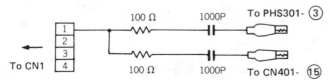

13-10 *Zenith VM6150 supply and take-up reel shorting cable.* Zenith

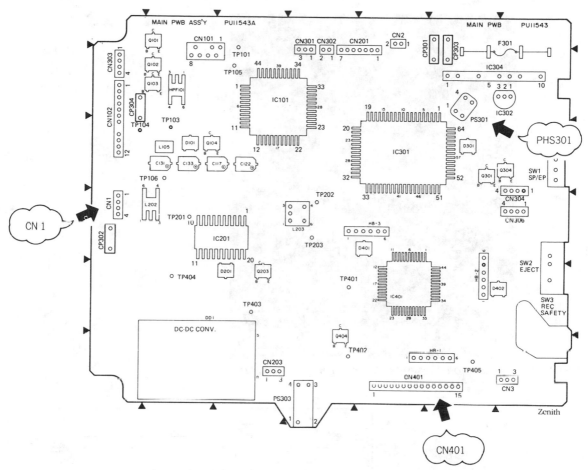

13-11 *Zenith VM6150 chassis location of CN1 plug, PHS301, and CN401 socket.*

Pentax PV-C850A Auto Focus Circuits   Before tearing into the camera, place auto focus switch on auto. Place a white cardboard a foot from the lens assembly and notice if the lens assembly moves. Take it away, and the assembly should move again. If not, check the infrared transmitting diode with the infrared diode tester. This diode, with the phototransistors, are located at the front and bottom of the lens assembly in most cameras.

Remove camera covers to get at the auto focus board and LED. Check the voltage (7.2 V) at the B + switch Q2AF (FIG. 13-14). Measure the +5 volts at pin 3 of the 5 V regulator (IC3AF). The 5 V regulator may be leaky or open with low or no voltage at pin 3. Next, check the voltage applied to the auto focus IC1AF. Likewise, measure the voltage at LED driver Q4AF, pre-amp IC4AF and voltage at pins 2 and 13 of IC1AF (3.6 V). This voltage is sent to the focus motor drive IC2AF. Check the motor voltage at pins 5 and 8 of

13-12   *Auto focus motor assembly located on Quasar VM10 camcorder.*

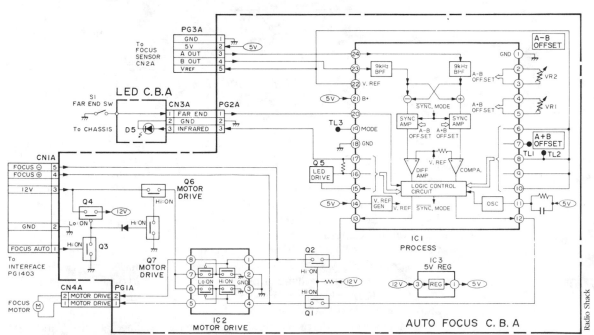

13-13   *Realistic 150 auto focus circuits.*

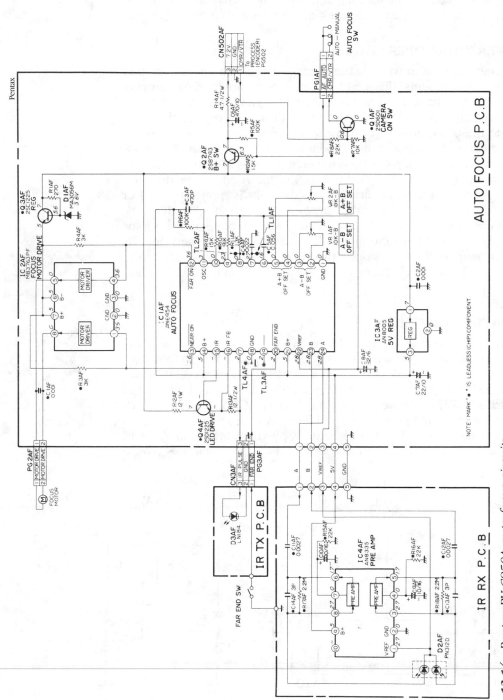

13-14 *Pentax PV-C850A auto focus circuits.*

the focus motor. Remove motor plug and check the focus motor with low ohmmeter continuity resistance for open motor winding.

NO POWER ZOOM OPERATION

The iris, auto focus, auto white balance, and power zoom circuits are tied together in some models. If none of these functions are working, suspect improper supply voltage. Press and hold the tele (T) and wide (W) switches. Notice if the lens assembly moves out or in. Check the regulated voltage supplied to the zoom drive IC or transistors.

In the Canon VM-E2NA (8 mm) zoom operation, the zoom circuits independently work off the 5-volt power source (FIG. 13-15). When the tele (T) switch is pushed, 5 volts is applied to pin 8 of the zoom motor drive IC. Likewise, when the side (W) switch is pressed, 5 volts is applied to pin 1 of the zoom drive IC 4005. Check the supply voltage at pin 13 of IC 4005. When the tele switch is pressed, measure the 5 volts at pin 8 and check for 4.3 volts at pin 9 going to the motor. If voltage is going in and none is coming out, suspect IC 4005. Suspect the motor when voltage is applied to the motor terminals. Check the motor terminal for continuity with the ohmmeter.

IRIS CONTROL CIRCUITS

Usually the iris circuits are controlled from the AGC and ALC module. If the iris unit does not function, scope the AGC and iris detector waveforms entering the iris board module or IC (pins 13 and 19). Check the CLP3 waveform (pin 18) from the timing generator and the VD waveform (pin 9) of the iris driver IC721. Measure the supply voltage on IC721 (FIG. 13-16). Check the continuity of the iris motor drive and field coils.

The iris detector and AGC signals are applied at pins 2 and 12 of IC 1404 in the Realistic 150 iris circuits (FIG. 13-17). First check the B+ voltage

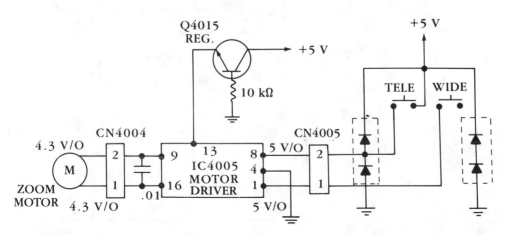

13-15 *Zoom motor circuits in the Canon (8 mm) VM-E2NA camcorder.*

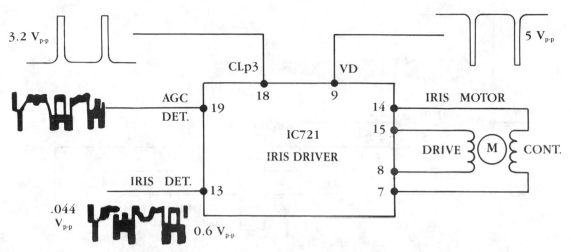

13-16 *The iris circuit in the Sony CCD-M8E/M8U camera circuits.*

(pin 1) with no iris movement. Notice the drive coil winding of the motor is supplied by +9 volts and is tied to pin 9. Measure the damping voltage at pin 7 and 8 of IC 1404. Check the continuity of the damp and drive coils of the iris motor with the low ohmmeter scale. Low drive voltage may indicate a leaky iris drive IC.

CAPSTAN DOES NOT ROTATE

The following symptoms might occur in the Zenith VM 6150: the tape is inserted and after about 2 seconds, it unloads and indicates "drum emergency." There is no take-up action. About 1 second after power is on in RED LOCK, unloading and drum emergency occurs, and it ejects the cassette. These symptoms indicate that there is no drum or capstan motor rotation. Check SP302, the dc-dc converter, and there might be a broken belt. If the motor is operating and there is no action, check for broken or off capstan motor belt.

When only the capstan motor does not rotate in short REW, short FF, REW, FF, idler shift, and unloading, the signal is normally controlled from the mechacon circuits.

The control signal for REC/PLAY is controlled by the servo circuits. Check CN401, D301, dc-dc converter, IC601, CN601, IC301, and D/A circuits (FIG. 13-18). Notice the capstan FWD voltage is 2.5 V, and in the stop position, 5 V is at pin 10 of CN401. Check for open motor field continuity with ohmmeter.

RCA CPR100 Capstan Motor Circuits   The capstan motor is controlled by IC driver IC604 (FLOWCHART 13-2). If the FF/REW rotation is normal and there's no CW/CCW rotation, check the voltage at IC901. If no FF or REW, check the 12 V supply source at pin 7 of IC604. In play (or forward) mode,

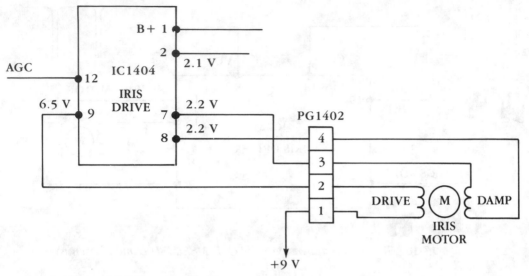

13-17   *Realistic 150 iris motor circuits.* Radio Shack

the capstan B+ voltage at pin 8 of IC604 is 2 V. With FF operation, the capstan B+ voltage at pin 8 of IC604 is 4.6 V (FIG. 13-19). Check motor coil continuity with voltage applied to the motor. Measure the forward and reverse motor voltage applied to the motor. Suspect capstan motor if voltages are present.

DOES NOT EJECT OR LOAD

In the RCA CPR300 camcorder, when loading begins, the main brake releases both reels. The tape from the cassette is loaded by the guide roller. During unloading, the pressure roller is the first thing released. The main brake prevents the tape from fluctuating and take-up brake is on to prevent tape from pulled out of the take-up reel (FIG. 13-20).

Press the EJECT switch. The system control IC provides the load and unload signal to the loading motor driver IC. Notice if the loading motor is running when unloading, the motor system ejects the mechanism and door (FLOWCHART 13-3). Check the supply voltage on the loading motor driver IC102. Check the voltages on pin 13 (unloading) and pin 4 when loading IC102. If voltage is present, check the motor connector and motor winding for continuity (FIG. 13-21). When the cassette housing does not raise or the cassette eject system does not function with the motor rotating, suspect mechanical problems with the cassette housing or take-up loading rings. Double-check the eject mechanism for bent or out-of-line lever and door.

CYLINDER MOTOR DOES NOT OPERATE

In many camcorders, the drum (cylinder) and capstan motors operate from the servo system. A problem symptom may be that when the tape is inserted, it loads for 1 or 2 seconds and then unloads. There is no take-up or

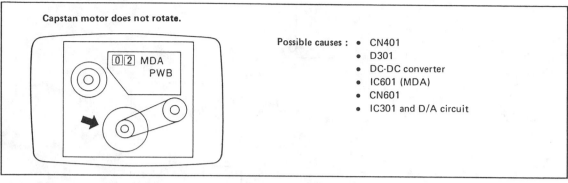

Capstan motor does not rotate.

Possible causes :
- CN401
- D301
- DC-DC converter
- IC601 (MDA)
- CN601
- IC301 and D/A circuit

Notes:

- The capstan motor is normally controlled from the mechacon, except for some situations when it is controlled from the servo circuit. This switching is performed by the CAP. REF. CTL signal at IC301 pin 47.

	Mechacon CPU voltage	Operations
1) Controlled from mechacon	IC301 pin 47 : L IC301 pins 63, 64, 1, 2 : D/A voltage	Short REW, Short FF, REW, FF, Idler shift, Unloading
2) Controlled from servo	IC301 pin 47 : H IC301 pins 63, 64, 1, 2 : L	REC/Play

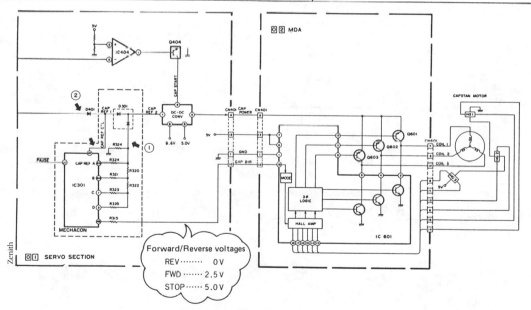

13-18 *Zenith VM6150 "Capstan Does Not Rotate" troubleshooting data.*

drum rotation. Check CP302, dc-dc converter, servo, belt, and drum motor in the Zenith VM6150 servo system for no drum rotation (FIG. 13-22).

The signal from the main servo system is applied to pin 13 of cylinder motor driver IC551. The driver voltage is fed to the three windings on the cylinder motor out of pins 10, 11, and 12 (4.4 V). Likewise, the cylinder FG

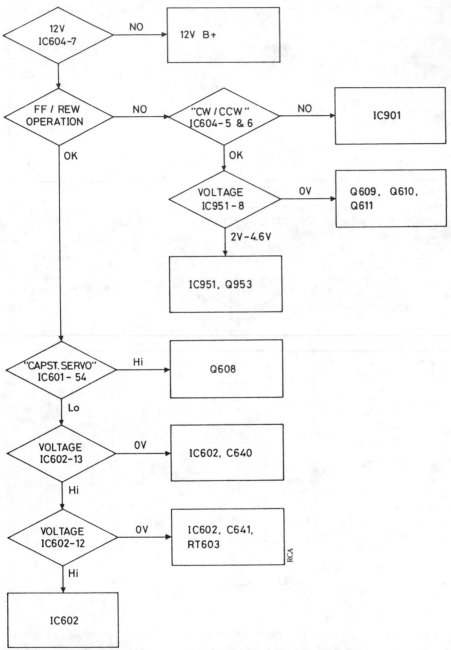

Flowchart 13-2   *RCA CPR100 capstan motor flowchart.*

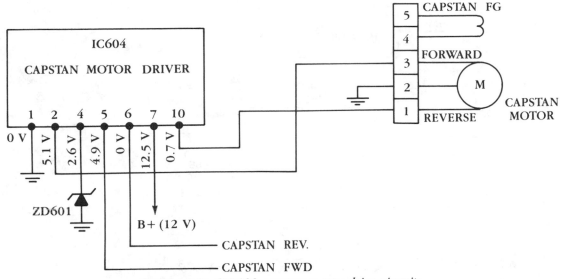

13-19 *RCA CPR100 capstan motor drive circuits.*

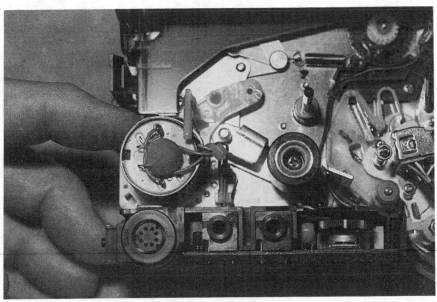

13-20 *Loading motor in RCA CPR300 camcorder.*

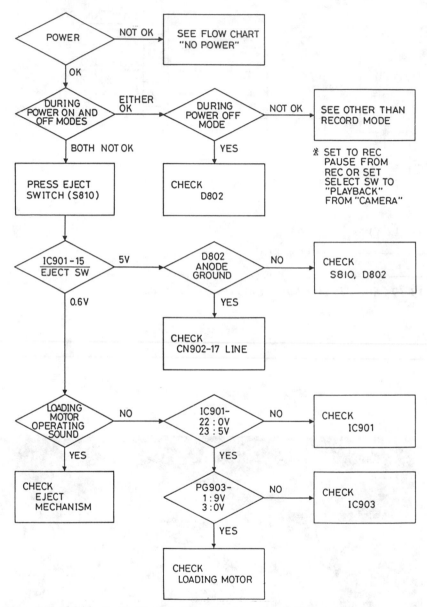

Flowchart 13-3 *Realistic 150 "Cassette Not Ejected" flowchart.* Radio Shack

and PG pulse from the cylinder motor assembly 13, 14, and 15 are taken from pins 3 and 4 of the cylinder motor drive circuits (FIG. 13-23). Check the input signal, measure B+ voltage on pin 13 (6.9 V), check the driver voltage output to cylinder motor terminals, and check the cylinder motor winding with the ohmmeter.

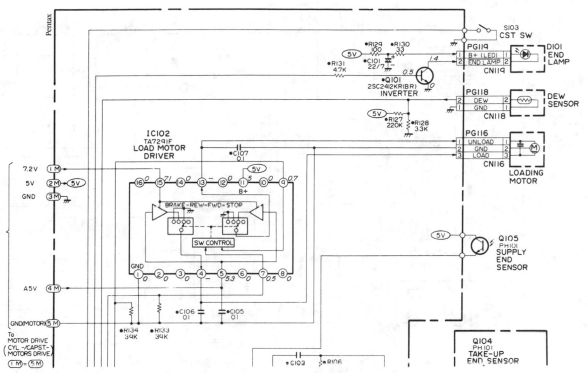

13-21 *Pentax PV-C850A loading motor circuits.*

ABNORMAL ROTATION OF DRUM MOTOR

The drum or cylinder motor does not rotate properly during recording. Check the servo speed control circuits in the Zenith VM6150 VCR. Check for zero volts at pin 37 of IC401. Take a drum PG waveform at pin 17 of IC401 (FLOWCHART 13-4). Inspect the FG waveforms at pin 8 of CN501. Check the drum pickup head.

DETECTORS NOT WORKING

When none of the trouble detection indicators work, suspect a defective system control IC (FLOWCHART 13-5). If no end lamp, check the end lamp voltage at pin 30 of IC901 (15 V). Then measure voltage applied to end LED. Suspect bad connecting cable contacts, no system control applied voltage or defective LED. Do not overlook an LED drive transistor.

If there's no supply reel or take-up sensor operation, check the B+, comparator IC, and system control IC. In the RCA CPR100 and Realistic 150 models, 5 volts is applied to the reel sensor circuits (FIG. 13-24). Do not overlook a defective sensor.

If the supply end sensor fails to work, measure the voltage at pin 12 (5 V) to Q123. The sensor signal is applied to the comparator IC (2.5 V). The

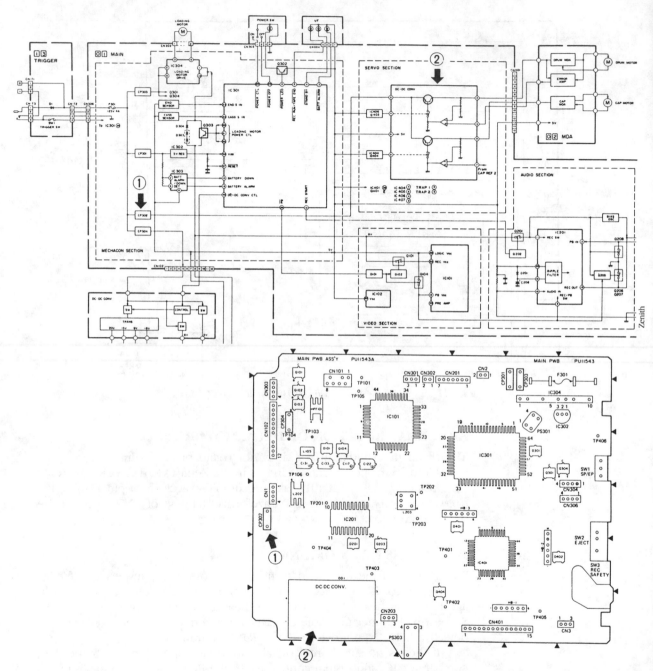

13-22 *Check CP302, the dc-dc converter, servo, belt, and drum motor in Zenith's VM6150 if no drum rotation.*

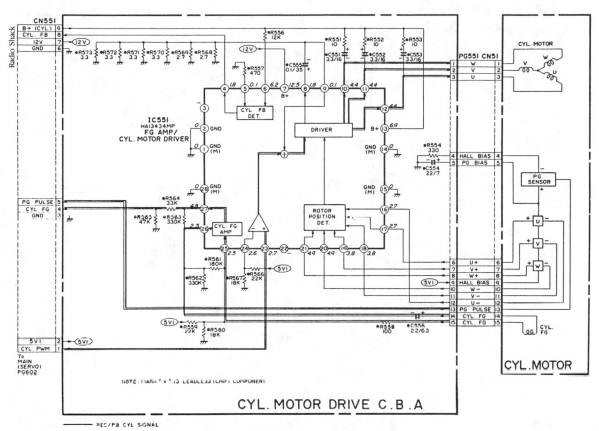

13-23 *Realistic 150 cylinder motor drive circuits.*

signal controlling the comparator IC is taken from pin 18 of the system control IC901. Make sure supply end light is lit. Test the supply end sensor with a transistor tester.

The VCR may not operate with a flashing dew test LED. The drum does not rotate during loading. Some times in unloading, the system stops for 5 minutes or so or shuts off. Check for a defective dew sensor or IC controlling the dew sensor circuits (FLOWCHART 13-6). Sometimes, when all LEDs flash, that indicates dew warning. When only some LEDs flash with no operation, that indicates an emergency mode, which requires service.

IMPROPER WHITE BALANCE

Check the incorrect white balance flowchart (FLOWCHART 13-7). In the RCA CPR100 process video circuits, measure the voltage at TP1107 off of pin 4 of IC1102 (1.4 V to 1.5 V). If no voltage, check supply voltage to IC1102 (B+, 9 V) pin 11 (FIG. 13-25). IC1102 may be defective with normal supply voltage and no voltage at TP1107.

Measure the voltage pin 15 of IC1104 (auto white balance IC). Check the voltage at pin 5 (2.9 V) of IC1104. If voltage is zero, inspect RM1101

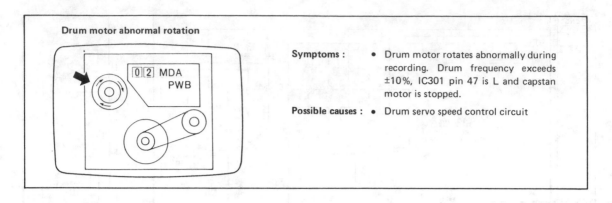

Drum motor abnormal rotation

0 2 MDA PWB

Symptoms :
- Drum motor rotates abnormally during recording. Drum frequency exceeds ±10%, IC301 pin 47 is L and capstan motor is stopped.

Possible causes :
- Drum servo speed control circuit

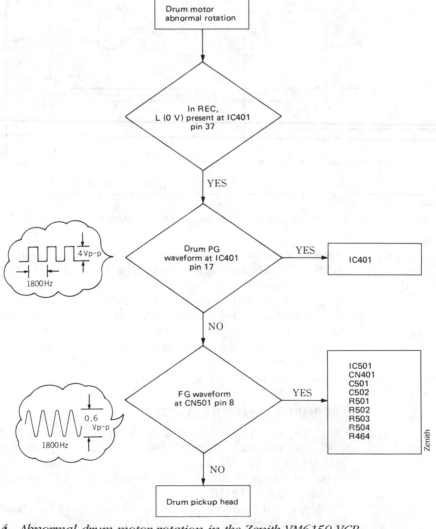

Flowchart 13-4 *Abnormal drum motor rotation in the Zenith VM6150 VCR.*

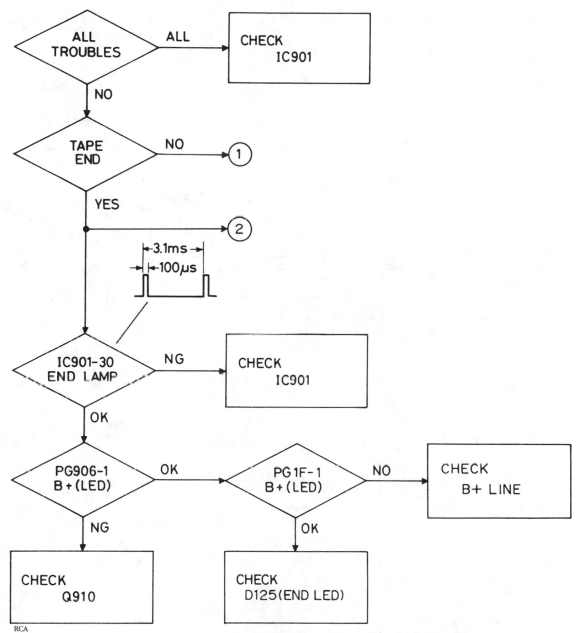

Flowchart 13-5 *RCA CPR100 "Does Not Detect Trouble" flowchart.*

TROUBLE SENSOR SCHEMATIC DIAGRAM

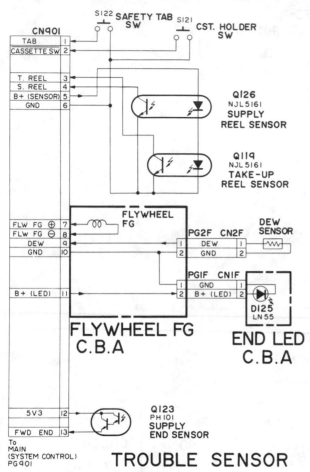

END LED P.C. BOARD (TOP VIEW)

END LED
C.B.A

END LED P.C. BOARD (BOTTOM VIEW)

END LED
C.B.A

13-24 *Realistic 150 trouble sensor circuits.* Radio Shack

(setup control). IC1104 may be defective if voltage is on pin 5 (2.9 V) and not on pin 15. Recheck voltages on pin 18 (0.3 V) and pin 19 (0.2 V). If no voltages are measured here, test voltages on IC1107.

NO ON-SCREEN DISPLAY

Check to see if any of the screen display lights are on. If not, inspect battery display, apply dc voltage to external battery jack, or exchange the battery. Does the display light up (E—F) with any tape rotation? Readjust the battery circuits. Make sure the camcorder is set to camera and record mode. If no display, check the 9- or 5-volt supply voltage. Measure voltages on power switches, overdischarge transistors, and regulators in the power dis-

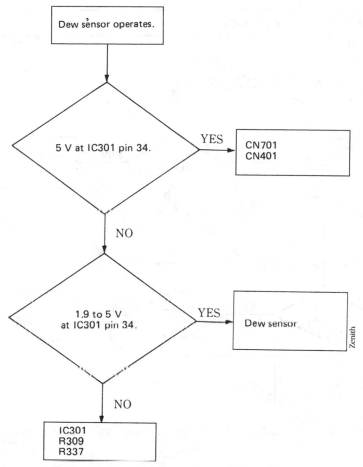

Flowchart 13-6   *Zenith VM6150 "Dew Sensor" flowchart.*

tribution. Check voltage on pins 29, 52, 53, and 26 (FIG. 13-26). Improper voltages may indicate defective system control IC.

NO VIDEO MONITOR

To check for lack of video monitor, check voltages and waveforms on the main video amp, A/V output, and luma process IC. Set select switch to camera mode. Aim the camera at the color bar chart. If EVF monitor not good, check IC301 and EVF circuits. Check video at A/V output, pins 1 and 8. Check pins 10 and 12 of IC301 for video signal (FIG. 13-27). If no signal, measure B+ voltage on IC301 and suspect IC301.

With no video on TV set or color monitor, check the video at pin 19 of IC201 (1 V_{p-p}). With no video, measure the voltage at pin 25 of IC201 (5 V). If no voltage, check the 5-volt supply line source (FIG. 13-28). If no voltage,

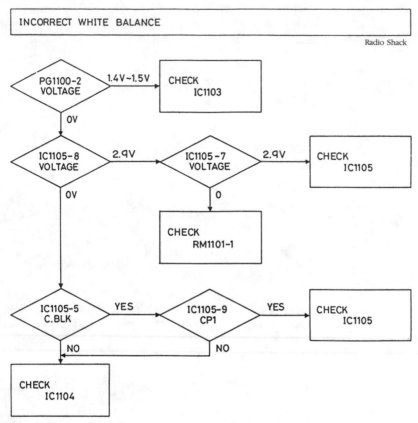

INCORRECT WHITE BALANCE

Radio Shack

Flowchart 13-7 *Realistic 150 "Incorrect White Balance" flowchart.*

check pin 24 of IC201 (video 210M p-1). Proceed to pin 15 of IC201 to look for video signal (1 V_{p-p}). Suspect IC201 if video waveform is at pin 15.

NO VIDEO RECORDING

A no-video-recording flowchart is shown in FLOWCHART 13-8. In the RCA CPR100, check the FM signal and voltage on head switch preamp (IC203), luminance process circuit for luma and video (IC201), detail enhancer for luma (IC206), and horizontal noise/video and luma (IC205).

Set the select switch to CAMERA and place in record mode. Check the FM signal at pin 25 of IC203 (FIG. 13-29). Now test for FM signal on pins 5, 11, 16, and 20 (3.5 to 4.2 V_{p-p}). If voltages are normal, check the video heads and tape. If no output voltages, check for 5 V on pin 26 of IC203. Zero volts at pins 26 and 24 indicates no 5-V source at pin 23. Suspect IC203 with 5 volts at pin 24 and recorded video out. Notice the playback (PB) and REC arrows in the schematic.

Go to the luminance circuits with no FM signal at pin 18 of the luma process IC201 (FIG. 13-30). If no luma signal on pin 7, suspect IC201. Test for

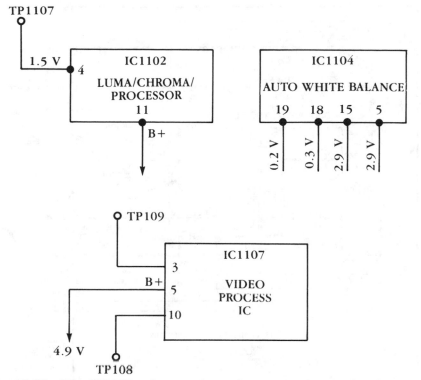

13-25 *RCA CPR100 voltage and waveform test points in the white balance circuits.*

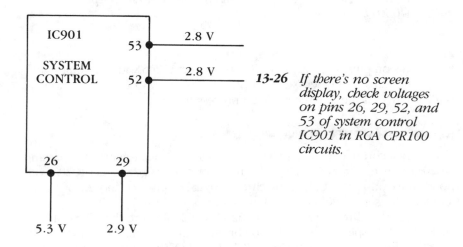

13-26 *If there's no screen display, check voltages on pins 26, 29, 52, and 53 of system control IC901 in RCA CPR100 circuits.*

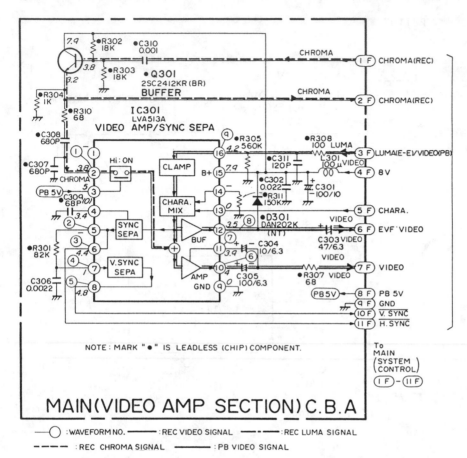

13-27 *Realistic 150 video signals on main video amp/sync separator (IC301).* Radio Shack

waveforms on pins 6, 7, and 10 of IC206. Suspect IC206 with no luma signal. Check the luma and video signal at pins 24, 26, and 27 of I201. No video at pin 27 may indicate a defective luma process IC201.

NO CHROMA RECORDING

Trace the chroma recording signal from the head-switching preamp (IC203), chroma process IC, and IC1104 (FLOWCHART 13-9). Suspect IC203 with no chroma on pin 5. Check for chroma signal at pins 21 and 22 of IC202. Measure the supply voltage (5 V) on pin 25 of IC203 (FIG. 13-31).

Check the chroma signal at pin 22 of IC202. Measure the PB 5-volt line (B+, 12 V). Suspect IC202 with no chroma signal at pin 27 (FIG. 13-32). Measure the chroma signal at pin 10 of IC1104 and Q301. Check for 5 V at pin 4 of IC1104. Suspect IC1104 if zero voltage and no recording chroma.

LUMINANCE/CHROMA (LUMINANCE) SCHEMATIC DIAGRAM

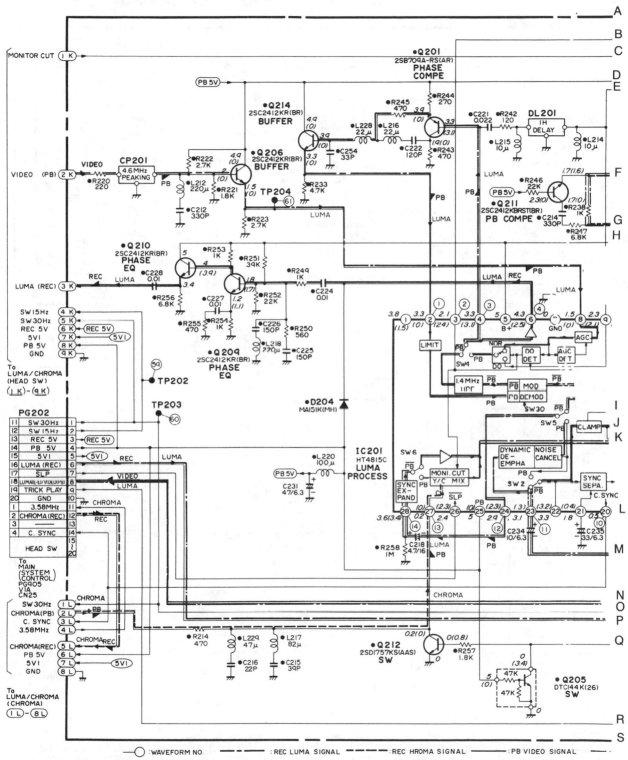

13-28 *Check luma signal and voltages on luma process (IC201) pins 15, 19, 24, and 25.*

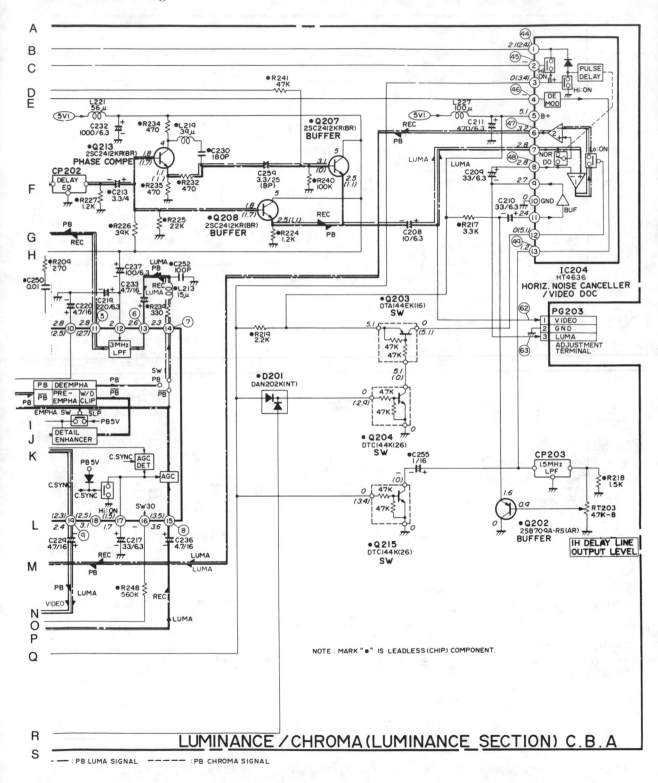

LUMINANCE / CHROMA (LUMINANCE SECTION) C.B.A

— : PB LUMA SIGNAL   ----- : PB CHROMA SIGNAL

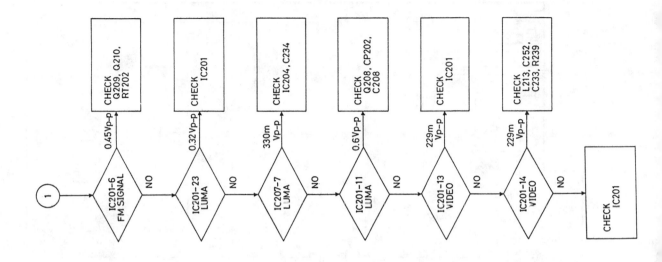

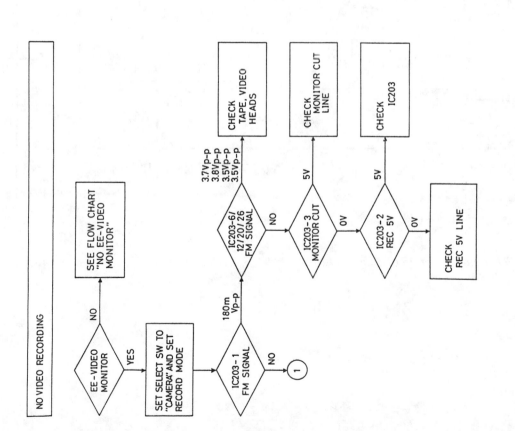

Flowchart 13-8 *Realistic 150 "No Video Recording" flowchart.*
Radio Shack

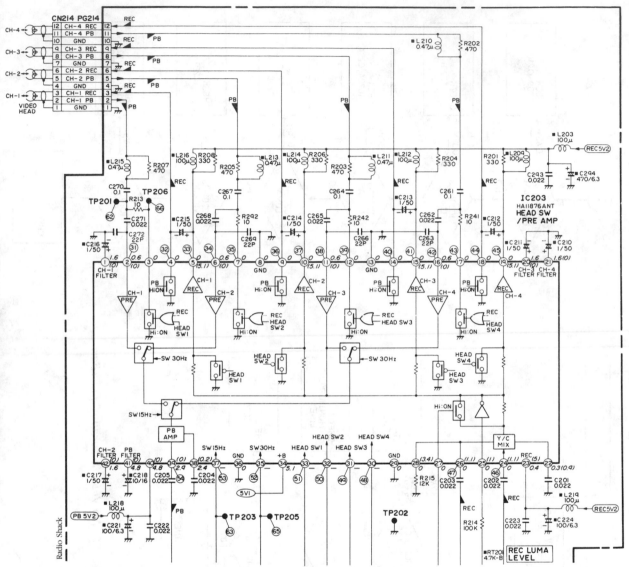

13-29 *Check for FM signal at pin 25 of IC203. Also check pins 5, 11, 16, and 20 for no video recording.*

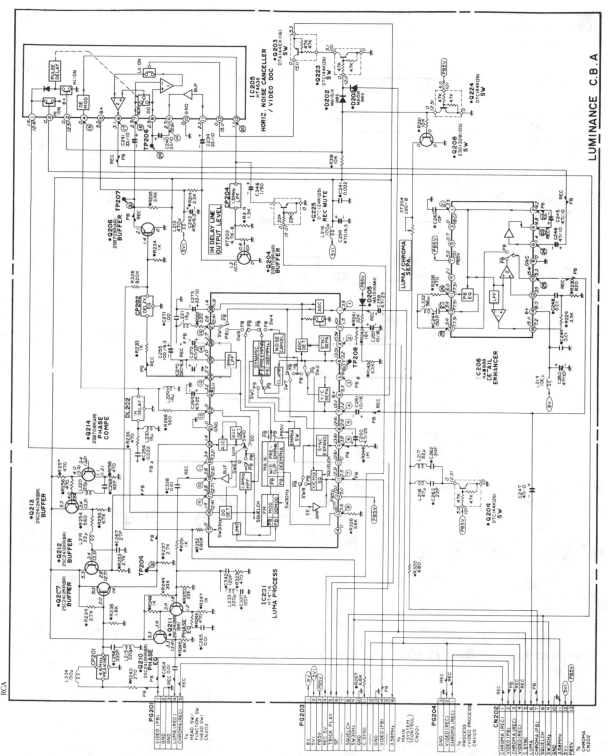

13-30 *Check for an FM signal at pin 18 of luma process (IC201) If no luma signal on pin 7, suspect IC201.*

NO CHROMA RECORDING

Radio Shack

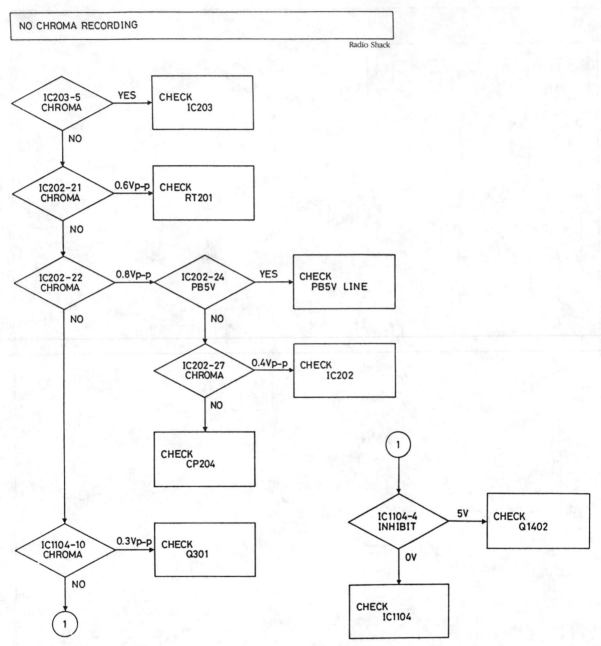

Flowchart 13-9   *Realistic 150 "No Chroma Recording" flowchart.*

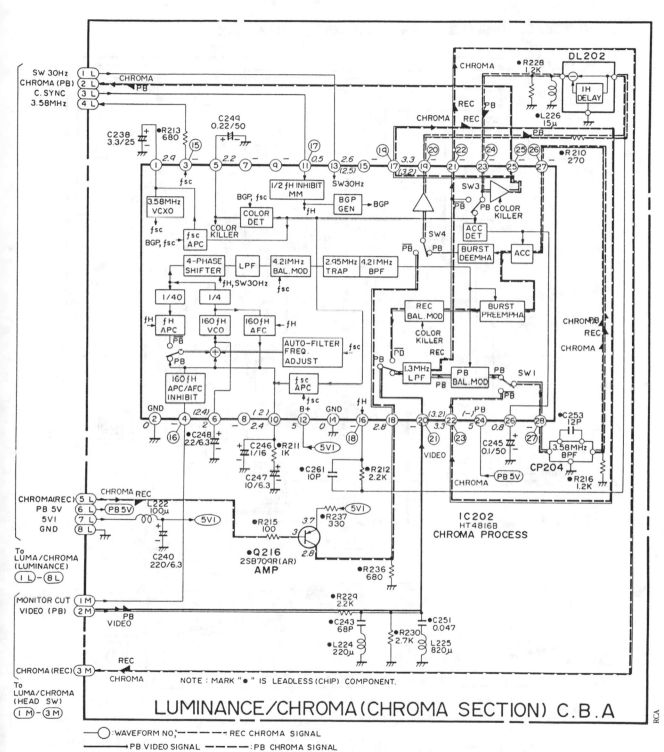

13-31 *Check chroma signal at pins 21 and 22 of IC202.*

LUMINANCE/CHROMA (HEAD SW) SCHEMATIC DIAGRAM

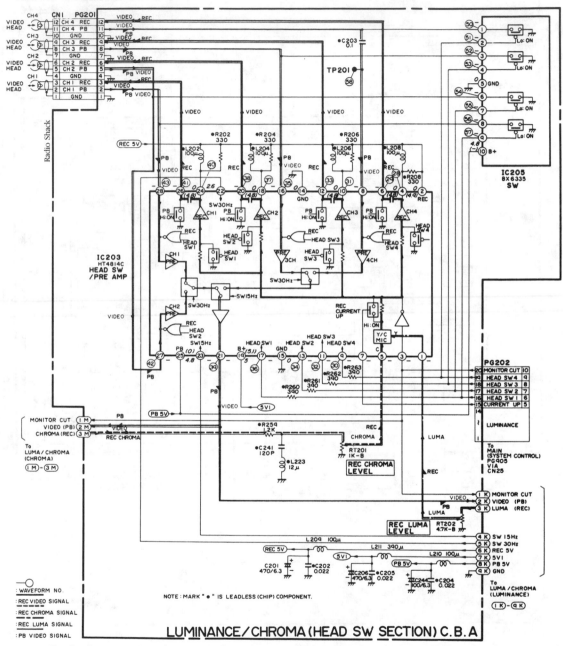

13-32   *Check chroma recording signal at pins 22 and 27 on the chroma process IC202.*

NO CHROMA PLAYBACK

To test for chroma playback, check the signal waveform and voltages on the luma process and chroma process ICs. Check for chroma playback signal at pin 27 of IC201 (FIG. 13-33). If no chroma signal, suspect IC201. Next check for chroma playback signal at pin 25 of chroma process (IC202). Check pin 23 and if no signal, measure continuity of delay line (DL202). Suspect IC202.

Measure the voltage at pin 24 (5 V) of IC 202. Check for chroma signal on pin 20 and suspect IC202. Measure and check the PB 5-volt supply source with no or low voltage at pin IC202. Do not overlook a leaky IC202 with low supply voltage.

NO VIDEO PLAYBACK

The lack of a video playback signal is checked from the tape heads back through luminance/chroma and luminance circuits. Turn on power switch and place in play mode. Test by the numbers (FIG. 13-34). Check for FM signal at TP204. Check 5-volt power source (pin 25) of IC203 with no FM signal. Test for FM signal at pin 21 of IC 203. If no signal, check waveform at TP202 (SW 15 Hz). Check for SW30Hz signal at TP203. Run continuity test on video heads. Inspect for clogged areas. Now suspect IC601.

Go to pin 28 of luma process (IC201) if FM signal is found at TP204 and no video playback. Test supply source on pin 25 of IC201 and suspect leaky IC201 or power source for low voltage. Check for luma signals at pins 23 and 11 of IC201. If no luma signal at pin 11, check for FM signal at pin 2 and 4 of IC201. Suspect the luma process IC201 with no FM or video playback signal. A defective or dirty video head may produce rainbow color effects in the recording.

NO PICTURE

Set select switch to camera mode. Check for random noise in EVF or monitor (FLOWCHART 13-10). Check the following stages by the numbers. Go directly

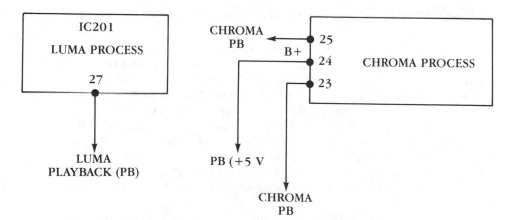

13-33 *Check chroma signal on IC202 and luma signal on IC201 for no chroma playback.*

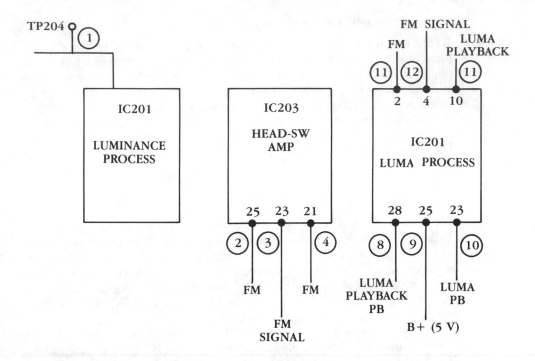

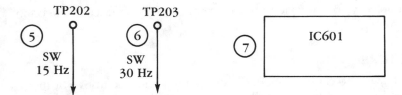

13-34 *Check by the number for no video playback (PB) on TP204, IC203, TP202 and TP203, IC601, and IC201.*

to IC 1003, pins 2 and 5 if random noise is seen without picture. (1) Check for cyan and green signals coming out of the MOS or CCD sensor IC1001. Is there a waveform on pins 9 and 16 of IC1006? (FIG. 13-35). If not, suspect IC1003. (2) Proceed to pins 12 and 13 for signal out of IC1006. Suspect IC1006 if no signal. (3) Check for the B+ supply source of IC1006.

Check for WHF and YEL signal at pins 2 and 5 of the white and yellow preamp (IC1002). If no signal, check MOS or CCD sensor IC1001. Proceed to terminals 1 and 8 of IC1006. If no signal, suspect IC1002. With signal, check pins 4 and 5 of IC1006 (yel/wht). If no output signal, suspect IC1006. Check terminal block (PG1100) connections pin 6 (luma). If no luma signal, proceed to IC1102 (5).

Check for luma signal at pins 3 and 15 of IC 1102 (luma filter enhancer). Trace signal to pins 11 and 12 of IC1103 (6). Suspect IC1102 if no

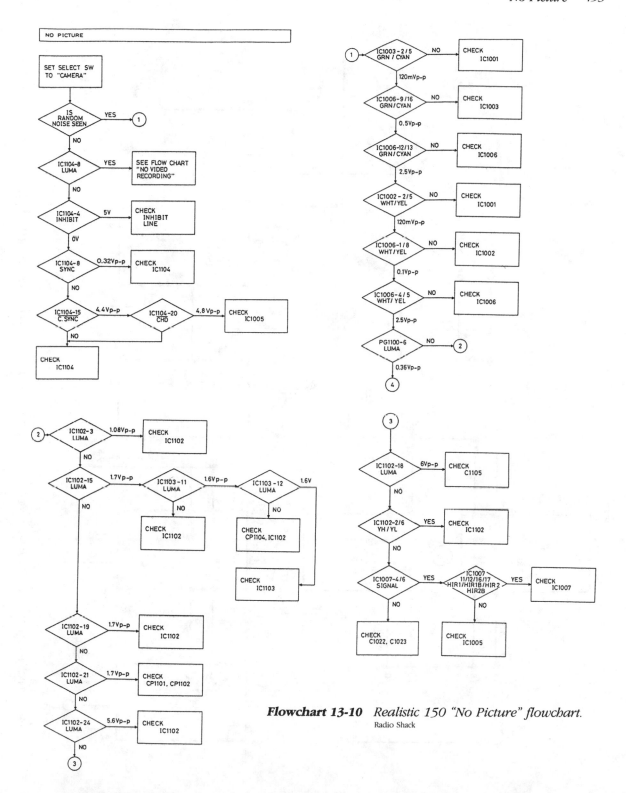

Flowchart 13-10 *Realistic 150 "No Picture" flowchart.*
Radio Shack

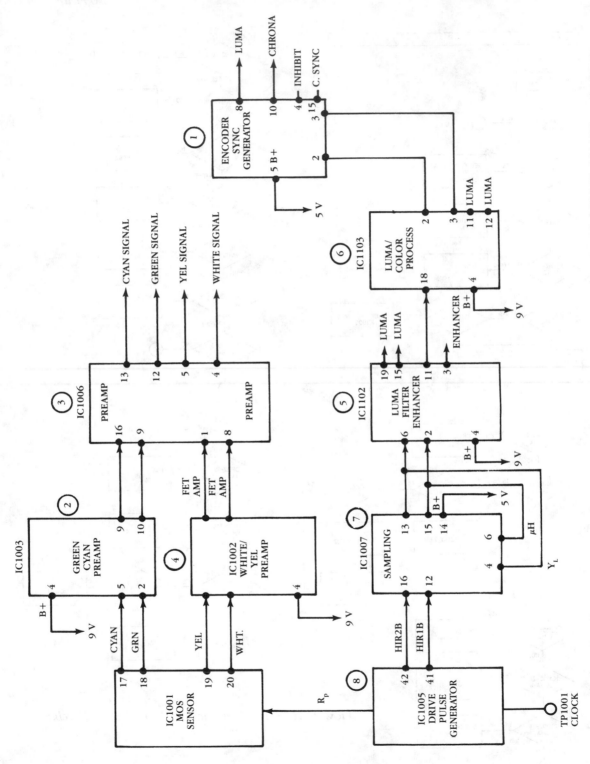

13-35 Check for no picture by the numbers on IC1104, IC1003, IC1006, IC1002, IC1102, IC1103, IC1107, and IC1005.

signal is on pins 18 and 11. Proceed to IC1102 pin 19 with no signal at pin 15 of IC1102. If no signal, check terminals 21 and 24 of IC1102. Double-check the YL/YL signals at pins 2 and 6 of IC1102. Suspect IC1007 if no signal (7). Finally, check for luma and chroma signal at pins 8 and 9, respectively. With signal going into IC1104 and no chroma or luma (color or luminance) coming out, suspect IC1104.

Go back to the encorder/sync generator (IC 1104) when no random noise is seen and check pin 8 for luma signal. If no 5 volts on pin 4 and 5, suspect 5-volt source. Check for signals on pins 8, 15, and 20 of IC1104. Suspect IC1104 if no signal is on pins 20 and 15. Signal tracing the waveforms on each IC component will turn up the defective section. Then take voltage measurements to locate the defective component.

NO COLOR

If a color flowchart is handy, check off the following IC stages to locate the defective component (FLOWCHART 13-11). The IC components involved are encoder/sync generator, luma/chroma, chroma amp/filter, and color matrix. In this Realistic 150 model, start with the three colors: red, blue, and green—at terminal board PG1100. Now troubleshoot the chroma ICs by the numbers (FIG. 13-36).

- Check the green, red, and blue signals at pins 5, 4, and 3 of PG1100. Try to readjust red, blue, and green setup controls.
- Go to pins 2 and 3 of IC1104 to check the R Y and B Y signals.
- If no signals, check IC1103 pins 2 and 3 or suspect IC1103. Measure the B+ at pin 1 (9 V).
- Check for chroma at pin 10 of IC1104. If no color, check pin 4 and 5 V line (B+). Suspect IC1104 with no voltage.
- When no red, blue, and green are at PG1100 connector terminal, check for red, blue, and green at pins 6, 5, and 4 at IC1101. Check IC1101 with low or no voltage.
- Check for color signals at pin 14, 15, 13, 12, 16, and 17 going to IC1100. If no signals, suspect IC1100 and IC1101.

NO AUDIO RECORDING

Check the audio block diagram and schematic for audio problems (FIG. 13-37). Inspect the microphone. Sub the external microphone to eliminate the regular mike. Most camcorder microphones are condenser types. Can you hear the audio in the earphone monitor?

The audio system may be checked by injecting 1 kHz audio signal in the microphone jack. Signal trace the audio record circuits. Place the unit into record mode. Check for audio waveform at TP201 (FIG. 13-38). Suspect a defective or clogged head with weak or no waveform. Test pin 8 and 1 of IC201 for audio signal. If no signal on pin 8, check pins 19 and 16 of IC201. If sound input is heard at pin 16 and not on pin 8, suspect IC201 or supply voltage source (pin 20, 5 V).

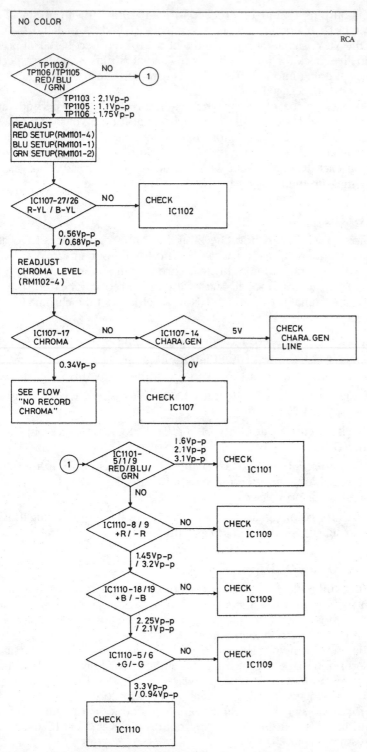

Flowchart 13-11   *RCA CPR100 "No Color" flowchart.*

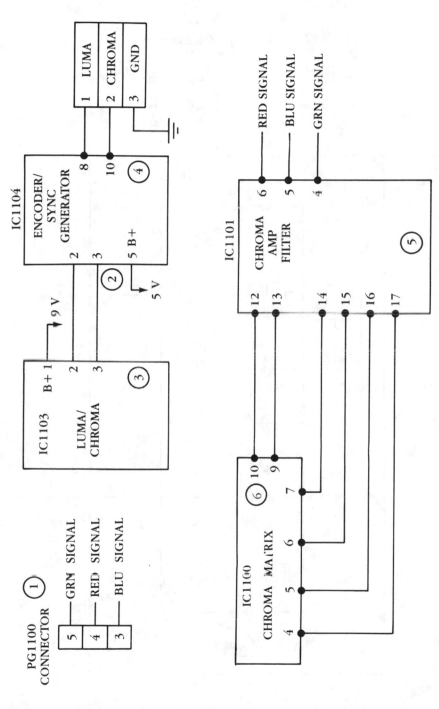

13-36 Check by the numbers of no color with PG1100, IC1104, IC1101, and color signals, IC1101, and IC1100.

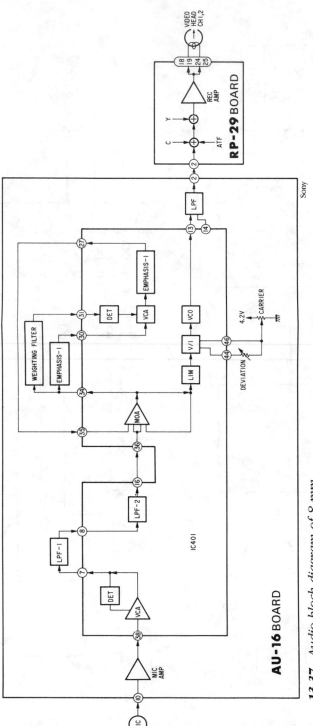

13-37 *Audio block diagram of 8 mm.*

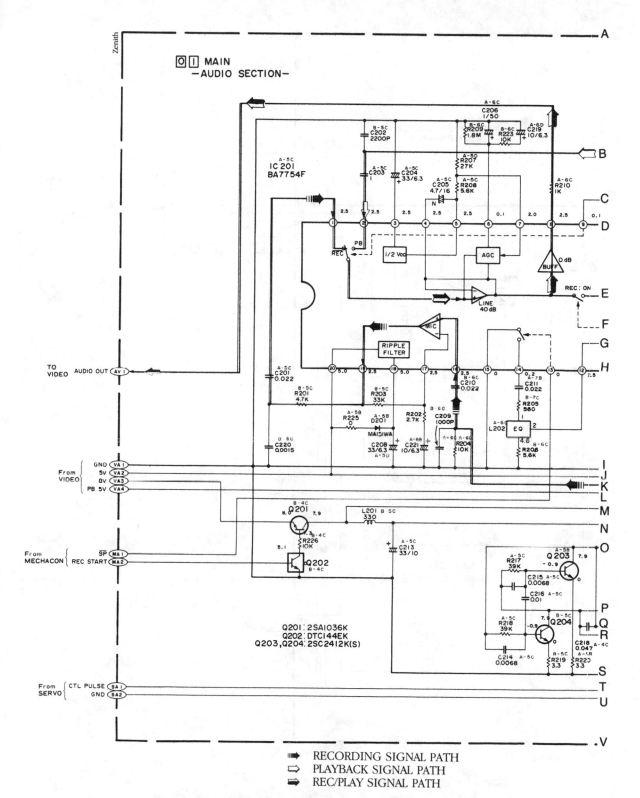

13-38 *Zenith VM6150 audio schematic diagram with waveform.*

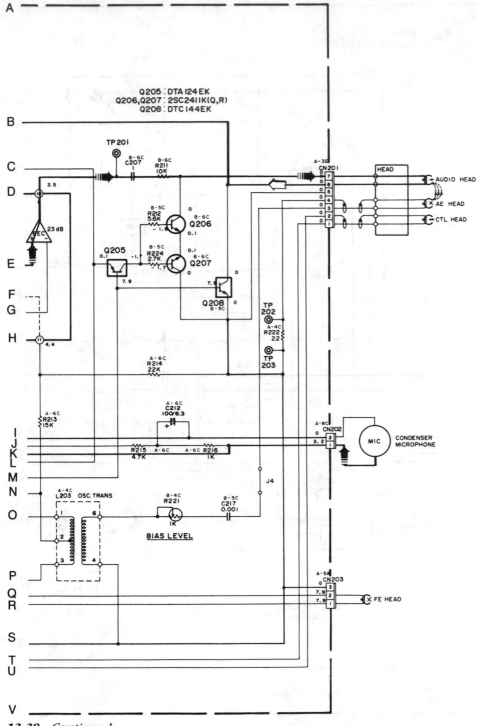

Q205 : DTA124EK
Q206,Q207 : 2SC2411K(Q,R)
Q208 : DTC144EK

A

B

TP 201

C   C207   R211
           B-6C   B-6C
                  10K

D   2.5   A-3E
                                           CN201

                          B-5C   7   HEAD
                          R212   B-6C   6   AUDIO HEAD
                          5.6K   Q206   5
                                   -1.8   4
                                           3   X AE HEAD
                          B-5C   2
     0.1   Q205   -1.7   R224   B-6C   CTL HEAD
                          2.7K   Q207
E   1.7

F   7.
G   Q208
                          B-5C   o
H   4.4

          A-6C
          R214
          22K

          1   TP 201
          2 Vp-p   2 Vp-p

                          2   TP
                                     202
                                     A-4C
                                     R222
          IC201-8pin   2.2
          1 Vp-p

                          3   TP
                                     203

          IC201-1 pin
          70 mVp-p

          A-6C   A-6C
          R213   A-6C   CN202
          15K   C212
I   100/6.3   2
J   +   3.2   1   MIC   CONDENSER
K   R215   A-6C A-6C R216   MICROPHONE
          4.7K   1K
L

M

N   J4

          A-4C
O   L203 OSC.TRANS   B-4C   B-5C
          1   6   R221   C217
                                    0.001
          2   1K

                          BIAS LEVEL
          3   4

P   A-5A
Q   CN203
                                       3
R   7.9   2
                                7.9   1   X FE HEAD

S

T
U

          4   CN203-2 pin
                     15 Vp-p

V

13-38 *Continued*

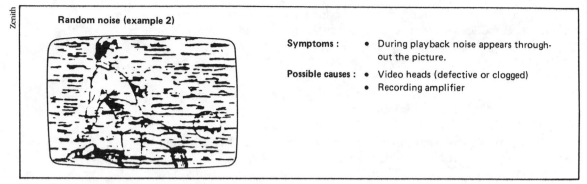

Zenith

Random noise (example 2)

Symptoms :
- During playback noise appears throughout the picture.

Possible causes :
- Video heads (defective or clogged)
- Recording amplifier

Note: If both head channels are defective, random noise appears throughout the picture.

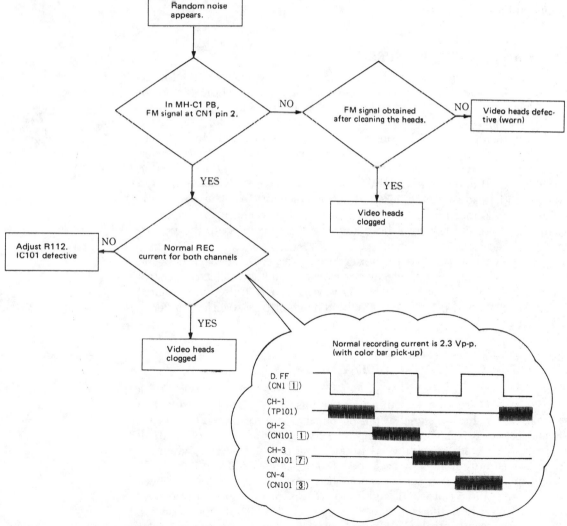

Flowchart 13-12 *Random noise during playback (PB).*

Improper bias may cause poor or distorted sound. Check the bias level setting (R221). Check the bias oscillator waveform at connector CN203. Suspect a defective bias oscillator section if signal is weak or improper. Measure the voltage on Q203 and Q204.

NO AUDIO PLAYBACK

Set the select switch to playback mode (PB). The playback signal from the tape head may be scoped at pin 2 of IC201 (see (FIG. 13-38). Check the amplified signal on pin 8 of IC201. If a signal is going in and not out, suspect IC401 or the power source (B+ 5 V, pin 20). Some audio circuits have a playback level control. Make sure it's adjusted properly. Signal trace the audio out (AV1) to the video circuits. Check the signal with proper waveforms on the audio schematic.

NOISY AND JITTERY PICTURE

Random noise in the whole picture may be caused by defective or clogged video heads. Random noise often occurs throughout the whole picture in both channels. Clean the video heads. Replace the video heads if worn (FLOWCHART 13-12).

Intermittent noise in the prerecorded tape may be a defective cassette or poor cylinder sync and CTL recording pulse. Load the VCR with a blank tape and place VCR in record mode. Check for good C. sync waveform at pin 80 of IC601 and CTL-REC pulse at pin 19 (FIG. 13-39). The voltage in servo control and head-switching IC601. Intermittent audio may be caused by poor wiring connections around the audio head. Also check for poor lead connections around full-erase head and where they connect to the pc wiring.

Noisy synchronous picture noise during play back, at the top of the picture, may result from a defective or clogged head and defective control recording circuit. Check the recording waveform, CTL pulse, and clogged CTL head (FLOWCHART 13-13). Check CTL head height. Do not overlook a defective tape.

NOISE IN PICTURE DURING PLAY MODE

This noise may be caused by improper speed of the capstan motor. Check the FG and FG frequency in the servo circuits. If the speed is faster than normal, check the FG signal at pin 30 of servo control (IC601). If no FG signal, suspect IC602. Check the capstan servo signal at pin 54 of IC601. If more than 2.5 volts, check the FG frequency at pin 11 of IC602. When the frequency is more than 568 Hz, suspect IC601, search, or SLP (FIG. 13-40).

Suspect the capstan servo system when capstan speed is lower. Check the voltage at pin 54 of IC601, and if more than 2.5 volts, suspect improper FG frequency. Check the FG frequency at pin 11 of IC602. If more than 568 Hz, suspect servo control IC601, search, or SLP.

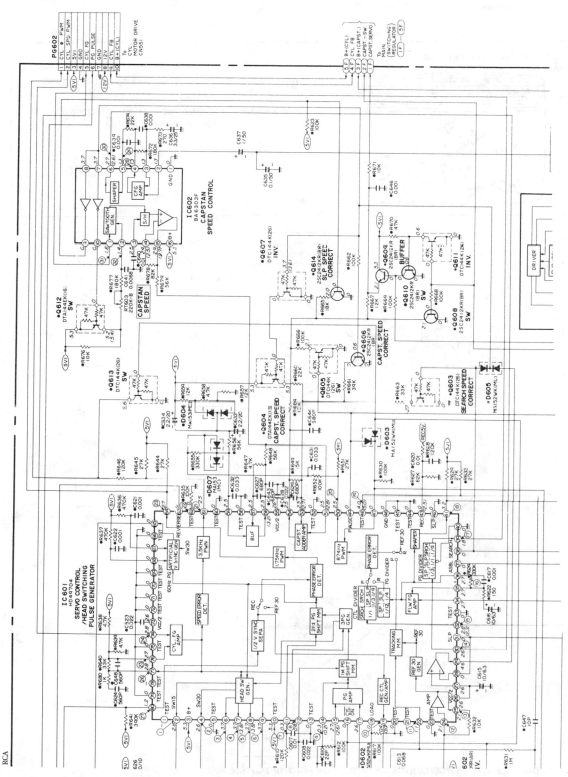

13-39 Check for cylinder sync and CTL recording pulse at servo control IC601 for intermittent noise on prerecorded tape.

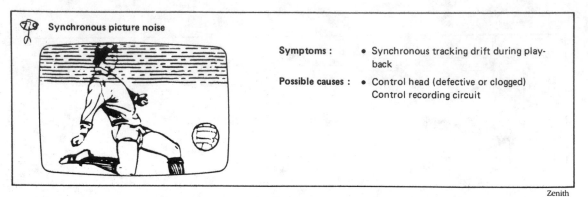

Synchronous picture noise

Symptoms :   • Synchronous tracking drift during play-
                   back

Possible causes : • Control head (defective or clogged)
                   Control recording circuit

Zenith

Synchronous
tracking drift

In REC,
waveform at TP405   —NO→   IC401

3.5Vp-p
33.3ms

YES

CTL pulse
at CN201 pin 1   —NO→   IC401

33.3ms
5 Vp-p

YES

Waveform normal
at CN201 pin 1   —NO→   CTL head

Spike appears.
Normal :
No spike
Disconnected :

YES

CTL head clogged
Check CTL head height.
Tape defective

Flowchart 13-13 *Synchronous picture noise during playback.*

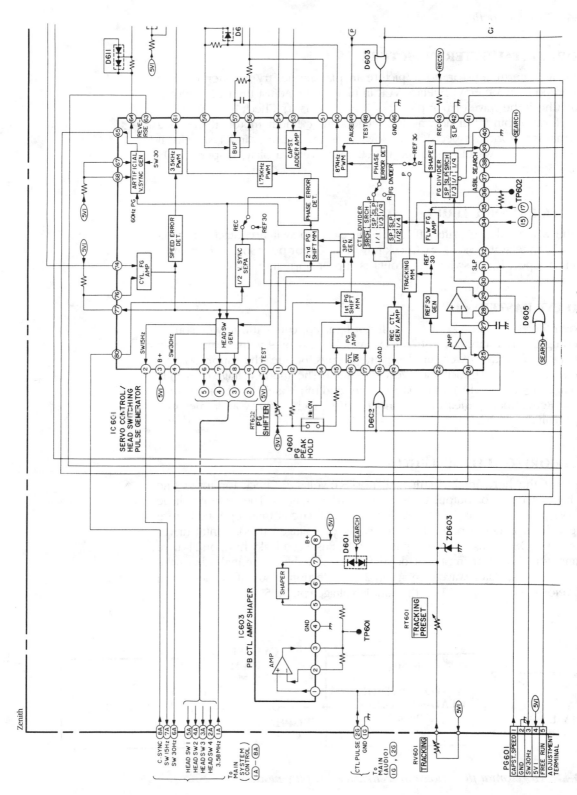

13-40 Check the FG and FG frequency signal with noise in picture during playback.

HORIZONTAL JITTER IN PICTURE

With an intermittent or noisy picture in play mode, try another cassette recorded by another VCR. Place VCR in play mode. Adjust the tracking control. Check the waveform at pin 12 of IC601 (FIG. 13-41). Check the CYL phase waveform at pin 17. If no waveform, check the cylinder motor. If there's a normal waveform, suspect IC601. Now check the phase cylinder waveform at pin 64. If no waveform, suspect IC601. If waveform okay, suspect IC605 (pins 5 and 7).

WHITE BALANCE DRIFTS

If the white balance drifts off, check the close-up switch contacts and soldered connections (FIG. 13-42). Check pin 10 of IC4 for poor soldered connections. Suspect IC4 if switch and contacts appear normal.

NO EVF RASTER

When the electronic viewfinder will not light up, check the power source feeding the EVF circuits. The voltage may be 5, 8 or 9 volts. If no supply voltage, check the power supply or line circuits. Besides the supply source, voltages on the CRT socket are very important. The anode voltage (pin 1) is from 2 to 3 kV (2.7 kV), pin 2 is 376 volts, and pin 3 is 330 volts (FLOWCHART 13-14). Remember to measure the anode voltage with a 3000-volt dc meter or high-voltage probe.

NO HORIZONTAL DEFLECTION

Suspect the horizontal circuit with no CRT voltage. Check for input line voltage at pin 5 of output transformer T801 (FIG. 13-43). The heater voltage across pins 3 and 7 is 16.3 volts. The horizontal circuit must operate before the voltage is developed. Check for collector voltage on horizontal driver transistor Q803. Fuse may be open (TF801). Suspect a leaky horizontal drive transistor (Q803) or improper drive voltage at the base terminal. Check the horizontal oscillator waveform at pin 2 of deflection IC801. If no deflection waveform, suspect IC 801 or the supply voltage (pin 4, 5.3 V).

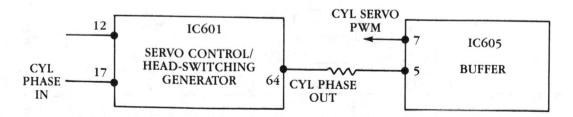

13-41 *Horizontal jitter/noise in picture during play mode.*

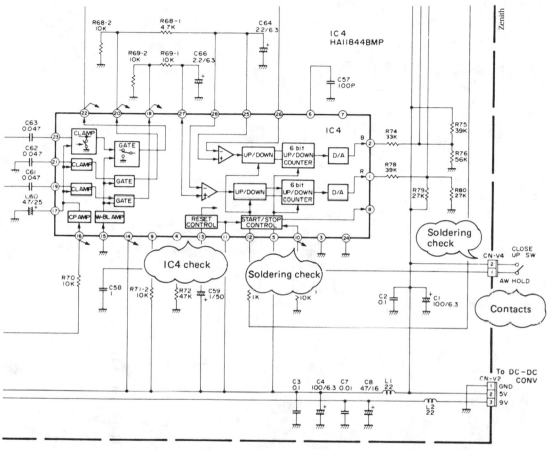

13-42 *Check close-up switch, connections, and IC4 when white balance drifts.*

NO VERTICAL DEFLECTION

It's possible to have a raster with only a white line or not enough height. Start with the deflection IC801 and take a waveform at pin 16. The vertical deflection circuits are all inside the IC, including vertical driver or output. Readjust the vertical size control (RT803). Suspect open vertical yoke winding or poor connections at PG802 if waveform at pin 1 is only a horizontal white line. Take critical vertical voltage measurements on pins 12 through 18.

NO OR WEAK VIDEO

Check the video signal from pin 3 (0.2 V_{p-p}) of connector (CN801) to pin 10 of IC801 (1.4 V_{p-p}). Here the video signal is amplified out of pin 11 to video amp (Q802). Do not overlook defective coupling capacitors C804, C808, and C814 for weak video. Suspect Q802 with adequate video signal on the base

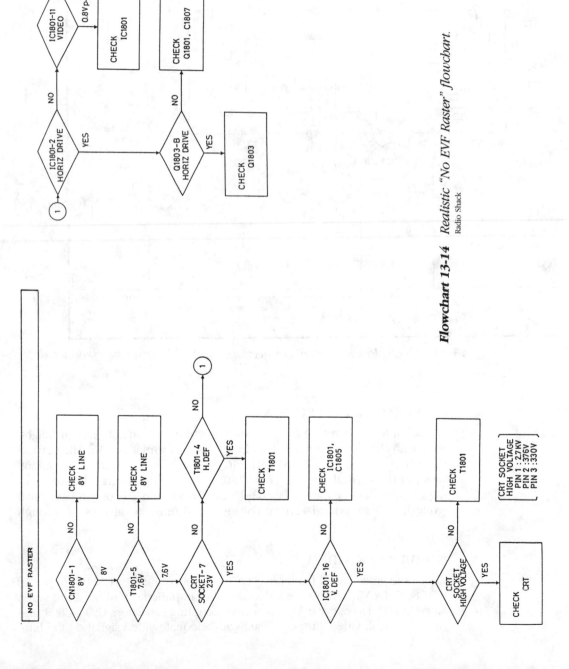

Flowchart 13-14 *Realistic "No EVF Raster" flowchart.*
Radio Shack

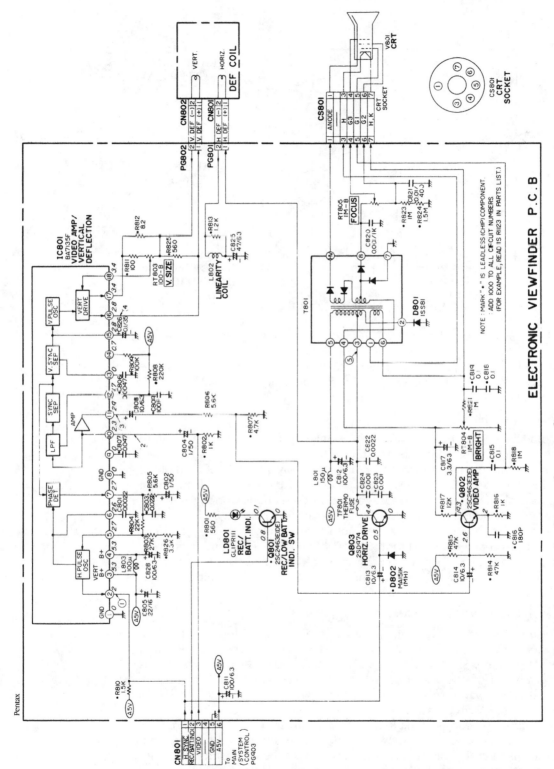

Pentax

ELECTRONIC VIEWFINDER P.C.B

13-43 Pentax PV-C850A electronic viewfinder schematic diagram.

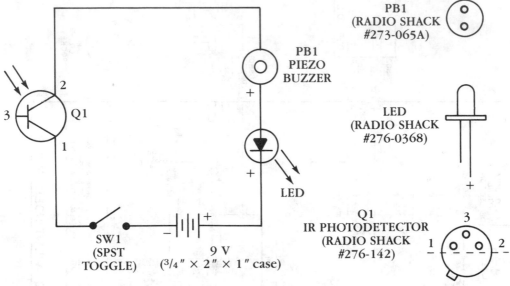

13-44   *Infrared auto focus sensor indicator schematic.*

and very little on the collector terminal. For poor brightness, check the brightness setting of RT804, R821, and the voltages at G1 and G2.

INFRARED INDICATOR

A homemade infrared indicator may be made out of only a few parts to indicate the infrared diode is working in the auto focus circuits (FIG. 13-44). Simply hold the sensor device about one inch away from the infrared diode inside the camera. This diode is often located at the bottom and front of the lens assembly. When the auto focus and infrared diode is working, a pulsating sound is audible in the piezo buzzer. Moving the infrared indicator away from and then close to the infrared auto focus diode may cause the lens assembly to rotate back and forth. Although the pulsating sound is not very loud, it does indicate the auto focus infrared diode and driver circuits are ok. No sound indicates a defective infrared LED or auto focus circuits.

IMPORTANT WAVEFORMS

Critical waveforms are very important in signal tracing or locating defective circuits in the various camcorder circuits. The block diagram of the 8 mm camera section is shown in FIG. 13-45. The imager and SSG circuits waveforms are given in FIG. 13-46. Waveforms of the mechacon circuits are in FIG. 13-47. Critical VHS-C waveforms of the servo circuit are in FIG. 13-48. Fig. 13-49 shows the VHS-C MDA circuit waveform.

Critical waveforms of the luminance and chroma (Y/C) circuits are indicated in FIG. 13-50. Fig. 13-51 shows the luminance and chrominance circuit waveforms of a VHS camcorder. The waveform of the electronic viewfinder circuits are in FIG. 13-52.

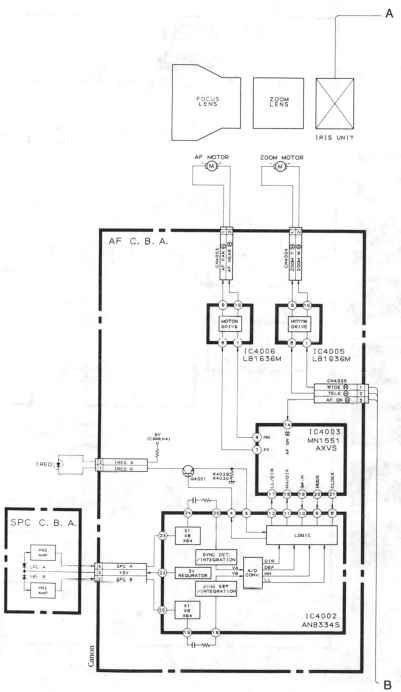

13-45 *Waveforms on block diagram of Canon's (8 mm) camera section.*

A

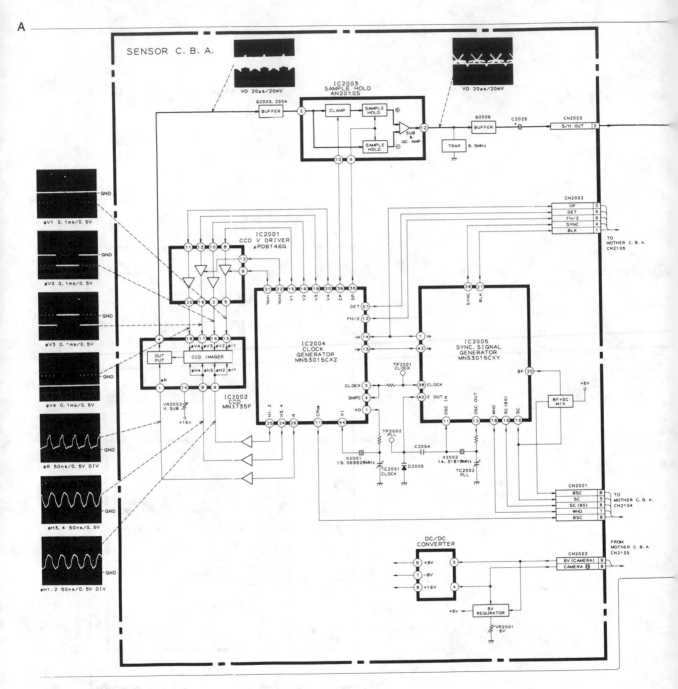

13-45   *Continued*

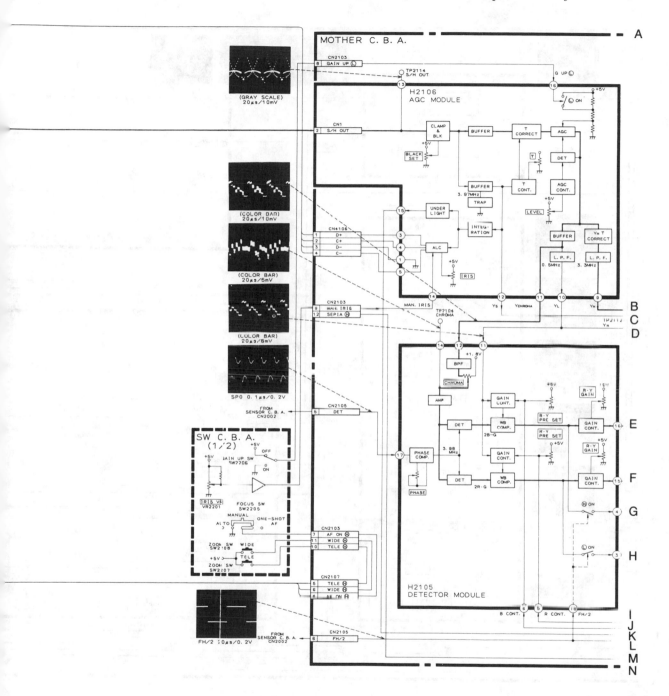

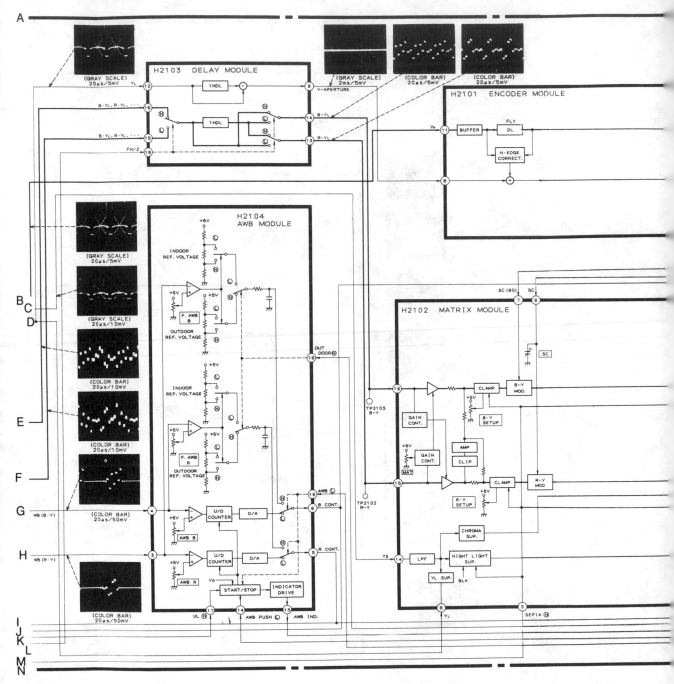

13-45   *Continued*

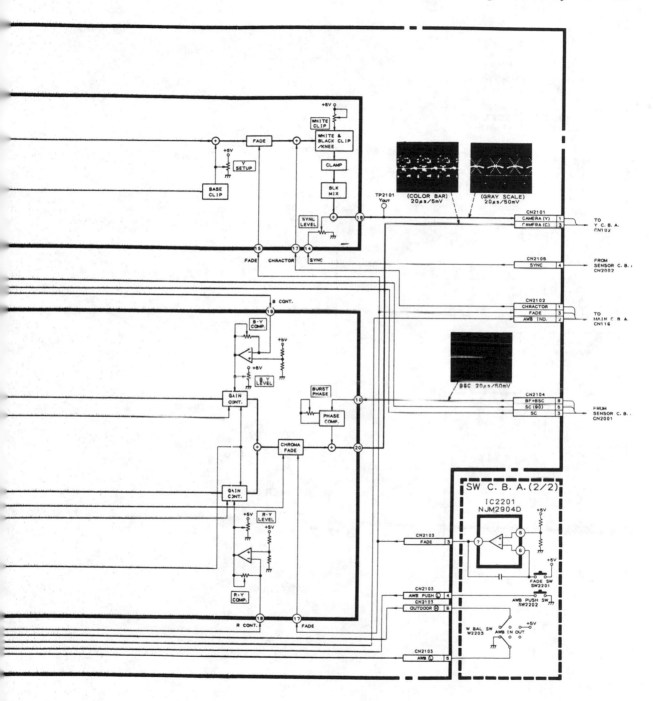

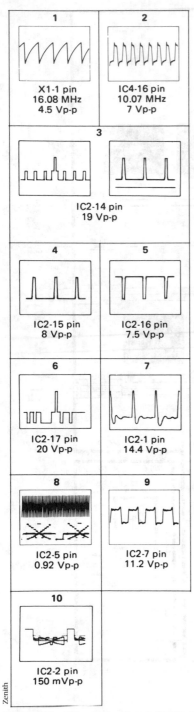

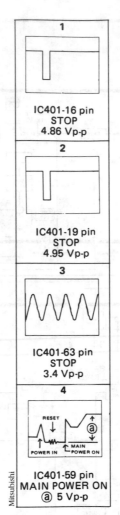

13-46   *Zenith VM6150 (VHS-C) waveforms of imager and SSG circuits.*

13-47   *Waveforms of mechacon circuits in the Mitsubishi HS-C20U camcorder.*

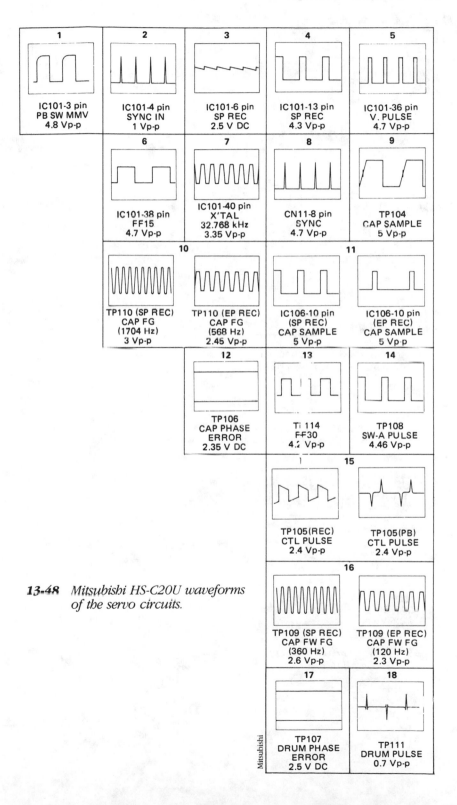

13-48 *Mitsubishi HS-C20U waveforms of the servo circuits.*

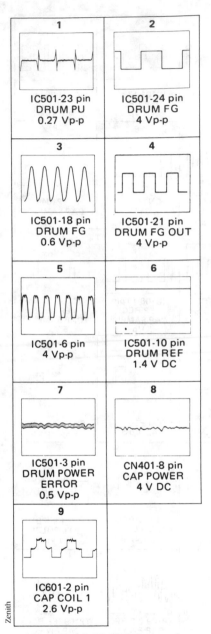

13-49 *Zenith VM6150 waveforms of the MDA circuits.*

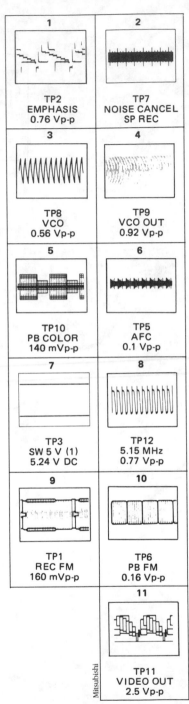

13-50 *Luminance and chroma (Y/C) circuit waveforms of Mitsubishi HS-C20U camcorder.*

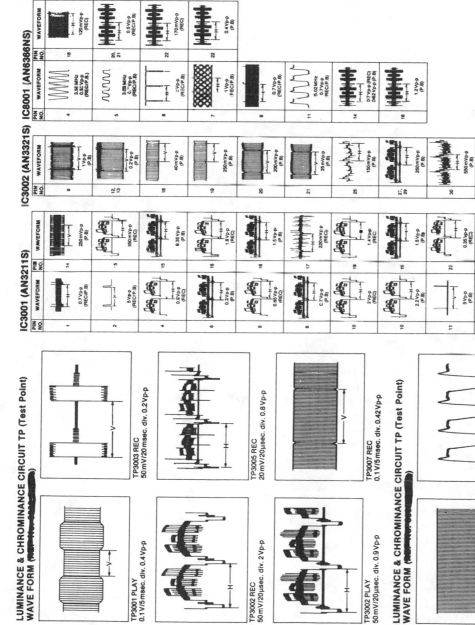

13-51 *General Electric 9-9605 (VHS) luminance and chrominance waveforms.* Thomson Consumer Electronics

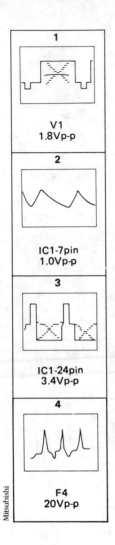

13-52 *Electronic viewfinder waveforms in the Mitsubishi HS-C20U camcorder.*

Chapter **14**

Power Supplies

There is a lot more to the camcorder power supply than a battery. The camcorder may be operated from a battery or ac power source. The ac power supply may consist of switching, constant voltage, constant current, voltage protection, and voltage regulation circuits. Besides supply a dc voltage for operating the camcorder, the batteries may be charged (FIG. 14-1). Also, inside the camcorder you may find battery discharge and alarm circuits with power circuit control.

AC POWER SUPPLY

There are several different voltages generated from the ac power pack (6, 7.2, 9, and 12 V). Most ac adapters provide dc power for camcorder operation and a battery-charging dc voltage. A typical power supply may furnish 6 volts dc out at 1.2 amps. When used as a battery charger, the charging voltage may be 10.5 volts dc at 1.2 amps. The Mitsubishi HS-C 20 V model operates on 9.6 volts at 1.2 amps and the RCA CTC100 operates at 12 volts dc (FIG. 14-2).

Canon VM-E2NA Power Adapter The Canon power pack and charger consists of the ac power circuit, switching, constant voltage, constant-current charging, and protection circuits. The ac power input circuit applied through a power receptacle passes through the noise filter and is rectified with a full-wave rectifier D1 (FIG. 14-3). The rectified power is then smoothed by C8 before being applied as a dc power. The dc power is fed to T1 and Q3 where it is alternately switched according to the output of pin 2 (approximately 50 kHz) of IC1 and is converted into pulse current. When the current flows through T1, a voltage appears at P5, and a dc voltage is formed at D7, C20, and L2, which provides output-regulated voltage.

The switching circuit consists of all components in the primary side of transformer T1 (FIG. 14-4). At power on, the start-up circuit (Q1 and Q2) turns

14-1 *The small battery pack may fit on the back side of the camcorder or plug into an external battery jack and ac adapter.*

14-2 *The battery slips onto the backside of the ac battery/charger adapter to be charged.*

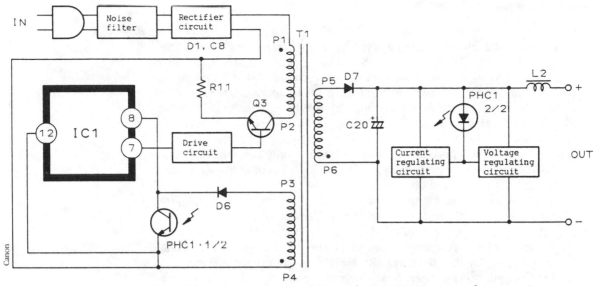

14-3 *The primary circuit of Canon's VM-E2NA power adapter unit.*

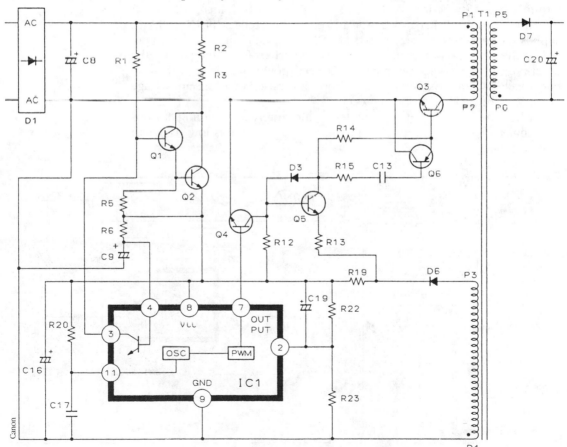

14-4 *The switching circuit of the ac power supply in Canon's VM-E2NA power adapter.*

on through R1, R2, and R3, and now a voltage is applied to pin 8 of IC1. This causes the PWM signal (approximately 5 kHz) to appear at output terminal 7 of IC1. The PWM signal passes through the drive circuit (Q4 and Q5) and is applied to the base of the switching transistor Q3 to activate Q3.

After IC1 is activated, the voltage appearing at P3 of T1 is applied to pin 8 as a power voltage for IC1. Q6 forcibly applies a reverse bias to the base of Q3 to reduce loss of switching time. The start-up circuit stops when the voltage at pin 4 of IC1 becomes 1.4 volts due to the time constant of R6 and C9. This causes the voltage level at pin 3 of IC1 to become low (Lo), and thus Q1 and Q2 are turned off.

The constant voltage circuit is in the secondary winding of T1 (FIG. 14-5). The error amp 2 in IC2 serves to regulate the output voltage to a constant value. The voltage appearing at ZD3 is divided by R6 and R37 and applied to the (+) terminal as a reference voltage. Likewise, the negative (–) terminal voltage is divided by R39, R40, and VR1 via R38 as a reference voltage.

If the output voltage rises, it will be suppressed by the following circuits. A rise in output voltage increases the voltage at the error amp (–) terminal, providing a drop of the error amp output, which increases of current flow through PHC1 diode. The increase of current at PHC1 collecter applies the increased voltage to pin 12 of IC1, shorting pin 7 at IC1 output during the low (Lo) duration. This expands the drive of Q4 being on for the duration, shorting switching transistor Q3 on, providing a drop in the output voltage. When the output voltage drops, it is raised to a constant voltage of 6.0 V by reversing the above procedure.

When the same circuit is connected to the battery for charging, it stops the regulated voltage in the following manner: C terminal is low (Lo) with

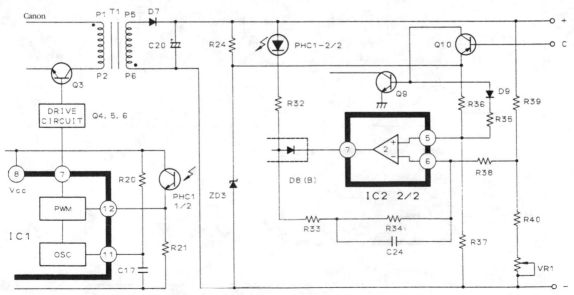

14-5   *The constant-voltage circuit (during operation) of Canon's VM-E2NA power supply.*

Q10 turned on with an increase of the error amp (2) reference voltage within IC2. The circuit is now used as a voltage limiter of 11.5 volts.

The error amp 1 in IC2 serves to regulate the current to a constant value (FIG. 14-6). During charging, the voltage appearing across ZD3 is divided by the combined resistance of R26, R26, and R27. The divided voltage is then applied to the (+) terminal as a reference voltage. This is done when terminal C (Lo) turns on Q10 and Q9.

The charging current is converted into a voltage when it flows through R31, with the converted voltage applied to the (−) terminal as reference voltage via R30. This circuit operates in the same manner as the voltage-regulating circuit. The charging current is returned at a constant value of 1.2 amps by changing the output duty ratio at pin 7 of IC1 so that the reference voltage at the (−) terminal is kept constant.

During operation, it is connected to the camcorder, and the current regulating operation automatically stops. C terminal is high (Hi) with Q10 and Q9 turned off, which increases the reference voltage error amp 1, and D8 is turned off.

The protection circuit consists of IC1 and surrounding components (FIG. 14-7). The overcurrent status is detected at pin 5 of IC1 by converting the current flowing through collector of Q3 into a voltage appearing at R10 and R11. When the voltage at pin 5 exceeds the set value, the latch circuit in the IC is activated to stop outputting the PWM signal.

When the secondary side of T1 is shorted, the voltage at P5 of T1 drops. The PHC-2 goes off because the voltage appearing across ZD2 drops, while PHC-2 on the light receiving side is open to increase the base voltage of Q8.

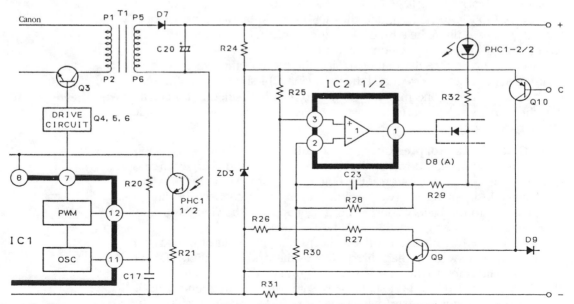

14-6 *The constant-current circuit (during charging) of Canon's VM-E2NA power adapter.*

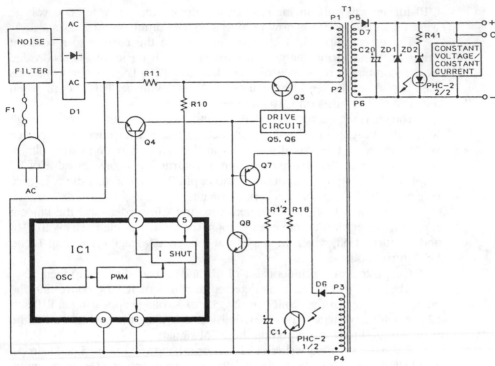

14-7   *The protection circuit of the Canon VM-E2NA power pack adapter.*

This lowers the output voltage of Q8 so that the voltage at the base of Q5 is pulled until Q5 is turned off, and thus Q3 stops the switching operation. When Q8 starts pulling the base of Q7, it turns on. Then Q8 is turned on via R17. Thus the thyristor operation is performed.

In order to restore the output voltage, the cause of the overloading or shorting should be removed, and the voltage at C14 should be sufficiently discharged for about one minute with the power plug pulled out. Remember, the primary side is protected by fuse (F1) if a faulty part is found inside the ac power supply.

RCA CPR100 Ac Adapter/Charger Circuits   The RCA power supply adapter may be broken down to the primary, adapter, and charger circuits (FIG. 14-8). Locking grooves are on the bottom side of the charger in which the battery locks in place. Two flexible shorting pins connect the output charging unit to the battery source. A red light appears showing the battery is charging, and when charged fully, LED302 comes on.

L1 is the ac line filter network that keeps line noice out of the adapter circuits (FIG. 14-9). AC is applied directly across the bridge rectifiers (D101). The dc voltage is fed to the inverter circuit (Q1 and HIC1). Current flows to HIC1 from resister R3, and Q1 starts to oscillate. The high-frequency voltage is applied across the primary winding (2 and 3) of transformer T1. The

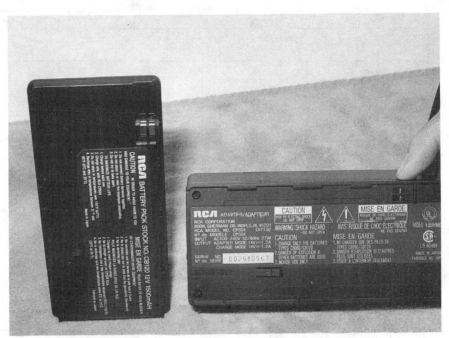

14-8 *RCA's CPR100 ac adapter/charger unit with battery.*

produced voltage in the secondary winding of T1 is fed back to HIC1 with D6, Q4, and T2. Oscillation occurs at approximately 80 kHz.

The secondary voltage across pins 6 and 4 of TV are applied to D4 and D6 (FIG. 14-10). The voltage is rectified by D4 and filtered with C12 and L3.

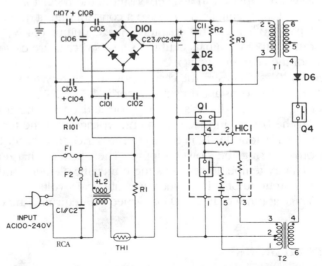

14-9 *The primary circuit of the RCA CPR100 adapter/charger circuitry.*

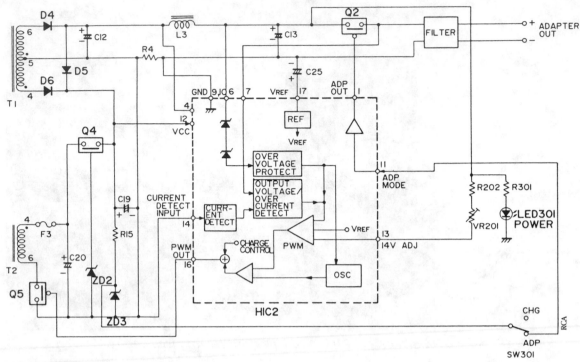

14-10 *The RCA CPR100 adapter/charger (adapter) circuit.*

Capacitor C13 provides additional filter of the ripple voltage. This voltage is applied to Q2, Q4, and HIC2.

When SW301 is placed in adapter position, the regulator 14 volts dc is found at the output terminals. To receive a constant output, the output voltage is fed back to HIC2. This adapter voltage output (14 V) cannot be checked at the output terminals until the sense switches are closed with the battery out of the charger (FIG. 14-11).

When SW301 switches to the charge position, battery sense SW3 is activated (FIG. 14-12). The constant output current is 1.2 or 0.7 amps, depending on the setting of SW2, which is switched off and on mechanically by the battery. With the battery in place, no output voltage is at the terminals, for Q2 is turned off. Diode D201 is connected in series to prevent the battery current from entering the power supply. When battery charging is completed, the battery temperature opens the bimetallic element in the battery. The voltage output automatically increases above 16 volts with the battery removed. Thus, at pin 6 of HIC2, Q3 is turned off, returning the output to 0 volts.

BATTERY CHARGING

Many of the small batteries last an hour or less with constant camcorder operation. The battery may last longer with intermittent operation. As the

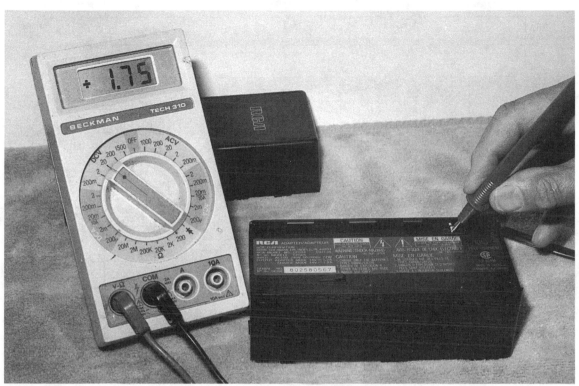

14-11 *The sense and interlock switches must be closed to measure any dc voltage from the ac voltage power adapter.*

battery becomes older and charged many times, the charged time becomes less than one hour. Most camcorders have a flashing light, indicating the battery is getting weak. In the RCA CPR300, the green recording light in the viewfinder begins to blink. If left on too long, the camcorder circuits will shut down, leaving the camcorder inoperative. Either insert a new battery or the ac adapter unit to provide camera operation. Always, take at least two batteries when out shooting scenes away from the power receptacles.

You may find a lead acid or NiCd battery operating the camcorder. Most of the later ones use the NiCd battery. Do not leave the discharged battery sit for a long time without charging. Some camcorder operators fully discharge the NiCd battery with a small 10-watt resister and a pair of alligator clips. These batteries will last a long time by simply charging them up after you are done with the camcorder. Most present-day ac adaptors shut off when the battery is fully charged, preventing overcharging of the battery. Most small batteries charge within one hour.

BATTERY DETECTION CIRCUITS

Although the battery detection circuits are found in the camcorder and not in the ac adaptor/charger, these circuits are discussed here because the de-

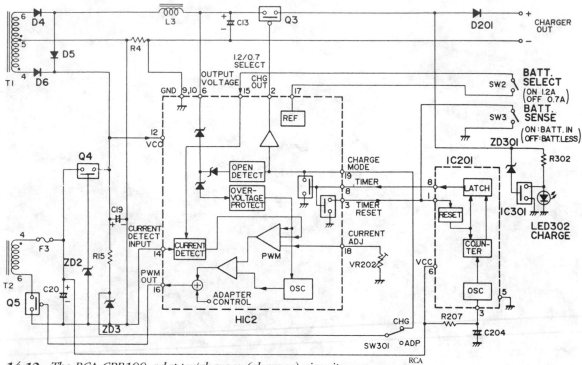

14-12 *The RCA CPR100 adapter/charger (charger) circuits.*

tector is activated by battery shutdown. Many of the camcorders (large or small) have some indicating device when the batteries are getting weak. It's usually located in the electronic viewfinder (EVF). Either the recording, battery indicator, or battery lines flash when the battery is getting low. In some camcorders, the unit shuts down within a few seconds. Sometimes you can eject of the cassette, and in others you must insert a new battery or apply the ac adaptor for any type of operation.

Pentax PV-C850A Battery Detection Circuit   This unit detects the battery teminal voltage and indicates it in the EVF bar graphics. If the battery terminal voltage has dropped to a certain limit, operation is interrupted to stop the mechanism and prevents improper operation (FIG. 14-13).

It consists of the subsystem control microprocessor IC902 and comparator IC904. IC904 compares the battery terminal voltage divided by RT901 with a reference voltage (VR) produced by D/A conversion from pin 9 and 10 of IC902. VR is varied until it becomes equal to or higher than VB. The battery voltage is detected from D/A data of VR when VR is equal to or higher VB. The battery terminal reference voltages are found in TABLES 14-1 and 14-2.

Realistic 150 Battery Overdischarge Detcction Circuits   The battery overdischarge detection (ODC) circuit monitors the battery terminal voltage, detects overdischarge, displays characters in the EVF screen to indicate

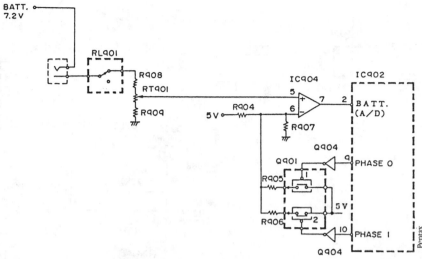

14-13 *Pentax PV-C850A battery detector circuit.*

**Table 14-1. Reference and Battery Terminal Voltages
(Pentax PV-C850A)**

Microprocessor Outputs		Reference voltage (IC902-6)	Battery terminal voltage
Pin 9	Pin 10		
1	0	3.07V	7.3V
0	1	2.85V	6.85V
0	0	2.73V	6.5V

Pentax

**Table 14-2. Battery Voltage and EVF Indication
(Pentax PV-C850A)**

Battery terminal voltage	Indication in EVF
Over 7.3V	(E --- F)
7.2V - 7.0V	(E--)
Under 6.85V	(E-) ('-' flashes)

Pentax

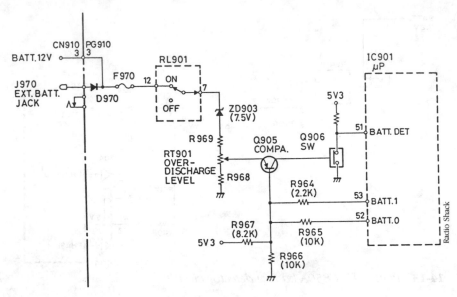

14-14   *Realistic 150 battery overdischarge detection circuits.*

discharge, and if the voltage is less than normal, it turns the power off. In the VTR mode, "power-off" corresponds to "stop." If in the camera mode, "power-off" corresponds to "record pause."

Battery power (12 V) passes through the fuse (F970) and a latch relay (RL901) to a zener diode (ZD903, 7.5 V), which causes a voltage drop of about 7.5 V (FIG. 14-14). It is then applied through RT901 (overcharge level) to the emitter of the comparator (Q905). Q905 compares the voltage with the reference voltage.

The reference voltage is generated by the digital-to-anolog converter controlled by BATT. outputs (2 bits of data—Batt 1 and Batt 0) from the IC901 and is applied to the base (inverting type) of the comparator (IC905). When the BATT. output of the system microprocessor (IC901) is high, the resistors connected to the output pins are connected in parallel with R967 (8.2 Ω), and the reference voltage is changed, depending on the battery output as shown in TABLE 14-3.

Table 14-3.   Reference and Battery Terminal Voltages (Realistic 150)

Outputs		Reference Voltage	Battery Terminal Voltage
BATT.1	BATT.0		
1	0	4.26V	12.3V
0	1	3.45V	11.6V
0	0	2.75V	10.9V

Table 14-4. Battery Voltages and Displays (Realistic 150)

Battery Voltage	μP Output Mode	Display in EVF Screen
More than 12.3V	No change	"E---F"
12.3V to 11.66V	No change	"E--"
11.65V to 10.9V	No change	"E-" ("-": blinks)
Less than 10.9V	Power off	

Radio Shack

When the battery voltage is applied to the emitter (noninverting input) of the comparater (Q905), it becomes lower than the reference voltage applied to the base of Q905. The output of the switch (Q906) goes high, and IC901 detects battery voltage and judges whether the battery is discharged. The results of this judgement make the output of IC901 as shown in TABLE 14-4.

Sony CCD-M8E/M8U 8 mm Battery Detection Circuit The battery-down circuit indicates when the battery is low in the camcorder (FIG. 14-15). When the BAT DWN signal becomes low (L), the voltage drops to more than the rated voltage in the circuit where the unregulated 6 V level is detected. The time of detection began when the POWER signal is low (L) and the loading motor does not operate.

The off period begins when the low battery is detected during battery insertion operation in the TAPE RUN and the BAT DOWN LED (REC LED) flashes for 30 seconds and the key acceptance as the machine operation stops. When either EJECT, REC, STBY or CCD-SW is pressed after the LED turns off, the LED starts flashing for 30 seconds.

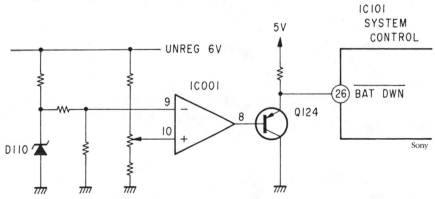

14-15 *Sony CCD-M8E/M8U battery detection circuits.*

When the battery down detection is noted during the REC period, the TAPE RUN/BAT DWN (REC LED) flashes for one second. This informs the operator that only one second of recording is possible before shutdown. After the one-second time interval, the mode changes to the READY Mode and the keys other than the eject key cannot work. Now only the loading and unloading operations are working until the battery is replaced.

If the battery down is detected in the STBY period, the mode changes to the READY mode and the TAPE RUN/BATT DWN (REC LED) flashes at 4 Hz. Again, only the unloading and loading functions operate until the battery is replaced.

Ac Adapter/Charger Circuit Adjustments   The ac adapter and charger output voltage must be properly adjusted for accurate and safe voltages in operating the camcorder or charging the batteries. First determine the battery operating voltage and adjust the output of the adapter voltage accordingly. Although each manufacturer has their own adjustments, the following methods indicate how it is done. Adjustments should also be made for required correct current charging.

Canon VM-E2NA Adapter Voltage Adjustment   Open up the control terminal during camcorder operation. Connect the (+) side of a digital voltmeter or DMM to the terminal (+) and the (−) side to the negative terminal of the meter. Turn VR1 until the digital voltmeter reads 6.5 V ± 0.0 V (FIG. 14-16). This adjustment should be made under a no-load condition.

Radio Shack 150 Adapter Voltage Adjustment   The adapter voltage adjustment is made with a DVM or DMM. Measure the voltage at the adapter terminals (FIG. 14-17). Place a 20-ohm, 10-watt resistor across the voltage adapter terminals as a load. Locate the voltage adapter control VR201 (FIG. 14-18). Now set the camera/charge switch to the camera position. Connect the DVM across the 10-watt resister. ADjust VR201 for 13.95 V ± 0.05 V.

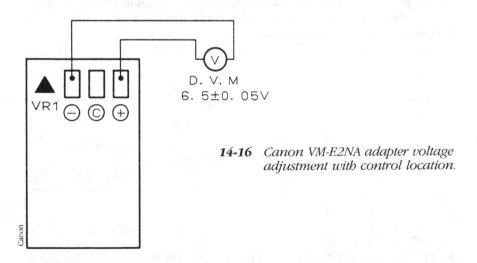

14-16   *Canon VM-E2NA adapter voltage adjustment with control location.*

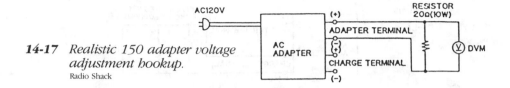

14-17 *Realistic 150 adapter voltage adjustment hookup.*
Radio Shack

Radio Shack 150 Adapter Charge Current Adjustment Set the camera/charge switch to CHARGE position. Set the battery select switch 2 to the ON position. Connect a 10-ohm 10-watt resistor between the (+) and (−) charge terminals (FIG. 14-19). Connect a 270 μF, 50-volt electrolytic capaciter across the 10-watt resistor. Connect the DVM or DMM across the resistor for testing. Adjust the charge current control (VR202) for 12 V ± 1 V. Now the proper voltage and charging current is adjusted for operation. These two checks should be made after repairing any adapter unit. Usually the battery operation voltage is much lower than the charging voltage.

Minolta C3300 Battery Alarm Adjustment This adjustment is made to set the battery alarm lamp so that it starts blinking at 9.2 volts. The oscilloscope and digital voltmeter is used with the alarm adjustment. Locate test point pin 6 of IC404 (FIG. 14-20). Place camcorder in the record mode with 9.2 Vdc to the battery terminals. Rotate R436 to the position that potential

CIRCUIT BOARD LOCATION AND

IDENTIFICATION

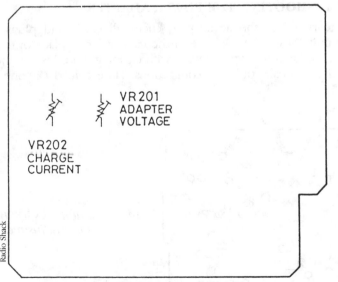

14-18 *Locate the adapter (VR201) and charge current control (VR202)*
on the timer board of the Realistic 150 camcorder for adjustment.

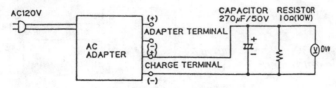

14-19 *Realistic 150 charge current adjustment hookup.* Radio Shack

charges from low to high (oscillation is observed at the changing point). Now check the battery alarm display of the tape counter starts blinking.

OTHER BATTERY CONNECTIONS

Besides connecting the small battery or ac adapter to the camcorder, the reset may be operated with the outside battery pack or auto car battery adapter/charger. Many camcorders have a separate jack where the external power can be plugged in (FIG. 14-21). Some camcorders have a car battery charger that plugs into the cigarette lighter.

The camcorder may be operated from the car battery adapter or the unit will charge up those batteries while shooting pictures in remote areas. The 12 V car battery voltage is lowered or raised according to the camcorder operating voltage. The car battery charger may have a shutdown, voltage detector, current detector, and detection timer circuits like the ac adapter (FIG. 14-22). Follow the manufacturer's service literature for correct output voltage and charging current adjustments of the car battery charger adapter.

TROUBLESHOOTING THE POWER ADAPTER

Before tearing into the ac adapter, check all cords and plugs. Most ac adapter units fit on the backside of the camcorder in place of the battery. Clean all slip-pressure-type contacts with cleaning fluid. Inspect the dc output cord for breaks or poor connections. Place a load (20-ohm, 10-watt

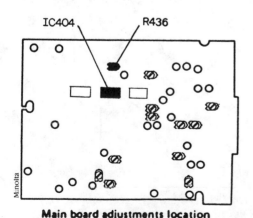

14-20 *Minolta C3300 battery alarm adjustment.*

Main board adjustments location

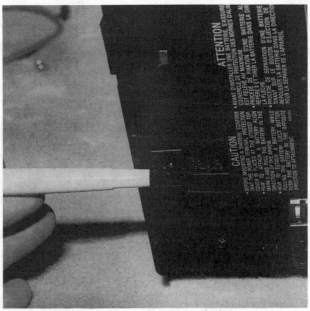

14-21 *The pen points to an external battery jack connection when connecting the outside battery pack to the RCA CPR300 camcorder.*

resistor) across the charging output terminals and measure the output volt ages.

Determine if the ac adapter is dead in both voltage and charge. If the unit supplies voltage but no charging of batteries, suspect a dirty voltage/charge switch. If the adapter is entirely dead, remove the top cover and inspect the fuse (FIG. 14-23). Replace the blown fuse with exact amperage.

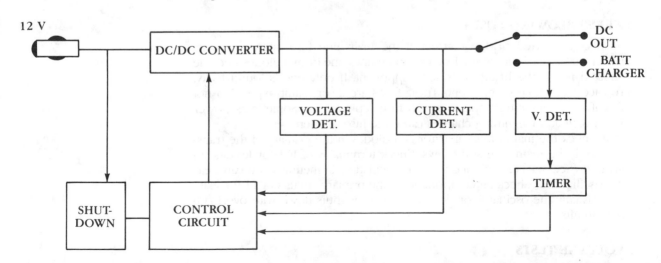

14-22 *A typical block diagram of a car battery voltage/charger adapter.*

14-23 *The inside view of the RCA CPR300 voltage/charger adapter. Locate fuse in bottom right-hand corner.*

Take a close look—sometimes there are more than one fuse in these adapters.

Next, check for ac voltage across the bridge rectifier unit (FIG. 14-24). Measure the dc voltage across the large filter capacitor. Do not overlook interlock or sense switches that open up if a battery or the adapter is not plugged into the camcorder. These switches should be closed during troubleshooting procedures. After removing the cover, place the battery into position or clip leads across these switches (FIG. 14-25).

KEEPS BLOWING FUSES

Suspect a shorted bridge rectifier if the main line fuse keeps opening. Check across each diode for leakage. Sometimes one or two diodes become shorted inside the bridge rectifier component. If only one is found leaky, replace the whole component. These fuses are 2- or 3-amp types. Do not fret if the adapter unit operates with fuse replacement. Sometimes power line overload or lightning charges cause the fuse to open.

Check the main filter capacitor and diodes in the primary of the transformer if the main fuse still blows. Check terminal 3 of IC1 for leakage to ground (See FIG. 14-24). Notice if IC1 is oscillating. Sometimes you can hear the oscillations. Check all components in the primary circuits of T1 for leakage. Usually the oscillator or dc-to-dc convertor shuts down with overloading circuits.

VOLTAGE TESTS

Measure the voltage at the cathode terminal of diode (D8). No voltage here indicates an overload, or the primary oscillator circuits are not operating.

3.1 SCHEMATIC DIAGRAM

0 1 MAIN BOARD

IC 1
STR11006

AC-IN
100~240V
50/60Hz

SW 1

F1
2A 250V

L1

VA1

C1
0.22

D1
S2VB60

C2
1500P

C3
1500P

C4
100/400

C6
0.047

R5
220

141.8

0.21

0.21

-0.1

0

R10
0.56
(2W)

R11
1K

C12
10/16

-1.52

Q1
2SB793AQ, AR

R2-1
150K
(1W)

R3-1
100K
(1W)

R4
100K
(1W)

C5
0.1/250

D2
RU1P

R2-2
150K
(1W)

R3-2
100K
(1W)

C8
0.033

C9
4700P

D5 EU1Z

R7
56

C10
10/16

R8
33(1/2W)

R9
(1/2W)

R6
10

C7
0.047

D3
EH1Z

D4
EU1Z

C11
0.01

D6 EU1Z

T1
P1

P2

S2

S1

B1

B2

PHC1   0N3105

0 3 LED

D16
LN28RP

D17
LN28RP

R45
1.5K

C29
0.1

R28
470

12.3

11.2

11.9

11.3

12.0

Q3
2SB793AQ, AR

Q4

D13
MA105IM

R34
2.2K

R35
2.2K

R29
180
(1/2W)

R30
180
(1/2W)

Q5
2SD636Q, R

0.7

R36
2.2K

R37
2.2K

0

0.7

-0.1   0

TF1

Q7
2SD1273P

R31
150   90°C

2.1

0

Q6
2SD636Q, R

IC 3   AN6780

INPUT CIRCUIT   TO EACH BLOCK

OUTPUT
CIRCUIT

F/F
15

F/F
2

F/F
1

VOLTAGE STABILIZER

INPUT CIRCUIT   OSCILLATOR

5.1

5.1

6.7

6.7

R40
100K

NOTE: Unless otherwise specified;
1. All resistance values are in ohms (1/4 W).
2. To measure voltages at T1 primary side, measure with
   D1 (−) grounded, at T1 secondary side, measure with
   LED board (1) grounded.
   Connect a battery pack BY-C101
3. Shaded ( ) parts are critical for safety.
   Replace only with specified parts nombers.

14-24 *The complete circuit diagram of Mitsubishi HS-C20U camcorder voltage/charger adapter unit.* Mitsubishi

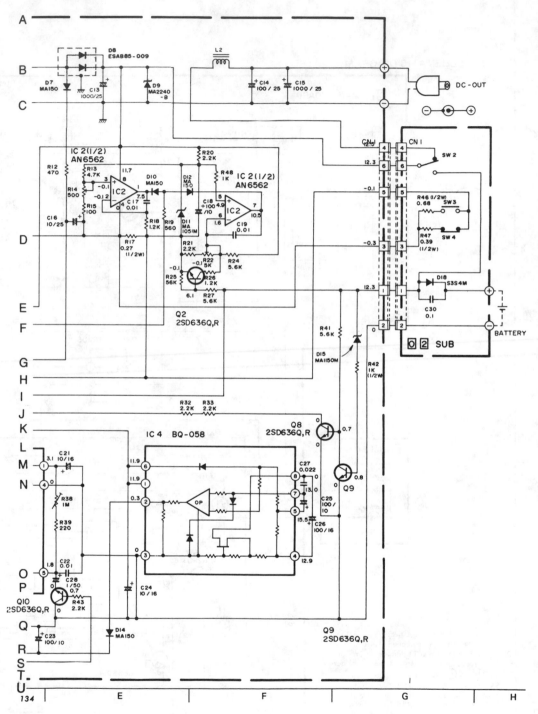

14-24 *Continued*

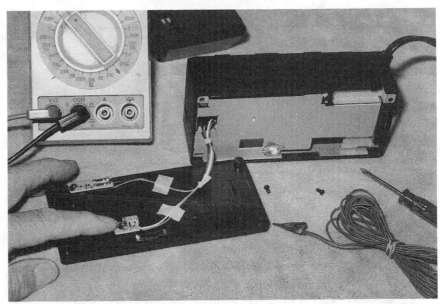

14-25 *Clip leads across the sense and interlock switches are on the top cover of the ac adapter.*

Remove S2 lead of the secondary from T1 to isolate the secondary circuits. Now take voltage measurements on IC1 and Q1. Very low voltage at pin 3 of IC1 may indicate a leaky IC. Higher-than-normal voltage at pin 3 may show that IC1 is open or not oscillating. Proceed to the secondary circuits if dc voltage is at the collecter terminal of D8.

RANDOM TRANSISTOR AND DIODE TESTS

A quick method to check for a leaky or shorted diode or transistor is to make a random check with each semiconductor on the board. Place the DMM to diode or transistor test and check the resistance across each diode. All diodes, including zener types, can be checked with this method. Double-check components around the diode if one is found leaky so you are sure another component is not indicating the leakage instead of the suspected component.

Check the transistors with a common base check to the collector and then the emitter terminals for leakage or open conditions. Like the diode, the good transistor should only have a low resistance measurement in one direction. The transistor may be open if no measurement. Use the regular transistor tester if one is handy. Most transistors in the ac adaptors are npn types, but check to be sure.

CHECKING ICs AND OTHER COMPONENTS

You may find two to four IC components in the ac adapter. One is used as a primary control oscillator, while the others are found in the voltage control

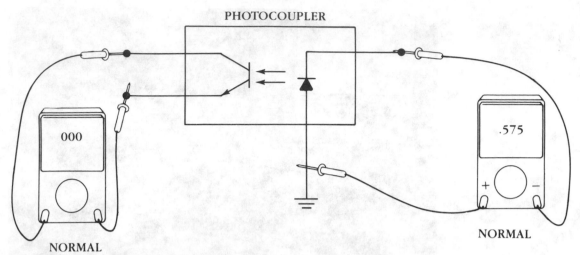

PHOTOCOUPLER

000

.575

NORMAL

NORMAL

14-26   *Checking the photocoupler unit with the DMM diode test.*

and charging current circuits. Voltage measurements on the IC may turn up a leaky IC. A low voltage (V_{cc}) supply pin of the IC may indicate the IC is leaky. Remove the pin lead from the foil with solder wick and take another voltage test. Measure the pin of the IC to common ground for a low resistance (under 1 kΩ). Replace the leaky IC with the low-resistance measurement of the supply voltage pin terminal.

The photocoupler enclosed in one component can be checked with the diode test of the DMM (FIG. 14-26). Check the diode like the regular fixed diode with the DMM diode test. Now check the phototransistor side in the same manner. The diode should have a low measurement in one direction and no measurement across the emitter and collector terminals on the transistor side. Very low measurement indicates a leaky photocoupler.

BATTERY WILL NOT CHARGE

The battery may be "used up" or the battery charger is defective (FIG. 14-27). If other batteries charge on the adaptor/charger, suspect a defective battery. Try completely discharging the battery. Now try to recharge it. After a couple of hours, if the battery does not charge up, discard it. (Do not place it in a fire to destroy it.)

Check the voltage output of the charger with a load made up of resistors across the battery charge output terminals. Very low voltage output may indicate a defective charging circuit or charge/voltage switch. Notice if the adapter provides operating voltage for the camcorder. Inspect the charge/voltage switch for poor contacts. Shunt the switch contacts with alligator clips. Suspect a defective IC charge circuit with no charge voltage. Inspect the diode in series with the voltage and charge lead terminal for open or burned conditions. Measure all voltages on the IC (power switch) terminals and compare with the schematic (FIG. 14-28).

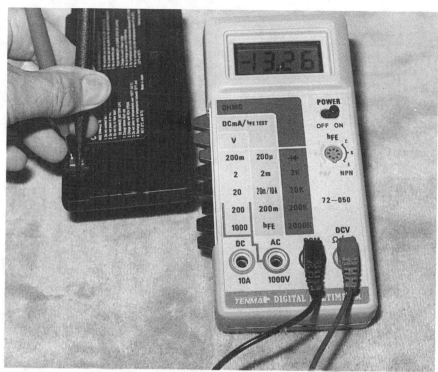

14-27 *Measuring the voltage at the battery pack terminal to see what condition it is in.*

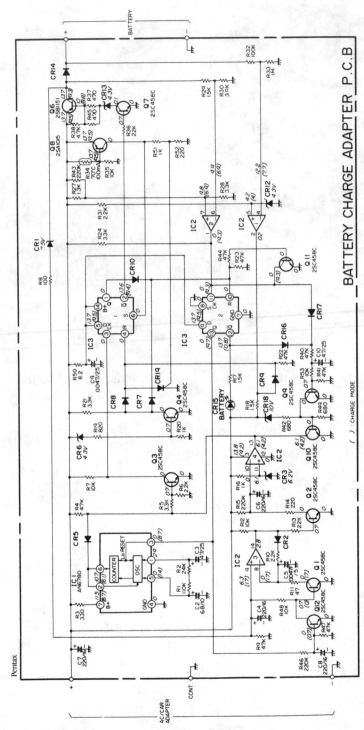

14-28 Measuring all voltages on the IC components in the battery charger adapter circuit of the Pentax PV-C850A camcorder.

Appendix **A**

Abbreviations

Sometimes only an abbreviation is used on the manufacturer's schematic diagram or service literature. Here is a list of the most-used abbreviations to help you understand the various camcorder circuits. They are listed in alphabetical order.

AC	alternating current
ACC	automatic color control
A/CTL	audio control
ADC	analog to digital converter
ADD	addler
ADJ	adjusting
ADUB	audio dubbing
AE	audio erase
AEF	automatic editing function
AFC	automatic frequency control
AFT	automatic fine tuning
AGT	automatic gain control
AH	audio head
AHD	audio high-density disc
AL	after loading
ALC	automatic level control
ALM	alarm
ALU	arithmetic logic unit
AM	amplitude modulation
AMP	amplifier
ANT	antenna
APC	automatic phase control
APL	average picture level
A/S/M	audio/servo/mechacon

ASSY	assembly
ATT	attenuator
AUD	audio
AW	automatic white
AUX	auxiliary
B	base or blue
BAL	balance
BATT	battery
BBD	bucket brigade device
BCD	binary-coded decimal
BEG	beginning
BF	behind focus or burst flag
BFP	burst flag pulse
BIT	binary digit
BLK	black or blanking
BLU	blue
BNC	bayonet connector
BOT	beginning of tape
BPF	bandpass filter
BRK	brake
BRN	brown
BRT	brightness
BT	band tuning
BUFF	buffer
B/W or BW	black and white
C	color, capacitance, or collector
CAL	calibration
CAP	capstan or capacitor
CAR	carrier
CRR	carrier
CASS	cassette
CC	cassette compartment
CCD	charge-coupled device
CCT	circuit
CDS	cadmium sulphite
CD	count down
CE	chip enable
CF	ceramic filter, correct focus, or color frame
CFG	capstan frequency generator
CFVSEL	capstan frequency-to-voltage converter select
CH	channel
CHG	charge
CHROMA	color
CLK	clock
CLR	clear
CMD	command

CMOS	complementary metal-oxide semiconductor
CNT	count or counter
COL	color
COM	common
COMB	combination or comb filter
COMP	comparator, composite, or compensation
CONN	connector
CONV	converter
CP	circuit protector or clamp pulse
CPC	capstan phase control
CPU	central processing unit
CTC	crosstalk channel
CTL	control
D	drum, digital, diode, or drain
D/A	digital-to-analog
DAC	digital-to-analog convertor
dB	decibel
DC	direct current
DD	direct drive
DEC	decoder
DEMOD	demodulator
DET	detector
DEV	deviation
DFRS	drum free-running stop
DG	differential/gain
DISCR	discriminator
DL	delay line
DLY	delay
DOC	dropout compensator
DOD	dropout detector
DP	differential phase
DPC	drum phase control
DYAC	dynamic aperture control
E	edit or emitter
EDP	electronic data processing
E-E	electric to electric
EF	emitter follower
EMP	emphasis
EN	enable
ENC	encoder
ENV	envelope
EO	error out
EOP	end of play
EP	extended play
EQ	equalizer
ES	electronic switch

ESNS	end sensor
EXP	expander
EXT	external
F	farad or fuse
FADV	frame advance
FDP	fluorescent display panel
FE	full erase
FET	field-effect transistor
FF	fast-forward, flip-flop, or front focus
FG	frequency generator
FI	field index
FIX	fixed
FM	frequency modulation
FMA	FM audio
FR	field recording, frame, or rusible resistor
FREQ	frequency
F-V CONV	frequency-to-voltage convertor
FWD	forward
FWDS	forward search
G	green or gate grid
GCA	gain control amplifier
GEN	generator
GND	ground
GRN	green
GRY	gray
H	horizontal, high, henry, or hour
HB	high bride
HBF	horizontal burst flag
HD	horizontal drive
HG	hall generator
HPF	high-pass filter
Hz	hertz
IC	integrated circuit
ID	identification pulse
IF	intermediate frequency
EFR	infrared
IFT	intermediate frequency transformer
IMS	images
IND	indicator
INH	inhibit
INS	insert
INT	internal or interrupt
INV	inverter
I/O	input/output
IR	infrared
L	low or left

LCD	liquid-crystal display
LED	light-emitting diode
LIM	limiter
LIN	linearity
LL	low light
LLD	low-light detector
LOAD	loading cassette
LP	long play
LPF	low-pass filter
LSB	lower sideband
M	motor
MAX	maximum
MDA	motor drive amplifier
MECHACON	mechanism control
MIC	microphone
MIN	minimum
MIX	mix or mixing
MM or MMV	monstable multivibrator
MNOS	metal nitride-oxide semiconductor
MOD	modulator or modulation
MOS	metal-oxide semiconductor
MPX	multiplex or multiplexer
MR	magnetic resistor
MS	mode select
MUT	muting
MUX	multiplex or multiplexer
NAND	not AND
NC	not connected
NFB	negative feedback
NLN	nonlinear
NO	normally open
NOR	normal, or not OR
NR	noise reduction
OP	operation
OPAMP	operational amplifier
ORN	orange
OSC	oscillator
PB	playback
PBLK	preblanking
PC	pulse counter or photocoupler
PCM	pulse-code modulation
PD	phase detector
PG	pulse generator
PGM	program
PHS	photosensor
PI	photointerrupter

PIF	picture intermediate frequency
PLA	programmable logic array
PLL	phase-locked loop
PLS	pulse
P or POS	position or positive
p-p	peak-to-peak
PR	pinch roller
PREAMP	preamplifier
P/S	pause/still
P.SET	preset
PSC	pulse-swallowing control
PU	pickup
PUT	programmable unijunction transistor
PWB	printing wiring board
PWM	pulse width modulcation
PW or PWR	power
Q	quality factor
R	red
RA	resistor array
RAM	random-access memory
R/B	red and blue
REC	recording
REF	reference
REG	regulator or regulated
REM	remote
REMOCON	remote control unit
REV	reverse
RF	radio frequency
R/P	record/playback
RPT	repeat
RS FF	RS flip-flop
RST	reset
RT	rotary transformer
RUN	running
RY	relay
SAW	sawtooth or surface acoustic wave
SC	subcarrier or simulcast
SCH	search
SEL	select
S or SENS	sensor
SEP	separator
SF	source follower
SFF	short fast follower
S/H	sample and hold
SIF	sound intermediate frequency
SN	signal-to-noise ratio

SOL	solenoid
SOS	sound on sound
SP	standard play
S PLS	sampling pulse
REV S	reverse switch
REW	rewind
S/S	slow/still
SSG	sync signal generator
SSNS	start sensor
STD	standard
SUP	supply
SW	switch
SWD	switched
SYNC	synchronization
SYNCON	system control
T	target
TAL	tally
TBC	time base connector
TC	time code or tension control
TEN	tension
TF	thermal fuse
TIM	timing
Tk or TRK	tracking
TNR	tuner
TP	test point
TR	transistor, trimmer, or transformer
SR	supply reel
SREW	short rewind
UL	unloading
UNREG	unregulated
UNSW	unswitched
V	volt or vertical
VACT	video action
VCO	voltage-controlled oscillator
VCXO	variable-control crystal oscillator
VD	vertical drive
VF	viewfinder
VIF	video intermediate frequency
VLT	violet
VR	variable resistor
VS	video and sync
VSCH	variable search
V/T	video/television
VXO	variable crystal oscillator
W	watt
WARN	warning

W & D	white and dark
W BLK	wide blanking
WHT	white
TRANS	transformer
T/T	tuner/timer
TU	take-up
YEL	yellow
WV	working voltage
XTAL or X.TAL	crystal
Y	luminance
ZFE	zero frame editing

Appendix **B**

Camcorder Manufacturers

AIWA
35 Oxford Dr.
Moonachie, NJ 07074

CANON
One Canon Plaza
Lake Success, NY 11042

CHINON
43 Fadem Rd.
Springfield, NJ 07081

CURTIS MATHES
1220 Champion Circle
Carlton, TX 75006

ELMO
70 New Hyde Park
New Hyde Park, NY 11040

FISHER
1200 West Walnut St.
P.O. Box 9038
Compton, CA 90224

GENERAL ELECTRIC
Box 1976
Indianapolis, IN 46206

GOLDSTAR
1050 Wall St.
Lyndhurst, NJ 07071

HITACHI
401 W. Artesia Blvd.
Compton, CA 90220

INSTANT REPLAY
2951 South Bay Shore Dr.
Coconut Grove, FL 33133

J. C. PENNEY
National Parts Center
6840 Barton Rd.
Morrow, GA 30260

JVC
41 Stater Dr.
Elmwood Park, NJ 07407

KODAK
343 State St.
Rochester, NY 14650

KYOCERA
411 Sette Dr.
Paramus, NJ 07652

MAGNAVOX
Phillips Consumer Electronics
(Philco) and Sylvania
P.O. Box 967
Greenville, TN 37944-0967

MINOLTA
101 Williams Dr.
Ramsey, NJ 07446

MITSUBISHI
5757 Plaza Dr.
Box 6007
Cypress, CA 90630

NEC
1255 Mechael Dr.
Wooddale, IL 60191

NIKON
623 Stewart Ave.
Garden City, NY 11530

OLYMPUS
Crossways Park
Woodbury, NY 11797

PANASONIC
One Panasonic Way
Secaucus, NJ 07094

PENTAX
35 Muerness Drive East
Englewood, CO 80112

QUASAR
P.O. Box 967
Greenville, TN 37944−0967

RADIO SHACK
National Parts Center
900 East Northside Dr.
Fort Worth, TX 48106

RCA
Thomson Consumer Electronics
P.O. Box 1976
Indianapolis, IN 46286

RICOH
5 Didrick Place
West Caldwell, NJ 07006

SANYO
SFS Corporation
1200 West Walnut St.
P.O. Box 9038
Compton, CA 90224

SEARS
Sears Tower
Chicago, IL 60684

SHARP
Sharp Plaza
Mahwah, NJ 07430

SONY
Sony Dr.
Park Ridge, NJ 07656

TEKNIKA
353 Route 46 W.
Fairfield, NJ 07006

TOSHIBA
82 Totowa Rd.
Wayne, NJ 07470

VIVITAR
1630 Steward St.
Santa Monica, CA 90406

ZENITH
1900 Austin Ave.
Chicago, IL 60639

Glossary

ac Alternating current, which is supplied from the ac wall plug or outlet. The camcorder may be operated from the power line with the ac adapter or power pack.

ACC Automatic color control. A switch that sets the color level on many TV receivers and video monitors.

AFM Audio frequency modulation, a method that provides a wide range of sound recording in both Beta and VHS systems.

AFC Automatic frequency control. The AFC circuit locks the TV or FM receiver to a station with the strongest signal.

AGC Automatic gain control. Like the auto or home radio, a certain signal level must be maintained. The camcorder AGC controls the signal level at all times.

AM Amplitude modulation. On the regular broadcast band, 550 to 1600 kHz are AM stations.

antenna A device to pick up the signal for best TV reception.

APC Automatic phase control. A circuit that keeps the color and luminance signals in phase to prevent jittery or wavy pictures.

aperture The opening in the camera that permits light to enter. The size of this opening is controlled by an adjustable setting called the the iris. The smaller the number that corresponds to the aperture, the larger the size of the "hole"

aspect ratio The ratio of height to length.

audio Audible sound. In camcorder recording, the sound is recorded at the top of the video tape.

automatic rewind A process that automatically brings the videocassette back to the beginning (found in some VCRs and camcorders).

automation Automatic operations performed by the camcorder.

A/V Audio/video systems or jacks.

azimuth The angle of the tape head with the tape. The tape must run in a straight line with the tape head to prevent poor-quality recording or playback. An adjuster for the tape head is usually located at the side of the tape head.

band   A band of broadcast frequencies such as the AM band (550 to 1500 kHz) or the FM band (88 to 108 MHz).

barrel distortion   Lines that bend in the picture that appears like you are looking through a barrell.

Beta   One of the first tape formats provided by Sony Corporation. The Beta cassette will not play on a VHS VCR, nor will a VHS cassette play with the Beta VCR machine.

bias   A bias voltage is applied to the audio tape when recording to reproduce higher frequencies.

black and white   A picture with no color—only black, white, and grey shades.

block matrix   A picture tube with black surrounding each bead color upon the face of the CRT, used to bring out a brighter, clearer picture.

boom   A long arm or pole that holds a microphone suspended over the subject.

burn   A permanent image on the front of a CRT. To avoid this, keep the lens cover over the camera at all times when using a video camera that has a tube as pickup device.

cable   The TV signal is brought through a cable system instead of the TV antenna. Cables are used to tie the camcorder, VCR, and TV receiver together to play back the recorded cassette.

camcorder   A separate camera and recorder were used in the early video days. Now both are available in one unit.

camera   The part of a camcorder made up of a lens and pickup device that is either a tube or solid-state component (CCD or MOS) that views the subject, transforms it into electronic signals, and places the images on tape to be replayed by a camcorder or video cassette player.

camera cap   A device to place over the lens opening to protect the lens and pickup device when the camcorder is not operating.

capstan   The capstan is a shaft that revolves at certain speeds to move the tape from the cassette across the tape head. Usually, the tape is held against the capstan with a rubber pinch roller, like in the audio cassette player.

capstan servo   The electronic control circuit that controls the capstan motor with proper speed in relation to the video drum tape and drive capstan.

cassette   A two-reel holder that contains video or audio tape. The video tape comes in three different formats: VHS, Beta and 8 mm.

cassette cleaner   A cassette with dry or liquid material that cleans the heads and tape paths of a VCR or audio cassette player.

CATV   Color TV signals that come through a cable to your house from a cable company are called cable TV or CATV. You must pay for these TV signals instead of using your own outside antenna.

CCD   Charge-coupled device. A solid-state chip that usually detects a subject as the vidicon tube in the early cameras.

character generator   A small device that generates titles and numbers on the video tape electronically.

chroma Chrominance or color. The three primary colors are red, green, and blue.

chromium dioxide A component used in making video and audio tapes.

color system The National Television Standards Committee (NTSC) system for American Television uses 525 lines and a 60 field, while the United Kingdom supports a Phase Alteration Line (PAL) and the French (SE CAM) system uses a 625-line, 50-field format. The European system is not compatible with the U.S. system.

color burst sensor A color burst sensor may be found in the VCR to tell when the burst signals are present and can be edited out of the old black-and-white movies.

color temperature Kelvin is the unit of color temperature, which is the degree of heat needed for a perfect black body to emit light. The higher the temperature, the bluer the light; the lower the temperature, the redder the light.

closed circuit A TV system with a camera and receiver are connected together by microwave or cable. Production broadcasting uses close circuit methods.

coaxial A shielded cable with a solid conductor in the center of the cable. The shielded cable prevents outside spurious signals from entering the TV or recorded picture.

comet-tailing When the camera or object moves, red or blue streaks may tail a bright object.

common A common ground, found in most electronic circuits, is a common point to return the electronic circuit.

consistency The variation in quality among different batches of tapes.

continuous loop A tape system in which the endless loop is repeated, such as the early telephone answering machines.

contrast Comparing the bright and dark areas of the picture. Too much contrast may result in a dark picture while very little contrast may be washed out.

control track The cue or sync track at the bottom of the tape. The control signal is recorded to automatically correct the tape speed.

convergence Positioning the three colored beams to shine through a shadow mask and onto each color bead (pixel) for the best picture.

counter A means of pinpointing a starting and stopping point on the tape.

crosstalk Audible or visible interference in the audio or video cassette player. Improper adjustment of tape head in the audio cassette may produce crosstalk.

CRT Cathode ray tube. A picture in the TV receiver. The electronic viewfinder of the camcorder may have a tube for viewing the scene.

cue To start and stop the tape at a certain position on the tape.

dB Decibels. A measurement of sound.

dc Direct current. A dc battery is used to power the camcorder.

degausser An electromagnetic ring of wires to clean up color impurities of the shadow mask of the picture tube. The magnetic poles of the earth and man-made devices such as a carpet sweeper or speaker may magnetize the shadow mask, producing impurities in the color picture.

depth of field   The range of focus at the desired lens opening. The higher number of the camera provides a great depth of field. The lower number provides a wide opening, producing a narrow depth of field.

dew sensor   A device with circuitry that automatically tells you the dangerous level of moisture in the camera. The camcorder should not be used while the dew sensor is flashing or on.

diffusion filter   A filter applied to the front of the lens that gives a soft appearance.

digital   A digital VCR has special effects such as freeze frame, picture in picture, and solarization.

diode   A semiconductor that prevents current from flowing in only one direction. Also called a *rectifier*.

dipole   "Rabbit ears" antennas are simple dipole. The dipole element of the TV antenna is the rod where the cable or flat lead-in wire is attached.

dropout   Little white streaks across the picture as the recorded tape is played. Dropouts often occur at the beginning and end of the tape. Dropouts may be caused by poor or contaminated tape.

dub   To transfer the image and sound from one tape to another or to change various sections of the recording. Sound may be dubbed upon the tape at a later date.

drum   A cylindrical component with heads that records the video picture.

dynamic range   The range from the softest to the loudest sound that can be recorded. The larger the number, the wider the dynamic range.

EVF   Electronic viewfinder. Actually, the tube and circuits are similar to a small TV set. Some camcorders have the electronic viewfinder, while others have an optical viewfinder.

edit   To add or take away scenes from a tape.

eject   To release the videocassette from the VCR, camcorder, or audio cassette player.

EP   Extended play. Refers to the speed where six hours of recording may be done on a T120 VHS cassette.

erase   To remove material or scenes from the audio or video cassette.

erase head   The erase head removes all previously recorded material from the tape as the camcorder, camera, or VCR is recording new material.

fast forward   A means to make the tape move faster in a forward mode.

fast search   The VCR or camcorder is operated at a faster speed so you can see the recorded material.

ferri chrome   A compound of chromium and iron dioxide material that produces high-quality video and audio tapes.

ferric oxide   Iron compound used in manufacturing video and audio tapes.

flagging   Bending of the picture at the top or bottom. In the TV camera, flagging occurs most often at the top of the picture.

flutter   Audio distortion.

flyback   The horizontal transformer in the TV receiver or electronic viewfinder.

flywheel   A large wheel found on the end of the capstan drive assembly. Most flywheels are rotated with a drive belt.

foot candle   The amount of light provided by a candle at the distance of one foot. The unit of light intensity.

foot-lambert   The unit of measurement of brightness. One foot-lambert is equal to 3.426 candelas per square meter.

flutter   Uneven speeds in tape that causes a wavy picture or sound.

FM   Frequency modulation. FM modulation removes most of the pickup static in radio reception.

formulation tape   The actual magnetic compound deposited upon the recording tape.

frame   A single picture. The VCR may have a device to stop the tape to view certain frames.

frequency response   The dynamic range that a medium may record (in decibels). The normal frequency response of audio cassette tape is from 20 to 20,000 Hz, while the average frequency response of video cassette tape is from 45 to 12,000 Hz.

F-stop   The setting of the lens opening. The larger the number, the smaller the opening, and the smaller the F-stop, the larger the lens opening.

fuse   The fuse protects the circuits inside the TV set, VCR, audio cassette, and camcorder. Most fuses are in a small, round, glass enclosure.

generation   The master tape is the first-generation recording.

ghost   Another or several images alongside the original. TV signals bouncing off of various subjects produce ghosts in the picture. Improper cable hookup may produce lines in the pictures.

glitch   Interference malfunction that may flash on the screen of a video or audio recording.

ground   Earth or a common reference point in the circuit.

ground plug   A three-prong ac plug in which the large prong is grounded to protect the operator.

hardware   The VCR is referred to as the hardware and software is the cassette that plays in the VCR.

harmonic distortion   Unwanted sounds or overtones in music.

head   The electromagnetic device that records, erases, or plays back tapes in the VCR, camcorder, or audio cassette player.

helical scan   The diagonal playback or recording system that places video frequencies on the tape. The tape spins at an angle to the cassette tape.

hertz (Hz)   The measurement of frequency equal to one vibration. 1000 cycles per second (Hz), or 1 kHz.

high Z   High impedance. A crystal microphone may have high impedance, while a dynamic mike may have low impedance output.

hue   The tint of a color picture. The tint control in a TV receiver varies the hue of the colored picture.

horizontal resolution   The more horizontal lines there are, the sharper the picture. European scanning lines are 625, while the U.S. standard contains 525 lines.

HQ   High quality. Usually, a camcorder or VCR with HQ specifications produces a higher quality image in chrominance and lumanance noise reduction and white-clip circuits.

IC   Integrated circuit. A chip with many different components in one body, used extensively in the camcorder, VCR, and other consumer electronic products.

IF   Intermediate frequency. The IF transformer in the radio or TV receiver is between the tuner and detector circuits.

infrared remote   A hand-held remote control unit that controls the TV, VCR, video disc, and audio disc players. The infrared remote transmits infrared beams of light, which are picked up by a receiver and control circuit.

image lag   When the camera is moved quickly from one subject to another, it produces a ghost or streak on the screen.

impedance   The unit of ac resistance. The output impedance of the amplifier must match the speaker impedance. The cables used to connect the TV antenna and VCR to the TV receiver have 75-ohm and 300-ohm impedances. The shielded cable is 75 ohms, while the flat wire is 300 ohms.

index   An electronic marker on a tape (a point for fast rewind, record, or play).

interference   Static or noisy unwanted signals.

IPS   Inches per foot. The speed of the tape during recording and playback.

kinescope   Refers to the TV picture tube. Also called a CRT.

iris   Controls the size of the opening of the lens assembly (aperture), which determines the amount of light entering the camera.

lag   A trace of light behind a moving object or when the camera is moved quickly from one scene to another.

laser   A concentrated beam of high-frequency light. A laser beam is in compact disc players for reading an audio disc.

LCD   Liquid-crystal display. Found in audio and video products.

lead-in   The flat wire or cable that brings in the TV signal to the back of the TV receiver.

LED   Light-emitting diodes. Found throughout the camcorder and VCR as indicators.

lens   A piece of curved glass that lets light pass through it, striking the film in a camera, pickup tube, or solid-state device in the video camera or camcorder.

load   To place a videocassette into the VCR or camcorder.

LP   Long play. The T-120 video cassette will play four hours of program material.

low Z   Low impedance. The speaker may have a low impedance of 4, 8, or 10 ohms.

L-125   A Beta Cassette with 15 to 45 minutes playing time.

L-250   Beta cassette with 1 to 1 ½ hours playing time.

L-500   Beta cassette with 2 to 3 hours playing time.

L-750   Beta cassette with 3 to 4 hours playing time.

L-830   Beta cassette with up to 5 hours of recording.

luminance   Brightness. The luminance circuits are in camcorder, VCR, and TV receivers.

lux   Measurement of light sensitivity. A camcorder with a 7 lux is more sensitive than one with a 20 lux setting.

M loading   The tape from a VHS format is wound around the heads in an M-like fashion.

macro   The macro lens is used to take close-up pictures.

MDS   Multipoint distribution system. A cable TV system with scrambled signals.

microwaves   Electromagnetic waves with a small wavelength, such as in satellite transmission and those in the microwave ovens used for cooking.

ME   Metal evaporated tape. Metal tape is in the 8 mm video cassette.

monitor   The television set may be called a TV monitor when connected to the VCR. A monitor may resemble a TV set without a tuner but has direct hookup to input video signals.

MOS   Metal-oxide semiconductor. The electronic solid-state chip used to pick up the picture instead of a tube. Pentax, Radio Shack, and RCA have MOS pickup devices in their camcorders.

MP   Metal particle. Found in the 8 mm video cassette tape.

MTS   Multichannel television sound. The TV or VCR with MTS decoder will allow you to hear stereophonic broadcast format.

muting   A circuit that blanks out video or audio signals in recording or playback.

newvicon   A tube pickup device used in the early home video cameras.

nicad   Nickel-cadmium. The battery made up of nickel-cadmium material can be charged over and over again.

noise   A distorted, unwanted signal in audio and video systems. Noise may appear intermittently or all the time in a poor recording.

NTSC   National Television Standards Committee. The committee who sets standards in the TV industry.

ohm   Unit of electrical resistance. Resistors are rated in ohms.

oscilloscope   An electronic testing device used to observe waveforms in electronic circuits.

overscan   Portions of the picture you do not see at the edges of the picture tube.

PAL   Phase Alteration Line. The 625-line color TV system found in Great Britain.

pause control   The pause control is used to stop the recording or playback of an unwanted program.

PCM   Pulse Code Modulation. The method used in 8 mm video or stereo systems.

PET   Polyethylene tesphalate (Mylar). The plastic base used for recording tape.

pixel   Picture element. Thousands of tiny light-sensitive spots on the CCD pickup device.

play   The play button is pushed when you want to watch what was recorded.

power   The amplifier may have 100 watts of power to drive several speakers. The power plug may be referred to as the ac outlet.

power supply   A voltage source that supplies power to the VCR or camcorder. Often, the power supply circuitry changes ac to dc voltage.

probe   The DMM or VOM has test probes to check voltage or resistance in the various circuits.

programming   The VCR may be programmed for hours or days of monitoring the TV signal.

rainbow effect   Wiggly color lines found in the picture from poor erasure of the previous program.

random excess   Provision to use the tuner in a scan mode (to go through the channels at random).

record   To put audio or video material onto the tape or disc.

rewind   To bring back the tape to a starting position.

resolution   The clarity of the picture. The higher the number in horizontal lines, the better the resolution. The American system has 525 lines.

RF   Radio frequency. The frequency at which radio and television frequencies are broadcast. External RF energy in the picture or sound may be caused by a strong unwanted signal feeding into the radio or television receiver.

saticon   A popular pickup device used in home video cameras.

scanning   There are 525 scanning lines in the U.S. system and 625 scanning lines in the United Kingdom broadcast system.

search   The video cassette or video disc player may have speed search, cue, and review functions to enable the operator to quickly locate a special segment of the recording.

se cam   The 625-line color system used in France.

sensitivity   The degree of input signal in RF or audio signal.

sensor light   Lamp bulb indicating the unit is ready to operate. A dew sensor light in the camcorder indicates when moisture is inside the head area.

separation   The degree the right and left channels are apart.

servo   A control circuit that regulates the speed for the rotating drum or motors inside the VCR, disc player, or camcorder.

shotgun mike   A highly direction microphone used to pick up audio at a great distance.

sine wave   Fundemental wave used in testing audio and video consumer products.

skewing   Bent visual distortion of the upper portion of the picture caused by rapid fluctuation of signal on the tape. Also, the angled motion of the tape.

SLP   Super long play. The slowest speed found in VHS, VCR, and camcorders.

S/N   Signal-to-noise ratio. The comparison of good signal with unwanted signal. The audio amp with the highest signal-to-noise ratio produces the least noisy sound.

snow   Black and white specks on the TV screen due to weak or poor reception.

software   The video cassette is referred to as software. The VCR is referred to as hardware.

SP   Standard play. A two-hour T-120 VHS tape rotates at SP speed.

speed   The rate the tape passes the tape head. Often rated in inches.

splice   Connecting two pieces of tape. Sometimes used in editing material.

stereo   Two separate channels of audio. The stereo amp has a left and right audio channel.

sync   Synchronizing signals. The recordings at the bottom of the tape are synchronizing signals. Sync pulses are in the TV set or monitor to keep the picture from going horizontally or vertically.

tape   A narrow, plastic-coated material with oxide compounds with magnetic quality. Both audio and video are recorded on tape.

tape head   A coil with a magnetic core that makes and takes off magnetic impressions of audio and video.

tint   Sometimes referred to as the hue control. The tint control of a TV receiver varies the color of a person's face.

tracking   There are audio and video tracks on the recording tape. The tape head may be adjusted for optional tracking of the tape.

tracking control   A control that slightly changes the alignment of the tape head so it will accurately align with the video tracks on the tape.

transistor   A semiconductor device that operates somewhat like a tube. Many transistors may be found in the IC component.

tuner   The front end of the VCR, radio, or TV set that picks up and tunes in each station.

UHF   Ultra high frequency. The stations found in the TV set from 14 to 83 channels. A special antenna is needed to pick up UHF channels.

U loading   The loading pattern of the tape in the Beta system.

VCR   Video cassette recorder.

VHF   Very high frequency. The VHF channels of the TV set are from 2 through 13.

VHS   Video home system. The most popular video format, developed by JVC.

VHS-C   A small cartridge using the VHS format. The VHS-C cassette must be placed in the adapter to play into the VCR.

video disc   A flat disc used to record audio and video information.

video disc player   A large unit that plays the video disc through the TV set.

vidicon   The early popular video pickup tube found in commercial and home cameras.

VIR   Vertical internal reference. A system used in some TV receivers for automatic hue control.

VTR   Video tape recorder.

white balance   The primary video colors, red, blue, and green, must be blended correctly for a white rendition.

white balance control   This control sets the colors for the camera by a switch or automatically.

wow and flutter   A variation of tape speed may produce wow and flutter in the sound or video of a recording.

zoom   A wide angle lens that can take a picture far away. Manual or motorized power zooming may be found in the camcorder. Often, the consumer home video cameras have a zoom ratio of 3:1 or 6:1.

Index